T0386167

GERMAN WOMEN'S WRITING OF THE
EIGHTEENTH AND NINETEENTH CENTURIES
FUTURE DIRECTIONS IN FEMINIST CRITICISM

# LEGENDA

LEGENDA, founded in 1995 by the European Humanities Research Centre of the University of Oxford, is now a joint imprint of the Modern Humanities Research Association and Routledge. Titles range from medieval texts to contemporary cinema and form a widely comparative view of the modern humanities, including works on Arabic, Catalan, English, French, German, Greek, Italian, Portuguese, Russian, Spanish, and Yiddish literature. An Editorial Board of distinguished academic specialists works in collaboration with leading scholarly bodies such as the Society for French Studies and the British Comparative Literature Association.

# MHRA

The Modern Humanities Research Association (MHRA) encourages and promotes advanced study and research in the field of the modern humanities, especially modern European languages and literature, including English, and also cinema. It also aims to break down the barriers between scholars working in different disciplines and to maintain the unity of humanistic scholarship in the face of increasing specialization. The Association fulfils this purpose primarily through the publication of journals, bibliographies, monographs and other aids to research.

**Routledge**
Taylor & Francis Group
LONDON AND NEW YORK

Routledge is a global publisher of academic books, journals and online resources in the humanities and social sciences. Founded in 1836, it has published many of the greatest thinkers and scholars of the last hundred years, including Adorno, Einstein, Russell, Popper, Wittgenstein, Jung, Bohm, Hayek, McLuhan, Marcuse and Sartre. Today Routledge is one of the world's leading academic publishers in the Humanities and Social Sciences. It publishes thousands of books and journals each year, serving scholars, instructors, and professional communities worldwide.

www.routledge.com

# German Women's Writing of the Eighteenth and Nineteenth Centuries

## Future Directions in Feminist Criticism

EDITED BY HELEN FRONIUS AND ANNA RICHARDS

LEGENDA

Modern Humanities Research Association and Routledge

2011

First published 2011

Published by the
Modern Humanities Research Association and Routledge
2 Park Square, Milton Park, Abingdon, Oxon OX14 4RN
711 Third Avenue, New York, NY 10017, USA

LEGENDA is an imprint of the
Modern Humanities Research Association and Routledge

Routledge is an imprint of the Taylor & Francis Group, an informa business

© Modern Humanities Research Association and Taylor & Francis 2011

ISBN 978-1-906540-86-9 (hbk)

# CONTENTS

❖

# ACKNOWLEDGEMENTS

This current volume is the outcome of a two-day conference on German women writers of the eighteenth and nineteenth centuries, held in Exeter College, University of Oxford, in 2008. We would like to thank the John Fell OUP Research Fund for the award which provided generous financial support for this conference. This allowed us to bring together scholars from the USA and other European countries, in addition to UK-based researchers. The Faculty of Medieval and Modern Languages at the University of Oxford also granted some funding, for which we are indebted. We are grateful to the School of Arts Research Fund of Birkbeck College, University of London, for funding the subvention which made the publication of this book possible. Most of the chapters in this book began life as papers at the conference. We would like to thank the contributors for their cooperation and hard work in preparing the volume for publication, and the other scholars who attended the conference for their illuminating discussions, which have enriched this collection. We owe thanks to Graham Nelson at Legenda for his kind patience and support and to Sue Dugen for her careful work on the index.

# NOTES ON THE CONTRIBUTORS

**Jennifer Askey** received her PhD in Germanic Languages and Literatures at Washington University in St Louis in 2003, writing on girls' literature and the narrativization of nationalism. She is Associate Professor of German in the Department of Modern Languages at Kansas State University, where she has worked since 2005. She teaches all levels of German language as well as nineteenth- and twentieth-century literature. Recent publications include an article on the celebration of Sedantag in a Berlin girls' school in the 1880s in the *Women in German Yearbook* (2008) and a chapter on the nineteenth-century textbook and children's book publisher Ferdinand Hirt & Sohn in *Publishing Culture and the 'Reading Nation'* published by Camden House in 2010.

**Hilary Brown** is Lecturer in German at Swansea University. Her research focuses on German women's writing and translation/reception studies. She has published widely on German women as translators and mediators of foreign literature in the seventeenth and eighteenth centuries. Her monograph on *Benedikte Naubert (1756–1819) and her Relations to English Culture* appeared in 2005, and a second monograph, *Luise Gottsched the Translator*, is forthcoming with Camden House.

**Annette Bühler-Dietrich** teaches German literature at the University of Stuttgart. Her research interests include: German drama and theatre since the nineteenth century; the interrelation of medical discourse and literature in the nineteenth century; migration literature in the nineteenth century as well as today; literature and modernism; cultural and literary religious formations. She is the author of *Auf dem Weg zum Theater: Else Lasker-Schüler, Marieluise Fleißer, Nelly Sachs, Gerlind Reinshagen, Elfriede Jelinek* (2003) and she co-edited *Glaube und Geschlecht: Fromme Frauen, spirituelle Muster, religiöse Traditionen* (2008) with Ruth Albrecht and Florentine Strzelczyk. Recent articles are on *Dogville*, Heinrich Mann, Homi Bhabha, and the nineteenth-century actress Clara Ziegler.

**Anne Fleig** is Professor of German Literature with a special emphasis on gender studies at the German Department of the Freie Universität Berlin. Her research focuses on a wide range of German authors from the eighteenth century to the present day. She has worked on eighteenth-century women writers, such as Friederike Sophie Hensel, Caroline Luise von Klencke, Christiane Karoline Schlegel, and Charlotte von Stein (in *Handlungs-Spiel-Räume: Dramen von Autorinnen im Theater des ausgehenden 18. Jahrhunderts*, 1999), and she has also edited and republished plays by Mariane Sophie Weikard, Juliane Hayn, Friederike Helene Unger, and others. Anne Fleig is particularly interested in questions of sex/gender, the body, sports, and emotions in literary and cultural history and has recently published articles on Heinrich von Kleist, E. T. A. Hoffmann, Gottfried Keller, Irmgard Keun, Marieluise Fleißer, John von Düffel, and

Arno Geiger, covering topics such as masculinity, dance, and laughter. Her latest book deals with Robert Musil's aesthetics of sport and modern culture (*Körperkultur und Moderne: Robert Musils Ästhetik des Sports*, 2008).

**Helen Fronius** is Lecturer in German at Worcester College, Oxford. She studied at the University of Oxford as an undergraduate and a graduate student, and has taught there for several years, as well as at the University of Cardiff and Birkbeck College, University of London. She has published articles on women authors in the late eighteenth century, as well as a monograph, *Women and Literature in the Goethe Era (1770–1820): Determined Dilettantes* (Oxford: Oxford University Press, 2007). She has also co-edited a collection of essays with Anna Linton which arose from a major AHRC research project, 'Representations of Women and Death in German Literature, Art and Media after 1500'. The volume (*Women and Death: Representations of Female Victims and Perpetrators in German Culture 1500–2000*) appeared with Camden House in 2008. She has also published on, and is currently working on, representations of infanticide in German society and literature in the later eighteenth century.

**Anke Gilleir** is Associate Professor of Modern German Literature at the University of Leuven (Belgium). She has published on German women's literature (eighteenth–twentieth century), minority literature in Germany and Europe, gender and literature/ literary theory, literature and politics, and the historiography of literature. Her publications include: Anke Gilleir, Alicia Montoya, and Suzan Van Dijk, eds, *Women Writing Back / Writing Women Back: Transnational Perspectives from the Late Middle Ages to the Dawn of the Modern Era* (Leiden and Boston: Brill 2010); Anke Gilleir and Margarete Susman, 'Staat, Literatur oder nochmals zum deutschen Intellektualismus', *German Quarterly*, 82.4 (2009), 483–503; Anke Gilleir, 'Habeas corpus. On the Meaning of the "Ethnic" Body in the Literature of Tahar Ben Jelloun and Feridun Zaimoglu', in *Seeking the Self — Encountering the Other: Diasporic Narrative and the Ethics of Representation*, ed. by Tuomas Huttunen, Kaisa Ilmonen, and Elina Valovirta (Cambridge: Cambridge Scholarly, 2008), 198–210; Anke Gilleir, Eva Kormann, and Angelika Schlimmer, eds, *Textmaschinenkörper: Genderorientierte Lektüren des Androiden* (Amsterdam: Rodopi 2006).

**Katharina von Hammerstein** received her PhD in German Studies at the University of California, Los Angeles (UCLA) in 1991 and is Full Professor at the University of Connecticut. Her research interests include postcolonial approaches to representations of black men and women in German and Austrian literature, ethnology, and visual arts *c.*1900; feminist analyses of European women's self-inscriptions into literary, social, and political discourses *c.*1800; interdisciplinary readings of women's self-(re)presentations as political practice in nineteenth- and early twentieth-century public discourses; and New Historicist approaches to German Romanticism. Her publications include an edition of Peter Altenberg's *Ashantee* (2007); editions of articles by Frieda von Bülow (2008) and her *Reisescizzen und Tagebuchblätter aus Deutsch-Ostafrika* (2009); a monograph on Sophie Mereau (1994), a three-volume edition of her work (1997), and a co-edited anthology *Sophie Mereau: Verbindungslinien in Zeit und Raum* (2008). She has also published on Louise Aston, Hedwig Dohm, and Franziska zu Reventlow.

**Stephanie Hilger** is Associate Professor of Comparative Literature and German at the University of Illinois at Urbana-Champaign. Her research focuses on gender, class, and race in eighteenth-century British, French, and German literature. She is the author of *Women Write Back: Strategies of Response and the Dynamics of European Literary Culture, 1790–1805* (2009). Her articles have appeared in journals such as *Lessing Yearbook, Eighteenth-Century Studies, Colloquia Germanica, Neophilologus, College Literature, French Review, Seminar,* and *Women in German Yearbook.* Her current project, 'The Warrior and the Traveller: Women in the French Revolution', examines the depiction of socially and politically active women in German literature during the thirty-year period following the French Revolution.

**Susanne Kinnebrock** is Professor of Communication Theory at the Department of Language and Communication Studies of RWTH Aachen University. Her research interests include the history of journalism and mass media, women journalists, gender representations in mass media, journalism research, narrative journalism, and narrative persuasion. She is Chair of the Communication History Division of the German Communication Association and Vice-Chair of the Communication History Section of the European Communication Research and Education Association. She has published a biography on Anita Augspurg and various volumes on the history of media and journalism. At present she is preparing a book on the history of political women's magazines.

**Anna Richards** is Lecturer in German at Birkbeck College, University of London. She has published a number of articles on German women's writing from the eighteenth to the twentieth centuries and on the relationship between medical history and the novel. Her book, *The Wasting Heroine in German Fiction by Women 1770–1914,* was published by Oxford University Press in 2004, and a collection of essays edited with Clare Bielby, *Women and Death 3: Women's Representations of Death in German Culture since 1500,* appeared with Camden House in 2010. Her current research project is an interdisciplinary study of mourning and sensibility in the late eighteenth century.

**Timon B. Schaffer** MA studied Communications and Gender Studies at the University of Vienna.

**Charlotte Woodford** is the Fellow in German and a Director of Studies in Modern Languages at Selwyn College, Cambridge. Her book *Nuns Writing History in Early Modern Germany* appeared with Oxford University Press in 2002. Since then, she has worked on fiction in the late nineteenth century, publishing on Fontane, Marie von Ebner-Eschenbach, and a lesbian poet in Ebner's circle, Marie von Najmajer. She is working on a project on the late nineteenth-century German bestseller and writing a book on German women's novels in the same period.

**Linda Kraus Worley** is a professor at the University of Kentucky. She has published on numerous women writers of the eighteenth and nineteenth centuries including Sophie von La Roche, Therese Huber, Louise von François, Marie von Ebner-Eschenbach, and Gabriele Reuter. Other research interests include fairy tales, travel literature, and faculty careers. In addition to her teaching in German Studies, she is affiliated with the Gender and Women's Studies department. She also directs and helped develop a university-wide graduate certificate programme aimed at preparing future academic staff for the many facets of a career in higher education.

# INTRODUCTION

# Studying Eighteenth- and Nineteenth-Century German Women Writers

## Feminist Criticism Past, Present, and Future

*Anna Richards*

According to some of its most prominent exponents, feminist literary criticism is in trouble. Susan Gubar diagnosed 'critical anorexia' in the discipline in 1998;[1] more recently, in 2008, Toril Moi lamented the fact that, unlike in the early years of second-wave feminism, when literature by women was a central focus of theoretical exploration, today women's writing and literary criticism are 'a marginal topic in feminist theory'.[2] Gubar and Moi occupy different positions within feminist literary criticism, but they attribute what they see as the decline of the field to the same source: to poststructuralist concepts of gender, and in particular to the theories of Judith Butler. After situating Gubar and Moi's diagnoses in the context of the history of feminist criticism, I aim in this introductory chapter to establish whether a similar pessimism is justified with regard to feminist scholarship on German women writers of the eighteenth and nineteenth centuries, whether our field is in decline. I examine the relationship between critical work on early German women writers and feminist criticism more generally, and identify the recent trends and current emphases in our field. The essays in this volume, which arose from a conference held in Oxford in 2008 as part of the German Women Writers of the Eighteenth and Nineteenth Centuries conference series, exemplify many of these important new directions.

## Feminist Literary Criticism since the 1970s

In the early days of second-wave feminist literary criticism, the 1970s and 1980s, scholars in Europe and the United States launched an attack on the canon and on established ways of reading it. Critics such as Kate Millett drew attention to the misogyny inherent in many well-known texts by male authors.[3] As well as denying the supposed apoliticism of the historical criteria for canonization, feminist critics began the long project of rediscovering neglected women writers from the past, interpreting their work in its patriarchal historical context, and evaluating its gender ideology. Women authors whose writing appeared to contradict or protest against traditional concepts of femininity were particularly prized. Meanwhile, starting in the 1970s, and influenced by psychoanalysis and Derridean deconstruction, French feminist theorists[4] including Hélène Cixous, Luce Irigaray, and Julia Kristeva focused on the gendered nature of language and/or speculated about an 'écriture féminine' [feminine/female writing] which expressed — or would express — a femininity hitherto excluded from patriarchal discourse.

Feminist literary scholarship soon faced challenges from within and from outside the discipline. French feminist theory was accused of essentialism and of bearing little relation to 'real' women's writing. Because of their refusal to overlook the gender-political implications of 'great' literature by men, and their attempts to reconstruct a forgotten female literary tradition which did not necessarily conform to established aesthetic criteria, other branches of feminist scholarship were accused of flattening or ignoring aesthetic value. By the late 1980s and the 1990s, black and lesbian feminist critics were arguing that their typically straight, white, middle-class feminist colleagues promoted a universalized concept of woman at the expense of recognizing the manifold differences between women, and set about rediscovering their own alternative traditions. These pluralist impulses did not, however, challenge the validity — or the political imperative — of taking the literary history of one sex as a subject of enquiry. Judith Butler did that in the late 1980s and 1990s, arguing in her works 'Performative Acts and Gender Constitution' (1988), *Gender Trouble* (1990), and *Bodies that Matter* (1993) that, like gender, sex itself was a discursively produced category, which was constituted, legitimized, and made to *appear* essential by means of its repeated performance by individuals.[5] For feminists to focus on the status specifically of women — or for feminist literary critics to study women writers — on the grounds of their sex was to perpetuate an ontologically unfounded and oppressive gender polarization.

Gender studies, a discipline concerned with the creation in discourse of femininity and masculinity and their potential alternatives, has proliferated in universities in the wake of the poststructuralist challenge to fixed concepts of gender or sex identity, seemingly at the expense of women's studies.[6] According to critics such as Gubar, poststructuralist approaches strip feminism of its political imperative. As regards literary criticism, they invalidate the feminist recuperation of historical, embodied female writing subjects and their works.[7] The work of early women writers, in the context of gender studies, risks being understood as one site for the location and dissemination of knowledge about gender amongst many. Feminist critics who pursue the traditional task of recovering women writers are in danger of appearing naively essentialist. This is why, according to Moi, the study of women and aesthetics has become 'marginal' to feminist theory.

Other feminist critics paint a more positive picture than Gubar and Moi of the current state of feminist literary criticism. According to Ellen Rooney in her introduction to the *Cambridge Companion to Feminist Theory* (2006), 'critical anorexia is nowhere evident'.[8] Such critics point out that there has been a proliferation of new approaches in recent years, including hybrid forms such as postcolonial feminist theory and deconstructive feminism.[9] The conflicts within the discipline, they argue, are a sign of vigour rather than decline.

## Feminist Criticism on German Women Writers of the Eighteenth and Nineteenth Centuries

How does the progress of feminist criticism on German women writers of the eighteenth and nineteenth centuries compare with developments in feminist literary criticism and feminist literary theory more generally? A little later than some colleagues working on Anglo-American writers, beginning in the 1980s, feminist scholars including Barbara Becker-Cantarino, Gisela Brinker-Gabler, Ruth-Ellen Boetcher Joeres, and Helga Meise — many of them 'Auslandsgermanistinnen' (Germanists living outside Germany) — began the process of 'recovering' early German women writers who had received little or no attention in traditional German literary history and reconstructing their historical context.[10] An essential early step in this process was the biographical and bibliographical work of establishing which women wrote and what writing existed: the *Lexikon deutsch-sprachiger Schriftstellerinnen 1800–1945*, for example, a bibliographical work which lists publications by, and includes short biographies of, women writers of the nineteenth and early twentieth centuries, appeared in 1986.[11] Women authors including Sophie von la Roche (1730–1807), Therese Huber (1764–1829), Fanny Lewald (1811–89), and Gabriele Reuter (1859–1941), to name only some, gradually became recognized names amongst many Germanists and in some cases found their way onto university reading lists. Occasionally their works were reissued in new editions: in 1987 Anita Runge began editing the 'Frühe Frauenliteratur in Deutschland' (Early Women's Writing in Germany) series, published by Olms, starting with Caroline Auguste Fischer's *Die Honigmonathe* (The Honeymoon, 1802). Sophie von La Roche's *Geschichte des Fräuleins von Sternheim* (History of Lady Sophia Sternheim, 1771) was edited by Becker-Cantarino for a Reclam edition in 1983[12] and issued in two English translations, one modern and one from the eighteenth century, in the early 1990s, facilitating its inclusion on syllabi outside Germany.[13] As well as a recognition of the restrictions under which early women writers laboured and the inevitable influence on their writing of patriarchal gender ideologies, the critical approach adopted by German scholars during this early period in second-wave feminist criticism often involved 'reading between the lines' of primary works for 'subversive' content.[14] In keeping with trends in feminist literary criticism as a whole, early German works such as *Elisa, oder das Weib wie es seyn sollte* (Elisa, or Woman As She Should Be, 1795), an anonymously published novel advocating extreme female self-sacrifice which is generally accepted to be the work of Caroline von Wobeser (1769–1807), held a certain interest for feminist critics as negative examples of patriarchal doctrine and conditioning. In general, however, 'die guten' [the good ones], to use Sigrid Weigel's words — that is, the 'protofeminist' ones — were more popular than 'die schlechten' [the bad ones], who simply reproduced patriarchal ideas.[15]

What emerges clearly from a consideration of publications since the 1980s is that, although scholars often divide the development of feminist literary theory into distinct phases, the history of critical textual work being carried out by feminist scholars in our field displays a good deal of continuity. In particular, the early work of 'recovering' little-known women writers and discussing the emancipatory aspects of their work which began in the 1980s has continued up to the present day. But the theories about a female language or 'écriture féminine' which emerged in the 1970s and 1980s made little impact in our field; secondary literature in which feminist critics attempt to apply these ideas to the works of eighteenth- and nineteenth-century German women writers has been fairly rare. An exception is Brigitte E. Jirku's *Wollen sie mit Nichts ... ihre Zeit versplittern?*, published in 1994, in which she argues that the expressive, emphatic language of *Empfindsamkeit* (sensibility) employed in many novels by women in the late eighteenth century can be interpreted as a kind of 'écriture féminine'.[16] The problem with this kind of approach, the reason perhaps for the comparative lack of interest among feminist critics of early German women's writing in 'écriture féminine', is the similarity between theoretical concepts of 'authentically' feminine or female self-expression and eighteenth- and nineteenth-century *patriarchal* conceptions of what a 'feminine' language — and female nature — *should* be: emotional, 'fluid', lacking in form. It is not surprising that feminist critics of later periods, during which patriarchy's ideological construction of the feminine has been less restrictive, or feminist scholars theorizing about the potential *future* of women's writing, have engaged more enthusiastically with the theory of 'écriture féminine' than critics in our field.

Similarly, the debates which took place in the late 1980s and 1990s about the false universality of the female subject of feminist criticism, debates led in the main by black and lesbian critics, may have seemed less relevant to scholars of eighteenth- and nineteenth-century German women writers than to feminist colleagues working on other countries and periods. However, they were not entirely without impact: a new pluralism was evident in our field as well. If feminist critics continued in the main to research white, middle-class German women writers, they nevertheless became more interested in questions of class, race, and ethnicity.[17] Travel writing by German women of the eighteenth and nineteenth centuries, and the confrontation with the Other and subsequent re-examination of the self which this involved, has been the subject of much secondary literature.[18] The 1990s also witnessed a diversification of sources and contexts in research on early German women writers. The focus on historical contextualization which has always characterized much of the scholarship in our field broadened, and critics also considered a wider range of non-literary texts such as women's journalistic activities or their autobiographical writings.

Just after the turn of the century, in an article in the *Women in German Yearbook* of 2001, Boetcher Joeres offered a largely positive diagnosis of the state of feminist criticism on nineteenth-century German women writers. Commenting on the volume of critical work and the variety of approaches adopted, she argued that the field 'seems at the moment to be in an active and energetic phase'.[19]

## Current and Future Perspectives

Ten years on from Boetcher Joeres's evaluation, does the picture remain a positive one? Despite the efforts of feminist critics during the last thirty years, early German women writers still lack a substantial presence on university syllabi and in the canon and it is still difficult to obtain modern editions of most of their works. Many critics feel that the increasing popularity of gender studies, with its separation of gender discourses from particular writing subjects and its lack of commitment to the literariness of the literary text, has eclipsed the feminist literary critical project. There is a sense that we need to embark on new directions in order to prevent the gradual decline of our field.

At first, some of the new directions being taken may seem rather conservative, in keeping perhaps with what is referred to as our 'postfeminist' age.[20] Boetcher Joeres picked up on this mood in her otherwise positive analysis of the field in 2001, arguing that 'something is missing': political engagement, the acknowledgement of relations of power which is 'absolutely central to any feminist work'.[21] Recent trends may appear to lack the focus on feminist politics which characterized earlier feminist criticism; they may seem to scholars such as Boetcher Joeres insufficiently to acknowledge women's historical oppression. As the essays in this volume demonstrate, however, the commitment to feminism remains.

In our opening chapter Anne Fleig discusses some of the problems afflicting criticism in our field today and offers some suggestions for the future. She acknowledges the volume of work that continues to be produced in some areas, in research on the women's novel, for example. However she suggests that a certain stagnation is discernible. Gender studies, focusing on the production of knowledge in discourse, has tended to overlook questions of female authorship and to detract attention from early women authors, and it has often employed the term 'gender' in unexamined, simplistic ways. She recommends a 'return to the author', but one which does not involve essentialist readings. On the contrary, both sex and gender, Fleig argues, should be investigated in their different historical constructions. Feminist critics should not solely consider the position of early women's writing on the map of gender or sex ideology, however; they should also consider it for its own sake, for its particular aesthetic qualities, independent of its sexual politics. Questions of genre also merit more attention.

Fleig's call for a non-essentialist approach to historical female author figures is in one sense in keeping with the emphasis which feminist literary criticism has placed on historical contextualization from the outset. Feminist critics of eighteenth- and nineteenth-century German women writers have long interpreted their works not as isolated artefacts transcending their age, but as the product of a particular historical moment; they have not read the work of women writers as the pure expression of an ahistorical 'inner self'. Even when feminist critics have uncovered a 'protofeminist' message between the lines, this should not be confused with their identifying an 'authentic', essentially female essence. After all, it is well known that the rise of the woman writer in the late eighteenth century was contemporaneous with a new polarized understanding of gender, propagated by medicine, philosophy, and anthropology, of which the modern concept of 'woman' as physically and psychically directly opposed to 'man' was a product. Feminist criticism has long shared with poststructuralism an understanding of the historical nature of 'natural concepts', as Rey Chow points out,[22] and problematized any simplistic sense of the author as a unified, self-determining subject.[23] As Fleig's chapter suggests, however, much work remains to be done on the way early texts help construct and comment on the construction of gender and sex identity. For example, the fascinating eighteenth- and nineteenth-century discourses on female dress and its function as a producer, as well as an indicator, of female 'nature', merit more attention.

Like Fleig, Anke Gilleir calls for a move away from certain aspects of gender studies and a return to an apparently more traditional study of literature in her chapter 'From Word to World and Back: Literary Studies and Gender Studies'. Gilleir argues that as gender studies has made the study of literature more culturally oriented, not only has the focus on women and their work as the subject of study abated, the specific literariness of the literary text — those formal and imaginative aspects which distinguish it from other cultural forms — has also been overlooked. The study of women's literature as literature, in her view, has been abandoned before it ever began in earnest in the academy. She proposes that more attention be paid to the formal qualities of women's literature among feminist critics, which would not be 'a sign of academic regression', but a means of rescuing women's writing in academia.

Both Fleig and Gilleir recognize that the approaches they advocate rely on the continued recovery of neglected women writers and on the wider availability of their texts. As Susanne Kord writes in *Women Peasant Poets in Eighteenth-Century England, Scotland and Germany* (2003), the 'monumental task' of tracing a reception history of authors who fell outside the male, middle-class aesthetic parameters established in the eighteenth century is by no means yet complete.[24] And in recent years there has been little evidence of 'critical anorexia' or stagnation with regard to this kind of research:[25] the project of unearthing neglected women writers is still being actively pursued. Several lesser-known authors such as Ernestine Voß (1756–1834), Louise Brachmann (1777–1822), and Friederike Brun (1765–1835) have been the subject of recent studies, which often take a fairly traditional approach, offering biographical information, introducing readers to little-known works, and explaining the reasons for their neglect.[26] In 2006, an invaluable resource for feminist critics in the field was published: Gudrun Loster-Schneider and Gaby Pailer's *Lexikon deutschsprachiger Epik und Dramatik von Autorinnen 1730–1900*, providing bibliographical information and content summaries of works by German-speaking women of the eighteenth and nineteenth centuries and short commentaries on them by scholars in the field.[27] As regards the better-known early German women writers, feminist critics continue to expand our knowledge of their work. The interest in La Roche, for example, has broadened well beyond her most successful early novel *Geschichte des Fräuleins von Sternheim*. In *Meine Liebe zu Büchern: Sophie von La Roche als professionelle Schriftstellerin*, published in 2008,[28] Barbara Becker-Cantarino discusses La Roche's many fictional works and her journalistic writing, conduct books, travel journals, and letters. For the first time La Roche's entire, fifty-year-long correspondence with Wieland is examined, rather than just the letters associated with the publication of *Sternheim*. By means of careful readings and historical contextualization, Becker-Cantarino arrives at new conclusions about the complexity of La Roche's relationship with Wieland and about the educative value of her works for female readers.

The continued discovery of new authors and sources has led, and will continue to lead, to a revision of some of the assumptions made in the early days of feminist literary criticism. For example, in the last decade there has been a new emphasis among some feminist critics on the inclusion of early German women writers in, rather than on their exclusion from, literary history. In an early article by Boetcher Joeres, published in 1986, she argued that while the 'pessimistic' approach of focusing on the oppression of early women writers is likely to be politically 'liberal', 'optimistic' criticism, which emphasizes their scope for participation on the literary scene, is likely to be politically 'conservative'.[29] Recent publications by feminist scholars such as Helen Fronius illustrate that Boetcher Joeres' evaluation of the politics of these critical approaches does not necessarily hold today.[30] In her monograph *Women and Literature in the Goethe Era (1770-1820): Determined Dilettantes* (2007), Fronius takes issue with the emphasis set by some early feminist research on women writers around 1800, arguing that critics made the mistake of equating the period's proscriptive statements about gender roles with social reality and therefore concluded that women authors were more silenced than was the case. In fact, she demonstrates, German women were writing in significant numbers and often actively pursuing the publication of their work in business-like fashion. In our volume Fronius makes a powerful case for the continued importance of recovering neglected works and historical sources which enable us to gain a more accurate picture of women's literary activity. We may be familiar with the existence of many early women writers, she argues, but only in a small number of cases has their work been analyzed in depth. By going back to the archives, back to the primary sources, it is possible to trace ways in which women participated in intertextual dialogues and contributed to the discourses of their day. She demonstrates for example that women contributed to the *Teutscher Merkur (German Mercury)*, a journal edited by Christoph Martin Wieland in the late eighteenth and early nineteenth centuries, in greater numbers, and more consistently, than is often assumed, and that in these contributions they sometimes expressed their views on gender relations in direct and challenging terms.

Another emerging trend in our field similarly involves the 'return to the text' advocated by Fleig and Gilleir, but sets it in a new literary context. As a natural extension perhaps of the long-established interest in women's travel writing, many feminist critics are attempting to understand the work of German women writers in a European context and establish a cross-cultural female literary tradition. The field of comparative literature has traditionally focused on canonized works by men; in 1994 Sarah Webster Goodwin wrote that it had until then proved 'a tough Bastille for feminists to storm'.[31] Recent feminist comparative research has set new emphases, eschewing the inscription of certain texts within an established European tradition of 'great' — and therefore widely influential — works in order to examine the historical construction of aesthetic value and the place of women in the literary marketplace, to consider relationships and interactions between women writers from different countries, and to investigate their 'free' translations and adaptations of works from other languages as creative activities in their own right.[32] A number of research groupings have pursued such topics. In 2007 an international research group entitled 'New Approaches to European Women's Writing 1700–1900' was established at the University of Utrecht to trace a tradition of women writers which transcends national boundaries. A volume entitled *Translators, Interpreters, Mediators: Women Writers 1700–1900* (2007), arising from a conference at Chawton House Library and edited by Gillian Dow, focuses on the translation activities of women at this period and includes two German authors, Luise Gottsched and Therese Huber.[33] In 2010, the British Women in German Studies (WIGS) conference was held in collaboration with Women in Spanish, Portuguese, and Latin American Studies (WISPS), with a keynote speech by Professor Carol Tully on nineteenth-century German women writers' Hispanism and translations of Spanish works.[34] In our volume, Hilary Brown, the author of a monograph on English influences on Benedikte Naubert's work,[35] discusses the advantages of considering German women's writing in a comparative light. She argues that comparisons with women writers from other countries can provide a more sympathetic or 'supportive' context than comparisons with male German contemporaries. At the same time, considering the 'intercultural transfer' which took place between women writers — translation activities, for example — could lead to a revision of the role played by women in the literary history of the eighteenth and nineteenth centuries and help rescue them from the margins of the discipline. Women's writing, from this comparative perspective, both belongs to a specifically female tradition and is included in mainstream cultural history.

As Fronius argues in her essay in this volume, an important task for twenty-first-century feminist literary criticism is to expand our knowledge of early women's writing by paying attention to works which, because of their 'unfeminist' politics, their 'triviality', or their obscurity, have been ignored up to now. Against the tendency of much early feminist criticism in our field, several essays in this volume investigate works which might typically be designated 'conservative' in terms of their gender ideology. Like 'optimistic' feminist research, this focus on less 'progressive' texts should not be equated with a lack of political engagement. It involves a sensitive appreciation of texts and their particular characteristics, and furthers our knowledge of women's literary participation.

In her essay Stephanie Hilger investigates *Virginia oder die Kolonie von Kentucky* (*Virginia, or the Kentucky Colony*, 1820) by the little-known Henriette Frölich and concludes that, in proto-feminist terms, the novel situates itself in 'unsettling' fashion between the poles of 'progressive' and 'conservative'. Employing the concept of 'writing back' from postcolonial theory, Hilger shows that the novel stands in intertextual relationship with texts by Goethe. In implicit contrast to Goethe's autobiography, Frölich describes her text as 'mehr Wahrheit als Dichtung' [more truth than fiction]. According to Hilger, Frölich may be a marginal woman writer, but she 'writes back' to Weimar Classicism, thereby both engaging and questioning its conventions.

Charlotte Woodford's chapter is a consideration of a genre typically considered 'conservative': the sentimental novel. She analyses the ways in which the ethos of renunciation is employed in two works, E. Marlitt's *Goldelse* (Gold Elsie, 1866) and Gabriele Reuter's *Liselotte von Reckling* (1904). While Marlitt rewards her heroine's capacity for self-sacrifice with a happy marriage based on middle-class values, Reuter in her 'anti-romance' problematizes the sentimental idea that renunciation empowers women, at the same time as criticizing unrestrained, 'modern' egoism. *Goldelse* can be read as a 'conservative' novel, but both works, Woodford argues, fulfil an important function for their female readers, affirming their desires, broaching the subject of sexuality, providing a source of escape, and fashioning figures for identification, and both are complex in their engagement with the ethical dilemmas of the modern age.

For Linda Kraus Worley, the adjective 'conservative' can be unhelpful. It is sometimes used in stereotypical or superficial ways which fail sufficiently to situate the work in question in historical context. For example, the novel *Lotti, die Uhrmacherin* (Lotti the Watchmaker, 1880), one of Marie von Ebner-Eschenbach's lesser-known works, may seem at first sight to plot a conventional life-course for its urban protagonist, ending her story with marriage and a family. Kraus Worley asks why such a conclusion should necessarily be read as 'antifeminist'. In fact, she argues, read in the context of discourses on city life in the nineteenth century, Ebner-Eschenbach's novel carves out a niche for its heroine in which she can experience the advantages of modern city life and of a profession without sacrificing a sense of community.

Annette Bühler-Dietrich in her essay 'Contestations of Normativity: Rereading Nineteenth-Century Authors with Current Moral Philosophy' draws on Judith Butler's recent publications. Bühler-Dietrich compares Butler's thoughts on the subject's dependence on the Other and on alternative modes of gender with writings on gender and sexuality by two turn-of-the-century German-speaking women writers, Laura Marholm and Rosa Mayreder, both of whom pursue a definition of femininity which is in contradiction to the normative gender ideals of their time. Bühler-Dietrich points out that it is the 'antifeminist' Marholm who prefigures something of Butler's understanding of 'ethical enmeshment with the other', writing against individualism and insisting instead on the subject's undoing by sexuality and her reliance on the other for her identity.

Other contributions to our volume focus on 'conservative' texts in order, not so much to highlight their individual qualities, as to illustrate the power and the mechanisms of patriarchal or racist ideology. Like Hilger, Katharina von Hammerstein draws on ideas from postcolonial theory in her analysis of Frieda von Bülow's autobiographical writings. Bülow was an unconventional woman and an active promoter of women's rights, but her experience of gender oppression did not lead to empathy with people ethnically different from her. While enjoying the increased freedom which colonial life offered to white women when she spent time in East Africa at the end of the nineteenth century, in her writings Bülow emphasized the alterity of colonial subjects, including women, and even revelled in their exotic Otherness. In doing so, Hammerstein argues, she bolstered her own sense of identity and established a patriotic sense of community between herself and her European readers. Reading Bülow's texts helps us to understand the ways in which, at this period, feminism could be complicit with racist and colonialist ideas, and may prompt us to ask questions about our own geographical and gender allegiances.

Jennifer Askey turns her attention to a so-called 'trivial' genre, girls' literature, to shed light on the process of gender socialization in the nineteenth century. She writes that popular stories for girls by authors such as Ottilie Wildermuth, Brigitte Augusti, and Clementine Helm often portray young female protagonists, figures of identification for readers, who care for the sick and needy. These heroines are typically rewarded for their efforts with some degree of power in the sickroom and with romance, marriage, and integration into the adult world. Such narratives thus accommodate both the conservative pedagogic imperatives of a society dependent on strictly prescribed gender roles and the desires and fantasies of adolescent female readers. This kind of literature, Askey argues, is by no means protofeminist, but its analysis as an instrument for women's formation in the nineteenth century is clearly of value in feminist terms.

As demonstrated by the contributions by Hilger and Hammerstein, which draw on postcolonial theory, and that of Askey, which is influenced by cultural studies, feminist criticism in our field continues to incorporate methodologies from other disciplines in order to provide new contexts and interpretative models for texts. Other recent studies have discussed the relationship between literary works and early educational theory,[36] medicine,[37] legal history,[38] fashion,[39] and the feminist movement.[40] In our volume, Susanne Kinnebrock and Timon B. Schaffer use a methodology taken from communication studies in order to draw some general conclusions about eighteenth- and nineteenth-century German women writers, instead of focusing, as much criticism has done in the past, on exceptional individuals. They analyse a late nineteenth-century collection of biographies for information about where women writers typically lived, their marital status, social background, occupation, and publication activities. In doing so they arrive at some new insights: for example, women writers often wrote for magazines and publications aimed at both sexes, rather than writing exclusively for women, as contemporary sources sometimes claimed. Using a social-sciences approach, Kinnebrock and Schaffer's chapter fills in some important gaps in our knowledge of women writers as a collective, thereby fleshing out the context for the examination of particular figures as well as identifying broader trends.

In the last ten years feminist literary criticism on German women writers of the eighteenth and nineteenth centuries has not stagnated as regards the volume of scholarship being published. Some critics, however, have experienced a sense of fatigue with traditional feminist approaches, which are accused of yielding the same results over and over again, regardless of the texts in question. Gender studies, focusing on the construction of femininity and masculinity in various discursive fields, of which literature is one, has offered productive new insights but has arguably also deflected attention away from female authors and the aesthetic qualities of their writing. Certain feminist scholars are now calling for a move away from gender studies back to a more concentrated focus on women and literature. Critics including those represented in this volume are tracing a comparative European tradition of women's writing, studying 'conservative' authors, focusing on the formal or aesthetic qualities of texts, and suggesting that women authors around 1800 were not as disadvantaged as we have supposed them to be. The commitment of such scholars to the feminist political project remains undiluted; their concern is to bring to light neglected women's writing, offer a nuanced, sensitive understanding of its particular characteristics, and broaden our historical understanding of women's experience. It is hard to imagine that the place which early German women writers have now gained in literary history and in academia thanks to feminist research can be lost again, but our research must continue to pose questions of the premises of feminist literary criticism and to evolve in new directions if this still marginal place is to expand.

## Notes to the Introduction

1. Susan Gubar, 'What Ails Feminist Criticism?', *Critical Inquiry*, 24.4 (1998), 878–902 (p. 901).
2. Toril Moi, ' "I am not a woman writer": About Women, Literature and Feminist Theory Today', *Feminist Theory* 9.3 (2008), 259–71 (p. 259).
3. Kate Millett, *Sexual Politics* (New York: Doubleday, 1970).
4. The designation 'French' has been criticized as inaccurate: not all the theorists in question were French.
5. Judith Butler, 'Performative Acts and Gender Constitution: An Essay in Phenomenology and Feminist Theory', *Theatre Journal*, 40.4 (1988), 519–31; *Gender Trouble: Feminism and the Subversion of Identity* (New York: Routledge, 1990); *Bodies that Matter: On the Discursive Limits of 'Sex'* (New York, Routledge, 1993).
6. According to Nancy K. Miller, 'If Women's Studies becomes gender studies, then the *real* end of women in the institution will not be far off' ('The Text's Heroine: A Feminist Critic and her Fictions', in *Conflicts in Feminism*, ed. by Marianne Hirsch and Evelyn Fox Keller (New York: Routledge, 1990), pp. 112–20 (p. 118)).
7. Mary Eagleton asks, 'How could feminism take heed of the insights of poststructuralism and postmodernism without jettisoning its political project?' (*Figuring the Woman Author in Contemporary Fiction* (New York: Palgrave Macmillan, 2005), p. 17).
8. Ellen Rooney, 'Introduction', in *The Cambridge Companion to Feminist Literary Theory*, ed. by Ellen Rooney (Cambridge: Cambridge University Press, 2006), pp. 1–26 (p. 13).
9. See Gill Plain and Susan Sellers, 'Part III: Poststructuralism and Beyond: Introduction', in *A History of Feminist Literary Criticism*, ed. by Gill Plain and Susan Sellers (Cambridge: Cambridge University Press, 2008), pp. 210–13, here p. 210.
10. Helga Meise, *Die Unschuld und die Schrift: Deutsche Frauenromane im 18. Jahrhundert* (Berlin: Guttandin & Hoppe, 1983); *German Women in the Eighteenth and Nineteenth Centuries*, ed. by Ruth-Ellen Boetcher Joeres and Mary Jo Maynes (Bloomington: Indiana University Press, 1986); Barbara Becker-Cantarino, *Der lange Weg zur Mündigkeit: Frau und Literatur (1500–1800)* (Stuttgart: Metzler, 1987); Lydia Schieth, *Die Entwicklung des deutschen Frauenromans im ausgehenden 18. Jahrhundert: Ein Beitrag zur Gattungsgeschichte* (Frankfurt am Main: Lang, 1987); *Deutsche Literatur von Frauen*, ed. by Gisela Brinker-Gabler, 2 vols (Munich: Beck, 1988); *Untersuchungen zum Roman von Frauen um 1800*, ed. by Helga Gallas and Magdalene Heuser (Tübingen: Niemeyer, 1990).
11. *Lexikon deutschsprachiger Schriftstellerinnen 1800–1945*, ed. by Gisela Brinker-Gabler, Karola Ludwig, and Angela Wöffen (Munich: Deutscher Taschenbuch Verlag, 1986).
12. Sophie von La Roche, *Geschichte des Fräuleins von Sternheim* [1771], ed. by Barbara Becker-Cantarino (Stuttgart: Reclam, 1983).
13. Sophie von La Roche, *History of Lady Sophia Sternheim*, trans. by Crista Baguss Britt (New York:

State University of New York Press, 1991); Sophie von La Roche, *The History of Lady Sophie Sternheim*, trans. by Joseph Collyer, ed. by James Lynn (London: Pickering & Chatto, 1991).

14. See e.g. Ruth-Ellen Boetcher Joeres, '"That girl is an entirely different character!" Yes, but is she a feminist? Observations on Sophie von La Roche's *Geschichte des Fräuleins von Sternheim*', in *German Women in the Eighteenth and Nineteenth Centuries: A Social and Literary History*, ed. by Ruth-Ellen Boetcher Joeres and Mary Jo Maynes (Bloomington: Indiana University Press, 1986), pp. 137–56.

15. Sigrid Weigel, 'Der schielende Blick: Thesen zur Geschichte weiblicher Schreibpraxis', in *Die verborgene Frau: Sechs Beiträge zu einer feministischen Literaturwissenschaft*, ed. by Sigrid Weigel and Inge Stephan (Berlin: Argument, 1983), pp. 83–137 (p. 84).

16. Brigitte E. Jirku, *'Wollen sie mit Nichts ... ihre Zeit versplittern?': Ich-Erzählerin und Erzählstruktur in von Frauen verfassten Romanen des 18. Jahrhunderts* (Frankfurt am Main: Lang, 1994).

17. E.g. Jeannine Blackwell, 'Sophie von La Roche and the Black Slave Poet Feuerbach: A Study in Sentimentality, Enlightenment, and Outsiderdom', in *The Enlightenment and its Legacy*, ed. by Sara Friedrichsmeyer and Barbara Becker-Cantarino (Bonn: Bouvier, 1991), pp. 105–15; Irene Stocksieker Di Maio, 'Jewish Emancipation and Integration: Fanny Lewald's Narrative Strategies', in *Autoren damals und heute: Literaturgeschichtliche Beispiele veränderter Wirkungshorizonte*, ed. by Gerhard P. Knapp (Amsterdam: Rodopi, 1991), pp. 273–301; Thomas Mast, 'Gender, Class, Jewishness, and the Problem of Self in Fanny Lewald's *Jenny*: Jenny's "schielender Blick"', *Focus on Literatur: A Journal for German-Language Literature*, 2.1 (1995), 31–50.

18. Konstanze Bäumer, 'Reisen als Moment der Erinnerung: Fanny Lewald (1811–1889) *Lehr- und Wanderjahre*', *Amsterdämer Beiträge zur Neueren Germanistik*, 28 (1989), 137–57; Helga Schutte Watt, 'Woman's Progress: Sophie La Roche's Travelogues 1787–1788', *The Germanic Review*, 69.2 (1994), 50–60; Patricia Howe, '"Das Beste sind Reisebeschreibungen": Reisende Frauen um die Mitte des neunzehnten Jahrhunderts und ihre Texte', in *Reisen im Diskurs: Modelle der literarischen Fremderfahrung von den Pilgerberichten bis zur Postmoderne*, ed. by Anne Fuchs and Theo Harden (Heidelberg: Carl Winter, 1995), pp. 273–301; Monika Nenon, 'Nationalcharakter und Kultur: Die Reiseberichte von Sophie von La Roche', *Carleton Germanic Papers*, 24 (1996), 57–72; Margaret E. Ward, 'The Personal is Political — the Political becomes Personal: Fanny Lewald's Early Travel Literature', in *Politics in German Literature*, ed. by Beth Bjorklund and Mark E. Cory (Columbia: Camden House, 1998), pp. 60–82; Christina Ujma, 'England und die Engländer in Fanny Lewalds Romanen und Reiseberichten', in *The Novel in Anglo-German Context: Cultural Cross-Currents and Affinities*, ed. by Susanne Stark (Amsterdam: Rodopi, 2000), pp. 145–56.

19. Ruth-Ellen Boetcher Joeres, 'Scattered Thoughts on Current Feminist Literary Critical Work in Nineteenth-Century German Studies', *Women in German Yearbook*, 17 (2001), 225–44 (p. 226).

20. There is no consensus on the exact definition of postfeminism or its relationship to the political imperatives of the feminist movement. See Ann Braithwaite, 'The Personal, the Political, Third-Wave and Postfeminisms', *Feminist Theory*, 3.3 (2002), 335–44.

21. Boetcher Joeres, 'Scattered Thoughts', pp. 235, 231.

22. Rey Chow, 'Poststructuralism: Theory as Critical Self-Consciousness', in *The Cambridge Companion to Feminist Literary Theory*, ed. by Ellen Rooney (Cambridge: Cambridge University Press, 2006), pp. 195–210 (p. 205).

23. Mary Eagleton comments on the affinities between Roland Barthes's concept of 'the death of the author' and feminism, pointing out that 'from many feminist positions, the "birth" of the woman author never meant cultural dominance or control of meaning' (*Figuring the Woman Author in Contemporary Fiction*, p. 4).

24. Susanne Kord, *Women Peasant Poets in Eighteenth-Century England, Scotland and Germany: Milkmaids on Parnassus* (Rochester, NY: Camden House, 2003).

25. See Anna Richards, 'The Eighteenth Century', review chapter in *The Year's Work in Modern Language Studies 69 (2006 and 2007)* (London: Maney, 2008) and in *The Year's Work in Modern Language Studies 70 (2008)* (London: Maney, 2009), for details of many secondary works on German eighteenth-century women writers published in 2006, 2007, and 2008.

26. In 2006 Dagny Stemper published a monograph on the life, letters, poems, and essays of the little-known Ernestine Voß: *Das Leben der schleswig-holsteinischen Schriftstellerin Ernestine Voß (1756–1834): Eine Analyse zu Biographie und Werk auf der Grundlage ihres autographischen Nachlasses*

(Frankfurt am Main: Lang, 2006). In a monograph published the next year, Janet Besserer Holmgren focused on Louise Brachmann, Friederike Brun, Amalie von Imhoff, Sophie Mereau, Elisa von der Recke, and Caroline von Wolzogen: *The Women Writers in Schiller's 'Horen': Patrons, Petticoats, and the Promotion of Weimar Classicism* (Newark, DE: University of Delaware Press, 2007). See also Ruth P. Dawson, *The Contested Quill: Literature by Women in Germany 1770–1800* (Newark, DE: University of Delaware Press, 2002).

27. *Lexikon deutschsprachiger Epik und Dramatik von Autorinnen 1730–1900*, ed. by Gudrun Loster-Schneider and Gaby Pailer (Tübingen and Basle: Francke, 2006).

28. Barbara Becker-Cantarino, *Meine Liebe zu Büchern: Sophie von La Roche als professionelle Schriftstellerin* (Heidelberg: Winter, 2008).

29. Ruth-Ellen Boetcher Joeres, '"That girl is an entirely different character!"', 137-38.

30. Anne Fleig, 'Zwischen Ausschluss und Aneignung: Neue Positionen in der Geschlechterforschung zur Aufklärung', *Das achtzehnte Jahrhundert*, 26.1 (2002), 79–89; Helen Fronius, *Women and Literature in the Goethe Era (1770–1820): Determined Dilettantes* (Oxford: Clarendon Press, 2007); Maya Gerig, *Jenseits von Tugend und Empfindsamkeit: Gesellschaftspolitik im Frauenroman um 1800* (Cologne, Weimar, and Vienna: Böhlau, 2008).

31. Sarah Webster Goodwin, 'Cross Fire and Collaboration among Comparative Literature, Feminism, and the New Historicism', in *Borderwork: Feminist Engagements with Contemporary Literature*, ed. by Margaret Higonnet (Ithaca: Cornell University Press, 1994), 247–66 (p. 265).

32. E.g. Anna Richards, '"Double-voiced discourse" and Psychological Insight in the Work of Therese Huber', *Modern Language Review*, 99.2 (2004), 416–29; Gisela Arygyle, 'The Horror and Pleasure of Un-English Fiction: Ida von Hahn-Hahn and Fanny Lewald in England', *Comparative Literature Studies*, 44.1–2 (2007), 144–65; Peter Damrau, 'Eliza Haywoods *Geschichte des Fräuleins Elisabeth Thoughtless* (1756): Frühe Selbsterkenntnis und Ehekritik in der englischen Übersetzungsliteratur', *German Quarterly*, 82.4 (2009), 425–46.

33. Gillian Dow, *Translators, Interpreters, Mediators: Women Writers 1700–1900* (Oxford: Lang, 2007).

34. Carol Tully, 'Women on the Verge of a Cultural Breakthrough: German Hispanism, Translation and Gender in the Nineteenth Century', keynote speech at WIGS and WISPS Annual Conference on 'Friendship', held at Swansea University, 13 November 2010.

35. Hilary Brown, *Benedikte Naubert (1756–1819) and her Relations to English Culture* (Leeds: Maney, 2005).

36. Anja May, *Wilhelm Meisters Schwestern: Bildungsromane von Frauen im ausgehenden 18. Jahrhundert* (Königstein/Taunus: Helmer, 2006).

37. Anna Richards, *The Wasting Heroine in German Fiction by Women 1770–1914* (Oxford: Oxford University Press, 2004).

38. See e.g. Vanessa van Ornam, *Fanny Lewald and Nineteenth-Century Constructions of Femininity* (New York: Lang, 2002).

39. Julia Bertschik, *Mode und Moderne: Kleidung als Spiegel des Zeitgeistes in der deutschsprachigen Literatur (1770–1945)* (Cologne: Böhlau, 2005).

40. Chris Weedon, *Gender, Feminism, and Fiction in Germany, 1840–1914* (New York and Berne: Lang, 2006).

PART I

# New Approaches

# CHAPTER 1

# Forgotten Women Writers?

## Reflections on the Current State and Future Prospects of Gender Studies

*Anne Fleig*

From the start, feminist and gender-oriented literary studies have debated the complex interaction between the history of literature and gender relations. Extensive research has shed light on the work of women writers from former centuries. The findings of this research have also had an impact on discourses on authorship, the public sphere, and aesthetic appreciation. Yet research on the intellectual and artistic products of women is often met with indifference today. It is necessary now to evaluate the achievements of the first wave of feminist studies and question the future prospects of gender studies in order to forestall the historical amnesia of postfeminism. The institutionalization of gender studies as well as the profound change that universities — both in Germany and in other European countries — are currently undergoing must also be considered in this evaluation. The starting point for the following reflections is the observation that the remarkable triumph of *gender* as an analytic category in the humanities and in the social sciences has not been matched by a similar development in literary-historical studies. I will consider whether or not an interrelation between the triumph of gender in one research area but not another exists here, and, if so, which implications for research derive from it.

In the first part of this chapter, I will outline the historical development of, and current state of affairs in studies concerned with, respectively, literature produced by women writers and the conditions of female authorship. In the next step, I summarize the progression of gender studies, a discipline which has, to some extent, grown and flourished at the expense of the historically oriented women's studies. In the third, final part, I discuss future perspectives and possible ways of supplementing and building on the findings of gender studies specific to the eighteenth and nineteenth centuries. The purpose of this essay is to look ahead to future developments in that area of research which deals with the literature of women and men and which aims to situate that literature in its historical, social, and cultural context. This research will include the categories of both gender and sex. The main argument to be put forward is that there must be a 'return' of the female author in literary studies, in order to ensure the transmission and canonization of female authors' works in historical studies of literature, on the book market, and in schools and universities.

## The Current State of Gender Studies from the Point of View of Literary History

Since the late 1970s, especially since Silvia Bovenschen's 1979 study *Die imaginierte Weiblichkeit*, which was the starting point for a renewed interest in works by women writers in the German-speaking world, many female literary scholars have devoted themselves to the discovery and analysis of unknown — or rather forgotten — works by women as a contribution to literary history. This quest was initially inspired by the fact that many women saw themselves as part of the female collective, which made it a quest for their own past. It was driven by the notion of a political identity founded on contributing to the history of emancipation and to a change in current gender relations. But from the start, feminist scholars were fully aware of the paradox of equality and difference involved in a quest for historical women and a protest against their exclusion from history, which simultaneously reinforces the difference between men and women.[1] Early feminist scholarship in particular proved its legitimacy by dealing with the historical development of modern gender relations.[2]

After thirty years of research we know that women of the eighteenth and nineteenth centuries executed works in all genres and therefore gained access to the literary public sphere on various levels. While earlier feminist criticism assumed that women were excluded from all educational establishments as well as from discourses on authorship and genre, this notion has given way to a focus on women's complex and contradictory participation in cultural life and in the literary market, mainly due to developments in discourse history in the late 1990s.[3] At present, however, research on literature by women authors seems to be somewhat stagnant. The well-known studies of the works of female writers of the eighteenth and nineteenth centuries written in the 1980s and 1990s have only been taken up by subsequent scholars in a few cases.[4] Despite the fact that these studies existed in order to unearth women's writing, and despite the fact that they were explicitly intended to function as the foundation for further studies, these have failed to appear.[5] Works following in the footsteps of these foundational studies on works by female authors of the eighteenth and nineteenth centuries have remained rare. The change in perspective described above was itself a response to certain symptoms of fatigue within feminist scholarship and to one reproach in particular, namely that dealing with female literature led to nothing but a repeated 'Bestätigung eines historischen Mangels' [confirmation of their historical absence].[6] However, the change in perspective has had limited success.

It is true that some recent studies have continued to try to reveal the contradictory involvement of women in the literary scene. However, the revisions of former positions have not given new impetus to the investigation of female authors. Thus monographs dealing with individual genres can still be counted on the fingers of one hand. This applies to the large number of dramas as well as to women's letters and autobiographies. In comparison, research on the novel appears to be far more differentiated. It has advanced in terms of research on individual female writers,[7] genre considerations,[8] and in the application of approaches deriving from different fields, such as the concept of space.[9] One example of such developments can be found in Maya Gerig's recent study on socio-politics in novels by women writers around 1800. The programmatic title of Gerig's essay 'Jenseits von Tugend und Empfindsamkeit' (Beyond Virtue and Sensibility)[10] explicitly builds on the thesis of women's participation in public life and her study consistently elucidates this notion with regard to the issues of infanticide, child murder, and domestic abuse.

On the whole, however, it seems that there are few impulses in recent studies on literature written by women around 1800 that could generate further interest. It is most striking that each of the monographs mentioned in the previous two paragraphs is a doctoral dissertation, and thus stands at the threshold of institutional scholarship. These researchers often remain relatively unknown, lack institutional backing, and have not established a professional reputation which would lend weight to their findings.

There are various reasons for this apparent stagnation. The impression may have been conveyed that the fundamental work on women writers has been done and that the phase of discovery has been completed. This notion corresponds to the socio-political climate in which many believe that the demands of the second-wave feminist movement have been fulfilled and that equal rights for men and women have been achieved. In the era of postfeminism and postmodern gender discourse, the topic of inequality has fallen from favour, although in the context of the eighteenth century, for example, it remains an unavoidable question, given the class system and the different educational opportunities open to men and women in that period. Another dimension emerges with respect to those still dedicated to the feminist project. There are considerable discrepancies between developments in feminist theory in the areas of gender, queer, and postcolonial studies on the one hand and studies dealing with historical material on the other.[11] These discrepancies have hardly been reflected upon until today. Viewed in the context of the whole field, this fact results even more in a perception of women's literature as a mere side issue. Whilst authors like Goethe and Kleist now undergo a queer or postcolonial reading,[12] research on women writers is reproached for being essentialist. This is a charge to which publications on female authors are easily exposed. Questioning female identity and concepts of female authorship on the one hand brought about important insights into the contradictory processes of literary production and reception, but on the other hand it put gender studies with a historical focus on the defensive. However, the critique of essentialism has not been sufficiently strong to deconstruct concepts of male authorship as well. The thesis of the 'Death of the Author' (Roland Barthes) may have preceded the feminist sex/gender debate, but concepts of authorship are still hardly questioned where masculinity is concerned.[13]

Overall, then, it seems as if the marginalization of women writers of the eighteenth and nineteenth centuries is not gradually diminishing but instead is being perpetuated. In German universities, this also has been reinforced by the introduction of the bachelor degree, which has gone hand in hand with the subject's recanonization. In what follows, I shall illustrate the extent to which the establishment of gender studies is intertwined with the developments outlined above.

## The Development of Gender Studies

The introduction of gender studies to the German-speaking world took place at the same time as the perspective of feminist literary-historical studies was shifting from a focus on the exclusion of women writers from literary history to their participation in it. These developments proceeded from an emergent critique of earlier women's studies' problematic assumption of a female collective subject, and its overemphasis on a binary conception of sexual and gender difference. The essay 'Gender: A Useful Category of Historical Analysis' by the historian Joan Scott constructed gender as a relational category and thus opened up the discourse to a further self-reflexivity.[14]

Scott's concept of gender inaugurated a paradigm shift in the United States. A broader reception of Scott in the German-speaking world followed in the context of Judith Butler's *Gender Trouble* in the late 1990s. Next to Butler's text it was Scott's contribution which became a fundamental text for gender studies and heralded the start of the discourse-analytical and postmodern change in women's and gender studies respectively. This change involved a further differentiation of the object of study and a radicalization of feminist theories. Scott's text focused on two central questions: gender as a foundational feature of social interaction on the one hand and the importance of gender as a way of labelling power relations on the other.

Inge Stephan referred to Scott in her important 1999 essay '"Gender": Eine nützliche Kategorie für die Literaturwissenschaft', which appeared in a special edition of *Zeitschrift für Germanistik*. She argued that the use of gender as an analytical category would not simply add to the literary canon but question its very foundation.[15] In doing so, Stephan, however, oversimplifies the achievements of previous research in order to establish the category of gender as an innovative and predominant category for further research. At the same time, she emphasizes that gender studies is by no means in competition with feminist literary history and women's studies. It acts, rather, as a complement in her view.[16] However, she did eventually declare gender studies to be the leading field of research. This essay is of prime importance for exemplifying the change in scholarship that accompanied the institutionalization of gender studies. In this respect Inge Stephan herself employs the same logic of inclusion and exclusion she had previously rejected for the canon and for scholarship.[17]

The institutionalization of gender studies includes a change of questions, concepts, and historical perspective. This is particularly true for debates about conceptions of authorship and for work on the canon, as demonstrated by an article by Claudia Breger, Dorothea Dornhof, and Dagmar von Hoff published in the same special edition in which Stephan's essay appears. The article, entitled 'Gender Studies/ Gender Trouble: Tendenzen und Perspektiven der deutschsprachigen Forschung', focuses on the future prospects of gender studies with regard to literary studies. The historical approach, however, is not really touched upon in this otherwise very instructive article, and studies on the eighteenth century are not dealt with at all.[18] Instead, the first sentence of this article mentions 'institutions and forms of knowledge production' which shape gender relations. Consequently, dealing with gender, ethnicity, and sex is regarded as most relevant for the new field.[19]

There is clearly more to the transition from 'Geschlecht' to 'gender' than mere linguistic change; it is more than a mere matter of translation. The primacy of knowledge production as a subject of investigation means that questions of authorship become less important.[20] Gender as a category of knowledge mediates forms of knowledge production in discourses. In terms of the linguistic turn this mediation presupposes the discursive construction of both history and its subjects. The much-discussed relationality of the categories sex, gender, and ethnicity, something currently being debated in feminist theory as intersectionality, goes beyond the scope of this essay.[21]

Nonetheless, it is true to say that some simplification and distortion of the term *gender* have taken place despite all the theoretical efforts.[22] At the same time, historical problems as well as the analysis of social relations have ended up being somewhat neglected and the social construction of 'Geschlechterdifferenz' [sex/gender difference] has remained untouched.[23] In this respect, *gender* is perhaps not the useful category it once used to be, as Scott herself remarks at the start of the new millennium.[24] It is quite remarkable, though, that Scott's revision of the gender category has hardly received any attention in literary studies until now.

The category 'gender' appeals for many reasons: it allows scholars to avoid the term 'woman', thus neutralizing not only their own research topic,[25] but also the sex of female scholars themselves. The entry of women into academic institutions changes their relation to the structure of inclusion and exclusion, and may therefore cause a rejection of the status of 'other'.[26] This process of 'neutralization' can also entail a refusal to engage with the struggle for women as well as a rejection of the search for historical female predecessors.

It could be argued that the connection between gender relations and modern academic life does not allow for neutrality.[27] The alleged neutrality is legitimized in terms of supposedly increased scholarly and personal achievements on the one hand and a gain in complexity on the other hand. At the same time a certain historical amnesia is observable which is analogous with discourses on postfeminism. The essential contribution of women's studies to the development of gender studies is overlooked. Ultimately, the statement that gender studies is apparently neutral and has an intrinsic complexity is incompatible with the commitment to studying men's and women's literature, overcoming social constructions of gender differences, and finally establishing *one* literary history. The grammatical plural of gender studies itself highlights the diversity of concerns grouped under the same heading, which is interpreted as a gain in complexity. But what exactly gender studies consists of can scarcely be determined.[28]

To date, the category of gender has only on occasion effectively challenged literary history as a history of gender relations and it has not rewritten it successfully. Neither the problem of authorship nor that of historiography can be addressed on the level of gender. But the relation between sex and gender is very seldom taken into account. In this respect the promise that *gender* will be more differentiated than *Geschlecht* in German has not been fulfilled.[29] By focusing on *gender* the function and importance of sex are quietly disposed of; its historical constructedness is neither questioned nor registered.

Finally, it is certainly true that the concept of gender has been established at the expense of searching for traces of female cultural activity and dealing with female authors and their texts. In this regard, the stagnation in literary-historical studies on women and gender can be seen to be related to the institutionalization of gender studies, as well as to the predominance of the (often uncritically deployed) category of gender. Thus, one might say that institutionalization brings the claim of increased complexity and nuance, at the cost of an explicitly critical orientation and approach.

## The Future Prospects of Gender Studies

Employing the category of gender does not necessarily ensure a more differentiated notion of the production and reception of men's and women's literature.[30] In order to question traditional orders effectively, and to avoid reinforcing them unconsciously, interdependencies and overlaps between different categories must be taken into account. This applies to class and gender systems as well as to the newly formed concept of literary genre in the eighteenth century which led to an associated canonization.[31] When we analyse these overlaps it becomes apparent that female authors had room for manoeuvre, both in terms of their actions and in terms of participation in the diverse discourses which determine literary history.[32] Arguably the term gender is in danger of forfeiting its critical role and ending up as mere cliché owing to its often unreflective, uncritical overuse in various contexts. The term is at risk of losing its meaning by being used to describe anything from 'women' to 'relations between the sexes'. In addition, it seems as if the euphoria caused by the dissolution of identity and by the transgression of gender boundaries is slowly evaporating in the light of social problems caused by globalization.

This situation, however, also offers an opportunity since dealing with female authors and their texts always comprises a struggle with different aspects of inequality, too. Moreover, it forces us to reconsider exactly what we want to know, why we want to know it, and how this knowledge is formed. This applies to the category of gender in particular. In my opinion, there are at least four areas fertile for future research.

### Aesthetic textual strategies

Having documented women writers' contributions to all literary genres it is vital that we analyse the individual characteristics of each text in order to identify its specific qualities. The aim is not to limit the value of texts purely to their connection to a women's collective, something which has itself been disputed. Anna Richards provided an example of such an analysis with regard to Therese Huber's texts.[33] The restrictive reference to femininity or to a female identity must be relinquished and its problems exposed. It is necessary to analyse all issues articulated in the texts and to relate them to contemporary discourses, including men's texts. This approach is by no means confined to content. It is important to examine the aesthetic strategies of the texts, which have often been disregarded in favour of searching for their emancipatory qualities. In this context, concepts of modernity and the process of modernization which took place around 1800 and 1900 play an important part, and they are intimately connected to changes in gender relations.

### Relations between genre and gender

Genre relations as well as gender relations are changeable historical formations, which share some structural similarities owing to their alleged state as a natural fact. It is important not to lapse into essentialist thinking but to differentiate between the normative and practical levels, i.e. between which genres women actually chose to write in and what was being discussed as 'women's literature'.[34] Additionally, the history of genre takes place within the texts themselves and is therefore comparable to the problem of authorship.[35] Content and form need to be viewed side by side and need to be investigated from the point of view of the performativity of genre as well as the performativity of gender.

   With regard to the modern novel in particular, future research ought to investigate the correlation between the construction of maleness and the genre system. The notion of the modernist novel as a 'man's novel' should, for example, be reassessed. The assumption that gender differences were intensified around 1800 by the postulation of gender characteristics is currently mainly related to the portrayal of women as governesses of the female sex and educators in femininity. Young men in novels around 1800, in contrast, are sent into the wide world without needing to refer to masculinity as justification. On the one hand stories of male *Bildung* [formation] have always been regarded as universally valid, as masculine and human at the same time, and on the other hand they were ironically disrupted and their role in providing a paradigm of masculine identity was questioned — as was shown in Goethe's *Wilhelm Meisters Lehrjahre* (Wilhelm Meister's Apprenticeship, 1795–96). This interaction should be pursued further by looking at the challenge to identity that foils the consolidated bourgeois 'Geschlechtscharaktere' [gender identities/gender roles].

### Access to the public

For historically oriented research the question of access to the public has been a focal issue of feminist criticism from the outset. Material that has been unexploited so far, for example correspondence or contracts with publishing houses, could provide further information about ways of publishing or strategies for entering the literary marketplace. Recently Helen Fronius pointed out how women actively approached publishers in their letters, generally without false modesty. In some cases, they even used the conscious performance of femininity strategically, to attract the attention of male publishers to their literary products.[36] In this context it is also necessary to reflect upon the crucial role of the emerging bourgeoisie who set standards for canon formation which are still valid today. Pre-bourgeois society provided different forms, spaces, and possibilities for literary participation, which proves once more the historicity of the conditions of production. Or, to put it differently: women's access to the public sphere was not a problem until the bourgeois public sphere had self-consciously evolved.

*Conceptions of authorship*

An author's access to the public sphere is intimately connected with concepts of authorship. The biological sex of men and women does not necessarily correspond to the gender of the author. In this context Sigrid Nieberle posed the question: 'How does an author actually become female?'[37] After all, the female version of the term 'author' in German, 'Autorin', has been in circulation only since the eighteenth century and was then only used satirically.[38]

Besides gender there are historical, regional, genre-based, aesthetic, and theoretical aspects to the conception of authorship that have to be considered and to which literary studies have been paying attention for some time now.[39] Distinguishing between sex and gender allows for an important observation. Although authorship has been challenged in terms of the performative constructions of gender, the relevance of *sex* still remains unresolved.[40] The problem is exacerbated by the fact that having a name at all is considered essential to becoming an author and to being recognized by literary history. For women, however, anonymity also became an opportunity which allowed them to enter the literary market in the first place. Anonymity allows some measure of freedom and it also permits aesthetic play encompassing both the performance and the masquerading of sex. My plea for a return to the female author therefore implies that *sex*, not just *gender*, in its varying historical *constellations*, should be the subject of further research.

## Conclusion

As described above, problems of both content and method are directly connected with canon formation. Disregarding female authors means excluding sex and gender as a category for analysis from the conception of authorship altogether. The danger is that women writers and their texts may fall into oblivion again.[41] The availability of texts is an essential prerequisite for the reading and discussion of literature at universities, in schools, and in the media.[42] Only a reconstruction of authorship and the associated rereading of texts written by men and women can give rise to a revision of the canon. It is necessary to arouse the interest of male and female students by building on the work done to date, and to propel this project further by doing more differentiated research along the lines outlined above. Although the undergraduate students of today know that almost every topic has a 'gender angle', they typically have little or no knowledge of female authors of the eighteenth and nineteenth centuries. Finally, gender-based research ought to insist that the study of the historical experiences of men and women, which influence a variety of discourses, but which are simultaneously brought about by the very same discourses, is central to an understanding of social and individual development. The assumption that the project has been accomplished is naïve and dangerous. Gender studies ought to ensure that the historical experiences of men and women do not slip into oblivion, and that the lessons from the history of the academic discipline of women's studies are not forgotten. The phase of recovery can only be said to be complete when university syllabi consistently feature female authors, and when women writers are present on school curricula. That is when the work begins in earnest.[43]

## Notes to Chapter 1

1. See Claudia Honegger and Caroline Arni, 'Vorwort', in *Gender: Die Tücken einer Kategorie*, ed. by Claudia Honegger (Zurich: Chronos, 2001), pp. 7–13 (p. 9).
2. See Claudia Opitz, 'Nach der Gender-Forschung ist vor der Gender-Forschung: Plädoyer für die historische Perspektive in der Geschlechterforschung', in *Was kommt nach der Genderforschung? Zur Zukunft der feministischen Theoriebildung*, ed. by Rita Casale and Barbara Rendtorff (Bielefeld: Transcript, 2008), pp. 13–28.
3. See Anne Fleig, 'Zwischen Ausschluss und Aneignung: Neue Positionen in der Geschlechterforschung zur Aufklärung', *Das achtzehnte Jahrhundert*, 26.1 (2002), 79–89.
4. See for example Helga Meise, *Die Unschuld und die Schrift: Deutsche Frauenromane im 18. Jahrhundert* (Berlin: Guttandin & Hoppe, 1983; 2nd edn Frankfurt am Main: Helmer, 1992 [Marburg, 1983]); Katherine Goodman, *Dis/Closures: Women's Autobiography in Germany between 1790 and 1914* (Frankfurt am Main, Bern, and New York: Lang, 1986); Lydia Schieth, *Die Entwicklung des deutschen Frauenromans im ausgehenden 18. Jahrhundert* (Frankfurt am Main: Lang, 1987); Dagmar von Hoff, *Dramen des Weiblichen: Deutschsprachige Dramatikerinnen um 1800* (Opladen: Westdeutscher Verlag, 1989); *Untersuchungen zum Roman von Frauen um 1800*, ed. by Helga Gallas and Magdalene Heuser (Tübingen: Niemeyer, 1990); Susanne Kord, *Ein Blick hinter die Kulissen: Deutschsprachige Dramatikerinnen im 18. und 19. Jahrhundert* (Stuttgart: Metzler, 1992); Anita Runge, *Literarische Praxis von Frauen um 1800: Briefroman, Autobiographie, Märchen* (Hildesheim, Zurich, and New York: Olms, 1997).
5. See Kord, p. 11.
6. Jutta Osinski, *Einführung in die feministische Literaturwissenschaft* (Berlin: Erich Schmidt, 1998), p. 101.
7. See Birte Giesler, *Literatursprünge: Das erzählerische Werk von Friederike Helene Unger* (Göttingen: Wallstein, 2003).
8. See Anja May, *Wilhelm Meisters Schwestern: Bildungsromane von Frauen im ausgehenden 18. Jahrhundert* (Königstein im Taunus: Ulrike Helmer, 2006).
9. See Michaela Krug, *Auf der Suche nach dem eigenen Raum: Topographien des Weiblichen im Roman von Autorinnen um 1800* (Würzburg: Königshausen und Neumann, 2004).
10. See Maya Gerig, *Jenseits von Tugend und Empfindsamkeit: Gesellschaftspolitik im Frauenroman um 1800* (Cologne, Weimar, and Vienna: Böhlau, 2008); and *Schwellenüberschreitungen: Politik in der Literatur von deutschsprachigen Frauen 1780–1918*, ed. by Caroline Bland and Elisa Müller-Adams (Bielefeld: Aisthesis, 2007).
11. See also Annette Keck and Manuela Günter, 'Weibliche Autorschaft und Literaturgeschichte: Ein Forschungsbericht', *Internationales Archiv für die Sozialgeschichte der Literatur*, 26.2 (2001), 201–33 (p. 203).
12. See previous examples in *Outing Goethe and his Age*, ed. by Alice A. Kuzniar (Stanford, CA: Stanford University Press, 1996); *Queering the Canon: Defying Sights in German Literature and Culture*, ed. by Christoph Lorey and John Plews (Columbia, SC: Camden House, 1998).
13. See also Sigrid Nieberle, 'Rückkehr einer Scheinleiche? Ein erneuter Versuch über die Autorin', in *Rückkehr des Autors: Zur Erneuerung eines umstrittenen Begriffs*, ed. by Fotis Jannidis, Gerhard Lauer, Matias Martinez, and Simone Winko (Tübingen: Niemeyer 1999), pp. 255–72 (p. 259). Claudia Opitz wrote concerning historical studies: 'Weitergehende Reflexionen über die Dekonstruktion der Kategorie "Geschlecht" als eine, die "Frauen" und "Männer" als im wesentlichen binär gedachte Gruppen bzw. Weiblichkeit und Männlichkeit als Teile eines binären Zeichensystems umfasst, fehlen bislang weitgehend' [Further reflections about the deconstruction of the category 'gender' as one which tends to group 'men' and 'women' essentially as groups arranged in a binary fashion, or rather which tends to group femininity and masculinity as part of a binary codification system, are missing to date] (Claudia Opitz, '*Gender* — eine unverzichtbare Kategorie der historischen Analyse: Zur Rezeption von Joan W. Scotts Studien in Deutschland, Österreich und der Schweiz', in *Gender: Die Tücken einer Kategorie*, ed. by Claudia Honegger and Caroline Arni (Zurich: Chronos, 2001), pp. 95–115 (p. 98)).
14. Joan Scott, 'Gender: A Useful Category of Historical Analysis', *American Historical Review*

91.5 (1986), 1053–76 9German translation: 'Gender: Eine nützliche Kategorie der historischen Analyse', in *Selbstbewußt: Frauen in den USA*, ed. by Nancy Kaiser (Leipzig: Reclam 1994), pp. 27–74).

15. See Inge Stephan, '"Gender": Eine nützliche Kategorie für die Literaturwissenschaft', *Zeitschrift für Germanistik*, N.F. 1 (1999), 23–35 (p. 31).

16. See ibid., p. 34.

17. See ibid., p. 33.

18. See Claudia Breger, Dorothea Dornhof, and Dagmar von Hoff, 'Gender Studies/Gender Trouble: Tendenzen und Perspektiven der deutschsprachigen Forschung', *Zeitschrift für Germanistik*, N.F. 1 (1999), 72–113.

19. See ibid., p. 72.

20. See Christina von Braun and Inge Stephan, 'Gender@Wissen: Einführung', in *Gender@Wissen: Ein Handbuch der Gender-Theorien*, ed. by Christina von Braun and Inge Stephan (Cologne, Weimar, and Vienna: Böhlau, 2005), pp. 7–45, esp. pp. 29 ff.

21. See Gudrun-Axeli Knapp, '"Intersectionality" — ein neues Paradigma feministischer Theorie? Zur transatlantischen Reise von "Race, Class, Gender"', *Feministische Studien*, 23.1 (2005), 68–81; *Achsen der Ungleichheit: Zum Verhältnis von Klasse, Geschlecht und Ethnizität*, ed. by Cornelia Klinger, Gudrun-Axeli Knapp, and Birgit Sauer (Frankfurt am Main: Campus 2007).

22. As early as 1995 Renate Hof warned that the term 'gender' might become a cliché even before it developed a clear sense. See Renate Hof, *Die Grammatik der Geschlechter: Gender als Analysekategorie der Literaturwissenschaft* (Frankfurt and New York: Campus, 1995), p. 16.

23. See Rita Casale, 'Die Vierzigjährigen entdecken den Feminismus: Anmerkungen zur Epistemologisierung politischer Theorien', *Feministische Studien* 26.2 (2008), 197–207.

24. See Joan W. Scott, 'Die Zukunft von gender: Fantasien zur Jahrtausendwende', in *Gender: Die Tücken einer Kategorie*, ed. by Claudia Honegger and Caroline Arni (Zurich: Chronos, 2001), pp. 39–63 (p. 42) (English title: 'Millenial Fantasies: The Future of "Gender" in the 21st Century', in *Gender: Die Tücken einer Kategorie*, pp. 19–37).

25. See Keck and Günter, p. 232.

26. See Hof, p. 25.

27. For more detail, see Sabine Hark, *Dissidente Partizipation: Eine Diskursgeschichte des Feminismus* (Frankfurt am Main: Suhrkamp, 2005), p. 254; see Scott, 'Die Zukunft von gender', p. 55; for further approaches in feminist literary history see: Nieberle, p. 255, this is opposed by Osinski, p. 128.

28. See Hark, p. 258.

29. See Stephan, p. 28.

30. See Fleig, p. 83.

31. See Helga Meise, '"Hirnkinder": Gattungsvorgabe und hybride Schreibweise in Sophie von La Roches "Pomona für Teutschlands Töchter"', in *'bald zierliche Blumen — bald Nahrung des Verstands': Lektüren zu Sophie von La Roche*, ed. by Monika Lippke, Matthias Luserke-Jaqui, and Nikola Rossbach (Hanover: Wehrhahn, 2008), pp. 123–41.

32. See Nieberle, p. 261.

33. See Anna Richards, '"Double-voiced Discourse" and Psychological Insight in the Work of Therese Huber', *The Modern Language Review*, 99 (2004), 416–29.

34. See Anne Fleig and Helga Meise, 'Das Geschlecht der Innovation: Bedeutung und Reichweite der Verknüpfung von Gattungs- und Geschlechterdiskurs bei Gellert, Sulzer und Wieland', *Das achtzehnte Jahrhundert* 29.2 (2005), 159–78 (p. 176).

35. See ibid., p. 173.

36. See Helen Fronius, 'Der reiche Mann und die arme Frau: German Woman Writers and the Eighteenth-Century Literary Market', *German Life and Letters*, 56 (2003), 1–19.

37. Nieberle, p. 258.

38. See ibid., p. 258.

39. See *Rückkehr des Autors: Erneuerung eines umstrittenen Begriffs*, ed. by Fotis Jannidis, Gerhard Lauer, Matias Martinez, and Simone Winko (Tübingen: Niemeyer, 1999).

40. See Nieberle, p. 272.

41. See also ibid., p. 257.

42. On schools, see Franziska Schößler, *Einführung in die Gender Studies* (Berlin: Akademie Verlag, 2008), p. 17.
43. This chapter is a translation of the original German version. While in English an important distinction exists between 'sex' and 'gender', the German word 'Geschlecht' covers both sex and gender. In translating the article into English, therefore, we had to abandon the ambiguity implied in the German term 'Geschlecht' as well as in 'Geschlechterforschung' [sex/gender research].

CHAPTER 2

# From Word to World and Back:
# Literary Studies and Gender Studies

*Anke Gilleir*

In her essay 'Marble Paper: Toward a Feminist "History of Poetry"' (2004) Rachel
Blau DuPlessis offers a sustained and sophisticated analysis of Wordsworth's famous
ballad 'A Solitary Reaper' (1805–07). In the poem a speaker — often identified as
the poet himself — recalls how he witnessed a Scottish girl ('a solitary Highland
lass') who, while harvesting, sang to herself a 'melancholy strain' he was unable to
comprehend, yet which has enraptured him until the present day: 'Will no one tell
me what she sings?' In feminist literary criticism Wordsworth's poem is generally
considered as the articulation of male poetic dominance. The poet's gazing at an
unknown female figure signifies the possessive, even colonialist gesture which is
the condition of his 'sublime self-assurance', 'only rendered possible by the arduous
repression of the Other in all its forms'.[1] His transformation of the singing girl into
a poetical object can be interpreted as the muting of the female poet, whose song is
drowned out and appropriated. From this perspective Wordsworth's poem can be
compared to Wilhelm Meister's treatment of Mignon's song at the opening of the
third book of Goethe's *Wilhelm Meisters Lehrjahre* (Wilhelm Meister's Apprenticeship,
1795–96). Here the narrator recounts how Wilhelm grapples with the girl's peculiar
voice, language, and images in order to turn what he hears into a classical poem,
'Mignons Lied' (Mignon's Song), that is presented to the readers.[2] The image of the
muted female poet and of a feminine aesthetics suppressed by patriarchal culture
is familiar in feminist literary history. Yet interestingly Blau-DuPlessis inverts this
traditional feminist reading. She turns the protagonist into an autonomous poet,
'someone who has constructed her sung words, and possibly her melody',[3] and
Wordsworth's outcry 'Will no one tell me what she sings?' then becomes an utterance
of frustration at the resistance of the Other to being comprehended according to his
own terms. It is 'a sign of the unpossessionality of the female figure as autonomous
working artist, despite Wordsworth's repeated argument that she is a muse figure'.[4]
Blau DuPlessis's analysis moves from the fictional text to the historical conditions
of its time: she reconstructs the socio-economic and cultural situation of Gaelic-
speaking women who came from the Highlands to the south during harvest time
in the late eighteenth century and brought with them a language and music strange
to English ears. She moves from poetry to material history and back and inverts
Adorno's well-known hypothesis that the political force of lyrical poetry lies in its

otherworldliness.[5] She also transcends a number of dilemmas that have arisen in the field of feminist criticism in its disciplinary transition from *literary* criticism towards the more *culturally* engaged gender studies, which affected the focus both on women as prime objects of study and on literature as a medium. In that sense Rachel Blau DuPlessis's literary analysis is remarkable for its outspoken *feminist* perspective and its focus on the *female* figure/voice and on historical *women* and also because of the profound reading of the poetic language. Pointing out Adorno's 'unnerving logic' that considers a poem — in a negative way — as a historical phenomenon on the one hand, yet as a timeless form of music as far as its language is concerned on the other, she takes as a starting point the 'poem's subjectivity and tropes as temporally fixed' and revolves her process of interpretation around the 'complex, polyvalent force' of the language.[6] Programmatically she concludes:

> By conducting a reading by sociopoesis — the close reading of a text for what form, allusion, and diction tell us, and the examination of some version of the historical record to understand the woman behind the figure — we can begin a feminist analysis of poetry.[7]

Blau DuPlessis's scrupulous reading as the basis of her 'Feminist History of Poetry' functions as my starting point for some considerations on the state of feminist literary studies. My argument for the future of feminist criticism can be boiled down to the vindication of profound textual study, a move back from 'world to word' in a field where literary studies has come under pressure from cultural studies. Cultural studies has not only dethroned literature as a privileged object of culture, but also as an object requiring a disciplined approach. At the root of this lies the conviction that, especially in the case of the eighteenth and nineteenth centuries, literature has had an impact on human society and conduct, albeit an impact hard to qualify or even totally unintentional because of the formal — or idiosyncratic — nature of the text. Taking this into account, it is not surprising that we detect tension between the so-called 'formal' (Levinson) study of literature on the one hand, which refuses to take for granted the readily available, and politicized readings on the other, which consider the word of the poet as a repository of the power of the world.[8] In the field of feminist literary criticism the focus has never really been much on the indeterminacies of the written word. Too much had to be done before one could consider the alienating power of literary elements and templates that might be at work in the texts of female authors from before the rise of feminist consciousness: authors had to be unearthed, canons revised, texts published and read before they could be re-read over and over again for hidden scripts, be they conservative or subversive. Susanne Kord's work on Luise Gottsched, *Little Detours: Letters and Plays by Luise Gottsched* (2006), is an excellent example of this laborious academic enterprise. With the opening up of the field of (feminist) literary studies into diverse forms of cultural and identity studies the 'formal' study of women's texts has disappeared before it could become a standard operating mode. This chapter wants to consider the epistemological, institutional, and political aspects that characterize the change in discipline. Its concern is to save the enterprise of close reading and formal textual analysis for the future study of women's literature. This is done in spite of the awareness that the prior conditions for treating literature in such a way, especially as far as the German language field is concerned, hardly exist — even after more than thirty years since the beginnings of feminist literary criticism.

The 'progress' from feminist literary studies to gender studies has certainly enlarged the range of research topics and dimensions of knowledge. Yet as mentioned, this tendency to move from literary studies to cultural studies goes hand in hand with the marginalization of literature, not only as a recognized medium of meaning but also as a formal-linguistic artefact that demands specific skills in order to make it speak. Gayatri Spivak deals with this issue in *Death of a Discipline* (2003), her plea for a new form of comparative literature that breaks open the narrow European focus in favour of a more encompassing 'planetary' literary curriculum. Spivak finds this to be much more in tune with the present process of cultural globalization and also considers it a disciplinary move that might be able to stop the fashionable replacement of literary criticism with cultural studies, characterized by 'metropolitan language-based presentist and personalist political convictions, often with visibly foregone conclusions', i.e. a branch of study with a simplified view on language and a strong political agenda.[9] A sense of political consciousness in academia is to be applauded, yet it should be consistently self-critical and sustained. If we want to include literature in the curriculum of a more society-oriented university, Spivak argues, we should focus on the

> proper study of literature [that] may give us entry to the performativity of cultures as instantiated in narrative. Here we stand outside, but not as anthropologist; we stand rather as reader with imagination ready for the effort of othering [...]. (p. 13)

In *Death of a Discipline* Spivak does not focus on the transition from *feminist* literary studies to gender studies, but it is clear from her plea for a new concept of comparative literature in what sense literary studies as a discipline of text and language study is put under pressure by identity studies, blind to the fact that literariness may *constitute* meaning rather than merely reflect it. A proper reading of literary texts makes one already 'understand that the mother tongue is actively divided' (p. 20).

Within this field of shifting focus it is interesting to look at the study of women's literature and the position of feminist literary criticism, marginalized from an institutional point of view in countries like Germany and France and in general never really a hotbed for 'formalist' reading cultures. Literary studies as a theoretically reflective approach to an aesthetically conceived text (in the broadest sense of the word) with its formal structure and historical context is often considered incompatible with politically engaged readings that strive to reveal literature's ideological adherence. While what we call the formalist focus on literature tends to turn a blind eye to its social conditions, the ideological demystification of literature seems to disregard the specificity of its object. This is a well-known discussion that has been going on for some decades. It was recapitulated by Judith Butler, John Guillory, and Kendall Thomas at the turn of the millennium in the introduction to their volume *What's Left of Theory* (2000), as they argue for a cross-fertilization of the ethical and the formalist strands in literary studies:

> Whereas some argue that literature should remain cordoned off from social
> science and social theory, others are relieved that literature studies has moved
> toward a more active engagement with social issues, with race studies, practices
> of gender and sexuality, colonial space and its aftermath, the interstitial cultural
> spaces of globalization.[10]

It is striking to see how in this context the word 'gender' automatically places
literature in the hybrid space of socially engaged study, to which feminist literary
criticism, both as theoretical reflection and as the study of women's writing, has
to some extent belonged. In that sense it has always been in competition with
'established' literary studies. Differences first of all deal with matters of canonization
and aesthetics, but also as far as the *focus* on literature is concerned, there have been
rifts with symbolically dominant schools of literary criticism, not least since the rise
of theory as the core business of literary study since the late 1970s. This is not only
the case with women's literature, but the gap between political or ethical questions
in literary matters on the one hand, and 'formalist' or 'theoretical' readings of
literature on the other, has been most visible here. Elaine Showalter's well-known
sceptical remark in her essay 'Toward a Feminist Poetics' (1979) on the rise of a
'literary science' that spends 'more and more time mastering the theory, less and
less reading the books' is symptomatic in this respect.[11]

   Women's studies in literature started with serious arrears in matters of reading
material that could be made available to scholars and students (except for the
nineteenth-century British novelists) and that thus could become the object
of micrological discussions.[12] But apart from that, the academic attitude of the
established schools of literature that cherished either tradition and/or tackled the
blind spots of language idealism in a handful of sophisticated texts appeared unin-
viting to a politically conscious discipline such as feminist literary criticism. From
this perspective it is obvious that some affiliations existed between 'women's lit'
and cultural studies. With its less stringent body of theoretical texts and its inclusive
view of culture, cultural studies appeared as a discipline that could help to establish
or at least reinforce the institutional position of women's literature. Looking back on
the genesis and evolution of the study of women's literature at German universities
towards the end of her career in 2004, Ina Schabert concludes as follows:

> So we partly write like men, making gestures of objectivity, parading
> abstractions and complicated sentence structures, fitting our findings to
> prestigious theories [...]. The historical remoteness and esoteric character of a
> subject (such as medieval mysticism or early modern female writing) also help
> to convey academic prestige. So does the cloak of cultural studies.[13]

In an article published in *Tulsa Studies in Women's Literature* in 1991 Russell Reising
addressed the conflict between women's literary studies and established forms of
literary criticism and underscored how critics like Jonathan Culler

> situate the designation of a text as *literature* at the beginning of any theory
> of interpretation, though [they] refrain from addressing the complex issue of
> literariness [...]. The problem with such an assumption is that it elides the idea
> that to view a literary text or canon as a construct requires that we should grant
> it to be, in Terry Eagleton's concise phrase: 'fashioned by particular people for
> particular reasons at a certain time'.[14]

According to Reising the 'unwillingness to examine the ideological basis of notions such as literary competence and interpretative communities' (p. 72), which is absolutely necessary for the understanding of women's literature, can be countered by moving from 'word to world', i.e. by moving from an eclectic game of intertextual exchange between a handful of canonized texts toward a contextual framing of literature by a 'textuality that constitutes the fields of history, politics, economics, sexuality, or war' (p. 73). In other words, Reising proposes to abandon literary studies in the dominant scholarly sense of the word for a broader approach practised within cultural studies. The first move in this liberating process would be to 'jettison the very concept of literature [...] as well as the hermeneutic practices, priorities, and prohibitions associated with its existence' (p. 76).

Culler's injunction that we 'stay within the literary system as long as possible' is exactly the issue that feminism and all forms of cultural criticism need to address: 'For the literary system [...] virtually prohibits critical languages interested in re-situating literature and the related practices of reading, writing, and teaching literature within those material contexts that frame literacy and all literary production and consumption' (p. 74).

The reply to the canon of literary criticism, its scholarly jargon and cultural censorship, should consist of 'reading practices termed *incompetent*, readings aggressively interested in making whatever moves can be made from word to world' (p. 76). This is 'exactly the move cultural studies must make' (p. 74). More than ten years later Emory Elliott writes very much the same thing in the introduction to *Aesthetics in a Multicultural Age* (2002). The concept of aesthetics and interest in 'textual analysis and production' should be overruled:

> The major contribution cultural studies has made to more hermeneutically oriented disciplines such as English has been to bring literary interpretation to such issues as the processes of cultural exchange and the affective and economic relations that structure the transmission of cultural productions.[15]

Elliott stresses that in an academic field that opens itself up to the diversity of cultural production one needs 'new tools that will help us to understand what *those* writers and artists are doing' (p. 13). Instead of following the lines of 'traditional hermeneutics' (which in many discussions appears as a term that covers diverse literary theories), we are to coin 'a new system of analysis for describing the characteristics of art and literature and the feelings and intellectual pleasures they evoke in the diversity of the people we are today' (p. 14). Robyn Wiegman takes up the same problem in the case of women's studies in her discussion of Susan Gubar's — notorious — 1998 essay 'What Ails Feminist Criticism?' Starting from Gubar's fierce criticism of the idiosyncrasies of poststructuralist language philosophy, which has bereft feminism of any tangible object, Wiegman seeks a possible revival of 'the political imperative of feminism' in interdisciplinarity.[16] Susan Gubar herself pleads for the return to the 'critical coherency' that characterized 'the textual aesthetics and critical idioms of literary study'.[17] In an article published several years later she notes again: 'Curiously, too, in today's gender studies venues, literature and the study of literature — which played major roles at the inception of women's studies — have recently been supplemented and sometimes supplanted by other admittedly important areas of investigation'.[18] To Wiegman, however, interdisciplinarity is inherent to women's studies nowadays and should not be seen as a process of disintegration and, correspondingly, as an epistemological and political loss: 'We might understand the women's studies' incoherence as the condition of possibility for producing a feminist academic project that can rethink not simply the liberal understanding of difference as inclusion, but the politics and organization of knowledge as well'.[19] Wiegman's argument is similar to Reising's fifteen years earlier. Against the background of institutional politics where 'scholars [...] need to maintain their disciplinary identity in order to signify as an agent of knowledge',[20] interdisciplinary research as practised in identity studies may prove to be stimulating for women's studies. The fact that feminist criticism and even women's studies in general have come under strong pressure is reinforced by Wiegman's contribution to the *Modern Language Quarterly* volume 'Feminism in Time', where she repeatedly uses words like 'agony' and 'crisis' in her description of present-day 'feminism's academic institutionalization'.[21]

While Gayatri Spivak, underscoring the disappearing skill of proper reading, and Robyn Wiegman, negotiating a dialectic of difference and discipline, both explicitly speak from an American point of view, a similar tendency to move from feminist *literary* studies to cultural studies under the denominator of identity and difference can be noticed in Germany. Clearly the discipline of cultural studies in Germany has to be analysed against the background of an institutional and scholarly tradition that differs from the Anglo-American situation.[22] Yet as cultural studies was introduced and developed in the late 1990s in Germany, the idea of interdisciplinarity also became the basis of its academic profile and was equally adopted by gender studies. As was the case with its rise in Britain in the late 1960s, cultural studies in its German form goes hand in hand with a strong aversion to the cultural canon that has had an enormous symbolical dominance in German academic culture for over a century.[23] 'Entprivilegierung' [removal of privileges] and 'Gleichberechtigung' [equality] are common denominators for cultural studies and women's studies, certainly in the first phase of their academic institutionalization. In feminist literary criticism issues of aesthetics and poetics were often suspended in order to investigate the socio-historical conditions of women's cultural production. In her seminal historical survey *Deutsche Literatur von Frauen*, published in 1988, Gisela Brinker-Gabler points out in a very precise manner the importance of the academic critic's habitus as well as the relation between form, evaluation, and ethics:

> Das hier vorgeschlagene Konzept einer Untersuchung der Literatur von Frauen in ihrem jeweiligen historischen Kontext berücksichtigt die Variationsbreite literarischen Niveaus, der Gebrauchszusammenhänge und Schreibweisen. Daraus folgt als Konsequenz, daß literarischer Wert nicht nur auf eine ästhetische Qualität zu beziehen ist, sondern daß auch ethisch-soziale Wertkonzepte zu berücksichtigen sind. Der Wertungsvorgang ist weiter noch dadurch kompliziert, daß sich nicht — wie in der klassischen Werttheorie — die Aufmerksamkeit nur auf den Text richtet, sondern daß die Wertenden selbst und auch die jeweilige Wertungssituation, die von ästhetischen oder praktischen Wertmaßstäben gesteuert wird, zu berücksichtigen sind.[24]

[The concept we propose for the study of women's literature in its respective historical contexts considers the variations in literary standards, usages, and styles. As a consequence literary value is not only linked with quality, but socio-ethical values also have to be considered. The process of evaluation is even more complicated, because not only the text itself is considered (as in classical value theory), but the evaluators themselves and the situation in which they act, which is determined by aesthetic or practical standards, must also be taken into account.]

The underscoring of the 'broader' context of literary culture in research on historical women's literature has obvious political roots in the sense that it aims to uncover the gendered socio-ideological power relations of literary culture up to the late nineteenth century. Yet at times the 'historicist' approach seems to have a somewhat apologetic ring to it, arising perhaps from feminist critics' fear that historical literary texts produced by female authors may not provide material of sufficient aesthetic quality to be dealt with in a sophisticated manner. In the late 1980s German literary scholar Hannelore Schlaffer spoke plainly of women authors' lack of biographical and artistic greatness, which had unwittingly been revealed by the recent popularity of histories of women's writing: 'Wenn heute ein Buch nach dem anderen über die Geschichte schreibender Frauen erscheint, so ist das ein Gebot des Marktes, nicht eines der Sache'[25] [If one book after the other on the history of women authors is appearing nowadays, then that is purely for marketing reasons, not for intrinsic ones]. According to Schlaffer the problem is that of methodological imitation. Feminist historians repeat a male genre of heroic historiography that has, even as far as the genealogy of 'great men' is concerned, lost its plausibility. In the case of women it reveals the banality of their lives doubly painfully. Equally, their literature does not invite profound study:

Wie oft ist nicht schon die Mißachtung der Literaturwissenschaft gegenüber den Versen der Günderrode beklagt worden, einer Figur, die ohne ihr weibliches Liebes- und Lebensdrama im Dichterkreise nie Eingang in die Geschichte gefunden hätte. Männern, die so schlechte Poesie verfaßten wie sie, wurde ein Platz im Gedächtnis der Nachwelt nicht angewiesen.[26]

[How often have there not been complaints about the contempt of literary criticism for the verse of Günderrode, a figure who would never have made it into history without her female drama in love and life in the literary circles. Men who wrote poetry as bad as hers were not granted a place in posterity's memory.]

Obviously much can be said about Schlaffer's irritation with what she perceives as the mediocre literary quality 'typical' of women's literature from the Classical and Romantic periods. But she does not reject the idea that women authors should be rediscovered. What she does propose as a solution is a different research template. Literary historiography does not need 'Bilder von Heldinnen, sondern von tapferen Spießgesellen, keine Idole, sondern intelligente Porträts. Ihr literarischer Ort ist gerade der Essay'[27] [images of heroines, but rather of brave henchwomen, not idols but intelligent portraits. Their literary place is the essay in particular]. This is to some extent what Christa Bürger produced in her careful analysis of Romantic and Classical women authors, *Leben Schreiben: Die Klassik, die Romantik und der Ort der*

*Frauen*, published in 1990. In her 'miniature' portraits Bürger blended biography and literature, and compared genre and social codes in order to overcome the 'trivial' and explain the exclusion of women's literature from the canon. If the 'miniature' did indeed become a publication template for research on German historical women's literature, then it is more a reflection of its marginalized status (the obligatory chapter in every survey, if at all) than a hallmark of established authority.[28] Sustained and detailed research on women authors from the eighteenth and nineteenth centuries such as Susanne Kord's work on Louise Gottsched, Barbara Hahn's on Rahel Varnhagen, Katharina von Hammerstein's on Sophie Mereau, and Gudrun Loster-Schneider's on Sophie von La Roche did not lead to the introduction of women's literature into established literary studies. The move from literary criticism to cultural studies in the study of women's literature is part of a larger methodological shift after the linguistic turn, yet in my opinion it cannot be explained without considering some institutional aspects, some rules and power relationships in the academic field.

From this point of view it is interesting to compare the two editions of the gender studies survey published by Inge Stephan and Christina von Braun in 2000 and 2005 and see what happened to the position of literary studies in them. The first survey, *Genderstudien: Eine Einführung*, lists different scholarly disciplines and in each case explains the historical development of, and the main issues associated with, a gendered approach. All contributions chronicle how and when feminism entered the discipline and how the feminist view was eventually broadened by the introduction of the concept of gender, which could challenge *male* colleagues to consider the constructed nature of their gender identity as well.[29] One of the disciplines dealt with in the survey *Genderstudien* is literary studies. The chapter on literature, which also ends with the switch from woman to gender, deals with different aspects of feminism within literary studies: authorship, canon, genre, themes and motives, images, sex and body, method and theory. The last issue — method and theory — appears as a category in itself, suggesting that all the other questions concerning literature are outside theory and methodological reading. The introduction of gender as a concept that reveals even the most generally accepted aspects of human nature to be cultural constructions (Judith Butler appears as a key name) is considered a turning point in the study of literature. Gender implies a correspondence between all socio-historical acts and is inherently interdisciplinary, or, somewhat more specifically, it opens the field of literary study to a wider horizon of cultural studies. The alternative strategy, that of entering into a dialectical discussion with dominant literary theories, is not considered. *Genderstudien* corresponds with what Terry Eagleton describes as an elementary characteristic of literary criticism: it should always be a form of meta-critique that considers 'what codex and method we use and when'.[30] Stephan and von Braun do indeed display a high degree of meta-critique. Yet their disciplinary self-reflection leads to a different perception of the literary text, which simply becomes one element among others in a spectrum of cultural practices:

> Die Untersuchung von Gesten, Gefühlen und Wahrnehmungsweisen [gewinnt] eine neue Relevanz für die literaturwissenschaftliche Forschung, wobei die

kulturwissenschaftliche Neuorientierung in den 90er Jahren eine wichtige unterstützende Funktion bei der Hinwendung zu neuen Themen und Forschungsmethoden spielt (Gedächtnis, Erinnerung, kulturelle Praktiken, Liebesdiskurs, Mimesis, Alterität, Ethnizität etc.).[31]

[The study of gestures, emotions, and modes of perception gains a new relevance for literary studies, and the new cultural orientation in the 1990s has an important supporting role in the introduction of new themes and research methods (memory, remembrance, cultural practices, the discourse of love, mimesis, alterity, ethnicity, etc.).]

In institutional jargon a change of paradigm takes place: literary criticism — theory, poetics — is left for a new, still unoccupied position in the field of humanities.[32] In the volume *Genderwissen* (2005) neither literature nor literary studies are dealt with as separate issues. The very title *Genderwissen* — knowledge of gender/gendered knowledge — reveals the dominant perspective of the day: modes of knowledge and the question of how these interrelate with culture. This new *Handbuch der Gender-Theorien* deals with the dominant discourse of genetics and evolutionary history and with the mediatization of all knowledge: 'die Medien [bestimmen] sowohl über die Form der kommunikativen Vernetzung einer Gemeinschaft als auch über das gespeicherte Wissen einer Epoche' [the media determine the form of a society's communication network as well as the stored knowledge of each period].[33] The hypothesis that the medium makes the message is extremely relevant for literary studies, yet the fact that literature is a specific medium too is not considered in this book, nor, as Spivak acknowledges in *Death of a Discipline*, within literary studies in general.

It is interesting to notice that whereas in the German-language sphere two former protagonists of feminist literary studies have abandoned literary studies, the Anglo-American academy is witnessing a 'return to the aesthetic as a major preoccupation'[34] that opposes the flood of 'political' approaches. In his book *After Theory* Terry Eagleton reflects on the shifts in cultural and literary studies during the last decades and puts into perspective the tension between 'activist' strands of cultural investigation on the one hand and established 'autonomous' research on the other, in short, the tension between politics and theory. Eagleton emphasizes that some of the most important innovative insights from the last decades have come from feminism and gender studies. However, Eagleton says, ideological criticism, methods, and research in cultural studies have lost much of their former zeal and affiliated disciplines such as gender studies, postcolonial studies, and minority discourses must begin to assess themselves critically. They cannot 'afford simply to keep recounting the same narratives of class, race and gender, indispensable as these topics are'.[35] Obviously, Eagleton being Eagleton, this is not an argument for the return to a pre-critical mode of humanist thought. What he does seem to express, however, and in this sense his point is comparable to Spivak's plea for a new comparative literature, is a stronger consciousness of method and discipline at the basis of research, not least as far as literature is concerned. Ten years before Eagleton's somewhat ironic review of the state of the art, George Levine in the introduction to his volume *Aesthetics and Ideology* (1994) explicitly addressed this process:

Demystification of literature is not enough, the transformation of literature into textual evidence for anthropological and sociological commentary is not enough, and a commitment to the value of literature and formal analysis is not prima facie a politically suspect activity. Literature remains a subject worth studying 'in its own right' (however complicated the idea has become), and such study should exist both as part of the anthropological, sociological, historical, and cultural studies that now dominate, and parallel to them.[36]

An example of the 'one-sided' use of literature from an activist perspective according to Levine is Eve Sedgewick's seminal study *Between Men: English Literature and Male Homosocial Desire* (1985), which he considers 'a subtle and important project' that is however 'not seriously concerned with the formal properties of the works except as literary conventions confirm or shape the patternings in which she is interested'.[37] Just as Christa Bürger reflects on the dialectical relation between the literary text and the critic in the introduction to her book *Frauen Schreiben*, Geoffrey Harpham states in his contribution in *Aesthetics and Ideology*:

We seem to be approaching a maximum of theoretical confusion. I would argue, however, that we are also approaching the most definite and precise definition of the aesthetic that has yet been ventured — precisely as 'theoretical confusion', as the undecidability between object and subject, freedom and the repressive law, critical and uncritical passages, grievous and necessary misreadings, even art and ideology.[38]

Two aspects are important in this discussion. First of all there is the fact that dealing with 'poetics' means judgement and judgement always implies to some extent exclusion. Secondly, feminist literary criticism almost automatically seems to be on the activist side, which denies — or ignores — the formalist aspect of literature and evades questions that recognize literature's power to contain 'the unknown, the unknowable, the unforeseen, or even the unthinkable'.[39]

In the afterword to the 2004 *Critical Inquiry* volume 'Feminism in Time' Jonathan Culler considers the question of politics (feminism) and literature (formalism). In contrast to Sharon Marcus's conclusion that 'most literature professors now accept feminism as a valid mode of scholarly inquiry',[40] Cullers remarks somewhat ironically that owing to the success of women's studies programmes 'professors of English or history may feel no need to be involved' as women's literature and feminist issues fit comfortably in those 'other' departments.[41] Culler's own contribution to the study of literature from a gender or feminist perspective takes the literary text as the core of any question. His analytical example deals with lyrical poetry, the genre *par excellence* of poststructuralist discourse, which is yet totally marginalized in identity or cultural studies. His reading of Baudelaire's poems about prostitution hinges on an analysis of the poetical structure and rhetorics and looks at the 'discursive processes in which these poems, with their unusual thematic nexus of eroticism, virginity, and barrenness, participate' (p. 192). Considerable differences exist between Culler's analysis of Baudelaire from a feminist perspective and Blau DuPlessis's reading of Wordsworth: Culler looks at the poetical deformation of the historical discourse, while Blau DuPlessis looks from the poetical representation of the Other to the possible historical Other. Yet in a discussion about whether politically inspired questions addressed to literature should consider its formal, i.e. aesthetic or simply linguistic nature, Culler's and DuPlessis's profound readings are comparable and equally convincing.

The fact that literature's contribution to politics or, in a more general sense, knowledge, may precisely lie in its 'formal' dimension is reinforced in the German field by Ansgar and Vera Nünning, who reinscribe the 'technical' aspect of literary analysis into gender studies in their volume *Erzählanalyse und Gender Studies* (2004). In this book they record that literary texts are often reduced to their mimetical dimension when they are read with a feminist or gender focus. As Spivak would have it, they want to overcome the 'presentist mode' in identity studies. Just as Culler stresses the meaning of allegory in lyrical poetry, Ansgar Nünning and Vera Nünning stress the meaning of the narrative structure in prose literature: 'Ziel einer solchen erzähltheoretischen und kontextorientierten Erzählanalyse ist es, über die Untersuchung der Erzähl- und Repräsentationsformen literarischer Texte Einsicht in die kulturwissenschaftlich relevante Problemstellungen wie Geschlechterkonstruktionen zu gewinnen'[42] [The aim of this narratological and context-oriented analysis is to gain insight into culturally important questions such as constructions of gender by examining the forms of narration and representation in literary texts]. *What* is being said is *how* it is being said. From a somewhat different perspective Ansgar Nünning reinforces his argument about the importance of close reading in a recent contribution to the issue on 'Philology and Culture' of the periodical *Germanisch-Romanische Monatsschrift* (2009). In the face of the omnipresent dominance of life sciences in today's culture, Nünning points out that literature and literary studies should not retreat into a horticultural niche. Rather, literature should be regarded and approached as a medium that produces 'World images, world hierarchies, and orders of knowledge'.[43] It should not be looked at with a simplistic mimetic understanding but understood in its formal complexities; literary studies should focus on:

> die literaturspezifischen, symbolischen, narrativen, dramatischen und lyrischen Formen [...] durch die Literatur Lebenswissen nicht bloß wiedergibt oder verarbeitet, sondern durch sie verschiedene Lebensmodelle [...] inszeniert und alternative Weltbilder erzeugt.

> [the specific literary, symbolic, narrative, dramatic, and lyrical forms [...] through which literature not only represents or processes life science, but through which different models of life [...] are designed and alternative world images are constituted.][44]

The ability to read literature in a world that not only consists of genetic material, but also, as Nünning says, has mental and social dimensions into which literary texts may give insight, is most significant.[45] Reading literature in order to acknowledge it as an imaginary practice in the negotiation, mediatization, and criticism of identity construction, and reading works with their distinctive features, should, I think, in any case be part of the future of feminist literary criticism, not least for women's literature dating from before the rise of feminism. At the root of this lies the conviction that the literary encoding of ideas makes world and history look more complex, defies obviousness, common sense, and matters of fact, in short, the readily available. The integration of formalist analysis as part of the study of women's literature from the eighteenth and nineteenth centuries is not a sign of academic regression. Returning to the text would in this case reinforce the status of literature and literary studies, but similarly — and most of all — it would significantly redraw maps of literary culture, the genealogy of ideas, in short, add to the uncertainties of history, add to knowledge. An absolute precondition for this is the availability of literary texts by women authors, which has been an issue from the beginning of the study of historical women's literature in the 1970s. In Germany this problem was met by a number of new editions of work by women authors, albeit somewhat inconsistently and with variable standards and criteria. The series 'Frühe Frauenliteratur in Deutschland' (Early Women's Writing in Germany) (which includes authors such as Therese Huber, Caroline de la Motte-Fouqué, Benedikte Naubert, and Charlotte von Stein) published by the publishing house Olms-Weidmann since the late 1980s, for example, opted for reprints in Gothic script, whereas the publisher Ulrike Helmer chose new editions of historical literature (but printed fewer books). The road for women's literature from the eighteenth and nineteenth centuries to the well-known publishers with impressive marketing and distribution strategies is only open to texts that have been the object of consistent academic and public discussion for some time, and only a few texts have taken it, such as Sophie von La Roche's *Geschichte des Fräuleins von Sternheim* [History of Lady Sophia Sternheim] published by Reclam or Sophie Mereau's collected poems, prose, and letters published by DTV in 1997 (although already out of print now). Reprints appear mostly on the initiative of individual scholars, are often short-lived, and remain isolated. Digital and online publications have made older literature by women authors more widely accessible, yet, as any lecturer (and scholar) of literary history who wants to include historical women's literature on her/his curriculum will witness, printed books at affordable prices remain the best tools for the 'use', i.e. reading and rereading, of literary texts. If a literary text is only available in historical libraries or in an expensive, badly disseminated new copy it will retain an aura of uniqueness and so will to some extent be the work of literary criticism practised on it, forced to function as an illustration of ideas and hardly as the challenge to their articulation. Speaking pragmatically, women's literature from these centuries is doomed to be considered in a 'presentist mode', as matters always have to be *presented* instead of *discussed* for want of partners in the debate. Simon Richter's self-explanatory inclusion of Therese Huber's novels next to Kleist and Wieland in his study of the trope of the breast in German literature of the late eighteenth century, *Missing the Breast: Gender, Fantasy, and the Body in the German Enlightenment* (2006), shows how fertile and interesting the extension and deepening of the literary canon can be. But his approach is not mainstream in the discipline of *Germanistik*, at least not in Germany. In this light a survey on women's writing such as Gaby Pailer and Gudrun Loster-Schneider's *Lexikon deutschsprachiger Epik und Dramatik von Autorinnen* (2006) is of great importance. In contrast to the usual biographically framed presentation of historical women's literature, the editors have opted for a survey of abstracts of literary texts by women writers that were published between 1730 and 1900. As such, they do not merely widen the scope of knowledge of historical German literature, as the feminist historiography of literature has done from the late 1970s onward. By presenting women's literature *by means of literature*, they underscore the importance of the *text* as the core of literary study at a fundamental level. One example of an in-depth study of women's literature in what I have called the 'formalist' mode — digging into the linguistic and formal material of the literary texts, pondering its tropes and generic play — is Claudia Liebrand's *Kreative Refakturen: Annette von Droste-Hülshoffs Texte* (2008). Liebrand offers a profound reading of Droste-Hülshoff's lyrical poems as she searches for their articulation of gender and authorship. She moves from word to world and back again, stating that: 'nimmt man sie [die Gedichte] nur genau genug in den Blick [werden sie] zu Inszenierungsräumen, in denen das wieder auftaucht, was gerade nicht aufgerufen scheint: die Gender-Position der Dichterin[46] [if one considers these poems carefully enough, they become spaces of enactment where exactly that which seems not to have been evoked turns up, i.e. the gender position of the poet]. One could say that Droste-Hülshoff is an exception within feminist criticism as she has been a canonized author in literary history since her lifetime and her work is available in various editions. Yet Liebrand's analysis shows how much there is still to be discovered beneath the surface of the texts and what a different light a new reading sheds on the position of this well-known poet. The almost provocative simplicity of the word 'Texte' in the subtitle of this monograph, *Annette von Droste-Hülshoffs Texte*, is, I think, a significant statement on this subject.

## Notes to Chapter 2

1. Ann K. Mellor quoted in Rachel Blau DuPlessis, 'Marble Paper: Toward a Feminist "History of Poetry"', *Modern Language Quarterly*, 65.1 (2004), 93–129 (p. 112).
2. Johann Wolfgang Goethe, *Werke: Hamburger Ausgabe*, ed. by Erich Trunz, VII: *Wilhelm Meisters Lehrjahre* (Munich: Deutscher Taschenbuch Verlag, 1988), pp. 155–56.
3. Blau DuPlessis, p. 113.
4. Ibid., p. 117.
5. Ibid., p. 96.
6. Ibid., p. 117.
7. Ibid., p. 126.
8. See Marjorie Levinson, 'What is New Formalism?', *Periodical of the Modern Language Association*, 122.2 (2007), 558–70.
9. Gayatry Chakravorty Spivak, *Death of a Discipline* (New York: Columbia University Press, 2003), p. 8. Further references to this book are given after quotations in the text.
10. Judith Butler, John Guillory, and Kendall Thomas, *What's Left of Theory: New Work on the Politics of Literary Theory* (London and New York: Routledge, 2000), p. xi. An excellent survey of present tendencies in literary studies that focuses more on poetics is Levinson, 'What is New Formalism?'.
11. Quoted in Jutta Osinski, *Einführung in die feministische Literaturwissenschaft* (Berlin: Erich Schmidt Verlag, 1998), p. 50.
12. Anke Gilleir and Alicia Montoya, 'Introduction: Toward a New Conception of Women's Literary History', in *Women Writing Back/Writing Women Back: Transnational Perspectives from the Late Middle Ages to the Dawn of the Modern Era*, ed. by Anke Gilleir, Alicia Montoya, and Suzan van Dijk (Leiden and Boston: Brill, 2010), pp. 1–20.
13. Ina Schabert, 'No Room of One's Own: Women's Studies in English Departments in Germany', in *Periodical of the Modern Language Association*, 119.1 (2004), 69–79 (p. 74). Contrasting somewhat with this argument is Susan Gubar's remark on the present shift in focus from literature to other cultural media. Looking back on the development of feminist literary studies she makes

the following comment without offering an explanation: 'Curiously, too, in today's gender studies venues, literature and the study of literature — which played major roles at the inception of women's studies — have recently been supplemented and sometimes supplanted by other admittedly important areas of investigation' (Susan Gubar, 'Feminism Inside Out', *Periodical of the Modern Language Society*, 121.5 (2006), 1711–1716 (p. 1714)).

14. Russell J. Reising, 'Can Cultured Reading Read Culture? Toward a Theory of Literary Incompetence', *Tulsa Studies in Women's Literature*, 10.1 (1991), 67–77 (p. 72). Further references to this article are given after quotations in the text.

15. Emory Elliott, 'Introduction: Cultural Diversity and the Problem of Aesthetics', in *Aesthetics in a Multicultural Age*, ed. by Emory Elliott, Louis Freitas Caton, and Jeffrey Rhyne (Oxford: Oxford University Press, 2002), pp. 3–27 (p. 8). Further references to this article are given after quotations in the text.

16. Robyn Wiegman, 'Difference and Disciplinarity', in *Aesthetics in a Multicultural Age*, ed. by Emory Elliott, Louis Freitas Caton, and Jeffrey Rhyne (Oxford: Oxford University Press, 2002), pp. 135–56.

17. Wiegman, 'Difference and Disciplinarity', p. 138.

18. Gubar, 'Feminism Inside Out', p. 1714. The case Gubar makes in her 1998 article is on a different, almost opposite track from my own consideration of the evolution from feminist literary criticism to gender studies. Whereas I try to show that literary studies as a theoretically sophisticated discipline has been rejected by feminist criticism and identity studies, in favour of a more general cultural framework, Gubar considers as 'ailments' of feminism the work of critics such as Gayatri Spivak and Judith Butler, whose ardent adherence to poststructuralist conceptions of language have 'divorced feminist speculations from literary texts or [have] subordinat[ed] those texts to the epistemological, ideological, economic and political issues that supplanted literary history and aesthetic evaluation as the topics of writing about women' (Susan Gubar, 'What Ails Feminist Criticism?', *Critical Inquiry*, 24.4 (1998), 879–902 (p. 896)).

19. Wiegman, 'Difference and Disciplinarity', p. 138.

20. Ibid., p. 147.

21. Robyn Wiegman, 'On Being in Time with Feminism', *Modern Language Quarterly*, 65.1 (2004), 161–76 (p. 166).

22. Nor is the scope and position of women's studies in Germany comparable to the state of the discipline in the Anglo-Saxon world. A scan of the major German literary periodicals reveals the marginal presence of women's literature or gender matters. On this see Schabert, 'No Room of One's Own', p. 70.

23. Hartmut Böhme, Peter Matussek, and Lothar Müller, *Orientierung Kulturwissenschaft: Was sie kann, was sie will* (Hamburg: Rowohlt 2002), p. 108.

24. Gisela Brinker-Gabler, 'Einleitung. Frauen Schreiben. Überlegungen zu einer ausgewählten Exploration literarischer Praxis', in *Deutsche Literatur von Frauen*, 1: *Vom Mittelalter bis zum Ende des 18. Jahrhunderts*, ed. by Gisela Brinker-Gabler (Munich: Beck 1988), pp. 11–36 (pp. 32–33). Translations of citations are the author's own, unless stated otherwise.

25. Hannelore Schlaffer, 'Weibliche Geschichtsschreibung: Ein Dilemma', *Merkur: Deutsche Zeitschrift für europäisches Denken*, 40.3 (1986), 256–60 (p. 258).

26. Ibid., p. 259.

27. Ibid., p. 260.

28. As Toril Moi has indicated in terms borrowed from Bourdieu, the academic field and its rules function as a form of censorship that allows radical breaks with accepted forms no chance of survival, let alone symbolic authority. Toril Moi, 'The Challenge of the Particular Case: Bourdieu's Sociology of Cultural and Literary Criticism', in Toril Moi, *What is a Woman? And other Essays* (Oxford: Oxford University Press, 2001), pp. 300–12.

29. An important argument is also the fact that gender, in contrast to feminism, inherently contains a challenge to male colleagues to address the naturalness of identity issues and address 'die Konstruiertheit ihrer eigenen und der in Texten vermittelten Geschlechtsidentität' [the constructed character of their own gendered identity and the one mediated by texts, my translation] (Inge Stephan and Christina von Braun, 'Einleitung', in *Gender-Studien: Eine Einführung*, ed by Inge Stephan and Christina von Braun (Stuttgart: Metzler, 2000), pp. 9–15 (p. 11)).

30. Terry Eagleton, *After Theory* (New York: Basic Books, 2003), p. 124.

31. Inge Stephan, 'Literaturwissenschaft', in *Gender-Studien: Eine Einführung*, pp. 290–99 (p. 296).

32. In her excellent survey Jutta Osinski notices in a similar vein that the introduction of gender studies proved to be an escape from a theoretical 'potpourri' (*Einführung in die feministische Literaturwissenschaft*, p. 99).

33. Inge Stephan and Christina von Braun, 'Einleitung: Gender@Wissen', in *Gender@Wissen: Ein Handbuch der Gender-Theorien*, ed. by Inge Stephan and Christina von Braun (Cologne, -Weimar, and Vienna: Böhlau, 2005), pp. 7–45 (p. 23).

34. Wolfram Schmidgen, 'Reembodying the Aesthetic', *Modern Language Quarterly*, 66.1 (2005), 55–84 (p. 55).

35. Eagleton, *After Theory*, p. 222. In a comparable vein Terry Cochran remarks: 'Yet for all their reduced traditionalism, these newly fashioned ensembles — corpora of works constituted in reference to gender, culture, ethnicity, sexual proclivity, and so on — are clearly inscribed in the institutions that have so irrevocably moulded literary understanding' (Terry Cochran, 'The Knowing of Literature', *New Literary History*, 38 (2007), 127–43 (p. 129)).

36. George Levine, 'Introduction: Reclaiming the Aesthetic', in *Aesthetics and Ideology*, ed. by George Levine (New Brunswick, NJ: Rutgers University Press, 1994), pp. 1–30 (p. 16).

37. Ibid., p. 5. From an institutional point of view Peter Brooks points out that owing to the intense process of ideological and political consciousness-raising any critic had first and foremost to 'position him or her self as analyst and actor in an ideological drama, that not to do so is simply to be a bad-faith participant in hegemonic cultural practices' (Peter Brooks, 'Aesthetics and Ideology: What Happened to Poetics?', in *Aesthetics and Ideology*, pp. 153–67 (p. 157)).

38. Geoffrey Galt Harpham, 'Aesthetics and the Fundamentals of Modernity', in *Aesthetics and Ideology*, pp. 124–52 (p. 135).

39. Cochran, 'The Knowing of Literature', p. 120.

40. Sharon Marcus, 'Feminist Criticism: A Tale of Two Bodies', *Periodical of the Modern Language Association*, 121.5 (2006), 1722–1728 (p. 1722).

41. Jonathan Culler, 'Feminism in Time: A Response', in *Modern Language Quarterly*, 65.1 (2004), 117–94 (p. 180). Further references to this article are given after quotations in the text.

42. Ansgar Nünning and Vera Nünning, 'Von der feministischen Narratologie zur gender-orientierten Erzählanalyse', in *Erzählanalyse und Gender Studies*, ed. by Ansgar Nünning and Vera Nünning (Stuttgart: Metzler, 2004), pp. 1–32 (p. 12).

43. Ansgar Nünning, 'Welten-Weltbilder-Weisen der Welterzeugung: Das Wissen der Literatur und die Aufgabe der Literaturwissenschaft', *Germanisch-Romanische Monatsschrift*, 59.1 (2009), 65–90 (p. 68).

44. Ibid., p. 73.

45. Ibid., p. 79.

46. Claudia Liebrand, *Kreative Refakturen: Annette von Droste-Hülshoffs Texte* (Freiburg: Rombach, 2008), p. 13.

CHAPTER 3

# Chasing the Cloudy Woman

## In Praise of a Historical Approach to Women Writers

*Helen Fronius*

The history of women's writing has often been presented as a history of denial and exclusion from the literary sphere (by male editors, writers, and literary historians).[1] Scholars have frequently emphasized the general exclusion of women from public life. Karin Tebben argues that authorship was in itself a great threat to a woman's social respectability, and Susanne Kord deems female authorship a double risk: financial and personal.[2] Both scholars argue that this explains the frequently conformist nature of women's writing, and the disguised nature of subversive elements — where they exist at all. Barbara Becker-Cantarino even goes so far as to characterize the entire period of the Reformation to the Romantic era as 'eine Phase der Gesichts- und Geschichtslosigkeit für Frauen' [a phase during which women lacked a face and a history] because of their lack of participation in public discourse and public life.[3] The task of feminist criticism has been to diagnose, and to a certain extent to reverse, that process of exclusion. Ironically though, feminist criticism, consciously or unconsciously, had its own mechanisms of exclusion. Conservative women writers with dubious political beliefs, women who wrote in genres or styles which are no longer regarded fashionable, women whose writing was considered trivial even by female critics, women whose texts are hard to find and identify as theirs — such writers don't quite fit. This volume partly seeks to redress that imbalance, and to demonstrate the task which is still facing feminist criticism of the period. Other chapters show how investigations of conservative writers, marginal genres, and 'trivial' texts can yield important insights of feminist value. This chapter aims to show that the unearthing of new sources, of new texts, and the continued endeavour to contextualize women's work, remain crucial if the discipline is to flourish. I will show how valid conclusions about women's literary production cannot be drawn without a sufficiently broad source base. I will also argue that broadening that source base to include, among others, minor texts written by minor literary figures, adds to the depth of our understanding of the period, and of women's literary activity in general.

That a lot more spade work remains to be done is obvious. Susanne Kord's study of women writers and anonymity, now fifteen years old, concluded that more than 3,900 women authors published in the German-speaking countries in the 1700s and 1800s.[4] Her previous analysis of women dramatists listed 315 authors of the eighteenth and nineteenth centuries, who wrote over 2,000 dramas between them.[5] How many of those women are known to scholars of the period, even to feminist critics? And how many of their works have actually been the subject of scholarly scrutiny, let alone received the kind of literary analysis advocated by Gilleir in this volume? Helga Gallas and Anita Runge's 1993 bibliography of women's novels and stories published between 1771 and 1810 listed 110 female authors who published fiction in book form during those forty years. Altogether they published an impressive 396 books.[6] Again, how many of these have been the subject of any kind of in-depth scholarly scrutiny by one, let alone several, scholars? More than thirty years after feminist critics first turned their attention to female authors and their texts, coverage of the period remains piecemeal rather than comprehensive. This has several effects.

One is that unhistorical, and often unexamined, notions of women's writing in this period were able to persist for a long time without being called into question, simply because the groundwork which could have questioned certain notions had not been done. Anne Fleig's study *Handlungs-Spiel-Räume: Dramen von Autorinnen im Theater des ausgehenden 18. Jahrhunderts* (1999) shows how skewed our impression of the period can be, if we do not have the foundations on which to make informed assumptions. Her study was based on all available plays by women from between 1770 and 1800. The exploration of new texts enabled her to identify certain assumptions about the position of women dramatists in this period as a 'Fiktion der literarhistorischen Überlieferung' [a fiction of literary historical transmission].[7] Among these 'fictions' was the idea that women did not write many plays because of the inhibiting effect of the supreme aesthetic status accorded to drama. Fleig showed that this fiction derived more from modern scholarship than contemporary reality. The majority of eighteenth-century playwrights, both women and men, were far from inhibited by high aesthetic standards, and their works were more diverse than scholarship allowed.[8] The assumption that women's plays were more likely to be published anonymously, and less likely to be performed than men's plays, was also proved wrong by Fleig. At least half of all plays written by women were performed, which compares favourably to the performance ratings of work by male dramatists. Women's drama production rose parallel to men's drama production, in response to a general increase in the demand for new plays. The practice of submitting manuscripts anonymously meant that, in practice, an author's gender simply could not be used as a criterion for selection.[9]

In my own work published in 2007, I was able to show the benefits of using a broader range of primary sources. Taking into account both printed and unprinted primary sources, it was possible to demonstrate that women's reading and writing were less restricted than ideology has led us to expect, and that access to the literary market was far less dependent on gender than feminist scholars had tended to assume.[10] Women's position in the business of literature was in fact determined by other factors: the increase in readers, and the emergence of a literary market diverse enough to include both the demanding aesthetic of Weimar Classicism and the popular entertainments of romantic fiction. In spite of the well-documented disadvantages women faced through their lack of education and of financial and legal independence, there was demonstrably no generalized exclusion of women from the sphere of literature and culture, but rather a complex involvement on several levels — as readers, writers, public figures, teachers, actresses, translators, and correspondents.

There is a danger that we may overlook quieter voices, belonging to minor literary figures, expressed in minor texts, or published in minor, or hard to evaluate, outlets, such as literary journals. These texts add to the richness of our understanding of the period, of women's role in literary and cultural exchanges, and of the room for manoeuvre open to women at this time. Making visible women's complex involvement in cultural life is one of the tasks still facing feminist critics of the period; therefore, we need to continue to pay attention to the totality of sources. If we do not know the dramas women wrote, we cannot draw conclusions about why they hardly wrote any plays. Just because we have not looked for — or found — letters in which women haggle with publishers for favourable publishing conditions, that does not mean that women did not write such letters. As Fleig rightly pointed out, 'Wer Frauen aber nur im Haus sucht, kann sie woanders auch nicht finden' [If one only looks for women in the home, one can't expect to find them anywhere else].[11] If we do not continually seek to broaden our range of sources and scour the archives, we have no way of contextualizing the sources we do know. For example, how can we know whether the tropes of modesty women often employed in prefaces to novels masked reality or described it? Only by being able to compare them to a representative sample of prefaces from a different genre, such as drama, are we able to discern that this is not always how women represented their writing, and that the rhetoric of prefaces to novels may be genre-specific and therefore strategic.

Basing our work on a limited range of sources is potentially treacherous. For example, we have historically always been more aware of those women writers who were related to, married to, or acquainted with the great men of German literature (Wieland, Goethe, Schiller, Brentano, and so on). This told us two apparent facts about women writers. First, they were published through the largesse and patronage of great men. Secondly, they were stifled in their creativity by the strict ideals and high standards of such great men. Charlotte von Stein is the classic case.[12] But from such cases general conclusions have been drawn about the position of *all* women writers in the era — a disaster, as cases such as von Stein's are not only unrepresentative but also often exceptional. Women who did not have a male mentor via whom to approach a publisher were often better off than those who did.[13] They would naturally make their own advances without inhibition (because an alternative simply never existed). And like the vast majority of male writers (many of whom have also become obscure over the last two centuries), women authors did not always feel bound by the aesthetic norms of their age — insofar as they were even aware of them. The historical literary market is always much more diverse than the filtered-down, edited-out version of the literary market dealt with by literary scholars.

And yet, attention to the small-scale works of lesser literary figures can illuminate general questions about the position of women writers. To what extent were women able to appear to be contrary in their writing? Were they able to address a mixed gender audience? Were they able to contradict well-known male writers? How far were they able to engage in discourses of their day?[14] Were they able to stand up for, and defend, their sex against male prejudice? As an example of the kind of texts which tend to go unnoticed, I will examine women's writings on gender from the *Teutscher Merkur* (German Mercury) (*TM*).

In this period, if women wanted to publish their work without any threat to their social or financial standing, contributing to a journal seemed ideal. Journals allowed the publication of minor pieces that might not warrant stand-alone publication. They gave women access to a broader readership than individual works might command. Contributors, both male and female, could remain anonymous. Thus journals enabled women to participate in the debates of their day, Elisa von der Recke's articles in the *Berlinische Monatsschrift* (Berlin Monthly) being a good example of such participation.[15] The role of women's journals and female editors has been studied elsewhere and will not be the focus of this discussion.[16] Instead, I will highlight the possibilities for participating in intertextual dialogues offered to women by mainstream literary journals such as Wieland's *Teutscher Merkur* (after 1790 known as the *Neuer Teutscher Merkur* (New German Mercury)), aimed at a general, predominantly male readership.

The publication of Thomas Starnes's *Repertorium* brought women's contributions to the *Teutscher Merkur* (*TM*) to light; but since Ruth Dawson's article of 1984, these have received scant attention. During the lifespan of the journal, the work of thirty-one women writers was published. The majority of these contributions were poetry (twenty in all, with one contribution sometimes consisting of several poems). Only thirteen were prose texts. (Two women, Friederike Brun and Emilie von Berlepsch, published both poetry and prose in the *TM*.)[17] More than half of these women had published, or were about to publish, books in their own right. For them, the *TM* represented an opportunity to widen their readership, or to introduce themselves to the literary public before publishing a separate collection.[18] Women's work was published throughout the existence of the journal, from the first volume to the last. In the last year of the journal's life, no fewer than fifteen contributions from women were published, for the first time making up a significant proportion of the whole.[19] This appears to contradict the widespread notion that, after a brief heyday in the late eighteenth century, there was progressively less space for women on the literary market after 1800.[20] However, entire years went by without contributions from women: women's presence in the journal was still not overwhelming.[21]

Despite this, noteworthy texts did find their way into the journal. Two of these are remarkable partly because they constitute a response to texts written by men in earlier issues: women, by no means well-known authors, not only submitted contributions to the *TM*, but aimed at publicly contradicting men. In the first exchange, in 1782, a woman identified as Johanna Susanna Bohl wrote *Winde und*

*Männer: Antwort eines Frauenzimmers auf Dr. Sheridans Wolken und Weiber* (Wind and Men: A Woman's Riposte to Dr Sheridan's *Clouds and Women*), in response to Johann Gottlieb Kreutzfeld's translation of a poem by Sheridan, entitled: *Wolken und Weiber oder A New Simile for the Ladies, nach Dr. Sheridan* (Clouds and Women or A New Simile for the Ladies, according to Dr Sheridan).[22] Both poems are humorous in tone, but they quite explicitly address the vexed question of gender relations. There clearly is a serious undertone to this exchange. Bohl's poem is significant in that it sets out to redefine, from a female perspective, the gender relationship as previously characterized by a male author.

In *Wolken und Weiber* (Clouds and Women), the male poet is searching for a simile which will describe women 'in allen Punkten' [in every way].[23] Deciding on the image of a cloud, he proceeds to enumerate the ways in which women and clouds are alike. Both are unsteady and changeable, both in their attire and in their moods. Sometimes the slightest breeze can sway them; at other times, they stubbornly oppose the strongest winds. Like clouds, women can be light and cheerful or dark and threatening. They produce thunder and lightning — with their tongues — to make even 'der bravste Kerl' [the most courageous chap] cower as he would before a thunderstorm. And tears are to women as rain is to the clouds — a natural by-product of their existence. In contrast perhaps to these telling comparisons, Kreutzfeld contends that women's ideas lack substance and are, like clouds, built on air.

The comparisons become less playful when Kreutzfeld refers to the widely held belief that clouds brought with them 'Pest und Gift' [pestilence and poison], the equivalent of women's gossip: 'ein guter Name, sagt man auch, | Sterb' oft von einem Weiber-Hauch' [a good reputation, it is said, is often killed by a women's breath]. Also he contends that, analogous to clouds, women always obscure the horizons of men's vision. 'Ich seh, tritt sie mir vors Gesicht, | Dann keinen Himmel ausser — Ihr' [When faced with her, I see no other heaven, other than — her]. The poem's attitude to women is curious: it attempts humour in describing women's supposed character, but many of the characteristics mentioned are surely serious character faults. It is no surprise, therefore, that Johanna Susanna Bohl felt stung into writing a reply.

Her poem is a quick and direct riposte, as the subtitle indicates — *Antwort eines Frauenzimmers auf Dr. Sheridans Wolken und Weiber*. It does not dispute the relationship between the sexes as outlined in *Wolken und Weiber*, but rather challenges the interpretation of women's motives. The poem begins in a mock-polite tone: 'Wir danken ganz höflich für die Ehre | Dem Herren, der uns in die Sfäre | Des schön gestirnten Himmels versezt' [We would like to thank politely the gentleman who has granted us the honour of placing us in the sphere of the beautiful heavens].[24] She has searched for a simile to describe men, and has found the wind to be most suitable. 'Denn nichts unterm Monde schmiegt sich so an | Das wolkichte Weib, als der windichte Mann' [because nothing under the moon snuggles up to the cloud-like woman like the wind-like man]. Her poem ridicules the idea of womanhood propagated by Rousseau — that women's existence is only meaningful in relation to men.

Die Wolke bekommt erst vom Winde das Leben,
Muß nach Befehl sich bald senken bald heben,
Muß immer sich lassen treiben und jagen,
Nach ihres gestrengen Herrn Behagen,
Und dient ihm vielmahls nur zum Spiel,
Darf nicht gehn wenn und wohin sie will.
Denn öfters jagt nur zum Zeitvertreib
Der Windichte Mann das wolkichte Weib.

[The cloud only receives life from the wind,
has to rise and fall on command,
has to allow itself to be driven and hunted always
according to her severe master's whim,
and often serves only to amuse him,
is not allowed to go where and when she wants.
Because often the windy man chases
the cloudy woman just to pass the time.]

As this second stanza shows, women's dependence on men makes them changeable, for they are then easily exploited for men's amusement. Bohl then redefines the characteristics of clouds, in antithesis to Kreutzfeld's poem: far from wreaking havoc, clouds lessen the destructive force of the sun, and 'seegnen durch Einfluß das Feld und das Thal' [their influence blesses fields and valleys]. When the winds are pleasant and mild, clouds are gentle too. Unfortunately, winds are frequently anything other than pleasant, and resemble 'ein wütender Orcan' [an angry hurricane] instead. Men's temper and anger (often triggered by minor occurrences) are unleashed on women, 'So müssens die armen Wolken entgelten. | Da gehts an ein Brausen, ein Toben und Schelten' [and so the poor clouds have to endure a roaring, clamouring and scolding]. Whatever chaos might be caused by a black cloud, it is only because of the power of the wind. Were clouds unencumbered by the wind, she posits, they would not cause a disturbance to anyone. Clouds are helpless against the power of the wind, which in turn is described in threatening tones: it is 'schreckend' [terrifying], 'furchtbar' [terrible], 'gestreng' [severe], and 'ungestüm' [vehement]. She rejects the idea that women's gossiping destroys reputations, and suggests instead that 'alle Seuchen und Plagen [werden] | Von Winden durch die Welten getragen' [all diseases and plagues | [are] spread across the world by winds]. Men's destructive potential — inherent in their ability to corrupt innocent girls — is also hinted at: 'Sanftlockend bei Tage und Tödtend bey Nacht, | Verderbt er was sie lange gepflegt und bewacht' [gently seductive by day, and deadly by night, | he destroys what she has spent a long time preserving and looking after]. Bohl also rejects the notion that general statements can be made about women as though they did not exhibit any individual traits, 'Drum kann auch der Schluß nicht wahr und gemein | Auf alle Wolken zu machen seyn' [therefore the conclusion cannot be true and refer to all clouds] She ends the poem with a question:

Doch Eine Frage sey mir erlaubt,
Und die man nicht überflüßig glaubt.
Was wär denn ein solcher Gast [Mann] wohl werth,
Der Kraft und Vermögen uns aufgezehrt?

[...]
Bey dem man viel schmerzliche Nächte durchwacht,
Und Der Wirth und Wohnung noch lächerlich macht,
Ja was von dem allen das bitterste ist,
Den beissenden Spott noch mit Schmeicheln beschließt?

[But I may be permitted one question,
which shall not be deemed superfluous.
What would such a guest [man] be worth
who uses up our energy and fortune?
[...]
Who has forced one to be awake through many a painful night
and who has ridiculed the hostess and the house,
yes, and this is the most bitter thing of all,
who has concluded his biting scorn with flattery?]

Bohl gives the answer to the question herself, sounding a defiant note on which the poem ends: 'So wahr ich eine Wolke bin | Ich gäb nicht ein Tröpfchen Regen um ihn!' [As truly as I am a cloud, | I would not give a single drop of rain for him!]

Bohl's reply ensures that, appropriately, the last word on the subject of women belongs to a woman, not a man. Whilst humorous on the surface, Bohl nonetheless positioned herself in the literary sphere with a poem which examined, and found wanting, the male logic expressed elsewhere in the journal.

Of course, this is only one example of a woman participating in intertextual dialogue and contradicting the male perspective in public. There are others. In 1793, a woman wrote a poem on waltzing, in response to a male-authored poem published earlier in the *Teutscher Merkur*. In *Das Walzen* (On Waltzing), believed to have been the work of Friedrich von Köpken, the author rejected the fashionable waltz on two grounds: first, it was un-German, and secondly, immodest.[25] The dance is described as involving 'dieses wilde Schwingen | Wo sich Mann und Mädchen dicht umschlingen' [this wild swinging | during which men and women hold onto each other tightly], which contrasts with the traditional German virtues of 'Grazie und Anmuth' [grace and charm].[26] Waltzing is not worthy of the noble German people who are 'gewöhnt an Edelthaten, | Groß im Kriege' [used to noble deeds | and great in war]. German women, once gentle and virtuous, are singled out as especially depraved. Köpken sees worrying sexual overtones in the waltz:

Wie? Sie beben nicht mit scheuem Blick
Vor der Wilden Walzer dichten Reihen,
Die des Tanzes Grazie entweihen,
Vor den wüsten Orgyen zurück!

[What? You do not quiver with a modest gaze
before the tight rows of the wild waltz,
which desecrate the gracefulness of dance,
do not quiver before the wild orgies!]

The blame for this deplorable state of affairs lies with women. For Köpken, women are responsible for the moral health of the nation. The author ends the poem by appealing to the German people to return to their old ways, 'Dann erst, wenn bey sanften Reihentänzen, | Euch die Grazien mit Rosen kränzen, | Dann erst ist

Terpsichore versöhnt!' [Only then, when during gentle *ronde* dances | the graces give you roses, | will Terpsichore be appeased!]

Henriette Ernestine Christiane von Gilden anonymously published a poem in response to Köpken three months later, refuting his allegations of immorality. In *An den Verfasser des Gedichts: Das Walzen* (To the Author of the Poem: On Waltzing) she argues that the dance is not un-German, and an innocent pleasure. It was Köpken's judgement that was flawed: 'Schiefes Urtheil [trifft] unsere reinsten Thaten' [flawed judgement skews our purest deeds].[27] His judgement is discredited, not the dancers: 'Doch, wen schändet solch ein Blick?' [But who is disgraced by such a perspective?]. He is a 'Freudenstöhrer' [disruptor of pleasures], who cannot appreciate true beauty — he lacks an 'offnes Aug' und reine Güte' [open eye and pure goodness]. She insinuates that Köpken must be mixing with the wrong crowd, if immodesty is all he can see in the dance ('Wenn in deinen Kreisen | Man sich tummelt nach Bachanten-Weisen' [if the people of your acquaintance | dance like bacchantes]). 'Grazie and Anmuth' [grace and charm], the two qualities he had found lacking in the waltz, are in fact the ideal of its execution. He is clearly unable to appreciate the beauty and nobility of the 'seelenvolles Schweben' [soulful floating] of waltzing, 'Und so höhnt er kühn, das was er nie verstand' [and thus he mocks what he never understood]. To condemn the dance because of the dancers would be as illogical as condemning fine wine on account of the existence of drunkards. Gilden accuses Köpken of seeing 'die Schale statt dem Kerne' [the peel instead of the core]. This is the cause of his misguided criticism.

Her spirited defence of the waltz is interesting for several reasons. It shows that women did participate in general public debates about contemporary phenomena such as waltzing. Also, Gilden rejected the more specific charge of immodesty and immorality levelled against the female sex in Köpken's poem. Although this exchange did not ostensibly deal with gender relations, Gilden was spurred into speaking up for her sex and rejecting the criticisms Köpken made of women in particular. However, Gilden's male contemporaries do not seem particularly to have welcomed her intervention. Unlike Köpken's poem, Gilden's appeared accompanied by a number of disparaging footnotes by Wieland, in which he contradicts her and points out the poem's technical deficiencies. The metre is scrutinized ('die zwey fehlenden Sylben' [the two missing syllables]). A quotation from Voltaire, intended to end the poem with a bang, is dismissed ('Ich bitte um Erlaubniß hinzuzusetzen, daß Voltaire vielleicht auch hier [...] Unrecht haben könnte.' [I'd like to point out that Voltaire may be wrong, also in this matter]).[28] The editor explicitly conspires with Köpken to undermine the credibility of Gilden's argument because waltzing is 'auch mir verhaßt' [hateful to me as well]. Women could enter public debates, it seems, but not without potentially attracting the attentions of a censorious chaperone. Nevertheless, Gilden's poem and her pursuit of publication in a mainstream journal are noteworthy, especially as she too, like Bohl, engages in an act of 'writing back'. Despite the trivial nature and humorous tone of these contributions by Gilden and Bohl, they address crucial aspects of the relations between the sexes, and the status of women in particular.

Few substantial prose articles by women were published in the *Teutscher Merkur*. An exception is Emilie von Berlepsch's anonymous piece entitled *Ueber einige zum*

*Glück der Ehe nothwendige Eigenschaften und Grundsätze* (On a few Characteristics and Principles which are required for a Happy Marriage).[29] Published in two parts in the issues of May and June 1791, it is also accompanied by footnotes from the editor. In this case, however, the editor endorses the piece. It has been abandoned in a desk drawer for over ten years, he says, and is only now being published as a result of his intervention.[30] The essay is formally composed as a letter of advice from a woman to her soon-to-be-married younger sister. What is surprising about the essay is the way that, amongst the highly conventional mundane advice, Berlepsch makes an outspoken attack on traditional gender relations.[31] That the attack was somewhat hidden within an otherwise conventional article is perhaps explained by the mainstream masculine nature of the *Teutsche Merkur.*

Universal ideals of femininity might be noble, Berlepsch concedes early on, but they bring with them many problems. Gentleness ('Sanftmuth') in particular, so inextricably linked with femininity since Rousseau, is desirable in a woman, but real women do not conform to such universal ideals. It is therefore unavoidable ('da sich die Gesetze der Natur nicht umstoßen lassen' [because the laws of nature cannot be overturned], p. 68) that those women who are naturally of a more fiery temper will offend men's sensibilities. The problem here lies not with the women themselves, but with the ideals to which they have to conform. Furthermore, these ideals are misused for the purposes of oppressing and controlling women. Whilst gentleness is a good and noble idea, she criticizes 'den Mißbrauch des Ausdrucks sanft' [the misuse of the term gentleness]. More specifically, she opposes the prejudice 'welches den Weibern weder eignen Willen, noch Muth ihn auszudrücken, gestatten möchte' [which does not want to allow women their own will, or the courage to express it, p. 69]. Berlepsch's critique of the status of women in late eighteenth-century Germany was not anti-establishment in purpose. She wanted to ensure happier, better, and therefore lasting marriages. Her own experience of divorce in 1787, when she was thirty-two years old, undoubtedly influenced her. Like Johanna Susanna Bohl, she argues that women are in an undignified position, whereby they are worth nothing in themselves, and depend on men for everything. 'Natur und Gesellschaft, Vorurtheil und Nothwendigkeit, haben unsern Zustand so eingeschränkt, daß wir wenig durch uns selbst sind und seyn können' [Nature and society, prejudice and necessity have confined our condition to such an extent that we do not and cannot amount to much by ourselves, p. 75]. The lack of equality between partners results all too easily in a despotic relationship: 'Seelenherrschaft [...] muß in wilde Anarchie ausarten, sobald sie einen despotischen Anschein gewinnt, und bloß auf das Recht des Stärkeren sich gründen will' [Lordship over the soul results in wild anarchy as soon as it acquires a despotic appearance and founds itself solely on the rights of the stronger party, p. 76]. Men's rule over women might be less destructive if men were better equipped to be in charge, but, Berlepsch insists, this is not the case:

> Woraus besteht die größere Anzahl derjenigen, die sich anmaßen, Ehemänner und Hausväter zu werden? Theils sind es rohe, ungebildete Jünglinge, die nie Gelegenheit hatten das weibliche Herz zu studieren, oder, was noch schlimmer ist, nur aus seichten Romanen und Spottschriften, nur im Umgang mit der verworfensten Klasse der Weiber einige Kenntnisse davon erwerben [...]. (p. 77)

[What does the majority of those, who presume to become husbands and heads of families, consist of? Partly they are coarse, uneducated youths who have never had the opportunity to learn about the female heart, or what's even worse, who have only learnt about it from shallow novels and satires, and from associating with the most depraved class of women [...].]

Such men are not capable of properly treating women who are frequently handed to them at a tender and immature age ('ein zartes junges Geschöpf, das aus der Kinderstube in ihre Arme geworfen wird', [a delicate young creature who was thrown into their arms straight from the nursery], p. 78). Men do not possess the wisdom necessary to lead others ('Sie sollen Führer seyn? Ach die Blinden, die selbst eines Führers bedürfen!' [They want to be leaders? Oh the blind, who themselves require a leader!], p. 78). Many women also married civil servants, men who spent their lives 'in trocknen Amtsgeschäften' [in dry official business], where they had no opportunity to develop their 'Menschenkenntniß' or 'Biegsamkeit des Geistes' [understanding of mankind or flexibility of mind]. They are equally unsuited to be husbands in charge of young women (p. 79). Add to that all those men who were prevented by worries and concerns from devoting sufficient attention to their wives, and the number of husbands 'von denen eine schonende und großmüthige Behandlung sich erwarten läßt' [of whom one could expect considerate and generous treatment] was not great (p. 80).

Berlepsch continues: All-male society also created an atmosphere which precluded harmonious gender relations. In male company, even the least bearded youth learnt to repeat 'Spöttereyen, freche Scherze und hämische Anspielungen' [ridicule, impudent banter, and malicious insinuations]. Indeed, male society is so entirely based on communal disdain for the female sex that she wonders what else men would talk about: 'Würde nicht der Strom ihrer Unterredung versiegen, wenn nicht ein Stückchen aus der weiblichen Charakteristik Stoff zu lautem Gelächter hergeben müßte?' [Would the flow of conversation not dry up if a little observation about female characteristics did not yield loud laughter? (p. 81)]. But, she contends, male derision of the whole female sex is only supported by individual and exceptional instances. These are the instances which lie behind Ernst Brandes's arguments in *Ueber die Weiber* (On Women) — a text specifically cited by Berlepsch as poisoning relations between the sexes (p. 83).[32] Unlike many of her contemporaries, Berlepsch calls these unfounded prejudices against women by their proper name: misogyny. And so she maintains, 'Die nachtheiligen Folgen dieses misogynischen Tons auf Gesellschaft und Sitten überhaupt sind wohl nicht zu bezweifeln [...] doch ihr Einfluß auf das Glück der Ehe [...] wird vielleicht von vielen verkannt' [The negative consequences of this misogynist tone on society and morals in general cannot be doubted, but their influence on the happiness of marriages is perhaps recognized by many (p. 83)]. The misogynist stories, jokes, and anecdotes which fill men's heads naturally affect their behaviour towards women (p. 86).[33] Attitudes towards women which may have been acceptable in an earlier age were no longer appropriate in the late eighteenth century, a time of refinement ('allgemeine Verfeinerung und Ausbildung aller Ideen und Gefühle' [general refinement and development of all ideas and sentiments]). Men could no longer ignore women's needs, as these conditions had given women higher expectations ('höhere Bedürfnisse des Geistes und des Herzens' [higher requirements of the mind and the heart], p. 86).

Berlepsch could see only one solution to these problems in gender relations, and it resembles prevention more than a cure. Women's status must be altered; they must gain more '*Selbstständigkeit*' ([independence], p. 89, emphasis in the original). Berlepsch then elaborates on what this self-reliance might mean for women: 'Wir müssen, wir müssen allein stehen lernen! Wir müssen unsere Denkart, unsern Charakter in unsern eignen Augen so ehrwürdig machen, daß uns das Urtheil andrer in unserem geprüften und gerechten Urtheil über uns selber nicht irre machen kann' [We must, we must learn to stand alone! We must make our own way of thinking, our own character so noble in our own eyes, that the opinion of others cannot confuse our own tested and sound judgement of ourselves (p. 90)]. The strength of Berlepsch's feeling and the sense of the urgency felt by her is expressed in the repetition of 'müssen' [must]. There was no reason why German women should not be able to maintain their independent inner selves ('innere, geistige Existenz selbstständig und eigenthümlich' [inner, mental existence, independent and unique], p. 91). Many of the faults of women, such as their gossiping, would naturally be remedied if women were less restricted. Independence would act as a shield both against men's flattery ('der Weihrauch, den uns die Männer streuen' [the frankincense which men spread for us]), and men's criticism (p. 92). Berlepsch explicitly describes the late eighteenth century as a time of change, in which the old order was being replaced by a new one, thereby necessitating a renegotiation of gender relations. 'Die Frau ist nicht mehr bloß Haushälterin des Mannes und Gebährerin seiner Kinder; sie ist auch Erzieherin, ist Theilhaberin seiner oft sehr verwickelten Verhältnisse, und hat ihre eigene zuweilen nicht unwichtige Rolle im gesellschaftlichen Leben zu behaupten' [Woman is no longer simply a man's housekeeper and the bearer of his children, she is also a pedagogue, participates in his often very complicated circumstances, and has to maintain her own, at times not unimportant, role in society (pp. 100–01)].

The new role for women was, however, left tantalizingly indistinct. The remainder of the essay considers conventional questions of married life, and may well be part of the older essay written ten years earlier, whilst the section discussed here could have been written shortly before publication, under the influence of the French Revolution and the proclamation of human rights. But in her discussion of the duties of a housewife in part two, Berlepsch also insists on the dignity of women's familial role, and argues that housewives are unjustly forgotten, given the difficult nature of their task: 'diese Frau wird von der Welt übersehen, lebt unbekannt und stirbt vergessen!' [this woman is overlooked by the world, lives unrecognized, and dies forgotten!].[34] Berlepsch does not propose an alteration in the material circumstances of women's lives. But she does suggest that they may be able to establish an independent realm within themselves in which their sense of self is inviolable. This was a radical suggestion to make, and all the more radical for having been made in the unlikely context of Wieland's *Neuer Teutscher Merkur*. As these three examples show, women writers were able to scrutinize the often paradoxical notions of gender roles, as propagated in texts by men, by writing back.[35] The power relations inherent in the editorial and literary process are also evident in these examples — editors could choose to endorse or undermine women's writing as they saw fit. But that these women engaged with, and responded to, contemporary debates via the public medium of a literary journal is also undeniable. It is these complexities of women's positioning in the literary sphere which clearly come to light when we look further afield for examples of women's written expression.

Much writing about women in this period rehearses a narrative that Rebekka Habermas has called the 'Einbahnstraße des Leides' [one way street of suffering].[36] But it is possible to see beyond that, to see active conversation between the sexes instead of passively received monologues. A change in perspective, away from a one-sided analysis of oppression to a more complex consideration of opportunities and restrictions alike (based on a variety of sources, especially factual ones), is still required if we are to contextualize women's work fully. It has been, and continues to be, our task to reveal women's complex and often contradictory participation in literature and culture. If we regard the Enlightenment as a process of communication in which the rights of many groups were debated and negotiated (including, for example, the rights of Jews, the non-ruling classes, women, and children), then we can see the debate surrounding gender as a debate between the sexes, in which women also participated (and in which men often participated on women's behalf).[37] Highlighting this reciprocity is essential if we are not accidentally to reinforce women's exclusion. The emergence of new means of communication and forums for exchange (journals, reading societies, etc.) must be interpreted as benefiting not just men, but also women.

To do these sources justice, scholars must return to primary sources. Plenty remains to be rediscovered. The Nicolai Nachlaß [papers of the publisher Friedrich Nicolai] in the Staatsbibliothek in Berlin, for example, holds the letters of over ninety women correspondents, many of which have not been studied. And yet they are the most direct evidence we have of how women approached male publishers, pursued publication, and exploited the contemporary book market. New publications available to scholars will open up a large body of evidence which hitherto has been difficult to access. They are yet to be fully exploited in terms of making visible aspects of women's contribution to cultural life. Bernhard Fischer's *Chronologische Verlagsbibliographie* for Johann Friedrich Cotta's publishing house is one such publication.[38] It covers the years 1787–1832, and in three volumes lists not just the full titles of all of Cotta's publications, but also all the authors and contributors whom he published. In volume III, the register of authors lists the names of nearly seventy women whose writing Cotta published (not including those pseudonyms which have been impossible to identify, and which may well include some women). It includes authors, editors, translators, and contributors. This sample, based on one of the biggest and most important publishing houses of the era, is large enough to be statistically significant, an important criterion as explained by Susanne Kinnebrock and Timon B. Schaffer in this volume, and would allow general conclusions to be drawn, for example about the kind of contributions women wrote for journals (which genres? which themes predominate?), the number of contributions which, on average, women managed to have published, what kind of journals women wrote for (aimed at a mixed audience? or primarily aimed at a female readership?), and so on. Another bibliography has become available which also makes women's literary activity more transparent. Doris Kuhles's *Analytische Bibliographie* of the *Journal des Luxus und der Moden* (Journal of Luxury and Fashion) covers a very similar period of time (1786–1827), and although it focuses only on one journal, rather than the entire output of a publishing house, it nonetheless makes women's contributions to one of the major journals of the period readily accessible.[39] Volume III also contains a register of names. It has now become possible to work out how many women wrote for this journal and how their contributions developed over time (did they contribute a similar amount of material throughout the lifetime of the journal? or were there significant variations over the course of the forty-one years covered?). It is also possible to see how many women are reviewed in the journal, as actresses, singers, writers, or painters — in short, as participants in Germany's cultural life. The subject index is especially useful in that it guides the reader directly to articles which shed light on the gender discourse of the time (for example, there are references to articles on 'Gleichberechtigung der Frau' [equality of women], 'Mißachtung des Weibes' [disregard for women], and the like). These kinds of resources could undoubtedly bring less well-known voices to the attention of scholars. Moreover, they could allow us to make comparisons with other journals of the period, such as those published by Cotta. Making sources such as these more readily available is crucial if we are to appreciate the complexity of cultural life in this era. Digitalization projects currently running will be an enormous help in making these rare texts more widely available. Returning to the roots of feminist criticism on this period, by returning to the archives, is a fundamental step if scholarship on women writers is to remain fresh and vibrant. It is an essential prerequisite if we are to refocus on the female author as advocated by Anne Fleig in this volume. Without (re)visiting primary sources, we cannot leave the well-trodden path of scholarship that went before us, and we may end up simply going round in circles.

## Notes to Chapter 3

1. See for example *In the Shadow of Olympus: German Women Writers around 1800*, ed. by Katherine Goodman and Edith Josefine Waldstein (Albany: State University of New York Press, 1992); Barbara Becker-Cantarino, '"Gender Censorship": On Literary Production in German Romanticism', *Women in German Yearbook*, 11 (1995), 81–97; Barbara Becker-Cantarino, 'Goethe as a Critic of Literary Women', in *Goethe as a Critic of Literature*, ed. by Karl J. Fink and Max L. Baeumer (Lanham, NY and London: University Press of America, 1984), pp. 160–81; Barbara Becker-Cantarino, '"Outsiders": Women in German Literary Culture of Absolutism', *Jahrbuch für internationale Germanistik*, 2 (1984), 147–58.

2. Susanne Kord, *Ein Blick hinter die Kulissen: Deutschsprachige Dramatikerinnen im 18. und 19. Jahrhundert* (Stuttgart: Metzler, 1992), p. 27; Karin Tebben, 'Soziokulturelle Bedingungen weiblicher Schriftkultur im 18. und 19. Jahrhundert: Zur Einleitung', in Tebben, *Beruf: Schriftstellerin. Schreibende Frauen im 18. und 19. Jahrhundert* (Göttingen: Vandenhoeck & Ruprecht, 1998), pp. 10–46 (here p. 25).

3. Barbara Becker-Cantarino, *Schriftstellerinnen der Romantik: Epoche – Werk – Wirkung* (Munich: Beck, 2000), p. 27.

4. Susanne Kord, *Sich einen Namen machen: Anonymität und weibliche Autorschaft, 1700–1900*, Ergebnisse der Frauenforschung (Stuttgart: Metzler, 1996), p. 41.

5. See Kord, *Ein Blick*.

6. Helga Gallas and Anita Runge, *Romane und Erzählungen deutscher Schriftstellerinnen um 1800: Eine Bibliographie mit Standortnachweisen* (Stuttgart: Metzler, 1993), pp. 11–13.

7. Anne Fleig, *Handlungs-Spiel-Räume: Dramen von Autorinnen im Theater des ausgehenden 18. Jahrhunderts*, Epistemata: Reihe Literaturwissenschaft (Würzburg: Königshausen & Neumann, 1999), p. 281.

8. Ibid., pp. 1–4.

9. Ibid., p. 280.

10. See Helen Fronius, *Women and Literature in the Goethe Era, 1770–1820: Determined Dilettantes* (Oxford: Clarendon Press, 2007), and Helen Fronius, '"Nur eine Frau wie ich konnte so ein Werk schreiben": Reassessing German Women Writers and the Literary Market 1770–1820', in *Frauen und der literarische Markt 1780–1918*, ed. by E. Müller-Adams and E. Bland (Bielefeld: Aithesis, 2007), pp. 29–52.

11. Fleig, *Handlungs-Spiel-Räume*, p. 281.

12. Susan L. Cocalis, 'Acts of Omission: The Classical Dramas of Caroline von Wolzogen and Charlotte von Stein', in *Thalia's Daughters: German Women Dramatists from the Eighteenth Century to the Present*, ed. by Susan L. Cocalis and Ferrel Rose (Tübingen: Francke, 1996), pp. 77–98.

13. For examples, see Fronius, *Women and Literature*, and Helen Fronius, 'Der reiche Mann und die arme Frau: German Women Writers and the Eighteenth-Century Literary Market-Place', *German Life and Letters*, 56 (2003), 1–19.

14. Stephanie Hilger's study *Women Write Back: Strategies of Response and the Dynamics of European Literary Culture, 1790–1805* (Amsterdam and New York: Rodopi, 2009) asks similar research questions.

15. See for example Elisa von der Recke, 'An Herrn J. M. Preißler, Professor bei der kgl. dänischen Akademie der Künste, nebst Vorwort der Herausgeber und Nachschrift der Autorin', *Berlinische Monatsschrift*, 5 (1786), 385–98.

16. See for example Hugo Lachmanski, *Die deutschen Frauenzeitschriften des achtzehnten Jahrhunderts* (Berlin: Paul, 1900); Ulrike Weckel, *Zwischen Häuslichkeit und Öffentlichkeit: Die ersten deutschen Frauenzeitschriften im späten 18. Jahrhundert und ihr Publikum* (Tübingen: Niemeyer, 1998); Frank Schubert, *Die Stellung der Frau im Spiegel der Berlinischen Monatsschrift*, Abhandlungen zur Philosophie, Psychologie und Pädagogik, 150 (Bonn: Bouvier, 1980).

17. Statistics compiled using Thomas C. Starnes, *Der Teutsche Merkur: Ein Repertorium* (Sigmaringen: Jan Thorbecke, 1994).

18. Ruth P. Dawson, '"Der Weihrauch, den uns die Männer streuen": Wieland and the Women Writers in the Teutscher Merkur', in *Christoph Martin Wieland: Nordamerikanische Forschungsbeiträge zur 250. Wiederkehr seines Geburtstages 1983*, ed. by Hansjörg Schnelle (Tübingen: Niemeyer, 1984), pp. 225–49 (p. 229).

19. Ibid., p. 230.

20. Kord, *Namen*, p. 94.

21. Dawson, '"Der Weihrauch, den uns die Männer streuen"', p. 230.

22. Johanna Susanne Bohl, née Eberhardt (1738–1806), was the wife of the mayor of Lobeda, near Jena. Johann Gottlieb Kreutzfeld (1745–84) was a philosopher, librarian, and professor of poetry at the University of Königsberg.

23. All references are to [Johann Gottlieb Kreutzfeld], 'Wolken und Weiber oder A New Simile for the Ladies, nach Dr. Sheridan', *Der Teutsche Merkur*, May (1782), pp. 97–100. All translations in the text are the author's own, unless otherwise stated.

24. All references are to [Johanna Susanna Bohl], 'Winde und Männer. Antwort eines Frauenzimmers auf Dr. Sheridans Wolken und Weiber', *Der Teutsche Merkur*, July (1782), pp. 3–8.

25. Friedrich von Köpken (1737–1811) was a poet and civil servant in Magdeburg.

26. All references are to [Friedrich von Köpken], 'Das Walzen', *Der Neue Teutsche Merkur*, February (1793), pp. 216–18.

27. All references are to [Henriette Ernestine Christiane von Gilden], 'An den Verfasser des Gedichts: das Walzen. (Im 2ten Stücke des Teutschen Merkurs 1793, wie auch an Herrn Menschenschreck im Bürgerschen Musen-Allmanach dieses Jahres. S. 159)', *Der Neue Teutsche Merkur*, May (1793), pp. 95–97.

28. See footnotes on pp. 95, 96, and 97, signed 'W'. Wieland was of course famously a supporter of

Sophie von La Roche, Germany's most famous female author. He reflected on the phenomenon of women writers in Christoph Martin Wieland, 'Deutschland's Dichterinnen', *Neuer Teutscher Merkur*, (1803), pp. 258–74.

29. Emilie von Berlepsch (1755–1830). She began to publish in 1785; her first book was published in 1787, the year of her divorce. Among others, she published [Emilie von Berlepsch], *Caledonia: Von der Verfasserin der Sommerstunden. Eine malerische Schilderung der Hochgebirge in Schottland*, 4 vols (Hamburg: Hoffmann, 1802–04). Emilie von Berlepsch, *Sommerstunden* (Zurich: Orell, Gessner, Füssli und Compagnie, 1794).

30. See editor's footnote, p. 63. Emilie von Berlepsch, 'Ueber einige zum Glück der Ehe nothwendige Eigenschaften und Grundsätze', *Neuer Teutscher Merkur*, May (1791), pp. 63–102. All further references to this text appear in the text.

31. See Ruth P. Dawson, *The Contested Quill: Literature by Women in Germany, 1770–1800* (Newark; London: University of Delaware Press, 2002), pp. 258–63, for a discussion of the incongruities of Berlepsch's position.

32. [Ernst Brandes], *Ueber die Weiber* (Leipzig: Weidmanns Erben und Reich, 1787). He was also the author of Ernst Brandes, *Betrachtungen über das weibliche Geschlecht und dessen Ausbildung in dem geselligen Leben*, 3 vols (Hanover: Buchhandlung der Gebrüder Hahn, 1802).

33. See also Dawson, *The Contested Quill*, pp. 261–62.

34. Emilie von Berlepsch, 'Fortsetzung: Ueber einige zum Glück der Ehe nothwendige Eigenschaften und Grundsätze', *Neuer Teutscher Merkur*, June (1791), pp. 113–34.

35. See for example texts such as Ernst Brandes, 'Schriftstellerey der Weiber', in Brandes, *Betrachtungen über das weibliche Geschlecht und dessen Ausbildung in dem geselligen Leben* (Hanover: Buchhandlung der Gebrüder Hahn, 1802), pp. 1–87; Carl Friedrich Pockels, *Contraste zu dem Gemälde der Weiber: Nebst einer Apologie derselben gegen die Befehdung im goldenen Kalbe. Ein Anhang zu der Charakteristik des weiblichen Geschlechts* (Hanover: Ritschersche Buchhandlung, 1804); Carl Friedrich Pockels, 'Beantwortung der Frage: Dürfen Weiber gelehrte Kenntnisse haben? oder: Sind Weiblichkeit und wissenschaftliche Geistesbildung zu vereinigen? Ein Versuch', *Journal von deutschen Frauen für deutsche Frauen*, 1 (1805), 21–35; Christian August Fischer, 'Über den Umgang der Weiber mit Männern' (Leipzig: Gräff, 1800).

36. Rebekka Habermas, *Frauen und Männer des Bürgertums (1750–1850): Eine Familiengeschichte* (Göttingen: Vandenhoeck & Ruprecht, 2000), p. 19.

37. [Jakob Mauvillon], *Mann und Weib nach ihren gegenseitigen Verhältnissen geschildert. Ein Gegenstück zu der Schrift: Ueber die Weiber* (Leipzig: Dykische Buchhandlung, 1791); [Theodor Gottlieb von Hippel], *Ueber die bürgerliche Verbesserung der Weiber* (Frankfurt and Leipzig: [no publisher], 1794).

38. Bernard Fischer, *Der Verleger Johann Friedrich Cotta: Chronologische Verlagsbibliographie 1787–1832. Aus den Quellen bearbeitet* (Munich: K. G. Saur, 2003).

39. Doris Kuhles and Ulrike Standke, *Journal des Luxus und der Moden 1786–1827: Analytische Bibliographie mit sämtlichen 517 schwarz-weißen und 976 farbigen Abbildungen der Originalzeitschrift* (Munich: K. G. Saur, 2003).

# CHAPTER 4

# New Perspectives from Comparative Literature

*Hilary Brown*

Despite the best efforts of feminist critics, research on women's writing of the eighteenth and nineteenth centuries remains a marginalized aspect of *Germanistik*. A glance across to subject areas such as English studies shows that this is not the case across the board: English women writers of the period are much more part of mainstream teaching and research than our German ones. There appears to be greater public awareness of them, too, if we consider that prime-time television drama slots are just as likely to be given over to Austen or Gaskell as Dickens or Trollope, or that the Oxford World's Classics series would be unthinkable without Mary Shelley and George Eliot and the Brontës (and that it includes a fair number of their eighteenth-century sisters as well, such as Mary Hays, Elizabeth Haywood, Elizabeth Inchbald, and Charlotte Lennox). Why do women in German-speaking countries appear to have found it so much harder to get accepted into the canon? Is it something to do with their writing itself, or with the processes of reception and the writing of literary history? Could it be related to different critical traditions or even to different institutional structures in the United Kingdom and the United States? This chapter will argue that it can be fruitful to look beyond national boundaries and that one new way of approaching early German women's writing would be to consider it in a wider comparative context.

Two approaches will be discussed here. In the first part of the chapter, I will show how the traditional methodologies of comparative literature can usefully be applied to the study of German women writers. Secondly, I will refocus my definition of comparative literature, following critics such as Susan Bassnett, to take into account the various interrelated areas of intercultural transfer such as translation studies and reception studies.[1] I want to propose that comparative research could open up new perspectives on the work of early German women writers and may help to rescue these writers from the margins of our discipline.

Since its emergence in the nineteenth century, comparative literature has sought to provide new ways of understanding literature beyond the confines of national literary traditions. The term generally relates to the study of two or more authors or texts from different linguistic or cultural systems. It encompasses a range of methods and objects of study (and has frequently been agonized over as a result) but might typically involve comparing the treatment of themes and ideas in texts by writers from different countries, or comparing literary styles and trends across national boundaries. Comparatists might look for links between different literatures, and make pronouncements about the universality of human values and experience or the interconnectedness of world culture. Inevitably, much research and teaching has been pegged onto the Great Books of heavyweight male authors: Flaubert, Fontane, and Tolstoy might be analysed together (for their portrayal of adulterous women) or Richardson, Goethe, and Laclos (for their contribution to the development of epistolary fiction).

We surely have much to gain by putting women writers under the spotlight. Most generally, this might lead to fresh insights about the relationship between gender and authorship. It seems to be widely accepted that, in past centuries at least, women have produced literature in different circumstances from men, and their circumstances affected what they wrote. The so-called 'gynocriticism' pioneered by first- and second-wave feminists such as Virginia Woolf, Ellen Moers, and Elaine Showalter, with its emphasis on the social and historical context of women's writing, is still practised by many critics working on our period.[2] Most of them draw conclusions about women's writing by focusing on one particular country, and it would be revealing to broaden our view of the history of women's writing. If women really do produce their own brand of literature, might we find evidence of a female literary tradition which transcends national boundaries? If women use a distinct mode of discourse or 'genderlect', might we locate it at different times and in different places?[3]

More specifically, a comparative approach may offer new ways of reading and understanding early German women's writing. Historically, of course, the work of German women has often been measured against that of their male contemporaries and found to be inferior or 'trivial'. Placing the Helmina von Chézys and Amely Böltes alongside the Germaine de Staëls and Charlotte Brontës instead would allow us to view the woman writer in the 'supportive context' of other women writers.[4] There is certainly a strong case to be made for comparing German women of the eighteenth and nineteenth centuries with their European contemporaries. After all, this was a period in which cultural life in Europe was becoming distinctly cosmopolitan, and European literatures were evolving in close dialogue with each other. It was also the era in which women were entering the literary marketplace in large numbers for the first time across the continent.[5] The history of women in Europe in the eighteenth and nineteenth centuries can be viewed in a European framework. To some extent, women taking up their pens would have found themselves in similar circumstances, negotiating the same obstacles. The debates on the 'woman question' were Europe-wide, and there are many parallels between the situation of women across the continent with respect to domestic life, education, work, politics, and their participation in the public sphere. Historians write of the 'common themes and patterns pertaining to gender [which] appeared across the metropolitan centres of East and West Europe and [which] became definitive of a "European" experience'.[6]

And indeed there has been some intriguing research which has highlighted parallels between the work of German women and that of their European sisters.

Christine Cullens, for instance, has examined female novelists in England and Germany in the period 1752–1814 and finds myriad points of comparison. She states that 'women novelists writing in these two languages during this era used much the same range of subgenres and plots, and produced structurally and tonally similar works'. Her main idea is that women in this period had to 'watch themselves', and she regards the title of Frances Burney's novel *The Wanderer; or, Female Difficulties* (1814) as paradigmatic: 'The fictions of Burney and her less well known English and German female contemporaries all reflect on specifically *female* difficulties, the omnipresent limitations imposed by eighteenth-century standards of correct feminine behaviour and self-presentation'.[7] In her comparative study, Susanne Kord is able to provide a new interpretation of one of the most 'trivial' authors of all: the uneducated peasant poet Anna Louise Karsch who entertained crowds with improvised occasional verse. Kord explains how Karsch was part of a European trend and points to a band of more than twenty washerwomen, milkmaids, and serving girls who composed poetry in the same era on this side of the Channel. Kord's comparative work allows her to advance a theory about the development of aesthetic thought: she argues that the now-common concept of Art — identified predominantly with men and the middle classes — established itself in Europe in the eighteenth century not only in opposition to aristocratic culture but more strikingly in opposition to lower-class art forms.[8]

Drawing comparisons between German and other European women's writing will also help us to determine what is specific about the German tradition. For German women arrived later on the literary scene than their counterparts in, say, France or Britain. France and Britain had produced a good number of eminent female novelists by the mid-eighteenth century (including Madeleine de Scudéry, Marie-Madeleine de La Fayette, Françoise d'Issembourg de Graffigny, Aphra Behn, Charlotte Lennox, and Sarah Fielding), while the first novel by a woman in Germany did not appear until 1771 (Sophie von La Roche's *Geschichte des Fräuleins von Sternheim*). This situation was probably due in large part to the fragmented nature of the German states. Germany had no obvious political and cultural centre, and women would have found themselves isolated in their own domestic set-up, as Eda Sagarra explains: 'the regional diversity, poor communications and lack of a capital city prevented many intelligent and well-connected women from achieving the intellectual independence which a number of English and French women were able to enjoy'.[9] When the first generation of women writers began to emerge at the end of the eighteenth century, the cultural landscape was dominated in a way we do not find in France or Britain by one Olympian figure: Goethe. The aesthetic values promoted by Goethe and his (male) crowd sidelined women's art as dilettantish, affecting what women wrote and how their work was judged.[10] When we take these conditions into account, it becomes less surprising that the nineteenth century produced no German Austen or Eliot or Brontë. And the fact that it did not has probably influenced the way German women's writing has fared in scholarship since.[11] Comparative research of this kind can teach us much about the different factors which come into play in the production and canonization of literature by women.

Now, we should not embrace this comparative approach naïvely. We will inevitably have to confront some of the issues with which comparatists have long grappled. We can question the very assumptions which underpin comparative literary study, such as the idea of the distinct nation-state. We can question our own focus on gender: are we ghettoizing women writers by viewing them alongside other women writers? We can also reflect on the rigour of comparative literature's methods. Ideally, of course, comparatists require in-depth knowledge of more than one language and literature but in reality many turn to literature in translation and this may affect the research they are able to do. It may limit the comparatist's analyses to thematics, or distort readings if the source text has been 'domesticated' for the target audience (as they so often are, if Lawrence Venuti's critique is correct, at least for Anglo-American readers).[12] It may mean that the comparatist is not able to take account of untranslated sources such as letters, or to access a full range of secondary literature. One needs to give careful consideration to what one is actually comparing, too, and why. Comparatists have been criticized for having a tendency to use their own national literature as a starting-point, meaning their interpretations are in danger of being coloured by national bias and even chauvinism. We might find reasons to examine German women's writing in relation to French or English or Italian women's writing — but what could we illuminate by comparing it to Indian or African traditions?

Let us now turn to the second comparative approach mentioned at the beginning of the chapter. Rather than looking at women in their separate countries side-by-side, we can explore how they participated in intercultural transfer. In her seminal *Comparative Literature: A Critical Introduction* (1993), Susan Bassnett sets out a detailed case for comparative research to be pursued along these lines. Bassnett regards formalist comparative literature as highly problematic: it is the study of texts divorced from their contexts and it does not pay due regard to the role of translation in shaping world culture. She argues that comparative literature should rethink its relationship to translation studies, which she holds to be a more innovative discipline with a sounder methodology. Indeed, critics have begun to reassess translation in radical ways. Rather than viewing the act of translation as derivative or mechanical, they are placing new emphasis on translations as products of their cultural context and on the impact translations can have on native literary, political, and cultural traditions. They emphasize the creativity of the translator, and the potential for the translator to become visible in his or her creation: translation is regarded as 'a dangerous act, potentially subversive and always significant', and the translator as 'a powerful agent for cultural change'.[13] Bassnett argues that 'intercultural studies' — examining the politics of translation and reception — can teach us more than traditional comparative literature about the relationship between cultures and lead to exciting revisions of literary and cultural history.

An intercultural studies approach seems appropriate for our period, which was characterized at least initially by a new openness to the foreign. The Enlightenment was a European movement which saw greater mobility than ever before among the educated classes, vast networks of scholars and literati linking up Paris, London, Leipzig, and other major cities, and the swift exchange of ideas and publications between different language areas. What opportunities did women have to participate in cross-cultural interchange — as readers, mediators, and translators of foreign literature, as writers whose work was read abroad, as members of transnational networks?

There is a growing body of research in this area. Critics have begun to pay more attention to women's activities as translators, for example. They have identified large numbers of women in various European countries who rendered texts from one language into another, and they suggest that translation has had a special significance for women in the past. It appears that translation has often been deemed to be more socially acceptable for the fair sex than other literary activities. Women who translated could emphasize their role as a 'mere' mediator of someone else's words without appearing to trespass on the territory of the (male) author. Critics have shown how women sometimes appropriated the modest mask of translator to surprising ends. Female translators made careful choices about the texts they chose, how they framed them (through paratextual apparatus such as prefaces and footnotes), and their interventions in the source material. They manipulated other people's texts as a covert way of asserting their own agency. Among other things, this gave the translator the opportunity to add her voice to contemporary social, religious, or political debates. The Spaniard Mariá Romero Masegosa y Cancelada, for instance, reworked Françoise d'Issembourg de Graffigny's *Lettres d'une Péruvienne* (Letters from a Peruvian Woman) in the late eighteenth century, adding copious notes and altering several passages in the source text, in order to present a bold political vision for Spain's future which embraced the position of women, foreign policy, and religious reform.[14]

Further, critics have started to look at women in the context of reception studies more generally. The London/Cambridge research project led by Elinor Shaffer on 'The Reception of British and Irish Authors in Europe' has begun work on female authors of our period, with a volume on *The Reception of Jane Austen in Europe* appearing in 2007 and another on George Eliot in preparation. As Shaffer writes in the preface to the Austen volume: 'A whole submerged continent of women writers and translators may need to be rediscovered in order to redraw the comparative atlas'.[15]

It would undoubtedly be illuminating to turn our attention to women in Germany, for Germany was perhaps particularly alive to foreign influences in this period. At the beginning of the eighteenth century, Germany was a war-battered patchwork of territories without a coherent national identity. These territories did not share a common culture or even language: the ruling classes nearly always used French rather than German, and French or Latin were the preferred languages in most professions. The early decades of the century saw new efforts to modernize the country and promote the idea of a unified national language and culture. Germans looked abroad to more established nation-states for models — in particular France, later Britain. We find them immersed in reading, translating, imitating, and adapting foreign literature as part of a huge process of cultural renewal. We might think here of Johann Christoph Gottsched turning to French neo-classical playwrights in his mission to raise standards in the German theatre, or of Goethe's reception of Shakespeare and Ossian, or of the wave of interest in antiquity and translations from the Greek by Voss, Goethe, and Hölderlin, which was intricately bound up with the emergence of Weimar Classicism.[16]

How do women and their writings fit into these cosmopolitan trends? My own research on the eighteenth century indicates that numerous women turned their hand to translation. Indeed, it seems that women were as likely to produce translations as any other works, and many of the writers with whom we are now familiar engaged in translation at some point in their lives, such as Christiane Mariane von Ziegler (1695–1760), Luise Gottsched (1713–62), Sophie von La Roche (1731–1807), Friederike Helene Unger (1741 or 1751–1813), Benedikte Naubert (1756–1819), Dorothea Schlegel (1763–1839), and Therese Huber (1764–1829).[17] Often women would have worked in different circumstances from their male counterparts. On the whole, they did not move in the academic circles where foreign literature was first discovered, discussed, and translated. They did not enjoy the same freedom to travel and form useful contacts abroad. They might have been familiar with French (or English) but few would have been taught the classical languages, and they were unlikely to find themselves in a position like that of Goethe, who handpicked philologists to correct his attempts from Greek and Latin. There were certain areas in which they were particularly active, however. The rapid expansion in the book market in the late eighteenth century, for example, meant that there was a new demand for popular fiction from France and Britain — the translation of this type of literature was not highly regarded and became to some extent the province of the female translator.

Nevertheless, works such as Benedikte Naubert's *Elfriede oder das Opfer väterlicher Vorurtheile: Nach dem Englischen* (1788, *Elfrieda; or, Paternal Ambition*) and *Corelia oder die Geheimnisse des Grabes: Nach dem Englischen frey bearbeitet* (1802, *Corelia; or, The Mystic Tomb*) should not be too readily dismissed. Naubert — like other women such as Dorothea Margareta Liebeskind — was translating novels by Englishwomen, thus bringing into circulation a markedly feminine form of fiction. Liebeskind translated Elizabeth Inchbald (1753–1821), Charlotte Smith (1748–1806), and Ann Radcliffe (1764–1823); Naubert the likes of Phebe Gibbes (d. 1805), Susannah Gunning (1740?-1800), and Sarah Sheriffe (d. 1849). Naubert was probably allocated texts by her publishers rather than consciously alighting on literature by women, but the novels bear similar characteristics. They are sentimental tales à la Richardson: typically heroines must guard their virtue in a hostile world, in situations exacerbated by poverty, pressure to find a husband, and lack of social status or parental protection. After a series of trials and misunderstandings, the heroine is rewarded with matrimonial happiness and material possessions. The novels foreground female experience and vindicate feminine attributes — virtuous heroines exercise a power over men whose actions are reduced to their involvement in the mating game, good male characters are motivated by love alone, and corrupt male characters can be reformed by their contact with feminine virtue — offering readers a 'dream of female significance'.[18] These escapist fictions seem to have been consumed as avidly in Germany as in Britain: the translations were reviewed in major periodicals, ran to several editions, and became staple fare in the lending libraries. Significantly, Naubert was contributing to the spread of women's literature across Germany.[19]

There appear to be important links between women's translation work and their own writing. At a time when women's opportunities to publish were limited, translation seems to have offered them an acceptable way into print and furthered their literary careers (indeed, Susanne Kord suggests that even when they were not actually translating, many women in this period claimed to be publishing translations as a way of evading the taboos of original authorship[20]). It is striking that many women translated and then went on to write literature of their own. It seems that they used this intensive language work to develop their literary skills; venturing into print first with translations gave them the opportunity to acquaint themselves with the workings of the literary marketplace; and engaging with other people's texts could provide inspiration for their own. Sophie von La Roche, for instance, had been educated in French and had to master her native tongue in order to write her famous first novel. Her earliest piece was a short story written in French, 'Les Caprices de l'amour et de l'amitié' (The Caprices of Love and Friendship), which she then translated into German herself as practice before embarking on the larger novel project. As for Naubert, it seems that her work on English fiction (and in particular on Sophia Lee's 'female' historical novel *The Recess*) directly influenced the development of her own novel-concept.[21]

We do not find our women writers translating literary works only. Luise Gottsched, for one, produced a phenomenal number of translations over the course of her career, in fields ranging from drama and poetry to philosophy, history, archaeology, and even theoretical physics. Gottsched is now known primarily as a dramatist, and many critics are disparaging of her translation work, believing it to have been menial and unimportant and a distraction from her true calling as a writer. A handful of critics have discussed her literary translations, but the non-literary translations have been virtually ignored. In her monograph *Luise Gottsched: A Reconsideration* (1973), for example, Veronica C. Richel writes that 'Frau Gottsched's renditions of scholarly material, such as philosophical and historical tracts, are executed with competence and require no further comment'.[22] However, a more careful examination of these non-literary translations in their cultural and historical context casts Gottsched and her oeuvre in an unfamiliar and fascinating light.

For a start, Gottsched does not appear to have viewed translation as menial or second-rate or particularly feminine at all. She seems to have shared the early Enlightenment view of translation as a serious and useful undertaking which would help to breathe new life into German culture.[23] Like many at the time, she probably did not really make a distinction between translation and 'original' writing, and she does not appear to have favoured literature over other areas of intellectual endeavour: she herself claimed that she had a particular interest in philosophy, and we know that she had a lifelong passion for natural history and astronomy and spent many happy nights stargazing on her roof.[24] She was in an exceptional position to work on translations at the heart of her professor-husband's avant-garde, cosmopolitan circle in Leipzig.

Gottsched's non-literary translations form the bulk of her output. In the thirty-year period from *c.* 1730 to *c.* 1760, she turned reams of essays and studies by important figures of the European Enlightenment such as Voltaire, Châtelet,

Fontenelle, Shaftesbury, and Newton into German. Some translations were stand-alone works but others were titanic projects requiring months — and sometimes years — of effort. Gottsched often provided learned prefaces and notes to her translations: she seems to have been equally at ease handling Châtelet's theories on force, bodies, and velocity, and Newton's studies on chronology.[25] Working in all these areas obviously meant getting to grips with many different subjects and specialist vocabularies. We do not expect this kind of scholarliness from a woman in Germany at this time.

Gottsched's translations deserve our attention for three main reasons. First, she was making major works by French and English intellectuals available in German — often for the first time — in order to bring her countrypeople into contact with modern and sometimes hotly debated ideas (we need to remember that scientists and thinkers in the Enlightenment were starting to look at the world from a new, rational standpoint, and seriously unsettling the religious world-view which had dominated in Europe for centuries). Secondly, we have to admire Gottsched's boldness. We should not underestimate the dangers she faced in bringing some of these works to Germany: in this age of absolutism, there was still much resistance to rational, secular thought and it was not unknown for authors to see their books burned or find themselves thrown into jail. Thirdly, she was not just promoting a passive reception of Enlightenment ideas. Gottsched and her husband were aiming to nurture a culture of scholarship and criticism and debate across the German-speaking area akin to that which they saw thriving elsewhere in Europe. Ultimately, they hoped that their countrypeople would be encouraged to imitate and improve on the achievements of foreign writers and intellectuals and work towards making Germany a weighty presence on the European stage.

Let us take as an example Gottsched's *D. Eachards eines englischen Gottes-Gelehrten Untersuchung der Ursachen und Gelegenheiten, welche zur Verachtung der Geistlichen und der Religion Anlaß gegeben* (1740) (A Study of the Grounds and Occasions which have given rise to a Disdain for Clergymen and for Religion by the English Theologian D. Eachard), admittedly a somewhat underwhelming title, which perhaps accounts to some extent for the fact that it seems never to have been discussed in the secondary literature. Gottsched translated a number of works on philosophical and religious topics, and these often contained progressive ideas on subjects such as good and evil, morality, faith, God, and the Church. This one appeared at the height of the Gottscheds' fight against the dogmatism of organized religion. The Gottscheds objected to zealotry in any form, and laid emphasis instead on the importance of reason and the tolerance of different faiths; they launched an energetic campaign to reform the role of the clergy and homiletics in Germany. Gottsched's source text was *The Grounds and Occasions of the Contempt of the Clergy and Religion Enquired Into* by John Eachard, one-time Vice-Chancellor of Cambridge University, which had appeared in England some decades earlier but was highly relevant to the current situation in Germany. Eachard's text argues for simple, intelligent pulpit oratory using a lively mixture of wit and banter; Gottsched may have found it particularly appealing because it addressed a serious, even scholarly, issue in an accessible manner and thus had the potential to stir up wide debate. But she knew that it risked being denounced as facetious, anticlerical, and even atheistic, and she went to great lengths to ensure that her translation appeared in secret and anonymously. From this one example, we see that Gottsched's translations do indeed require further comment. Far from being a distraction from her 'proper' literary work, her translations were part of an ambitious and audacious programme aimed at bringing the Enlightenment to Germany and raising Germany's profile within the European republic of letters.[26]

Once we start looking at translation, we also stumble across women who may not necessarily be known to us as writers but in this light suddenly appear more interesting. There is the odd female classicist, for example, working in the shadow of a learned father or husband and able to make a valuable contribution to Germany's new craze for Greek and Latin literature: the obscure Fräulein von Erath (?–1776) with her acclaimed version of Cornelius Nepos's *De viris illustribus* (*On Distinguished Men*), or Ernestine Christine Reiske (1735–1798) with her remarkable volumes of Greek philosophy and erotica.[27] And who has heard of Julie Clodius (1750–1805), who pops up in some reference works with her never-reprinted novel *Eduard Montrefeuil* (1806)? Clodius translated one of the key texts of the English Bluestocking circle — Elizabeth Carter's *Poems on Several Occasions* — helping to promote feminist thought in Germany at an earlier stage than we would expect.[28]

Of course, the story of German women and intercultural transfer does not end there. It is not just translators who should concern us, but women who read and reviewed European literature, or corresponded with European colleagues, or mixed with them in the salons, or who wrote about their experiences of travel and exile. We should look at literature travelling in the other direction, too, and explore the reception of German women's writing abroad. There are swathes of uncharted territory.[29]

Together, studies along these lines can help us to revise our view of the part played by women in European cultural life. Much of this research is coming together under the aegis of an international research network directed by Suzan van Dijk and based at the University of Utrecht: the 'New Approaches to European Women's Writing' (NEWW) project. The NEWW research group aims to examine the position and influence of literary women before 1900 beyond the usual parameters of national literary history. It focuses on the role of women as translators and mediators of foreign literature, and on the reception of women's writing throughout Europe. The network has members in over twenty European countries and its activities include conferences, publications, and an online database. The *WomenWriters* database seeks to provide a map of the international reception of women's writing. Its entries on individual authors include biographical information and a list of the author's works with links to data about the reception of these works abroad (articles in the periodical press, translations).[30]

There are many reasons why the NEWW project is to be welcomed. It builds on research which has been done on women writers in their separate European countries. There is a vast amount of data to be gathered (establishing details about translations for even a single author, when so many publications at this time appeared anonymously or under pseudonyms, can be an intricate business), but by working collaboratively we can piece together the bigger picture. Patterns of contact and transfer often need to be plotted on an international level anyway: George Sand's reception in nineteenth-century Holland and Russia, for example, was shaped by the way she had been read and reviewed in Germany.[31] The project encourages us to look at a range of primary sources, and to move away from a focus on novels, plays, or poetry and the questions of 'quality' which continue to perturb scholars.[32] We may be able to reassess the importance of women who quietly beavered away on reviews or translations of foreign literature, or of now-forgotten writers who were popular in their own time and read throughout Europe. We may find that women dominated areas of European literary life which are not always accepted as significant in mainstream literary historiography, such as the late eighteenth-century market for supposedly lowbrow sentimental fiction.

In time, this research may lead as well to fresh insights about the 'rise' of the woman writer in Europe. Did women's writing in various countries develop in a cross-cultural context? We certainly find hints that women were responsive to the work of women abroad. It may be the case that they were particularly drawn to a type of foreign literature which reflected elements of female experience; they may have empathized with certain social and political concerns which were peculiar to their sex in this period. There were women who were fascinated by the work of their European sisters — they turn to it in their reading, for example, or feel compelled to translate it.[33] And one is struck by the fact that women often looked to more established female traditions elsewhere as they themselves gained opportunities to enter the literary sphere. It seems that many budding writers evoked illustrious women abroad — Madeleine de Scudéry, George Sand, Germaine de Staël — in an attempt to legitimize their activities or in their search for literary models.[34]

In conclusion, then, we have seen how comparative research can open up exciting new perspectives on women's writing. If German women writers of the eighteenth and nineteenth centuries are studied alongside their female contemporaries in other countries, this could expand and re-energize our field. In particular, it seems that we have much to learn from exploring how women's writing engaged with the cosmopolitanism which was so characteristic of much of this era. We may well be led to rethink women's contributions to cultural life. Ultimately, we may see German women writers emerging out of the margins of *Germanistik* and coming to occupy a prominent place in new accounts of European literary and cultural history.[35]

## Notes to Chapter 4

1. See Susan Bassnett, *Comparative Literature: A Critical Introduction* (Oxford: Blackwell, 1993) and Susan Bassnett, *Translation Studies*, 3rd edn (London: Routledge, 2002).

2. The term 'gynocritics' was coined by Elaine Showalter. See her 'Feminist Criticism in the Wilderness', in *The New Feminist Criticism: Essays on Women, Literature and Theory*, ed. by Elaine Showalter (London: Virago, 1986), pp. 243–70.

3. Louise Schleiner has outlined how one could use theories of cultural semiotics to discern specifically female elements in texts by early women writers. See Louise Schleiner, 'Voicing the Subject: Early Modern Women's Strategies within Discourse Domains', in *Writing the History of Women's Writing: Toward an International Approach*, ed. by Suzan van Dijk and others (Amsterdam: Royal Netherlands Academy of Arts and Sciences, 2001), pp. 163–69. In a more general discussion,

Margaret Higonnet has sketched out some of the natural associations between feminist literary criticism and comparative literature. Feminist critics view gender as one of the categories which structure the literary field and, because concepts of gender transcend national boundaries, this inevitably invites comparative analyses. Higonnet points out that feminist critics have begun to move beyond universalist positions towards cross-cultural gender studies (for example the study of non-Western marginalized literatures for comparative purposes). But there is still much work to be done to incorporate feminist approaches into comparative literature in the academy. Cf. Margaret R. Higonnet, 'Comparative Literature on the Feminist Edge', in *Comparative Literature in the Age of Multiculturalism*, ed. by Charles Bernheimer (Baltimore: The Johns Hopkins University Press, 1995), pp. 115–64.

4. Ruth Robbins, *Literary Feminisms* (London: Macmillan, 2000), p. 7. This is the approach taken by April Alliston, who examines eighteenth-century women writers in Britain and France and seeks to rehabilitate some less familiar ones by pointing to correspondences with their more canonical sisters. See April Alliston, *Virtue's Faults: Correspondences in Eighteenth-Century British and French Women's Fiction* (Stanford, CA: Stanford University Press, 1996).

5. See, for example, Jane Spencer, *The Rise of the Woman Novelist: From Aphra Behn to Jane Austen* (Oxford: Blackwell, 1986); Barbara Becker-Cantarino, *Der lange Weg zur Mündigkeit: Frau und Literatur (1500–1800)* (Stuttgart: Metzler, 1987); *Going Public: Women and Publishing in Early Modern France*, ed. by Elizabeth C. Goldsmith and Dena Goodman (Ithaca: Cornell University Press, 1995); Theresa Ann Smith, *The Emerging Female Citizen: Gender and Enlightenment in Spain* (Berkeley: University of California Press, 2006).

6. Barbara Caine and Glenda Sluga, *Gendering European History* (London: Leicester University Press, 2000), p. 1. Caine and Sluga examine some of the ideas about women which crossed national boundaries (such as women's place in the public sphere and the birth of feminism) and identify similarities in the historical situation of women in different countries (such as the dividing lines between 'male' and 'female' work which became more pronounced with increasing industrialization and the emergence of consumer capitalism). Cf. Karen Offen, *European Feminisms, 1700–1950: A Political History* (Stanford, CA: Stanford University Press, 2000).

7. Chris[tine E.] Cullens, 'Female Difficulties, Comparativist Challenge: Novels by English and German Women, 1752–1814', in *Borderwork: Feminist Engagements with Comparative Literature*, ed. by Margaret R. Higonnet (Ithaca: Cornell University Press, 1994), pp. 100–19 (p. 101 and p. 103). Cf. Christine E. Cullens, ' "Female Difficulties": Novels by English and German Women, 1755–1814' (unpublished doctoral dissertation, Stanford University, 1989).

8. Susanne Kord, *Women Peasant Poets in Eighteenth-Century England, Scotland and Germany: Milkmaids on Parnassus* (Rochester, NY: Camden House, 2003).

9. Eda Sagarra, *A Social History of Germany, 1648–1914* (London: Methuen, 1977), p. 406.

10. Cf. Katherine R. Goodman and Edith Waldstein, 'Introduction', in *In the Shadow of Olympus: German Women Writers around 1800*, ed. by Katherine R. Goodman and Edith Waldstein (Albany: State University of New York Press, 1992), pp. 1–27.

11. Research on English women's writing may have become mainstream more quickly because of its nineteenth-century beacons. Elaine Showalter describes how many early critics came to women writers via Victorian studies: 'Victorian studies was a field hospitable to a feminist presence early on, in its interdisciplinarity, its acceptance of women writers, and its friendliness toward women scholars and critics. Many young women graduate students in my generation were drawn to the Victorian period because it was the only period in which women were accepted as canonical writers. [...] Only later did the field of eighteenth-century studies become receptive to feminist analysis.' (Elaine Showalter, *A Literature of their Own: From Charlotte Brontë to Doris Lessing*, 2nd edn (London: Virago, 1999), pp. xxiii–xxiv)

12. Venuti analyses the history of translation in the West, concluding that translators in the English-speaking world tend to produce fluent, 'domesticated' translations, imposing their own cultural values on the source text and ignoring linguistic and cultural difference. See Lawrence Venuti, *The Translator's Invisibility: A History of Translation*, 2nd edn (London: Routledge, 2008). Venuti lays out his objections to the study of literature in translation in the academy in chapter 5 of *The Scandals of Translation: Towards an Ethics of Difference* (London: Routledge, 1998).

13. Bassnett, *Translation Studies*, p. 9.
14. See Theresa Ann Smith, 'Writing out of the Margins: Women, Translation, and the Spanish Enlightenment', *Journal of Women's History*, 15.1 (2003), 116–43. Cf. Susanne Stark, 'Women and Translation in the Nineteenth Century', *New Comparison*, 15 (1993), 33–44; Mirella Agorni, 'The Voice of the "Translatress": From Aphra Behn to Elizabeth Carter', *Yearbook of English Studies*, 28 (1998), 181–95; Sarah Annes Brown, 'Women Translators', in *The Oxford History of Literary Translation in English*, ed. by Peter France and Stuart Gillespie, 5 vols (Oxford: Oxford University Press, 2005 — ), III: *1660–1790* (2005), ed. by Stuart Gillespie and David Hopkins, pp. 111–20; Marie-Pascale Pieretti, 'Women Writers and Translation in Eighteenth-Century France', *French Review*, 75.3 (2002), 474–88; *D'une écriture à l'autre: Les femmes et la traduction sous l'ancien regime*, ed. by Jean-Philippe Beaulieu (Ottawa: Presses de l'Université d'Ottawa, 2004); Wendy Rosslyn, *Feats of Agreeable Usefulness: Translations by Russian Women 1763–1825* (Fichtenwalde: Göpfert, 2000). For a more general discussion, see Sherry Simon, *Gender in Translation: Cultural Identity and the Politics of Transmission* (London: Routledge, 1996).
15. Elinor Shaffer, 'Preface', in *The Reception of Jane Austen in Europe*, ed. by Anthony Mandal and Brian Southam, The Athlone Critical Traditions Series: The Reception of British and Irish Authors in Europe, 14 (London: Continuum, 2007), pp. vii–xi (p. ix). Reception studies in a transnational framework may challenge our views of writers and their writings and can offer a new dimension to our understanding of canonization. It is interesting, for example, that Austen was relatively neglected on the continent until well into the twentieth century (in contrast to novelists such as Walter Scott) and that her novels are still not regarded as 'world classics' in many countries. In France, she is so little known that even the recent blockbuster films are received and reviewed as 'costume drama' rather than as anything to do with a specific English author. See the three chapters by Isabelle Bour in *The Reception of Jane Austen in Europe*.
16. Cf. *Weltliteratur: Die Lust am Übersetzen im Jahrhundert Goethes*, ed. by Reinhard Tgahrt and others, Marbacher Kataloge, 37 (Munich: Kösel, 1982).
17. For portraits of some of these women as translators, see *Übersetzungskultur im 18. Jahrhundert: Übersetzerinnen in Deutschland, Frankreich und der Schweiz*, ed. by Brunhilde Wehinger and Hilary Brown (Hanover: Wehrhahn, 2008).
18. Janet Todd, *The Sign of Angellica: Women, Writing and Fiction, 1660–1800* (New York: Columbia University Press, 1989), p. 191.
19. See Hilary Brown, *Benedikte Naubert (1756–1819) and her Relations to English Culture*, Modern Humanities Research Association Texts and Dissertations, 63; Bithell Series of Dissertations, 27 (Leeds: Maney, 2005), ch. 2. For more on Liebeskind, see Monika Siegel, ' "Ich hatte einen Hang zur Schwärmerey...": Das Leben der Schriftstellerin und Übersetzerin Meta Forkel-Liebeskind im Spiegel ihrer Zeit' (unpublished doctoral thesis, University of Darmstadt, 2001) <http://elib.tu-darmstadt.de/diss/000222> [accessed 20 April 2010] and Marie-Luise Spiekermann, 'Dorothea Margareta Liebeskind (1765–1853): Übersetzerin zwischen wissenschaftlicher Literatur und Unterhaltungsromanen englischer Autorinnen', in *Übersetzungskultur im 18. Jahrhundert*, pp. 141–64.
20. Susanne Kord, 'The Innocent Translator: Translation as Pseudonymous Behavior in Eighteenth-Century German Women's Writing', *Jerome Quarterly*, 9.3 (1994), 11–13.
21. See Brown, *Benedikte Naubert*, ch. 3.
22. Veronica C. Richel, *Luise Gottsched: A Reconsideration* (Berne: Lang, 1973).
23. See her comments on her translation of Marie-Anne Barbier's tragedy *Cornélie, mère des Graques*, for instance: '*Cornelia*, das schöne Trauerspiel der Demoiselle *Barbier* hat meinen ganzen Beyfall an sich gezogen, ich habe die Uebersetzung unternommen, und mir alle Mühe gegeben das Original zu erreichen. Die große Tochter Scipions des Africaners, die vortrefliche Mutter der Gracchen, die Ehre ihres Geschlechts, hat mich schon längst gereitzet ihr erhabnes Beyspiel, und ihren tugendhaften Wandel, auch den Deutschen bekannter zu machen, und dieselben zur Nachahmung der großmüthigsten Römerin anzufeuren. Möchte das deutsche Theater es doch dem französischen nachthun, so werden die Auftritte dieser edlen Römerin mit dem Consul Lucinius die republikanischen Gesinnungen der ersten, in ihrer ganzen Stärke zeigen, die ich mit aller Sorgfalt zu übersetzen, mich bemühet habe.' (Letter of 1739, Luise Gottsched, *Briefe*, ed. by Dorothea von Runckel, 3 vols (Dresden: Harpeter, 1771–72), I, 246)

24. See her husband's biography of her in Luise Gottsched, *Der Frau Luise Adelgunde Victoria Gottschedin, geb. Kulmus, sämmtliche kleinere Gedichte*, ed. by Johann Christoph Gottsched (Leipzig: Breitkopf, 1763). This volume also contains her library catalogue, and we can see that she possessed books on many different subjects: history, geography, classics, mathematics, philosophy, religion, and physics, to name but some.

25. *Zwo Schriften, welche von der Frau Marquis von Chatelet, gebohrner Baronessinn von Breteuil, und dem Herrn von Mairan, beständigem Sekretär bey der französischen Akademie der Wissenschaften, Das Maaß der lebendigen Kräften betreffend, gewechselt worden*, trans. by Luise Gottsched (Leipzig: Breitkopf, 1741); *Neue Sammlung auserlesener Stücke, aus Popens, Eachards, Newtons und andrer Schriften*, trans. by Luise Gottsched (Leipzig: Breitkopf, 1749). The latter contains the piece: 'Herrn Isaac Newtons kurze Chronik von den Nachrichten der ältesten Dinge in Europa bis auf Alexanders des großen Eroberung von Persien. Aus dem Engländischen übersetzt'.

26. For more on the Eachard translation, see Hilary Brown, 'Luise Gottsched the Satirist', *Modern Language Review*, 103 (2008), 1036–50. For overviews of Gottsched's activities as a translator, see Hilary Brown, 'Luise Gottsched and the Reception of French Enlightenment Literature in Germany', in *Translators, Interpreters, Mediators: Women Writers 1700–1900*, ed. by Gillian Dow (Oxford: Lang, 2007), pp. 21–36 and Hilary Brown, ' "Als käm Sie von der Thems und von der Seyne her": Luise Gottsched als Übersetzerin', in *Übersetzungskultur im 18. Jahrhundert*, pp. 37–52. See also my forthcoming monograph on *Luise Gottsched the Translator*.

27. See [Fräulein von Erath], *Leben und Thaten verschiedener berühmter Feldherren. Nebst dem Leben des M. Porcius Cato, und Titus Pomponius Atticus* (Frankfurt and Leipzig: Kochendörffer, 1766); *Hellas*, trans. by Ernestine Christine Reiske (Mitau: Hinz, 1778); *Zur Moral*, trans. by Ernestine Christine Reiske (Leipzig: Buchhandlung der Gelehrten, 1782). For further information, see Hilary Brown, 'Women and Classical Translation in the Eighteenth Century', *German Life and Letters*, 59 (2006), 344–60, and Anke Bennholdt-Thomsen and Alfredo Guzzoni, *Gelehrsamkeit und Leidenschaft: Das Leben der Ernestine Christine Reiske, 1735–1798* (Munich: Beck, 1992).

28. See Hilary Brown, 'The Reception of the Bluestockings by Eighteenth-Century German Women Writers', *Women in German Yearbook*, 18 (2002), 620–31.

29. The most recent conference in the Women Writers of the Eighteenth and Nineteenth Centuries Conference Series addressed some of these areas: 'German Women's Writing in its European Context, 1700–1900', Institute of Germanic & Romance Studies, University of London, 25–26 November 2010. See <http://w01.igrscms.wf.ulcc.ac.uk/index.php?id=379> [accessed 19 April 2010].

30. The NEWW project website can be found at <http://www.womenwriters.nl>. For the *WomenWriters* database, see <http://neww.huygens.knaw.nl> [accessed 19 April 2010]. Much of the data at the moment relates to the reception of women writers in the Netherlands. Cf. *'I have heard about you': Foreign Women's Writing Crossing the Dutch Border*, ed. by Suzan van Dijk and others (Hilversum: Uitgeverij Verloren, 2004).

31. See Françoise Genevray, 'Vassili Botkine, George Sand et l'alliance intellectuelle franco-allemande', *Œuvres & Critiques* (special issue on 'George Sand: La réception hors de France au XIXe siècle'), 28.1 (2003), 49–75 and Suzan van Dijk and Kerstin Wiedemann, 'La nécessité d'une approche internationale de la réception sandienne: Des réactions allemandes réutilisées par la critique néerlandaise', ibid., 188–211.

32. Some scholars in English studies are arguing that we are now in a 'post-recovery' phase, and should face up to the issue of literary merit. See, for instance, Susan Staves's introduction to her recent *Literary History of Women's Writing in Britain, 1660–1789*: 'I do not agree with those who think that feminists must jettison the idea of literature or the idea of literary merit. I agree that new aesthetic values can be found in some previously devalued women's writing, but I do not agree with those who contend that we cannot make aesthetic evaluations of literary works that have any use or objectivity. Aesthetic or literary merit is an important principle of selection in my literary history. It cannot be a sin against feminism to say that some women wrote well and others wrote badly, that some were intelligent, reflective, and original, others dull, unreflective, and formulaic.' (Susan Staves, *A Literary History of Women's Writing in Britain, 1660–1789* (Cambridge: Cambridge University Press, 2006), p. 4). The NEWW approach resists categorizing women in these terms and engaging in the problematic business of promoting alternative female canons.

33. A recent conference at Chawton House Library aimed to explore the transnational links between literary women in Europe in the period 1700–1900. The proceedings are published in two volumes: a special issue of the journal *Women's Writing*, 18.1 (2011) ('Women Readers in Europe: Readers, Writers, Salonnières, 1750–1900') and *Readers, Writers, Salonnières: Female Networks in Europe, 1700–1900*, ed. by Hilary Brown and Gillian Dow (Oxford: Lang, 2011). For recent work on 'gynocentric translation' — women translating women and sometimes dedicating their translations to women — and how this helped to form a cross-cultural female literary tradition in the eighteenth century, see Julie Candler Hayes, *Translation, Subjectivity, and Culture in France and England, 1600–1800* (Stanford, CA: Stanford University Press, 2009), ch. 5.

34. Literature on this topic includes: Sabine Koloch, 'Madeleine de Scudéry in Deutschland: Zur Genese eines literarischen Selbstbewußtseins bürgerlicher Autorinnen', in *Gender Studies in den romanischen Literaturen: Revisionen, Subversionen*, ed. by Renate Kroll and Margarete Zimmermann, 2 vols (Frankfurt am Main: dipa, 1999), I, 213–55; Karin Baumgartner, 'In Search of Literary Mothers across the Rhine: The Influence of Mme de Genlis and Mme de Staël on the Writing of Helmina von Chézy', *Women's Writing* (special issue on 'Women Readers in Europe: Readers, Writers, Salonnières, 1750–1900'), 18.1 (2011), 50–67; Ursula Jung, 'The Reception of Germaine de Staël and George Sand among Female Novelists in Nineteenth-Century Spain', in *Readers, Writers, Salonnières*.

35. I am grateful to Gillian Dow and Duncan Large for their helpful comments on this chapter.

CHAPTER 5

# Women as Professional Writers:
# Evaluating Biographical Encyclopaedias

*Susanne Kinnebrock and Timon B. Schaffer*

## Introduction

It is almost impossible to make definite pronouncements about the number of German women who were writing and publishing in the nineteenth century. Too diverse are the forms of writing, too large the number of writers, too incomplete and androcentric contemporary statistics. This may be the reason why there are no collective biographies that can claim to give a representative overview of women writers of that time. Thanks to instructive individual biographies and illuminating analyses of work, we are well informed about individual writers, their circles, and their oeuvres. But it is problematic to draw conclusions from these individual examples or non-representative samples about the majority of German women writers, particularly as the total number of female writers — the universal set and the population parameters to put it in social science terms — are not known. When the contours of a population are unknown, a representative sample cannot be drawn and findings on individual members of a population cannot be generalized, since it is not clear to what extent the selected individual cases mirror the situation of the majority.

Consequently we get only vague answers to questions about the dominating milieux in which the majority of women writers grew up and lived. We don't know exactly where and what the *majority* of women writers published, or which genres and media platforms they preferred *generally*. To what extent did women writers have to make a living from their writings? Did they *mostly* regard themselves as professional or occasional writers? How did they *usually* deal with the prevailing model of true womanhood which did not allow for gainful employment? To what extent were women writers hiding behind pseudonyms? And what other strategies did they *normally* use to conceal or legitimize their professional activities as authors?

The study of collectives (rather than individual cases) and representative results are central issues in social sciences such as communication studies. This chapter tries to address the problems of representativeness by applying a methodology from communication studies to a rather unique corpus of sources: Sophie Pataky's encyclopaedia *German Ladies of the Pen*, which is based on a complete census of women writers in German-speaking countries at the end of the nineteenth century. A standardized content analysis[1] was conducted to explore the socio-demographics and sociality of women writers in 1900, their publishing activities, and their conception of themselves as professional writers.

To highlight the specificity and uniqueness of the evaluated set of data we first want to demonstrate the advantages of Pataky's collection of biographies compared to other biographical encyclopaedias on women writers. Their selection criteria, and the extent to which representative conclusions can reliably be drawn from them, will be critically examined. In the second part, the collective of German-speaking women writers is described in terms of socio-demographics, sociality, publication activities, and professional self-conceptions. Thus a new framework is provided for the analysis of the lives and works of individual women writers.

This chapter pursues two objectives: First, we want to provide some insights into what social science perspectives can contribute to women's literary history. And secondly we want to amend the history of women writers with representative data on German women writers at the end of the nineteenth century.

## Biographical Encyclopaedias and Collective Biographies of German-Speaking Women Writers at the End of the Nineteenth Century

Since the 1980s literary history has been affected, revived, and partly revised by insights from gender studies.[2] In the meantime numerous biographical dictionaries and collective biographies have provided us with a sense of how large the number of female authors and how diverse their oeuvre was. When we take a closer look at these biographical dictionaries and collective biographies, however, it becomes evident that they share a common problem: the collecting of biographies is preceded by tough selection decisions. Hiltrud Gnüg and Renate Möhrmann presented their compendium on women's literary history with this almost resigned remark:

> Einer einbändigen Frauenliteraturgeschichte sind notwendige Grenzen gesetzt. Will sie sich nicht nur in einer positivistischen Auflistung von Name, Daten, Werken, Fakten erschöpfen, muß sie auswählen. Sie kann nur exemplarisch verfahren und vermag in keinem Fall, das ganze Spektrum der von Frauen verfaßten Literatur angemessen vorzustellen. Insofern erhebt dieser Band nicht den Anspruch auf Vollständigkeit.
>
> [A history of women's literature within a single volume is necessarily limited. If it doesn't intend to rely exclusively and positivistically on a list of names, dates, works, and facts, it has to select. It can only refer to examples and is not able to present the entire spectrum of literature by women writers adequately. So the volume cannot claim to be exhaustive.][3]

When explaining that they could only include certain important examples of women's writing, Gnüg and Möhrmann mainly refer to the diversity of writings by female authors at this period. But the curricula vitae, living conditions, and professional environments of women writers were similarly diverse. In order to approach a more comprehensive history of women writers we should be aware of these multifaceted diversities, reflect on the criteria used to select a certain writer as an example for a group of writers or field of writing, and choose our examples very carefully. The findings and summaries of established encyclopaedias and socio-historical studies should always be analysed against the background of their actual sample and its representativeness.

In her very instructive social history of German writers from 1880 to 1933 Britta Scheideler, for example, mostly does not differentiate between female and male authors. Scheideler[4] examines the two sexes as a more or less homogeneous group, although the living and working situations of women and men differed dramatically at that time. Considering the completely different social position of nineteenth-century women (who were excluded from the public sphere, lacked access to educational resources, and regarded gainful employment as shameful), Scheideler's results can be used to illuminate our understanding of women writers only with great caution.

Another obstacle on the path to representative insights into women writers' typical life circumstances results from the scholarly concentration on women who worked full-time and exclusively produced literary works.[5] This is problematic insofar as gainful employment was especially frowned upon within the literate classes — within the bourgeoisie and the aristocracy where women usually had the ability to write well, in contrast to large parts of the working classes. Consequently, women writers often concealed that they were writing to make a living. The use of pseudonyms can be regarded as a way of hiding gainful employment as well as denying 'professional' status. Studies on a subgroup of women writers, female journalists, have shown that only a tiny fraction of the many German-speaking female journalists at the end of the nineteenth century were recognizable as full-time and professional.[6]

The distinction between female journalists on the one hand and women writers on the other hand points to an additional problem in identifying the universal set of women writers at the end of the nineteenth century. Many a writer did not exclusively present her work in books. Especially popular media like women's magazines, family magazines, and the feuilleton sections of newspapers published short pieces of prose, serialized novels, stories, and lyric poetry. Moreover, writers produced literary reviews and travelogues for journals, magazines, and newspapers. As result many writers worked as journalists as well.[7] The blurred boundaries between journalism and literature make it questionable to limit a representative sample to women writers who published primarily in literary media and were successful in terms of literary reputation. This was nevertheless done, for example by Elisabeth Friedrichs,[8] who collected more than 4,000 biographies of women writers, narrowing her sample again by excluding border-crossers such as women who primarily published travel literature, letters or biographies, as well as women who wrote on feminist, political, religious, or scientific issues. Distinctive groups of women writers, who worked either within a confined field of literature, or in a certain time or specific geographic area, have been investigated as a collective. Susanne Kord gave an illuminating review of female dramatists of the eighteenth and nineteenth centuries,[9] Brian Keith-Smith collected material on unknown women writers between 1900 and 1933,[10] and Sigrid Schmid-Bortenschlager recently published a history of literature focusing on a nationally confined area, on Austria and its women writers from 1800 to 2000.[11] These few examples illustrate attempts to analyse the history of women writers in more detail by limiting the sample size under investigation. Geographical restrictions especially should be reconsidered, however, since national boundaries have changed as well as political regimes and cultural affinities. At best a focus on language areas seems to be adequate.

In order to analyse Karl Wilhelm Franz Brümmer's encyclopaedia on contemporary writers (containing approximately 10,000 biographical portraits) as well as materials in Brümmer's archive of biographies (approximately 6,000 biographies), Lucia Hacker selected 140 letters to Brümmer with biographical data from his literary estate and compared them to the portraits in his encyclopaedia.[12] Hacker was able to give very interesting insights into women writers' family backgrounds, their motivation to write, and their way of living. Since she compared female biographies and modes of self-construction with male ones, Hacker was able to outline the gender-specific aspects of women writers' lives and work. However, Hacker did not draw a representative sample — and again the question has to be posed as to what extent her results can be generalized.

To sum up, a social history of German women writers has not yet been written, although different disciplines have approached the field applying various methods. Socio-historical approaches differentiate little between the sexes and mainly reconstruct the history of the male majority of writers.[13] This is partly due to the sources, because labour statistics often did not distinguish between men and women. Approaches by German literary scholars usually focus on individual cases illustrating the life and work of exceptional writers.[14] But they do not give a review of typical careers. Social scientists, finally, recognize the potential of numerous samples and their representativeness, but tend to concentrate on contemporaries rather than on historical populations. Since only a knowledge of the universal set allows for a positioning of the individual, further research should be aimed at reconstructing a complete census of a past population.

## Content Analysis of Sophie Pataky's *German Ladies of the Pen* (1898)

Considering the problems of finding and selecting biographical sources on women writers, Sophie Pataky's biographical encyclopaedia of women writers called *Ladies of the Pen* can be regarded as a rather unique source. This encyclopaedia differs from others because it illustrates the results of a *complete* census among German-speaking women writers collected between 1896 and 1898. The author of this encyclopaedia, Sophie Pataky,[15] writes in the introduction that she was motivated by the first international women's congress ever held in Germany (in Berlin 1896) to make women's contributions to the cultural production more visible.[16] As a consequence she started collecting data on women writers and their publications. She evaluated established bibliographies and compiled lists of all the German-speaking women writers and their published works from 1840 onwards, and then she evaluated biographical encyclopaedias.[17] Finally she contacted editors of other encyclopaedias on writers as well as representatives of writers' and women's organizations.[18] As a result of this extensive work Pataky was able to list the names and publications of 4,547 women writers,[19] most of them working in the second half of the nineteenth century. Besides authors of literary texts (lyricists, dramatists, and authors of prose)

Pataky registered women writers who produced guidebooks or non-fiction books as well as those who worked as journalists or translators. Occasional writers were also included in her sample, which might partly explain why Pataky found many more women writers than were listed in official population statistics.[20] Using her list, Pataky wrote letters to those women writers who were still alive asking them for biographical information. The portraits in the encyclopaedia are based mainly on the answers of 2,048 women writers who were active at the turn of the century.

Pataky's biographical portraits are arranged quite differently depending on the answers that she received from writers. The biographical notes are either very short (including only some basic information such as date of birth, current address, and preferred genres) or they stretch out over a few pages, containing much detailed information. Since parts of Pataky's literary estate are accessible,[21] it is possible to reconstruct Pataky's work on the letters and to see how she fitted them as biographical portraits into her encyclopaedia. A systematic comparison between the letters Pataky received and the portraits she published was drawn as a first step in this study. It revealed that Pataky only slightly adapted the wording of the letters. The portraits can be regarded as fairly authentic documents giving reliable insights into the life and work of women writers in German-speaking countries at the turn of the century.[22] Of the 2,048 active writers who were portrayed in Pataky's encyclopaedia, 1,440 women can be regarded as writers who mainly produced literature.[23] We excluded writers who exclusively or primarily wrote journalistic pieces. The other 1,440 women constitute the sample for our further analysis.

Contemporary critics, however, criticized the encyclopaedia for gathering up 'every woman who once had written or botched an article' instead of only selecting 'professional' and 'important' writers.[24] This misogynist remark points precisely to the encyclopaedia's outstanding quality — the portrayal of all the 'hidden' women writers who worked occasionally, without a contract of employment or possibly even completely unpaid.

## Method

A quantitative content analysis was conducted.[25] The dimensions of the analysis were demographics, social position (including milieu, education, and family background), occupation (including characteristics of employment and the writers' motivations), the opus (in order to find out about preferred genres and types of media), the writers' organizational networks (such as churches, social movements, or political parties), and, finally, references to gender stereotypes (to find out whether traditional or emancipated gender roles were explicitly mentioned).

## Results

### Demographics

Most German-speaking women writers at the end of the nineteenth century lived in Germany (73%), 19% lived in Austria (although Austria encompassed large parts of Central Europe at that time including Hungary and parts of Poland, Bohemia,

Slovakia, Slovenia, and Croatia) and — surprisingly, given the total population of the country — only 3% of German-speaking women writers lived in Switzerland.[26] Within these countries women writers tended to live in metropolises (27%) such as Vienna or Berlin or large regional centres (32%) such as Leipzig or Graz. Therefore, we can assume that women writers were 'urbanites' at a time when the majority of people still lived in the countryside or in small villages. In 1900, only 14% of the German population lived in metropolises and large cities.[27] A comparison between places of birth and the writers' actual residences, additionally, underlines the tendency among women writers to move to large cities. While the majority (62%) were born in the countryside or in small towns, approximately a third of these moved away.

Women writers tended to be older women, half of them single or widowed, who did not have to look after children. The average age was 47, which was old in terms of life expectancy at that time (48 years in Germany in 1901).[28] This comparatively high average age is not surprising if we consider the typical phases of a bourgeois woman's life. After marriage, these women usually stopped working and devoted the following decades to housekeeping and childcare.[29] It seems that reproductive work and professional work were not carried out at the same time, but during different phases of life. Women wrote primarily after their children had grown up. This might explain why children are rarely mentioned: Only 8% of the biographies contained (subtle) references to children. Presumably the lives of women were not dominated (any more) by childcare when they devoted their time to writing. Another explanation could be that women writers chose to submit descriptions of their professional lives instead of private biographies and therefore did not mention children. However, since the vast majority of these biographies contain a lot of other personal information — and thereby reflect a typical pattern of female identity construction at that time[30] — this explanation seems rather implausible.

Marital status is not always revealed, but if one concludes from 77% of the evaluated biographies to the whole sample, only 45% of the women writers were married and therefore could presumably rely on a husband to support them financially. The majority were either not married, widowed (15%), or even divorced (2%), something which might explain the necessity for many of these women to earn some extra money by writing.

*Social position*

Like their male counterparts, women writers around 1900 came from relatively educated bourgeois families — at least 83% of them. The professions of fathers and husbands were taken as indicators of milieu.[31] Within the group of bourgeois women writers, civil servants, pastors, merchants, and teachers constituted the main occupational family background. 14% of the women writers had an aristocratic background; only 3% grew up in working-class families. German-speaking women writers came from more socially elevated families than their male colleagues. According to the labour census of 1895 less than 6% of male writers came from aristocratic families in contrast to 14% of the women writers in Pataky's sample. The small number of writers with a lower-class background can be attributed to a lack of education. Individual autobiographies, such as the one by the Austrian socialist Adelheid Popp (1869–1939), illustrate the difficulties working-class women had to face when they started their writing despite being nearly illiterate.[32] An upper-class background often gave women access to private tuition, which compensated for the inadequacies in women's education in Imperial Germany and Austria,[33] and allowed them to write.

Milieux in Central Europe were also determined by religious affiliations. However, since there are few references in the encyclopaedia to the religious backgrounds of women writers, reliable results cannot be presented.

*Occupation*

Regarding the authors' occupation, it is remarkable that 51% of the women writers mentioned some gainful employment which did not necessarily include writing. 26% regarded writing as a full-time job, but only 3% could live exclusively from their literary work. More than 17% made their living by working as a teacher. It can be concluded that writing was an occasional or secondary occupation for most of the women writers. It is remarkable that many of them explicitly denied that they were writing to make a living. Considering, however, how many pieces they published, their denial that they wrote from necessity could be the result of their relatively upper-class background. At that time gainful employment was simply not appropriate for a Central European woman from the upper bourgeoisie or aristocracy.[34]

*Opus*

Looking at the key activities, it becomes evident that nineteenth-century women writers used many genres und wrote for very different types of media. It was not only the publishing houses that printed works by women writers — only 62% of the women published books and brochures — but also the emerging popular press. More than half of all women writers additionally wrote for periodicals, sometimes in several magazines and newspapers simultaneously. Half of the women writers who contributed to periodicals mentioned the titles of the journals, magazines, and newspapers which printed their works, and we can conclude that they published in very diverse periodicals, ranging from literary journals such as *Die Gesellschaft* (Society) edited by Michael Conrad, to family magazines such as *Die Gartenlaube* (The Arbour), women's magazines such as the *Deutsche Hausfrauen-Zeitung* (German Magazine for Housewives) edited by Lina Morgenstern, magazines for children and adolescents, political revues such as the *Deutsche Rundschau* (German Review), illustrated magazines like the *Berliner Illustrierte Zeitung* (Berlin Illustrated Magazine), and sometimes also fashion magazines or church journals. Women writers did not exclusively write for women and their publications were not restricted to women's and fashion magazines as clichéd contemporary sources often claimed.

As the fact that they published numerous publications in periodicals might indicate, women writers tended to produce relatively short, mostly narrative texts, namely novellas and short stories. 65% of all the women writers reported that they used these genres.

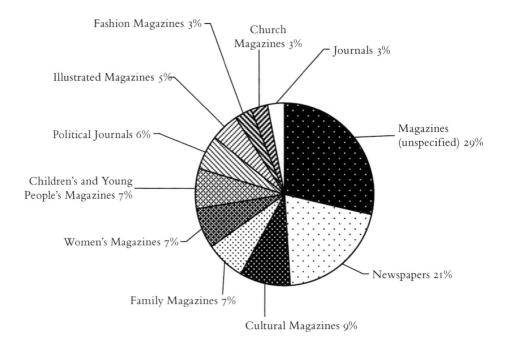

FIG. 1. Periodicals in which women writers published (n = 1,402; multiple coding)

As the next pie chart (Fig. 2) indicates, women writers were not restricted to a single genre; they used a variety of genres simultaneously, with 'women's novels', thought to be the most acceptable genre for women writers,[35] playing only a partial role. A third of the female writers wrote novels, a third poetry, a sixth respectively drama, children's literature, translations, and so-called feuilletons, reflective essays on cultural developments.

*Organizational networks*

Although the late nineteenth century was the age of corporatism in Central Europe, women writers at that time seem to have been little embedded in organizational networks. Political parties, the churches, and the labour movement do not seem to have been important networks for them. Nor can the feminist movement be regarded as an important point of reference, since it is mentioned in only 2% of the biographies.

*Reference to gender stereotypes*

The burgeoning feminist movement of the time did not necessarily provoke women writers to view or describe themselves in emancipated terms. Emancipated ways of living are rarely mentioned in the sample. The self-constructions of women writers do not focus on divorces, full-time employment, or other indicators of a self-determined life. 11% articulate their respect for traditional gender roles

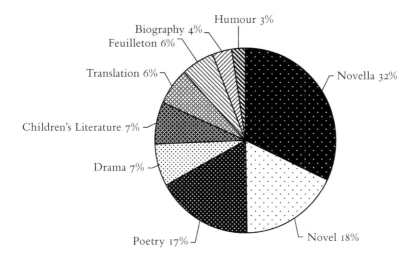

FIG. 2. Preferred genres in per cent (n = 1,440; multiple coding)

by emphasizing that they are women of virtue, devoted wives, and perfect housekeepers.

It is possible, however, that these traditional self-descriptions were a means of legitimizing their role as working women. Concerning the eighteenth century, Ulrike Weckel and Helga Brandes suggest a variety of similar strategies that female editors used to counterbalance an unconventional role as working woman in the public sphere.[36] As already mentioned, neither gainful employment nor public self-display were considered appropriate for bourgeois women in Imperial Germany and Austria.

## Conclusion

To date, much research into women's writing has remained on an *individual* level, studying well-known women writers or individuals who proved exceptional either for literary or for biographical reasons, such as women with connections to male writers or proto-feminist writers. What the study of women writers still sorely lacks are representative samples which can fill in details about female authors as a group. To fill in the blank spaces surrounding the exceptional individuals requires a different methodology drawn from the social sciences. What this chapter has shown is that biographical encyclopaedias can provide such a representative sample. They can reveal what was the norm, what was usual, what was the case for the majority.

This in turn helps us to assess those writers about whom we do know more, because they can now be evaluated not in a vacuum, but in a context filled with facts.

For example, despite all the barriers working women had to face at the turn of the century, the number of women writing was high, exceeding many contemporary estimates. Women writers mainly came from educated, bourgeois families and positioned themselves also within this milieu. Most of the writers seem to have worked part-time or only occasionally, and made their living in other fields such as teaching.

Many women writers crossed the boundary between literature and journalism at the end of the nineteenth century. The majority not only published books, but were also regular contributors to magazines and newspapers. From the wide range of genres that women writers used we can conclude that they were able to react flexibly to the demands of the literary market. Their work was very diverse, contrary to the stereotypical labelling of the work of women writers that can be found in nineteenth-century sources.

## Notes to Chapter 5

1. Content analysis is a research technique for the objective, systematic, and quantitative description of the manifest content of large numbers of texts (biographies in our case). Usually content analysis is used to determine the presence of certain words or concepts within texts. Researchers quantify and analyse the presence, meanings, and relationships of such words and concepts. To conduct a content analysis, the text is coded, or broken down, into manageable categories on a variety of levels — word, word sense, phrase, sentence, or theme in order to measure the attributes and evaluations of persons and issues. The cases within these categories are counted to reveal the quantity of certain attributes and evaluations within a large number of texts.

2. Margarete Zimmermann, 'Literaturgeschichte/Literaturgeschichtsschreibung', in *Metzler Lexikon Gender Studies/Geschlechterforschung: Ansätze — Personen — Grundbegriffe*, ed. by Renate Kroll (Stuttgart and Weimar: Metzler, 2002), pp. 237–38.

3. Hiltrud Gnüg and Renate Möhrmann, 'Vorwort', in *Frauen — Literatur — Geschichte: Schreibende Frauen vom Mittelalter bis zur Gegenwart*, ed. by Hiltrud Gnüg and Renate Möhrmann (Stuttgart: Metzler, 1999), pp. xi–xii.

4. Britta Scheideler, *Zwischen Beruf und Berufung: Zur Sozialgeschichte der deutschen Schriftsteller von 1880 bis 1933* (Frankfurt am Main: Buchhändler-Vereinigung, 1997).

5. E.g. Karin Tebben, *Beruf: Schriftstellerin. Schreibende Frauen im 18. und 19. Jahrhundert* (Göttingen: Vandenhoeck & Ruprecht, 1998).

6. E.g. Susanne Kinnebrock, 'Revisiting Journalism as a Profession in the Nineteenth Century: Empirical Findings on Women Journalists in Central Europe', *Communications: The European Journal of Communication Research*, 34 (2009), 107–24.

7. E.g. Susanne Kinnebrock, 'Schreiben für die (politische) Öffentlichkeit: Frauen im Journalismus um 1900', in *Frauen in der literarischen Öffentlichkeit 1780–1918*, ed. by Caroline Bland and Elisa Müller-Adams (Bielefeld: Aisthesis, 2007), pp. 143–67.

8. Elisabeth Friedrichs, *Die deutschsprachigen Schriftstellerinnen des 18. und 19. Jahrhunderts: Ein Lexikon* (Stuttgart: Metzler, 1981).

9. Susanne Kord, *Ein Blick hinter die Kulissen: Deutschsprachige Dramatikerinnen im 18. und 19. Jahrhundert* (Stuttgart: Metzler, 1992).

10. Brian Keith-Smith, *An Encyclopedia of German Women Writers 1900–1933: Biographies and Bibliographies with Exemplary Readings*, i–vii (Lewiston, NY: Edwin Mellen Press Ltd, 1997). See also Karin Tebben, *Deutschsprachige Schriftstellerinnen des Fin de siècle* (Darmstadt: Wissenschaftliche Buchgesellschaft, 1999).

11. Sigrid Schmid-Bortenschlager, *Österreichische Schriftstellerinnen 1800–2000: Eine Literaturgeschichte* (Darmstadt: Wissenschaftliche Buchgesellschaft, 2009). See also Helga Harriman, 'Women Writers and Artists in Fin-de-Siècle Vienna', *Modern Austrian Literature: Journal of the International Arthur Schnitzler Research Association*, 23 (1993), 1–19; Christa Bittermann-Wille and Helga Hofmann-Weinberger, 'Erstklassige Schriftstellerinnen zweiter Güte? Literarische Bestseller österreichischer Autorinnen vom 19. Jahrhundert bis zum Zweiten Weltkrieg', in *Biblos: Beiträge zu Buch, Bibliothek und Schrift*, ed. by Austrian National Library (Wien: Phoibos Verlag, 2005), pp. 19–39; Jutta Schulze and Petra Budke, *Schriftstellerinnen in Berlin 1871–1945: Ein Lexikon zu Leben und Werk* (Berlin: Orlanda-Frauenverlag, 1995).

12. Lucia Hacker, *Schreibende Frauen um 1900: Rollen, Bilder, Gesten* (Berlin: LIT, 2007).

13. E.g. Scheideler, *Zwischen Beruf und Berufung*.

14. See Sigrid Schmid-Bortenschlager and Hanna Schnedl-Bubenicej, *Österreichische Schriftstellerinnen 1880–1938: Eine Bio-Bibliographie* (Stuttgart: Heinz, 1982); Brian Keith-Smith, *German Women Writers 1900–1933: Twelve Essays*, Bristol German Publications 3 (Lewiston, NY: Mellen Verlag, 1993); Keith-Smith, *An Encyclopaedia of German Women Writers 1900–1933*.

15. There is very little biographical information available on Sophie Pataky. Pataky was born in 1860 in Podiebrad in Bohemia as Sophie Caroline Stipek and married the bookseller and publisher Carl Pataky (born 1844). The couple lived in Berlin and it was her husband's publishing house that published her encyclopaedia in 1898. In 1907 Carl and Sophie Pataky seem to have moved to Meran in South Tyrol. Carl Pataky died in 1914 in Reichenhall in Bavaria. Sophie Pataky's place and date of death are not known, and there is also no information on how some of her papers were transferred to the Archives of the German Feminist Movement in Kassel (Jank, n.d. [1999], online).

16. Sophie Pataky, *Lexikon deutscher Frauen der Feder: Eine Zusammenstellung der seit dem Jahre 1840 erschienenen Werke weiblicher Autoren, nebst Biographien der lebenden und einem Verzeichnis der Pseudonyme*, I (Berlin: Pataky [Eigenverlag], 1898), pp. v–vi.

17. Ibid., pp. vii–x.

18. Dagmar Jank [1999], *Anmerkungen zum Teilnachlaß von Sophie Pataky (1860_?) im Archiv der deutschen Frauenbewegung in Kassel*. Retrieved February, 18, 2009, <http://forge.fh-potsdam.de/~ABD/jank/sophie_pataky.pdf>.

19. Carmen Sitter, *'Die eine Hälfte vergißt man(n) leicht!': Zur Situation von Journalistinnen in Deutschland* (Pfaffenweiler: Centaurus, 1998), p. 112.

20. According to the German labour census of 1895 only 530 women from among 7,407 writers, private scholars [Privatgelehrte], and journalists wrote either as a main occupation or as a second job.

21. A number of Pataky's papers are housed by the Archives of the German Feminist Movement in Kassel (Stiftung Archiv der deutschen Frauenbewegung, Kassel).

22. The extensiveness of Pataky's search for women writers as well as the accuracy of the information in her portraits is confirmed by a comparison with the samples and the portraits in other biographical encyclopaedias. Marianne Nigg, for example, who published a collection of biographies on Austrian women writers five years before Pataky, drew on a nearly identical sample (but only included women writers living in Austria). Moreover, Nigg's biographical and bibliographical core information hardly differs from Pataky's, although Nigg's portraits are much shorter and therefore give less insight into the motivations and self-perceptions of women writers at that time. This is evident from a systematic evaluation of Nigg's biographical encyclopaedia which was completed in a graduate seminar at the Communication Department of the University of Vienna in 2008. See Marianne Nigg, *Biographien der österreichischen Dichterinnen und Schriftstellerinnen: Ein Beitrag zur deutschen Literatur in Österreich* (Korneuburg: Julius Kühlkopfs 1893); for further critical comparisons of biographical encyclopaedias see Hacker, *Schreibende Frauen um 1900*.

23. Originally Pataky's encyclopaedia included 2,716 entries with further biographical information. In all these cases the authors had either responded to Pataky's initiative or Pataky had collected their data from other sources. Since we wanted to focus on women writers who were still active in 1898, we did not take all 2,716 portraits into account: 669 portraits have been omitted because the authors were deceased. Three hundred and seventy-seven authors were left out either

because no date of birth was given or birth was dated prior to 1815. Presumably these women writers were too old to be still active or the date of death was just omitted. Since it was very unclear whether these authors actually lived and worked at the end of the nineteenth century, we preferred to delete these 'missing cases' from our sample. And finally those women who cited journalistic activities as their main focus (229 in number) were removed from the record.

24. *Centralblatt für Bibliothekswesen*, 1898, p. 82, quoted in Marianne Jacob, *Die Anfänge bibliographischer Darstellung der deutschen Literatur des 19. Jahrhunderts: Untersuchungen zur Vorgeschichte des Deutschen Schriftsteller-Lexikons 1830–1880* (Berlin: PhD, Faculty of Philosophy, Humboldt University, 2003), p. 142.

25. The content analysis was conducted by a gender historian specializing in the nineteenth century in order to capture the meanings conveyed by contemporary diction. We thank Helke Dreier from the University of Hagen for her careful analysis of the portraits.

26. At first sight the small percentage of Swiss women writers in Pataky's encyclopaedia might seem puzzling. It is not likely, however, that Pataky chose to exclude Swiss women writers. She had extensive contact with representatives of Swiss writers' and women's organizations (Jank, *Anmerkungen zum Teilnachlaß von Sophie Pataky*, online).

27. Hans-Ulrich Wehler, *Deutsche Gesellschaftsgeschichte*, III: *Von der 'Deutschen Doppelrevolution' bis zum Beginn des Ersten Weltkriegs 1849–1914* (Munich: Beck, 1995), p. 37.

28. Ibid., p. 38.

29. Ute Frevert, *Frauen-Geschichte zwischen bürgerlicher Verbesserung und neuer Weiblichkeit* (Frankfurt am Main: Suhrkamp, 2001), pp. 106–08.

30. Gisela Febel, 'Frauenbiographik als kollektive Biographik', in *Frauenbiographik: Lebensbeschreibungen und Porträts*, ed. by Christian von Zimmermann and Nina von Zimmermann (Tübingen: Gunter Narr, 2005), p. 139; Hacker, *Schreibende Frauen um 1900*, p. 24.

31. Only 74% of Pataky's portraits contain information on the professions of husbands and fathers, which helped us identify the social class women writers came from. In line with Scheideler's results, women writers did not form a completely homogeneous group. They belonged to various classes and milieus, but they predominantly came from educated, bourgeois families (see Scheideler, *Zwischen Beruf und Berufung*, pp. 15–16).

32. Adelheid Popp, *Jugend einer Arbeiterin* (Berlin and Bonn: Dietz, 1983).

33. Richard J. Evans, *The Feminist Movement in Germany 1894–1933* (London and Beverly Hills: Sage, 1976), pp. 17–21.

34. Gisela Bock, *Frauen in der europäischen Geschichte: Vom Mittelalter bis zur Gegenwart* (Munich: Beck, 2000), pp. 132–53.

35. Tebben, *Beruf: Schriftstellerin. Schreibende Frauen im 18. und 19. Jahrhundert*, p. 28.

36. Ulrike Weckel, *Zwischen Häuslichkeit und Öffentlichkeit: Die ersten deutschen Frauenzeitschriften im späten 18. Jahrhundert und ihr Publikum* (Tübingen: Niemeyer, 1998); Helga Brandes, 'Das Frauenzimmer-Journal: Zur Herausbildung einer journalistischen Gattung im 18. Jahrhundert', in *Deutsche Literatur von Frauen*, I: *Vom Mittelalter bis zum Ende des 18. Jahrhunderts*, ed. by Gisela Brinker-Gabler (Munich: Beck, 1988), pp. 452–68.

PART II

# Case Studies

CHAPTER 6

# Nineteenth-Century Sentimentality and Renunciation

## E. Marlitt's *Goldelse* (1866) and Gabriele Reuter's *Liselotte von Reckling* (1904)

### Charlotte Woodford

In literary criticism, *sentimental* is often a pejorative term. Sentimental novels are associated with 'unlikely plots, powerfully one-dimensional characters, [and] spending (of words, tears, lives of characters)'.[1] The term 'sentimental' to describe these aesthetic features, perceived by many critics as 'flaws', was (and is) an easy way of dismissing novels by women and demonstrating how apparently second-rate they are.[2] Such novels, however, should not be underestimated. By strongly identifying with the protagonists of the sentimental novel, readers were offered a way of better understanding their own domestic lives, and in the ethical awareness of the heroine, they saw their own values affirmed. As the twentieth century began, the reader of Gabriele Reuter's fiction engaged with the choices made by her heroines, and in doing so was rethinking the life-choices available to women in society outside the novel. This chapter will examine the romance *Goldelse* (*Gold Elsie*, 1866),[3] first novel of bestselling author E. Marlitt (pseudonym for Eugenie John), as well as Gabriele Reuter's popular novel *Liselotte von Reckling* (1904).[4] Particular attention will be given to the theme of *Entsagung* (renunciation), a theme embraced by the romance which is problematized in women's novels around the turn of the twentieth century.

In the romance, renunciation is a form of empowerment, the process through which the protagonist achieves autonomy and self-knowledge, and begins to engage in useful social activity.[5] There, renunciation is also a temporary state: the protagonists reap the reward for their willingness to renounce their love when they eventually declare their affection for one another and embrace. As such, the romance differs markedly in its treatment of the theme of *Entsagung* from near-contemporary works of poetic realism, where, according to Wolfgang Lukas, *Entsagung* is transformed into a pathological male fear of sexuality and ultimately the complete repression of desire.[6] Reuter's *Liselotte* critiques the value of renunciation, but also responds ambivalently to modern egoism.

It has been argued convincingly elsewhere that at the start of the nineteenth century, bourgeois values began to dominate the literary market and women writers, whose contribution became particularly prominent in this period, were forced into a 'ghetto', writing 'edifying, moralistic "women's literature" for women in support of "natural" gender roles'.[7] When women writers transgressed into the public sphere in order to write, they were supposed to be 'Priesterinnen der Sitte, der Ordnung und der Zucht' [priestesses of decency, order, and chastity]; their writings were expected to transfigure domestic life.[8] Joeres points out that 'middle-class German women writers never really left the private sphere, at least in terms of abandoning its primarily bourgeois ideologies and precepts'.[9] The German nation was to be founded on strongly gendered middle-class values: men, in the public sphere, were to be honourable, courageous and prepared to put the nation's interests before their own; women were to be chaste homemakers, quietly supporting their husbands' efforts. Reuter sums up the division (with some irony) in *Aus guter Familie* (From a Good Family, 1895): 'Für den deutschen Mann die Pflicht — für die deutsche Frau der Glaube und die Treue' [The German man needs to do his duty; the German woman needs faith and loyalty].[10]

In the late nineteenth century in Germany, industrialization and urbanization provided for a vast expansion of the book-buying market at the same time as creating a population with a need to come to terms with the conditions of this new age. The most successful novels were often powerfully melodramatic and fostered the reader's identification with protagonists and the values which they represented.[11] Works which were escapist and reassuring appealed particularly strongly to the mass market in this period of rapid social change. The mass market had a taste for the sentimental: Dickens's novels, with so many well-known emotive scenes, like the death of Little Nell in the *Old Curiosity Shop*, were widely read in Germany in translation.[12]

In the rapidly expanding market place which accompanied industrialization and urbanization from the 1860s onwards, journals such as the family periodical *Die Gartenlaube* (Garden Bower) or the evangelical Christian journal *Daheim* (At Home) achieved commercial success that had never previously been possible, with serialized fiction presenting models of ideal womanhood.[13] E. Marlitt, pseudonym for Eugenie John, became the house author of *Die Gartenlaube*. Her enjoyable romances, written at a very good pace with well-rounded and plausible characters, generated enormous profits for Marlitt and the journal's editor, Ernst Keil. In 1866, Marlitt's *Goldelse* became the first full-length novel ever to be serialized in the *Gartenlaube*, whose circulation was at that point 170,000 copies (it later doubled).[14] Additionally, her novels were subsequently published by Keil as highly successful books and were widely translated, selling well in the US and British markets too. Marlitt's novels reached what Todd Kontje calls 'something approaching a mass readership'.[15] Kirsten Belgum points out that realism in German is largely perceived as a middle-class male genre revolving around what she describes as 'the awakening and vicarious satisfaction of middle-class dreams'.[16] She argues convincingly that female novelists such as Marlitt need to be seen as part of the tradition of German 'realism'; Marlitt's novels foster that dream of prosperity and a happy home, with heirs to inherit the new wealth. The novels are the product of a new middle-class self-consciousness, asserting the values and gender roles through which the German nation was be founded, as Todd Kontje explores.[17] Reuter, on the other hand, engages critically with those values to explore the repression which she perceived as accompanying conformity to a restrictive middle-class code. For Marlitt, renunciation is the key to future prosperity; in Reuter's novels, it leads to exploitation and unhappiness.

In Marlitt's *Goldelse*, as in her other works, the ethos of *Entsagung* or renunciation is celebrated: it distinguishes the middle classes from aristocratic decadence and corruption. *Entsagung* is not restricted merely to the field of the erotic, but is part of a wider stoicism which affects every aspect of life. At the start of *Goldelse*, the young protagonist Elisabeth Ferber (the eponymous 'Goldelse' or Else) selflessly refuses to keep any of the money she earns as a music teacher, using it to feed and clothe the family. She willingly renounces her career as a music teacher to accompany her parents when they move to the castle of Gnadeck in Thuringia; she takes on sewing to help finance the move, and even has to suffer the loss of her beloved piano. She makes the sacrifices willingly: 'Doch *der* Schmerz war jetzt auch überwunden und lag hinter ihr, wie so manches, was sie schweigend entbehrt und geleistet hatte' (p. 20) [But *that* suffering had now also been overcome and lay behind her, like so much which she had silently renounced and achieved].

Elisabeth is descended loosely from a noble family whose line has been extinguished with the death some years ago of Wolf von Gnadewitz. He had wanted to marry Elisabeth's mother, his housekeeper and distant relative, but she preferred Ferber, a middle-class officer 'von ausgezeichnetem Charakter' (p. 7) [of excellent character]. In a characteristic act of vengeance, Gnadewitz left Elisabeth's mother in his will the dilapidated former family seat, Gnadeck, which for many years had been uninhabitable. Ferber's family eventually leave behind poverty in the city to renovate their inheritance, turning it into a middle-class home by demolishing much of the ruin which reminded them of former aristocratic decadence.

The exploration of the castle is a symbolic moment which marks the passing from one era to the next. The family imagine themselves to be like the suitors who unsuccessfully attempted to wake Sleeping Beauty: 'wir arbeiten uns mühsam durch Hecken und Gestrüpp, wie ehemals Dornröschens unglückliche Befreier' (p. 17) [we struggled laboriously through hedges and undergrowth just like the unfortunate suitors attempting to liberate Sleeping Beauty]. Instead of a 'Zauberschloß' (p. 29) [fairy-tale palace], they discover initially a dark threatening stone building: 'hier ist Tod, nichts als Tod!' (p. 30) [There is only death here, nothing but death!]. However, pushing open a gate, Elisabeth discovers a secret garden, teeming with the new life of spring:

> Zahllose Schmetterlinge flatterten durch die Luft, und über die riesigen Fächer der Farnkräuter zu Elisabeths Füßen liefen geschäftig goldglänzende Käfer. Ueber all dies Blühen und Treiben erhoben einige Obstbäume und mehrere schöne Linden ihre Kronen. (p. 31)

> [Countless butterflies fluttered through the air and beetles, gleaming with gold, swarmed busily over the giant tendrils of the bracken at Elisabeth's feet. The

crowns of a number of fruit trees and several beautiful linden trees towered over
this buzz of activity and flourishing of new life.]

Her uncle's maid Sabine tells stories of the rich, proud countess who used to live
in the castle and was 'hart und gefühllos wie Stein' (p. 35) [as hard and unfeeling
as stone]. In contrast, the vibrancy of the wildlife in the castle's hidden courtyard
matches Elisabeth's youthful exuberance.

Inside the castle, time has stood still. One room houses the tomb of a young
wife from the seventeenth century, testimony to the cruelty and sexual deviancy
of the former aristocratic owners. In a letter left among the woman's possessions,
an ancestor of Herr von Gnadewitz confesses to having kept the gypsy woman,
Lila, against her will, seduced her and then married her to legitimize their son,
after whose birth she pined away. The son is also revealed as Elisabeth Ferber's
ancestor. But while the local aristocrats expect that the Ferber brothers will now
present a legitimate claim to the title 'von Gnadewitz', Elisabeth declares proudly
to a horrified audience: 'ich bin eine Bürgerliche' (p. 230) [I am a middle-class
woman]. She continues: 'Wir lieben unseren Namen, weil er rein und ehrlich ist,
und wollen dies fleckenlose Erbteil nicht vertauschen gegen ein Gut, das sich aus
den Thränen und dem Schweiße anderer groß genährt hat!' (p. 231) [We cherish
our name because it is pure and honest. We would not exchange this immaculate
inheritance for one which has gorged on the tears and sweat of others]. The brothers
renounce their claim to the title, even though it would have enabled them to gain
in wealth and prestige.

In *Goldelse*, Elisabeth's love for the owner of Lindhof, Rudolf von Walde, is clear
to the reader when she springs forward selflessly to challenge an assassin, a former
servant with a grudge, who was waiting for Walde to pass by on his horse in order
to shoot him. Elisabeth disarms the servant whose gun is fired harmlessly into the
forest; he is later found to have committed suicide. This incident is similar to the
chapter in Elizabeth Gaskell's *North and South* (1855) when Margaret Hale throws
herself in front of factory owner Mr Thornton to protect him from the angry mob
of striking mill workers who have gathered at his gates. Walde makes the mistake
of assuming the protagonist's selfless heroism to be a *conscious* act of love. Elisabeth
has a sense of feminine propriety which exceeds her understanding of her desire
for the hero. Her behaviour betrays her love of Walde before she has consciously
acknowledged it, and thus, like Margaret Hale, she denies her love for him. Kirsten
Belgum describes how in Marlitt's novels 'female desire' is a powerful and mysterious
force which the protagonist cannot control.[18] Elisabeth claims proudly that she
would have behaved the same way for any man in danger: 'Ich habe einfach eine
Pflicht gegen den Nächsten erfüllt, und würde [...] ganz ebenso gehandelt haben,
wenn der Fall ein umgekehrter, und Linke [the murderous servant] der Bedrohte
gewesen wäre...' (p. 145) [I simply carried out my duty to my neighbour and I would
have behaved in just the same way if it had been the other way round and Linke
had been the one who was threatened].[19] In doing so, Elisabeth appears to deny her
love for Walde, leading to his disappointment and apparently inexplicable coldness
towards her. The sentimental narrative style indicates her confusion of mind; his
manner seems like 'ein unlösbares Rätsel' (p. 146) [an insoluble mystery] and she

wonders whether it would be better to avoid meeting him:

> War es ihr zu verdenken, wenn sie sich vornahm, dergleichen Konflikten künftig auszuweichen? ... Gewiß nicht ... Nun, zum Glücke war ja seine Abreise nahe ... zum Glücke? Der mittels Trotz und Stolz aufgerichtete Bau der Selbstbetrügerei zerfiel plötzlich vor diesem einen Gedanken. (p. 146)

> [Would anyone blame her if she were to try in future to avoid such conflicts? ... Certainly not ... Well, fortunately his departure was imminent ... Fortunately? The self-deceit, which she had carefully constructed through defiance and pride, crumbled suddenly at this one thought.]

The suspension points of the sentimental narrative suggest that Walde excites in Elisabeth an emotion too complex to convey in words; the modal particles in the German — 'gewiß', 'nun', 'ja' — enable the reader to infer the process of gradual realization of her love, as her self-deceit crumbles. Elisabeth gradually discovers what her uncle describes with pathos as 'die Macht, die uns selbst Vater und Mutter vergessen läßt um eines anderen willen' (p. 78) [the power which makes us forget even our father and mother for the sake of another]. Elisabeth has to discover love for herself through her emotional and physical responses to the hero. The narrative form of the romance encourages escapism by allowing space for the reader's imagination, through which the reader's own hidden longing can emerge, allowing the reader to echo Elisabeth's phrase: 'Aber was kann ich für meine widerspenstige Phantasie?' (p. 57) [But what can I do about my untameable imagination?].

Walde is also reticent in the expression of his feelings for Elisabeth and is prepared to renounce every claim to her love. His marriage to Elisabeth eventually provides a force of reconciliation which unites the classes in order that the common values of humanity should prevail, creating what Lucas refers to as the model of the 'Bürgeradel' [middle-class aristocrats], protagonists who are members of the aristocracy but whose values and morality are that of the middle classes.[20] In contrast to Walde's integrity, his distant cousin Emil von Hollfeld merely feigns *Entsagung* as a cover for his sexual incontinence. Rudolf's sister, the rich heiress Helene von Walde, is too ill to marry; Hollfeld encourages her to believe in his undying love for her, hoping to inherit her wealth after her inevitable premature death. However, in Helene's presence, Hollfeld is secretly wooing Elisabeth, who has been engaged to play piano duets with Helene. He pursues Elisabeth in an impertinent fashion. In a crucial scene at the climax of the novel, he tricks Elisabeth into meeting him alone in the pavilion away from the house. Elisabeth, whose trembling betrays her terror of the situation, is nevertheless stoically 'fest und ruhig' (p. 227) [constant and composed] in her refusal to give in to his desires. Hollfeld, by contrast, is 'blind vor Aufregung' (p. 228) [blind with arousal]. He catches hold of Elisabeth: 'Sie fühlte den heißen Atem ihres Peinigers über ihre Finger hinstreifen, sein Haar berührte ihre Wange, sie schauderte, aber alle physischen Kräfte versagten ihr buchstäblich' (p. 228) [She felt the hot breath of her tormenter touch her fingers, his hair touched her cheek, she shuddered, but all her physical strength literally failed her]. Hollfeld has lost all self-control: 'er lag völlig im Banne seiner Leidenschaft' (p. 229) [he was completely in the thrall of his passion]. Hollfeld, who until now had concealed his base desires ('seine niedrigen Neigungen', p. 229) from the eyes of the world, is beyond rational thought. Elisabeth is saved only by the arrival of Helene, Hollfeld's aunt, and Walde. The latter, seeing his beloved in the arms of another, assumes his love for Elisabeth is not reciprocated and decides to renounce his love, in order to permit Elisabeth's supposed happiness with Hollfeld. In this novel, the mood of renunciation and stoicism of the nineteenth century is affirmed, yet behind the corsets and the 'stiff upper lip' there is a strong sense of the power of physical attraction.

Novels published in family journals such as *Die Gartenlaube*, *Über Land und Meer* (Over Land and Sea) or *Daheim* had to make suitable reading for an innocent teenage girl, for whom the experience of desire was perhaps as mysterious as for Elisabeth in *Goldelse*, and whose sensitivities might be developed in the very process of reading novels. The above description of Hollfeld's attempt to seduce Elisabeth makes clear the physical proximity of the two figures and Hollfeld's hot breath on her fingers is a metonym for his excited physical caressing of her body. As Elisabeth is defending her virtue against Hollfeld, they are momentarily confronted through the window by the contorted face of a silent adversary, Bertha. She is a servant in her uncle's house and a distant relative; her name recalls the mad first wife of the hero, Rochester, in Charlotte Brontë's *Jane Eyre* (1847), whose very existence threatens Jane's marriage to Rochester. Elisabeth's curiosity has been stimulated throughout the novel by the mysterious Bertha, who never speaks and who latterly seems to want to harm Elisabeth. In the final chapter Bertha is revealed as the polar opposite of the virtuous Elisabeth. While the heroine resists Hollfeld's advances — and is rewarded by marriage to Herr von Walde — Bertha has carried out a lengthy secret love affair with Hollfeld, whom she claims promised to marry her. She becomes pregnant with his child (an unusual event in Marlitt's fiction, where there is subsequently very little reference to sexuality outside of marriage; in *Die Frau mit dem Karfunkelsteinen* (The Lady with the Garnets, 1885), for example, a seemingly illegitimate child turns out to be the product of a secret marriage). Hollfeld jilts Bertha to pursue Elisabeth.

The way in which Bertha's seduction by Hollfeld and pregnancy is revealed is masterful in its subtlety. Bertha is brought before the doctor in the final chapter, having received a blow to the head. The doctor, instead of treating the wound, enlightens the head forester, whom Bertha calls 'uncle', as to the cause of Bertha's unusual behaviour in recent weeks:

> Ihre Wunde war ungefährlich; aber der Arzt schüttelte den Kopf und warf einen seltsamen Blick auf den Oberförster, der mit besorgter Miene seine Manipulation verfolgte.
>
> Der Doktor war ein gerader Mann von etwas rauhen, derben Manieren. Er trat plötzlich auf den Oberförster zu und sagte ihm mit nicht sehr unterdrückter Stimme einige Worte.
>
> Wie von einem tödlichen Schusse getroffen, taumelte der alte Mann zurück, starrte den Doktor an wie geistesabwesend, und ohne auch nur eine Silbe zu erwidern, ohne einen Blick auf die Kranke zu werfen, schritt er zur Thür hinaus.
>
> 'Onkel, Onkel, verzeihe mir!' schrie das Mädchen mit herzzerreißender Stimme auf. (p. 249)

[Her wound was not dangerous; but the doctor shook his head and shot a strange glance at the head forester, who was watching the examination carefully with a look of concern.

   The doctor was a frank person with somewhat rough, coarse manners. He came over suddenly to the head forester and said a few words to him without greatly lowering his voice.

   The old man recoiled as if he had been fatally shot, stared at the doctor as if he had lost his senses and without uttering even a syllable, without casting a glance at the patient, he walked out of the door.

   'Uncle, Uncle, forgive me!', cried the girl in a heart-rending voice.]

A brief physical examination of Bertha reveals her pregnancy, the news of which Doctor Fels conveys to the uncle frankly, in words intended for Bertha as well as the uncle. While his words are delivered in a voice loud enough to be audible to the patient, in the text they are ironically suppressed altogether. The taboo on the treatment of sexual immorality is upheld. The uncle's shocked reaction and Bertha's cry for forgiveness convey the shame which Bertha has incurred. Later Bertha reports: 'Er hat dem Onkel meine Schmach mitgeteilt, ich hörte es ... Was soll aus mir werden!' (p. 251) [He revealed my shame to my uncle, I heard him ... What will become of me!]. News of Bertha's 'love-affair' with Hollfeld is mentioned openly by the omniscient narrator at a later point. Bertha's 'condition' is alluded to on a number of occasions. For example, the following situation delicately suggests that Bertha's pregnancy, as well as her abandonment, was the cause of her night wanderings and anti-social behaviour: 'Als sie endlich erkannte, daß sie es mit einem Ehrlosen zu thun habe, da wurden ihr die ganzen Schrecken ihrer Lage klar. Sie geriet in Verzweiflung' (p. 250) [When she eventually recognized that she was involved with a man who had no honour, the full horror of her situation was clear to her. She began to despair]. Bertha is described as 'das warnende Exempel' (p. 251) [a salutary example]; her own lack of self-control — as well as Hollfeld's sensuality — has been her downfall. As the novel's example of human frailty, she is refused entry to her uncle's house and her story only ends well when one of her uncle's employees offers to marry her and take care of her in her exile. She is persuaded to emigrate to the United States of America with her uncle's money. Her disappearance from the novel prevents its 'happy ending' being disrupted by the reminder of licentious behaviour. Sexual transgression, all explicit mention of which has literally been suppressed, can be made good through repentance and marriage, but only off the printed page, out of sight of bourgeois society.

   With their familiar theme of 'virtue rewarded' and despite the independence of the heroines, Marlitt's novels, on the one hand, put forward a restrictive ideal of femininity. It is not so much female agency as stoical resistance that brings about the resolution: Goldelse indeed ends up — like a fairy-tale princess — trapped in a tower by Bertha, in need of rescue by her handsome prince before her happy ending can occur. On the other hand, however, the integrity of Elisabeth and Walde, asserted time and again through the theme of renunciation, contrasts with the abuses of the old era. Elisabeth's self-control enables her to offer passive resistance to the moral corruption around her. Moreover, by repeatedly delaying satisfaction through the act of renunciation, Goldelse undergoes an important process of self-development, ultimately entering into the adult realm, where she can acknowledge and act on her attraction to the hero. In contrast to the fear of sexuality and failed or frigid marriages of the realist novel,[21] the union of Else and Walde is characterized by warmth and honesty and it seems inevitable that their first-born child will be followed by further offspring.

In contrast, *Liselotte von Reckling* subverts the romantic script by failing to reward the heroine with a happy and fulfilling marriage. Reuter was a devotee of Nietzsche and her works — notably *Aus guter Familie (From a Good Family*, 1895) — reject what Nietzsche described as 'das Ideal einer blöden entsagenden demüthigen selbstlosen Menschlichkeit' [the ideal of a senseless renouncing humble selfless humanity].[22] For Reuter, *Entsagung* is a form of masochism.[23] In *Liselotte von Reckling*, childhood neglect makes the protagonist repeatedly seek affirmation of her own self through a damaging devotion to others' needs. Her eventual marriage is one-sided and leaves Liselotte isolated. When her husband tells her plainly that he no longer feels any passion for her, Liselotte accepts this 'mit müder Entsagung' (p. 274) [with tired resignation]. But eventually, she seeks fulfilment through a new life on her own. In the manner of Nora in Ibsen's *The Doll's House* (1879), Liselotte learns to prioritize her 'duty to herself'.

In the wake of Nietzsche and Ibsen, and with the growing women's emancipation movement, women writers like Gabriele Reuter, or her contemporary Hedwig Dohm (for example in *Schicksale einer Seele* (Fates of a Soul), 1899), explored ways of living which overtly challenged bourgeois social norms. Divorce and separation, for example, were taboo subjects from the 1840s to the 1890s, the period characterized by a conservative bourgeois literary market.[24] Novels around the turn of the twentieth century begin more explicitly to explore divorce, separation, and the possibility of new sexual freedoms, even 'die freie Liebe' [free love] (*Liselotte*, p. 124). *Liselotte* also explores the search for new, post-Christian systems of ethical values through an engagement with the ideas of theosophy, a religious faith with origins in Eastern religious thought which emerged in the late nineteenth century in the United States. Gabriele Reuter draws attention to the dangers of the act of repression inherent in self-denial and renunciation. Her novels show women sacrificing their health and sanity for the sake of conformity to external ideals. For Reuter, the act of reading could be an act of resistance, providing women with a temporary escape from patriarchy. *Liselotte von Reckling* provides the ill-treated protagonist with an escape route from a repressive marriage through separation and divorce. Moreover, by writing openly about Liselotte's sex during her honeymoon, her miscarriage, the death of her newborn infant, and her regret at her husband's refusal to share her bed with her, the novel attempts to overcome the act of repression inherent in the reticence of the realist narrative.

*Liselotte von Reckling* begins in a gothic setting, an austere former abbey, where portraits on the walls of the nuns of yesteryear are riddled with bullet holes left by the French who once occupied the convent (and symbolic perhaps of Reuter's own disdain for conventional Christianity). The portraits once disturbed the young Liselotte. Now, however, it is her own fate which keeps her awake at night. She is grieving for her recently deceased father. Her mother, a former actress, lived the high life in Monte Carlo and is laden with debt. It is noteworthy, perhaps, that while Reuter in her first novel, *Aus guter Familie*, sought to depict the fate of a woman whom she considered 'typical', here she chooses a girl whose background is exotic and at a considerable remove from the reader's own experience. Liselotte is vulnerable and cut off from those who loved her. Her father's mother and relatives reside in the former abbey, and to them (in the light of naturalism, perhaps) she seems genetically tainted by her mother's compulsive behaviour and 'immoral' background. Towards the start of the novel, Liselotte falls in love with one of her male cousins, but she learns that he is forbidden from marrying her. Her grandmother embodies all the negative stereotypes of stoicism and self-denial; she withholds affection from Liselotte and exhorts her grandsons to emulate her. Merely in this brief outline of the opening sections of the plot of *Liselotte von Reckling*, the relation to Marlitt's melodrama and implausible twists of plot is abundantly apparent.

Reuter was an atheist and an admirer of French naturalism; she attempts to avoid the sentimental novel's depictions of cosy domesticity. However, in the chapter which narrates the onset of Liselotte's period of depression following the death of her newborn son,[25] Liselotte weeps as she finds the sleeve in her work-box of an outfit which she had carefully prepared for him to wear: 'Sie hielt das Stückchen feiner Leinewand zwischen ihren zitternden Fingern, stille Tränen schlichen über ihre Wange. Die Sehnsucht war wieder da, der Schmerz brannte neu und heiß' (p. 241) [She held the little piece of fine linen between her trembling fingers and silent tears fell on her cheeks. Her longing returned; her pain throbbed, new and intense]. In order to draw attention to the suffering and isolation which Liselotte experiences in marriage, the language of sentimentalism is employed. Yet there is no meaning to Liselotte's suffering as there often is in the romance; it does not make her a stronger person or bring her closer to God: it is simply meaningless pain, which others do not understand and which Liselotte must endure.

Reuter's novel retains close links to earlier sentimental novels through the presentation of a female protagonist with whom we are encouraged to identify, and through her sudden twists of fortune which shock or surprise us. Janice Radway identified the escapism and compensatory function of the romance and points out that 'romances are valuable [...] in proportion to their lack of resemblance to the real world'.[26] Marlitt's novels provide a temporary and highly enjoyable escape from the pressures of domestic life and contain 'a powerful element of fantasy and wish fulfilment'.[27] While Reuter eschews the 'happily ever after' of the heroine falling into the hero's arms, her rewriting of the romantic script retains its escapism. One thinks of the eponymous Ellen in *Ellen von der Weiden* (1900) making love to a 'dwarf-like' decadent artist in the mountains which were her childhood home or the fleeting, yet explicitly sexual honeymoon experience in *Liselotte von Reckling*. However, the last line of *Liselotte* makes reference to the romantic 'dream' of marriage and motherhood only to subvert it. When Liselotte has finally dispatched her husband, Count Lorenz von Altenhagen, the narrative concludes:

> Liselotte strich über ihre Stirn und stand lange mit gefalteten Händen, tief beruhigt. Der Traum war zu Ende — ein selig-schrecklicher, ängstigender, quälerischer Traum. Sie war aufgewacht — war bei sich daheim — im Frieden — in schöner, heller Einsamkeit. (p. 324)

[Liselotte cast a hand over her brow and stood for a while with folded hands, calm and composed. The dream had ended — a dream which was heavenly but terrible, terrifying and a torment. She had awoken and was at home — in peace — in beautiful bright solitude.]

With neat symmetry, the dream of a happy bourgeois family life pursued in the first part of *Liselotte* becomes a nightmare, as the second half explores the reality of her self-sacrifice in marriage. At the end, the contented future to which the protagonist looks forward is not the renunciation of her own needs in submission to a husband but the bliss of 'a room of one's own' and independence from others.

*Liselotte von Reckling* is an ambivalent novel. Liselotte is the opposite of the feisty, outspoken, and committed heroines who make Marlitt's novels so attractive. Having abandoned hope of marrying her cousin, Liselotte encounters her mother for the first time in several years and devotes herself to looking after her. Her mother throughout the novel wields power over Liselotte which derives from her very ineffectualness. Unable to manage her finances or her relations with others, she relies time and again on Liselotte to rescue her from difficulties. Liselotte needs to be needed; she is damaged by an absence of love in her formative years and conditioned to seek to earn love through self-sacrificing service to others. Her devotion to her mother is described as '[ein] heimliche[s] Martyrium' (p. 276) [a secret martyrdom]. Unstable and devious, Liselotte's mother is in thrall to a new religious cult, closely resembling theosophy, led by the charismatic Count Lorenz von Altenhagen. Mother and daughter follow Altenhagen to Berlin, where Liselotte befriends a young man paralysed in an accident, another devotee of Altenhagen's, to whose offer of marriage she almost succumbs out of a sense of pity, before her mother engineers a marriage between Liselotte and Altenhagen himself.

In *Liselotte*, Reuter explores the contemporary fascination with new religions and post-Christian morality. Reuter writes in her autobiography of her friendship in the 1890s with Rudolf Steiner, who went on to lead the theosophy society in Germany.[28] Reuter visited Nietzsche with Steiner and friends, after Nietzsche's descent into madness, to view the Nietzsche archive and gaze at the great man himself. Theosophy was linked closely to transcendentalism; in *Liselotte*, Altenhagen explains his belief that each human being 'nur sich selbst verantwortlich ist, und sich selbst erlösen kann' (p. 253) [is only answerable to himself and can redeem himself]. Another figure later adds: 'es ist der innerste Kern unserer Lehre, daß man nicht urteilen soll über den anderen, sondern dessen Gewissen den einzigen Richter sein lassen' (p. 267) [it is the innermost kernel of our teaching that one should not stand in judgement over another man but should allow his conscience to be his only judge]. These statements reveal that the new teachings stand in opposition to the message of renunciation and self-denial for which Nietzsche criticized Christianity. Inherent in the teaching is a strong individualism which contains its own dangers. In Reuter's novel, the sect, 'die Erneuerten' (New Humanity), led by Altenhagen, seems to fill the gap left by the religious uncertainty of the *fin de siècle* for Liselotte's self-centred mother, for the invalid who falls in love with Liselotte and attempts to exploit her pity for him, and for countless others who find the social and sexual code of conventional society to be overly restrictive. However, to

Liselotte Altenhagen's new ethical code begins to seem like self-indulgence. The movement gives him almost celebrity status. His edits a journal called *Stimme der Wahrheit* (Voice of Truth) and his book *Gedanken eines Erneuerten* (Thoughts of a New Man) becomes the talk of the town, sold on railway station platforms and discussed all over Berlin. His followers argue over its key tenets and eventually challenge Altenhagen over the leadership, with key figures leaving the movement to set up their own. When he is faced with opposition, the tyrant in Altenhagen becomes clear even to Liselotte:

> [Sie fühlte] im Ton seiner Stimme etwas Neues, Erschreckendes. Er hielt sich nicht wie bisher für einen suchenden Menschen unter anderen Suchenden, er betonte sich als einen, der mit besonderen Gnadengütern ausgestattet, hoch über ihnen stand und sich gütig zu ihnen neigte. (p. 271)

> [In the tone of his voice, Liselotte discerned something new, something shocking. He no longer considered himself to be a man searching alongside other like-minded men; his tone revealed him to be one to whom particular grace had been bestowed, who towered over the others and looked down kindly on them.]

Just as Stuart, the paralysed man, in his physical weakness came to recognize his power over Liselotte through her pity for him, Altenhagen, in 'service' to others, achieves tremendous power. When Stuart's mother weakens Altenhagen by with-drawing her financial support from his good causes, Liselotte replaces that income by willingly sacrificing her money and home comforts out of pity for him.

In his private relationship with Liselotte, Altenhagen sets the agenda, first using her as a sexual plaything before reverting to his former abstinence, sublimating all his sexual energy into writing his bestselling book. On his honeymoon, his earlier repression of sexual needs results in obsessive behaviour, as he and Liselotte rarely leave the bedroom. For Altenhagen, sex becomes another means of exploring his own power: 'Und dann kam die Überraschung, als das zarte Mädchen sich schauernd [sic] und doch mit einer glühenden Inbrunst unter seinen Willen beugte' (p. 196) [and then came the surprise as, with a shiver and yet with glowing fervour, the tender girl yielded to his will]. Liselotte revels in her own physicality but finds it impossible to shake off the idea that sexual feelings are shameful: 'dann schämte sie sich wieder der ihr so fremden Triebe und bangte vor irgend einer Strafe, die sie von einem erzürnten Gott treffen könne' (pp. 198–99) [then she would become ashamed once more of the desires which seemed so strange to her and afraid of some kind of punishment that might be sent by an angry god]. Soon afterwards on the point of their returning to Berlin:

> wurde Liselotte krank und der Arzt legte ihr für einige Wochen die strengste Ruhe und Schonung auf. Es war nur eine eben auftauchende Hoffnung vernichtet worden, — und doch erwachten beide Ehegatten aus dem Rausch, der sie umfangen hielt, und blickten sich verstört in die Augen. (p. 200)

> [Liselotte became ill and the doctor prescribed her the strictest rest and recuperation for several weeks. A recently emerged hope had been dashed, that was all — and yet both husband and wife were awakened from the intoxication which had enveloped them and they looked at one another perturbed.]

Liselotte has suffered a miscarriage: 'Hoffnung' (hope) was the standard German euphemism for pregnancy, the inevitable result of their weeks of daily sexual intercourse. The reference to it opens in German with the words 'es war nur' [it was only]. This is intended ironically; we are distanced from the event by seeing it through the eyes of the male doctor and husband. The description of miscarriage is a rare example of a novel of this period engaging with the biological reality of women's lives as childbearers, as opposed to the rosy tableau of mother and infant with which *Goldelse* closes. However, the link is made between the miscarriage and Liselotte's guilt at her enjoyment of physical lovemaking. Although from a narrative point of view the link is made only in Liselotte's mind, the reader's identification with Liselotte risks making it seem that Liselotte has indeed been punished for Altenhagen's excesses. Later, Liselotte, dwelling on the death of her baby, wonders whether 'ein kräftigerer Egoismus' [a stronger egoism] during her pregnancy might not have resulted in a healthier baby who would have been able to thrive (p. 277). As well as drawing attention in both cases to Liselotte's unnecessary and damaging guilt, Reuter highlights the fragile balance between selfless submission to others and damage to one's own interests.

Altenhagen does not resemble the hero of a Marlitt novel, cold and indifferent at first, but transformed by his love for the heroine. He seeks a wife who would sacrifice her own needs to his noble causes: 'die ihr Leben und ihr Herz ausschließlich seiner Arbeit und seinem Wollen hingab' (p. 165) [who would devote her life and her heart exclusively to his work and his wishes]. Liselotte believes in a Christian God and in the solemn nature of marriage vows; Altenhagen admits before their marriage that he condones adultery (p. 127). He is eventually seduced by the apparently exotic (but fraudulent) Daja Minstrel and leaves with her for America to explore the combined attractions of sex and orientalism. Liselotte embodies the dangers of the repression of the needs of the self in the service of others, while Altenhagen and his followers highlight conversely the ethical problem of pursuing the desires of your own ego at the expense of others' needs and using others as a means to an end.

While *Entsagung* for Marlitt is a positive state which leads to self-fulfilment, in Reuter's novel it is a symptom of repression and closely linked to masochism. Reuter's novel goes further than its critique of *Entsagung*; it also highlights through the figures of Altenhagen, the paralysed man, and Liselotte's mother the dangers of egoism. Altenhagen reveals the love of power which can be inherent in service to others; the paralysed man and Liselotte's mother highlight the selfishness which can be achieved even in weakness. In the nineteenth-century sentimental novel, of which Marlitt's *Goldelse* is an excellent example, physical weakness can result in inner strength of character which enables a protagonist such as Else to withstand the hostility of those around her. Marlitt's novel depicts a model of ideal womanhood — and passive resistance — achievable through willing subordination to others. Reuter's novel, on the other hand, perceives an ethical ambivalence in the achievement of power through weakness; in *Liselotte*, the figures of Altenhagen, the mother, and the invalid seem to echo Nietzsche's ideas in *Menschliches, Allzumenschliches* (Human, All Too Human, 1878), when he claims: 'das Mitleiden [...] ist insofern eine Tröstung für die Schwachen und Leidenden, als sie daran erkennen, doch wenigstens noch

Eine [sic] *Macht zu haben*, trotz aller ihrer Schwäche: die *Macht wehe zu tun'* [pity is in that respect a comfort for those who are weak and suffering, inasmuch as they recognize that they at least have one remaining *power*, despite all their weakness: *the power to cause pain*].[29] Goldelse's pity is unambiguous and a source of her moral strength; Liselotte's pity in contrast leaves her open to exploitation by others and is the cause of many sorrows. In the comparison, then, between Marlitt's romance and the anti-romance of *Liselotte*, the engagement of the women's novel with society's ethical values is brought more sharply into focus. While *Goldelse* reveals *Entsagung* as essential to the middle-class desire for social ascendancy, *Liselotte von Reckling* draws attention both to the dangers of neglecting one's own interests and the ambivalence of the egoism inherent in the ideas of modernity.

The sentimental novel, subject to closer examination, is a type of fiction whose effect on the reader is more important than the philosophical or literary sophistication of the narrative. Sentimentalism is characterized by the desire to create identification with protagonists (Reuter's novel does not always maintain this) in order that their ethical awareness (their honesty and integrity) or a sense of pity or injustice at the extent of their suffering be transmitted. Susanne Clark refers to the sentimental novel as characterized by an aesthetic of commitment.[30] Integral to the sentimentality of nineteenth-century novels, in the end, is the authors' belief that their works could participate in the rapid changes which were taking place in society at this time. Through identification the novels offered reassurance at a time of rapid social change with industrialization and urbanization. The conservatism of Marlitt's novel can be read as a response to a growing sense of the instability of the prevailing social order, yet it nonetheless affirms women's desires and provides an escape from the monotony of everyday life. Liselotte's story may be far from the reality of Reuter's readers' own lives. Yet through Liselotte's suffering, as in a tragic drama, the readers are offered the consolation of identifying with one who suffers like themselves in order perhaps to arrive at the catharsis which offers momentary alleviation of their sorrows. Marlitt's *Goldelse* and Reuter's *Liselotte von Reckling* are ultimately attempts by women not merely to write the society in which they lived within the confines of what was publishable in the period, but also to rewrite it, to transmit their commitment to others and so to fashion a new set of values for a new era.

## Notes to Chapter 6

1. Hildegard Hoeller, *Edith Wharton's Dialogue with Realism and Sentimental Fiction* (Gainesville: University Press of Florida, 2000), p. 31.
2. In Anglo-American literature, since the appearance of Jane Tompkins's pioneering study, *Sensational Designs: The Cultural Work of American Fiction 1790–1860* (New York: Oxford University Press, 1985) and Nancy Armstrong, *Desire and Domestic Fiction* (New York: Oxford University Press, 1987), many studies have highlighted the importance of the discourse of sentimentality for nineteenth-century popular fiction by men and women and its relationship with the development of the realist novel. In French literature, Margaret Cohen, *The Sentimental Education of the Novel* (Princeton, NJ: Yale University Press, 1999) examines the idealist novel, its sentimentality, and its relationship with Balzac. One of the few pieces directly addressing this topic in German literature is Anna Richards, 'Sense and Sentimentality? Margarete Böhme's *Tagebuch einer Verlorenen* (1905) in Context', in *Commodities of Desire: The Prostitute in Modern German Literature*, ed. by Christiane Schönfeld (Rochester, NY: Camden House, 2000),

pp. 98–109. See also Charlotte Woodford, 'Suffering and Domesticity: The Subversion of Sentimentalism in Three Stories by Marie von Ebner-Eschenbach', *German Life and Letters*, 59 (2006), 47–61.

3. Eugenie Marlitt, *Goldelse*, serialised 1866, first publ. Leipzig: Ernst Keil, 1867. The edition used here is Eugenie Marlitt, *Goldelse* (Berlin: Sammlung Zenodot Bibliothek der Frauen, 2007). Many of Marlitt's works are available online at <www.zenodot.de>. Translations of the titles of Marlitt's novels are those of the original English translations. All other quotations are my own.

4. Gabriele Reuter, *Liselotte von Reckling* (Berlin: Fischer, 1904). All quotations are taken from this edition.

5. See Wolfgang Lukas, '"Entsagung": Konstanz und Wandel eines Motivs in der Erzählliteratur von der späten Goethezeit zum frühen Realismus', in *Zwischen Goethezeit und Realismus — Wandel und Spezifik in der Phase des Biedermeier*, ed. by Michael Titzmann (Tübingen: Niemeyer, 2002), pp. 113–49 (pp. 138–46).

6. Lukas, '"Entsagung"', p. 143.

7. Barbara Becker-Cantarino, '"Gender Censorship": On Literary Production in German Romanticism', *Women in German Yearbook*, 11 (1995), 81–97 (pp. 93–94).

8. Faranak Alimadad-Mensch, *Gabriele Reuter: Porträt einer Schriftstellerin* (Berne: Peter Lang, 1984), p. 2, citing Heinrich Gross, *Deutschlands Dichterinnen und Schriftstellerinnen: Eine literarhistorische Skizze*, 2nd edn (Vienna: Carl Gerolds Sohn, 1882), p. 262.

9. Ruth-Ellen Boetcher Joeres, *Respectability and Deviance: Nineteenth-Century German Women Writers and the Ambiguity of Representation* (Chicago: University of Chicago Press, 1998), p. 261.

10. Gabriele Reuter, *Aus guter Familie*, 2 vols first publ. 1895 (Marburg: Verlag LiteraturWissenschaft.de, 2004), I, 19.

11. See Todd Kontje, 'History as Melodrama in Felix Dahn's *Ein Kampf um Rom*', in *The Late Nineteenth-Century German Bestseller*, ed. by Charlotte Woodford and Benedict Schofield (Rochester, NY: Camden House, forthcoming).

12. Alberto Martino, *Die deutsche Leihbibliothek: Geschichte einer literarischen Institution (1756–1914)* (Wiesbaden: Harrassowitz, 1990), pp. 404–06.

13. See Kirsten Belgum, 'Domesticating the Reader: Women and *Die Gartenlaube*', *Women in German Yearbook*, 9 (1994), 91–111 and Eda Sagarra, 'Gegen den Zeit- und Revolutionsgeist: Ida Gräfin Hahn-Hahn und die christliche Tendenzliteratur im Deutschland des 19. Jahrhunderts', in *Deutsche Literatur von Frauen*, II, ed. by Gisela Brinker-Gabler (Munich: Beck, 1988), pp. 105–19. Also Boetcher Joeres, *Respectability*, p. 237.

14. Todd Kontje, *Women, the Novel, and the German Nation 1771–1871: Domestic Fiction and the Fatherland* (Cambridge: Cambridge University Press, 1998), p. 184, citing B. K. Starcher, 'Ernst Keil und die Anfänge der *Gartenlaube*', *Seminar*, 17 (1981), 205–13 (pp. 212–13).

15. Kontje, *Women, the Novel, and the German Nation*, p. 184.

16. Kirsten Belgum, 'E. Marlitt: Narratives of Virtuous Desire', in *A Companion to German Realism*, ed. by Todd Kontje (Rochester, NY: Camden House, 2002), pp. 259–82 (p. 275).

17. Kontje, *Women, the Novel, and the German Nation*, pp. 185–87.

18. Belgum, 'E. Marlitt', p. 275.

19. 'You seem to fancy that my conduct of yesterday [...] was a personal act between you and me; and that you may come and thank me for it, in stead of perceiving, as a gentleman would — yes! A gentleman [...] that any woman, worthy of the name of woman, would come forward to shield, with her reverenced helplessness, a man in danger from the violence of numbers.' (Elizabeth Gaskell, *North and South*, Part I, ch. 24, p. 195)

20. Lucas, '"Entsagung"', p. 127.

21. See Lucas, '"Entsagung"', pp. 138–46.

22. Friedrich Wilhelm Nietzsche, *Jenseits von Gut und Böse* (1886), §212.

23. See *After Intimacy: The Culture of Divorce in the West since 1789*, ed. by Karl Leydecker and Nicholas White (Oxford: Peter Lang, 2007), especially Karl Leydecker, 'Divorce and the Rise of the Women's Novel in Germany', pp. 11–29 (p. 29).

24. See Chris Weedon, 'Of Madness and Masochism: Sexuality in Women's Writing at the Turn of the Century', in *Taboos in German Literature*, ed. by David Jackson (Oxford: Berghahn, 1996), pp. 79–95.

25. See Anna Richards, *The Wasting Heroine in German Fiction by Women 1770–1914* (Oxford: Oxford University Press, 2004), pp. 162–67.

26. Janice Radway, *Reading the Romance: Women, Patriarchy and Popular Literature* (Chapel Hill: University of Carolina Press, 1984), pp. 88–89 and 100.

27. Belgum, 'E. Marlitt', pp. 259–60.

28. Gabriele Reuter, *Vom Kinde zum Menschen* (Berlin: Fischer, 1921), pp. 446–60.

29. Friedrich Wilhelm Nietzsche, *Menschliches, Allzumenschliches*, 1: *Ein Buch für freie Geister* (1878), §50.

30. Suzanne Clark, *Sentimental Modernism: Women Writers and the Revolution of the Word* (Bloomington: Indiana University Press, 1991), p. 199.

CHAPTER 7

# Marie von Ebner-Eschenbach's *Lotti, die Uhrmacherin* and the City: Questioning the 'Conservative'

*Linda Kraus Worley*

The noted historian Alice Kessler-Harris poses a provocative question in the title of an opinion piece that appeared in December 2007. She bluntly asks: 'Do We Still Need Women's History?'.[1] Commenting on recent trends in the United States that have tended to shift scholarly attention away from women's history, she observes that the 1990s witnessed:

> both a dramatic integration of women's history into the historical vocabulary, and a transition from the subject of women to the issues of gender. Since gender involved turning to an exploration of the social systems that underlay the relationships of men and women, it seemed to many historians to be a retreat from the effort to uncover the history of women per se. Women as women receded into the background, as something more abstract called gender relations came to the fore. (p. B6)

Kessler-Harris notes that the study of the history of women is seen 'as having celebratory content — its effort is to find our lost ancestors and restore them to a place in our memories' (p. B7). She contrasts the study of women's history which 'can be accused of lacking objectivity — of having a feminist purpose' with the powerful analytic framework of gender which 'suggests a more distanced stance' (p. B7). Although she underscores the value of gender studies as it investigates 'how the organization of relationships between men and women established priorities and motivated social and political action' (p. B7), she nonetheless insists on the necessity for a continued focus on women's history. Positing that the history of women 'constitutes the original database for gendered interpretation', she concludes that from 'a scholarly perspective, few people would argue that we know enough about, or sufficiently understand, the minds of women over time to believe that our data are complete, or complete enough' (p. B7). One conclusion to be drawn from Kessler-Harris's essay is that our incomplete database must be augmented by research into the full range of women's experiences and writings, not just those that can be readily celebrated as 'progressive' or 'protofeminist'.

   The debates among historians such as Kessler-Harris are part of more general discussions in academia, including literary studies, about the limits and possibilities of both feminist studies and gender studies. Kessler-Harris's reminder that the database of knowledge about women is far from complete is particularly applicable to German-speaking women writers of the eighteenth and nineteenth centuries who have been labelled 'conservative'. In the desire to find protofeminist foremothers during the purported celebratory phase of feminist scholarship, many literary scholars of the 1970s and 1980s directed their efforts towards writers whose texts were seen to contain subversive content or radical forms. Those who did not readily fit into these categories tended to be ignored. In *Respectability and Deviance* (1998), Ruth-Ellen Boetcher Joeres recounts her own early experiences:

> We saw subversion at every level, in every veiled reference to gender in the literary texts we were recovering; we also chose, if possible, to write about progressive writers, if we could locate them, and if we didn't — if we, as I did on one occasion, chose to talk about middle-class writers whose views were moderate (and in that way much more typical of most German women writers of their time) — we were criticized (as I was) for not furthering the feminist project.[2] (p. xxvii)

The privileging of women writers seen as progressive has dovetailed with a more general aversion in German literary studies to ideologies and people labelled 'conservative' or 'reactionary'. One might conjecture that the dark shadow of the Nazi era has cast suspicion on 'conservative' or 'reactionary' writers and periods as complicit in Germany's turn to fascism. Conversely, that which is considered 'progressive' can be seen as avoiding this taint.[3] Thus Todd Kontje begins the introduction to his recent *Companion to German Realism: 1848–1900* (2002) with the pithy statement: 'German realism of the nineteenth century has a bad reputation'.[4] He analyses the opinions of earlier critics who contended that the 'mild and tepid' 'liberals' of the 'later nineteenth century could offer only the cozy comforts of an anti-modern *Heimatliteratur* [regional literature] or an elitist cult of genius that ignored questions of modern urbanization and the workers' movement' (pp. 1–2). Kontje asserts that the essays in the volume 'demonstrate that it is not only possible to reawaken slumbering classics but also to discover new life in pages once cast into the dustbin of literary history' (p. 21).

Other scholars also specifically aim to problematize the 'bad reputation' of certain nineteenth-century eras and writers. In *Modernism and Cultural Conflict: 1880–1922*, for example, Ann Ardis convincingly reminds the reader that realism is an artistic mode not necessarily involving conservative politics, whereas modernist art, conversely, does not necessarily imply revolutionary politics. Boetcher Joeres, looking at women writers of the nineteenth century, underscores that:

> because of the particular position of women in society, because of the layers of stereotypical presuppositions and labels attached to them, because of the patriarchal ideology that so often determines what we all think and how we all act — because of the confusion of labels and representations — it is necessary to remove past interpretive layers before I can see what other, less label-bound interpretations are possible. (p. 9)

Such labels include terms such as 'conservative', 'sentimental', and 'domestic'. These labels are particularly pernicious in that their twenty-first-century connotations often bear scant resemblance to their nineteenth-century range of meanings. Some current research aims precisely at re-examining these labels in terms of their use in contemporaneous discourse networks. Charlotte Woodford, for example, looks anew at the discourse of sentimentality as it is used in the fiction of Ebner-Eschenbach.[5]

Marie von Ebner-Eschenbach (1830–1916) was long positioned in the scholarly and popular press as a conservative writer of Austrian realism who embodied goodness and compassion in her texts and life. Her literary fate reflects many of the tendencies outlined above and, as such, has been the focus of recent revisions. Karlheinz Rossbacher looks to Ebner as a representative of Vienna's liberal Ringstrasse era and thus underscores the anachronistic use of the label 'conservative' when applied to Ebner by modern critics.[6] Susanne Kord notes that Ebner's image as an 'erzählende Großmutter' (storytelling grandmother) tends to dominate her reception.[7] Among the labels that have played a role in the image-making that accompanied and still accompanies Ebner's career, the repeated stereotyping of her as old-fashioned and 'conservative' stands out. Kord describes two 'literaturgeschichtlichen Ausschlußmechanismen' [exclusionary mechanisms of literary history] particularly complicit in the lack of notice paid to Ebner's writing: 'zum einen die Tradierung der Autorin als Einzelfall und zum zweiten die Festlegung der Autorin auf "subjective" Genres wie Briefe, Erzählungen, Aphorismen und Autobiographisches' [firstly, the tradition of positing the woman author as a unique case and secondly, the restriction of the woman author to 'subjective' genres such as letters, stories, aphorisms, and the autobiographical, p. 1]. Due to these tendencies, Ebner has been denied proper integration in the context of nineteenth-century literature and the full range of her writing has not been recognized.

Ebner's complicated reception has other dimensions as well. In 'The Making (and Unmaking) of an Austrian Icon: The Reception of Marie von Ebner-Eschenbach as a Geopolitical Case Study' (2008), I build on previous scholarship in order to show how changing social, cultural, and political needs, desires, and fears operated to create a larger-than-life Austrian icon in the post-1871 era while limiting Ebner-Eschenbach's literary presence to that of the author of *Dorf- und Schloßgeschichten* (Village and Castle Stories), a position which helped undermine her reputation as a serious writer.[8] Recent changes in Ebner's reception have been fuelled in large measure by the feminist-oriented research of the past few decades.[9] Even a cursory glance at this scholarship reveals that Ebner and her texts have been analysed in many ways: with an emphasis on the female artist (Rose), the female protagonists (Tanzer; Manczyk-Krygiel), Ebner's diaries, autobiography, and dramas (Goodman; Gabriel; Kord), her life story and reception (Klostermeier; Toegel; Pfeiffer, 'Kanon'; Worley, 'Icon'), and, most recently, the ethnic and political discourses woven into her texts (Rossbacher; Worley, 'Czech'; Seeling; Wandruszka).[10] In addition, individual texts have received close readings, often for the first time (Thum; Worley, 'Telling Stories'; Dietrick; Pfeiffer, *Ebner*).[11]

In spite of the considerable scholarly activity which has broadened our perception of Ebner's range and begun to dismantle stereotypes, there remain facets of Ebner's work that have received little attention. One such area is the role Vienna as a city plays in a number of her texts. Harriman notes that some critics have criticized Ebner's work as out of date because 'she seems oblivious to the realities of modern life which center on the pressing problems of the cities'.[12] The assertion that Ebner is oblivious to life in the modern city is simply false. Despite the fact that Ebner has traditionally been associated with tales set in the countryside, she must also be acknowledged as a Viennese 'insider' who wrote a number of texts set in Vienna. Her intimate knowledge of the city came from first-hand experience. From childhood on, she and her family regularly spent the winter months in Vienna. Her husband, Moritz von Ebner-Eschenbach, was a military officer, engineer, and inventor, whose last military post was to direct the military's so-called 'Geniekomittee' [Genius Committee] in Vienna. Her extended aristocratic family had connections with multiple segments of society; indeed, she records in daily diary entries the myriad social visits she both made and received (many of which were noted as unwelcome interruptions of her work). Personal contact with scores of writers as well as other cultural and journalistic trendsetters was a part of Ebner's literary career even before her rise to fame. Numerous Vienna-based notables such as Betty Paoli, Ferdinand von Saar, and Josef Breuer were good friends. Her position in Viennese society likely prompted the writer Paul Heyse to advise her to write 'einen Roman aus der wiener [sic] Gesellschaft' [a novel of Viennese society].[13]

By reading Ebner's Vienna-based fiction as part of an urban-based literature, we add to our knowledge of the 'minds of women over time' (Kessler-Harris, p. B7), including women labelled 'conservative', further broaden our understanding of Ebner, and gain insights into the creation, dissemination, and/or disruption of discourses regarding life in a city in the late nineteenth century.[14] The literature of the Austrian Ringstrasse era, which ran roughly parallel to the German *Gründerzeit* [founding era] and British Victorian periods, has tended to receive much less attention than that of the later Austrian fin-de-siècle. Rossbacher takes a powerful step in countering this neglect in his excellent book *Literatur und Liberalismus: Zur Kultur der Ringstrassenzeit in Wien* (1992). Concentrating on Ferdinand von Saar, Ludwig Anzengruber, and Marie von Ebner-Eschenbach, Rossbacher examines core themes such as the role of the nobility and the Ringstrasse itself, as well as images of women, Jews, and different nationalities as they are foregrounded in the literature of the era. He does not, however, specifically examine Ebner's *Lotti, die Uhrmacherin*, which by dint of its publication in the prestigious *Deutsche Rundschau* in 1880 is considered to be the work which marked Ebner's literary breakthrough in Germany. This short novel, set in Vienna, deals in substantive ways with issues closely related to life in a modern city.[15] *Lotti* sketches a model of a successful city community, contrasts competing economic systems, and looks at the fate of a single, working woman. In addition, the uses and disadvantages of history for life, to reference the title of one of Nietzsche's *Unzeitgemäße Betrachtungen* (*Untimely Meditations*, 1873–76), is a major theme of the book.

It is perhaps worth recalling that Vienna did not suddenly appear as a city of note at the fin-de-siècle, but, as capital of the Habsburg realms, had played a prominent role in Europe's cultural life for centuries. Indeed, in the middle of the nineteenth century, Vienna ranked third in size in Europe after London and Paris, boasting a population of approximately half a million people. The Ringstrasse, planned in the 1850s, was designed to replace the extant military ring of fortifications with a broad, open artery that could effectively move people and, if needed, troops. As such, it created urban spaces similar to those built in Paris by Baron Hausmann. Officially opened in 1865, the Ringstrasse encircled the old inner city, which subsequently began to take on museum-like qualities.[16] The aristocracy and clergy tended to live in this part of the city. By contrast, the newly erected government and cultural buildings on the Ringstrasse reflected the power and prestige of the middle classes, especially the upper middle class with its liberal politics. The Ringstrasse thus became the dazzling symbol of the 'new' Vienna.

Given this background, it is significant that Ebner, whose own apartment was located in the old inner city, sets *Lotti* there as well, rather than in the 'new' Vienna.[17] The first pages of the novel focus on Charlotte (Lotti) Feßler's city apartment. Lotti's bedroom is furnished with an old-fashioned, carved bed and masterfully crafted clocks, among which is a 'deutsche Stockuhr, eine solide Arbeit Meister Anton Schreibelmeyers' [a German bracket clock, a solid work by Master Anton Schreibelmeyer].[18] As her clocks chime six, she listens with 'unendlichem Wohlgefallen' (p. 1) [infinite satisfaction] to their concert, which reminds her that it is time to go to work. The text places Lotti squarely in a solid, 'old-German' world. The reader also immediately learns that Lotti is thirty-five years old, single, and a watchmaker who considers herself to be physically plain (pp. 1–2). This last fact connects Lotte with other 'plain' nineteenth-century heroines such as Brontë's Jane Eyre, Stifter's Brigitta, and François's Hardine von Reckenburg, all of whom are resourceful, strong, and intelligent women.[19]

The description of the apartment's living room continues in the same vein. The narrator's descriptions overlap with what the narrator reports of Lotti's attitudes toward her city apartment. Lotti's 'trauliches Gemach' (p. 2) [cosy chamber] looks out onto a small courtyard, thus allowing her to be part of both the capital city and nature:

> Es will etwas heißen, im Herzen der Zivilisation zu wohnen, im Mittelpunkt der Hauptstadt, tausend Schritte vom Dome, den zu sehen viele Leute tausend Meilen weit hergezogen kommen, und dabei von seinem Fenster aus Wetterbeobachtungen [...] betreiben zu können, Wolken und Vögel ziehen, und der Sonne und dem Mond ins Gesicht zu sehen. (p. 2)

> [It means something to live in the heart of civilization, in the centre of the capital city, a thousand steps from the cathedral, which many travel a thousand miles to see, and at the same time be able to conduct observations of the weather [...] to see clouds and birds pass by and look the sun and the moon in the face.]

The novel does not provide panoramic views of the city's streets or districts; however, the novel does portray Lotti scanning her neighbours' windows. These neighbours are part of her city community and their stories are briefly told (pp. 2–6). Lotti has interacted with each of these apartment dwellers and has earned their respect; she has, for example, thwarted the attempted suicide of one of her neighbours, a tailor.

These first pages suggest that the novel will follow the nineteenth-century European 'apartment-house' plot discussed in Sharon Marcus's *Apartment Stories: City and Home in Nineteenth-Century Paris and London* (1999).[20] Marcus defines this plot type as one which follows the fates of tenants who are linked in various ways. The tenants are often revealed to be kin; there may be marriages among them. Very often an inquisitive doorman (or woman) links the external world of the city streets with the interior world of the apartments. In fact Ebner's *Lotti* does not continue with this plot trajectory, but the early pages of the novel do foreground the importance of the community created around the courtyard formed by the apartment buildings. Therefore Ebner's text is to be read in the context of her era's concerns with such dangers of the modern city as alienation and lack of community.[21]

The city was the focus of such well-known nineteenth-century critics of modern life as Ferdinand Tönnies (1855–1936) and Camillo Sitte (1843–1903). Tönnies's *Gemeinschaft und Gesellschaft* (Community and Society, 1887) contrasts a *Gemeinschaft* based on feelings of togetherness and mutual bonds with an individualistic, impersonal *Gesellschaft* based on monetary exchange. Ebner's fellow Viennese, Camillo Sitte, voices concerns about the modern city in *Der Städtebau in seinen künstlerischen Grundsätzen* (City Planning According to Artistic Principles), first published in 1889. Sitte's imagined city stands in sharp contrast to the Ringstrasse ideals. He advocated urban design principles which would prioritize the creation of comfortable, enclosed, and intimate public spaces alongside irregularly shaped streets, all designed to create a sense of community and thus combat urban loneliness and fragmentation. Lotti's inner-city courtyard community prefigures the reforms of modern society proposed at a later date by Tönnies and Sitte.

After Lotti ends her morning round of neighbourly greetings, the narrator comments that Lotti, 'konservativ wie sie einmal ist' [conservative as she is], wishes only 'daß alles beim alten bleibe' [that everything stay the same].[22] Her wish to conserve relationships is echoed in her attitude towards her living quarters. She has kept her father's antique German furniture, his hand-annotated, eclectic assortment of books and valuable collection of pocket watches in her living room. The fact that this room is notably cramped does not bother her. While admiring the way she is able to squeeze so much into a small space, she also experiences it as cosy: 'Je länger sie es bewohnte, desto gemütlicher erschien es ihr' (p. 6) [the longer she lived in it, the cosier it appeared to her].

Lotti's apartment is not to be read merely as a marker of her modest means, but rather points to an antiquarian relationship to the past. It is useful to recognize that *Lotti* is part of a net of cultural discourses regarding the role, indeed the dominance, of history in nineteenth-century thought and lives. The second of Nietzsche's *Unzeitgemäße Betrachtungen* (Untimely Meditations), *Vom Nutzen und Nachteil der Historie für das Leben* (On the Uses and Disadvantages of History for Life), was published in February 1874 and is central to a full understanding of Ebner's novel. We know from her diary entries that Ebner read Nietzsche. She notes on 8 April 1874, five years before her extensive work on *Lotti*:

> Dann blieb ich allein, las noch u [sic] war ganz vergnügt, las: *Unzeitgemäße Betrachtungen* von Dr. Nietzsche. Ich bin voll Bewunderung u. fühle mich

dennoch abgestoßen. Der Styl [sic] ganz einzig. So wurde in deutscher Sprache noch nicht geschrieben.

[Then I stayed alone, read on and was completely happy, read: *Untimely Meditations* by Dr Nietzsche. I am full of admiration and feel nevertheless repulsed. The style is unique. No one else has ever written like this in the German language.][23]

In an appendix to her diary of 1884, she again writes concerning Nietzsche: 'Geb 1844 Verf[asser] von *Unzeitgemäße Betrachtungen* (vier Bände) ein unerhört merkwürdiger Geist [sic] Wird noch viele Rätsel aufgeben und viele auflösen' [Born 1844 author of *Untimely Meditations* (four volumes) an incredibly unusual mind [sic] Will pose many puzzles yet and solve many].[24] Nietzsche's taxonomy and critique of various types of history — the monumental, antiquarian, and critical — resonate in Ebner's *Lotti*.

In the first part of *Lotti*, the heroine's relationship to the antiques surrounding her brings only contentment. In *Vom Nutzen und Nachteil der Historie für das Leben*, Nietzsche describes the positive aspects of an antiquarian relationship to the world:

Die Geschichte gehört zweitens dem Bewahrenden und Verehrenden — dem, der mit Treue und Liebe dorthin zurückblickt, woher er kommt, worin er geworden ist; durch diese Pietät trägt er gleichsam den Dank für sein Dasein ab. Indem er das von alters her Bestehende mit behutsamer Hand pflegt, will er die Bedingungen, unter denen er entstanden ist, für solche bewahren, welche nach ihm entstehen sollen — und so dient er dem Leben. Der Besitz von Urväter-Hausrat verändert in einer solchen Seele seinen Begriff: denn sie wird vielmehr von ihm besessen. Das Kleine, das Beschränkte, das Morsche und Veraltete erhält seine eigne Würde und Unantastbarkeit dadurch, daß die bewahrende und verehrende Seele des antiquarischen Menschen in diese Dinge übersiedelt und sich darin ein heimisches Nest bereitet.[25]

[History thus belongs in the second place to him who preserves and reveres — to him who looks back to whence he has come, to where he came into being, with love and loyalty; with this piety he as it were gives thanks for his existence. By tending with care that which has existed from of old, he wants to preserve for those who shall come into existence after him the conditions under which he himself came into existence — and thus he serves life. The possession of ancestral goods changes its meaning in such a soul: *they* rather possess *it*. The trivial, circumscribed, decaying, and obsolete acquire their own dignity and inviolability through the fact that the preserving and revering soul of the antiquarian man has emigrated into them and there made its home.][26]

Lotti infuses the things bequeathed to her by her father, Meister Johannes Feßler, with filial piety. Her attachment to these historical objects, especially the timepieces, transcends the personal in that they are connected to the greater world of monumental history through the extensive glosses Johannes added to a book on the history of watchmaking. Next to every discovery in his craft, he had noted a concurrent event of world importance, thus linking the artisans with the great men of history. The effect of his glosses is not to commemorate the great deeds, but to gesture towards the parallel greatness of the craftsmen's deeds. Within this context, the watch collection has become a kind of totem invested with deep meaning. Lotti means to preserve it at all costs. The collection's museum-like character is underscored by the fact that Lotti's will stipulates it be bequeathed to a city museum.

The first chapters of Ebner's novel thus address issues of central importance in the nineteenth century. The reader glimpses a model of successful city life as practised by Lotti towards her neighbours. In addition, the value of an antiquarian relationship to history is underscored, especially when it values the work and lifestyle of traditional artisans. The importance accorded to the crafts is reflected in the fact that Ebner originally planned to call this novel *Kunst und Handwerk* (Art and Craft). Lotti, the artisan, can be seen as a kind of artist, as Rose argues in *The Guises of Modesty: Marie von Ebner-Eschenbach's Female Artists* (1994). In addition to this theme, the novel contrasts the artisan way of life with an exclusively profit-oriented realm, in this case, the world of publishing.

The artisan class experienced massive changes during the course of the nineteenth century as liberalism and capitalism put to rest corporatism. Indeed, as historian James R. Farr notes, 'Most artisans entered the nineteenth century with a corporate, communal sense of themselves, and exited without one'.[27] Guilds were abolished in Austria in 1859. This act undermined traditional artisan culture as it opened the trades to non-guild members. Corporatism had been far more than an economic system in that it provided artisans with a status-based identity rooted in community. Financial solvency, in particular owning one's own household, was the economic foundation of respectability. This independence was, according to Farr, the 'badge of respectable social rank for artisans, and thus was at the core of their identity and culture' (p. 100). As the century progressed, the artisan class bifurcated into propertyless wage earners and proprietary artisans, the small shopkeepers. *Lotti*, set in the 1870s, captures the clash between the artisanal work culture and the capitalistic market forces which would create a commercialized mass culture by the end of the century.

By means of a flashback, the novel reveals how the equilibrium of Meister Feßler's home and workplace, where both Lotti and her devoted adopted brother, Gottfried, had become accomplished watchmakers, was disrupted by the arrival of Hermann von Halwig. An aspiring poet, Halwig is intrigued by Feßler's craft and way of living. His enthusiasm embraces Lotti and they become engaged. Halwig pursues his art; however, as his writing becomes ever more popular, it becomes less artistic. When Lotti criticizes the direction his work is taking, he pulls away from her. She eventually breaks the engagement. Years pass and Lotti lives as a single working woman in independent, industrious contentment. A chance encounter with Halwig, now married, re-establishes their connection and allows her to see how the harsh demands of the modern publishing business have affected him. Halwig, goaded on by pressing financial needs stemming from the conspicuous consumption of his wife, Agathe, is forced to churn out one, hopefully best-selling, sensation novel after another. He works very diligently, but cannot meet his contractual quotas. His financial situation is driving him towards an even more inhumane contract, one that would oblige him to deliver three novels a year for the next ten years. This hectic pace, a hallmark of modern capitalist society, has taken its toll on his health, especially his nerves, which are 'bis zum Zerreißen gespannt' (p. 59) [stretched to ripping point]. Halwig recognizes to a limited extent his loss of autonomy, remarking at one point to Gottfried, '"ich lebe nicht — ich schreibe"' (p. 55) [I don't live — I write], commenting to Lotti on another occasion about the nature of his work: '"aber ich bin ein Sklave ... ein freiwilliger natürlich — einer der vernarrt ist in seiner Sklaverei"' (p. 53) [but I am a slave ... a voluntary one, naturally — one who is infatuated with his slavery]. In order for the products of his labours to remain popular and thus marketable, Halwig has had to bow to the tastes of the reading public. He tells Lotti '"dem Geschmack der Zeit muß man Konzessionen machen ... m a n m u ß [sic]"' (p. 64) ['one has to make concessions to the taste of the times ... o n e   h a s   t o']. His is no longer the solid, old-German economic environment within which the Feßlers laboured and still labour.

Meister Johannes Feßler was known for the quality of his work. Lotti and Gottfried continue the tradition and both are highly respected in Vienna for their skill. Other watchmakers, for example, often send their most difficult repairs to Lotti. Within this system there is room for a woman to be a masterful artisan, but a woman cannot officially obtain the rank of master. There are other gender-based inequalities as well. Gottfried had, for example, been sent to London to complete his education, whereas Lotti had to stay in Vienna.[28] Nevertheless, both are presented as successful, unalienated workers in charge of their own time and means of production. Gottfried becomes a proprietary artisan, opening his own shop which, significantly, has a glass shop window. This detail underscores that he plans to attract, among others, the new class of female shoppers as they walk the city streets peering into display windows. The sign he mounts on the store — 'G. und L. Feßler' — gives equal billing to Lotti. Although Gottfried is changing and adapting to the new economic realities, the novel gives no indication that he will forfeit his independent status and succumb to the nervous pace of the capitalist system. Indeed, Gottfried consciously plans to continue to place his craft above business considerations: 'Das neu errichtete Geschäft ließ sich vortrefflich an, und doch wollte er nicht so ganz Kaufmann werden, daß er am Ende seine Uhrmacherei darüber vernachlässigte' (p. 62) [The newly established store got off to an excellent start, and yet he did not want to become so completely the businessman that he would in the end neglect his watchmaking for it].

The discourses addressed above shed new light on the end of the novel. After learning that Halwig can be bought out of his contractual difficulties, Lotti sells the watch collection and has the proceeds secretly funnelled to him. Halwig and his wife immediately retreat to what they envision will be a country paradise far from the perils of the city. Lotti follows their open invitation, travelling by train to the Halwigs' country estate, but leaves without approaching them when she sees the pair arm in arm, fully wrapped up in each other. Events on the trip home reinforce her feelings of isolation. She is jolted out of her loneliness when she is met at the station by Gottfried, whose love she finally recognizes and returns. They marry soon thereafter and their peaceful union is made even happier after the birth of a son.

The novel's ending has been variously criticized. Rose, for example, argues that 'Conservative pressures on writers such as Droste-Hülshoff, Paoli, François and

Ebner-Eschenbach often prompted them to resolve the social tensions implicit in the construction of independent heroines by ending the narrative with a forced ideal of motherhood' (p. 104). Rose also reads Lotti's sale of the watches as an event which deprives her of her identity: 'for she had already lost her family — her father to old age, and her foster brother to his apprenticeship overseas — and now she has forfeited the property on which she based her professional life' (p. 106). Writing over a hundred years earlier than Rose, the writer Fanny Lewald, according to an entry in Ebner's diary, criticized the fact that in *Lotti* 'aus schwachherziger Liebe und Freundschaft einem Elenden geholfen wird' [a miserable person was helped from motives of weak-hearted love and friendship].[29] These criticisms are justifiable only if the novel is read within a framework that reads marriage and a family as a convenient, 'conservative', even sentimental ending to an otherwise protofeminist tale of an independent working woman artist, or which interprets Lotti's sale of the watches as an act of self-renunciation. Ebner herself explicitly responded to Lewald's reading by insisting in this same diary entry that it was not love, but 'Barmherzigkeit' [compassion] which motivated Lotti to help Halwig financially and that Lotti 'thuts wegen sich' (p. 25) [does it for herself]. The novel validates Ebner's assertion. For example, Lotti's actions fit squarely with her earlier compassionate behaviour towards her city neighbours. Even more to the point, Lotti's chance encounter with Halwig on a city street sets into motion a series of events that propel Lotti out of her comfortable cocoon in which everything remains the same. She now enters the changing stream of life, a world she has not yet experienced. Her act of selling the collection is, indeed, for herself.

In *Vom Nutzen und Nachteil*, Nietzsche does not stop with the 'Nutzen', the positive uses of an antiquarian relationship to life, but also underscores the 'Nachteil', the negatives that can impede an individual from living life fully. Because the antiquarian historical sense 'versteht eben allein Leben zu *bewahren* [sic], nicht zu zeugen' (p. 31) ['For it knows only how to *preserve* life, not how to engender it', p. 75], Nietzsche identifies dangers 'wenn die Historie dem vergangnen Leben so dient, daß sie das Weiterleben und gerade das höhere Leben untergräbt, wenn der historische Sinn das Leben nicht mehr konserviert, sondern mumisiert' (p. 31) ['when the study of history serves the life of the past in such a way that it undermines continuing and especially higher life, when the historical sense no longer conserves life but mummifies it', p. 75]. Although Lotti has been surrounded by ticking clocks, she has ironically been living in a realm where time has stopped. There is neither freedom of movement nor freedom to change in a space crowded by the furniture of the past, both literally and symbolically. Thus, Lotti's selling the collection does deprive her of an identity, but, I would argue, divests her of an identity that had begun to take on a museum-like quality. Her break with the past will allow her to live. Nietzsche also notes that from time to time an individual must have a critical relation to history: 'Er muß die Kraft haben und von Zeit zu Zeit anwenden, eine Vergangenheit zu zerbrechen und aufzulösen, um leben zu können' (p. 32) ['If he is to live, man must possess and from time to time employ the strength to break up and dissolve a part of the past', p. 75].

The process of selling the clocks is quickly completed: Lotti agrees on a price with an agent and the collection is gone. She does not particularly mourn its absence. Her journey into the changing stream of life continues quite literally when she journeys by train into the countryside to visit the Halwigs. Events on this trip give her new perspectives unobtainable in her museum life in the old part of the city. She finds herself in the exalted mood which 'beinahe jedes Stadtkind erfaßt, wenn es plötzlich aus seiner ummauerten in die unbegrenzte Welt versetzt wird' (p. 114) ['grabs almost every child of the city, whenever he is suddenly transported out of his walled world into the boundless world']. She paints a rosy picture of the benefits of nature and country life over city life. At first, she interprets all of her experiences through this filter: the beautiful day, the walk to Halwig's estate, her musings in the estate's grove of trees. When she recognizes that the Halwigs as a pair do not need her, she is forced to recognize the isolation inherent in her status as 'odd woman', one of those single working women George Gissing portrays in his 1893 novel *The Odd Women*.[30] An initially warm reception in the family of a stationmaster turns chilly when the stationmaster's wife learns that Lotti, rather than being part of a couple, is an old maid, an 'alte Jungfer' (p. 119) and as such is suspect. Her train compartment on the ride back, filled with a noisy group of friends, acts to magnify her feelings of isolation. There can be no doubt that these events, coupled with her sale of the watch collection, alter her life.

Choosing a life with Gottfried can be read as a retreat to a subservient, self-abnegating position as married woman and mother only if the broader cultural discourses woven throughout the novel are ignored. These discourses point to the fact that marriage and a child add to, rather than subtract from, Lotti's life. There is, for example, no indication that she will cease working as a skilled watchmaker or that the relationship of equals symbolized by the shop sign 'G. und L. Feßler' will end. There is no indication that she will cease creating a community of intimate neighbours in the city environment. These parts of her life will continue, but added to them will be other aspects of life previously absent such as passion and the birth of a child, which is itself a potent creation. Lotti no longer, in Nietzsche's words, merely conserves ['bewahren'] life, but creates it ['zeugen']. Although Nietzsche was almost certainly not thinking of the trajectory of a woman's life in his cultural critique, in this novel Ebner does. Ending the novel with marriage and motherhood need not be disparaged as 'conservative' or 'sentimental'. Lotti's story underscores that portrayals of positive life trajectories for women need not be limited to tales of rebellious heroines who run from entrapping and denigrating marriages or who become bohemian free spirits loose in a city.

The last paragraphs of the novel work against a stereotype the plot itself has evoked: the anti-urbanist belief that life in the country washes away the dirt associated in the popular imagination with city life. According to this script, life far away from the hectic pace and perils of the city should allow Halwig and Agathe to live contentedly. He would be free of publication pressures; she would regain her health. Indeed, during her ill-fated trip to the Halwigs' country estate, everything Lotti sees fits perfectly into this idyllic image. The Halwigs' blissful state in nature, however, does not last. Agathe gets bored and the couple quickly use up the money that was Lotti's gift. Even more tellingly, Halwig misses the nervous tension caused by deadlines as well as the excitement that comes with the creation of sensational plots. He feels 'Sehnsucht nach den Qualen und Wonnen seiner Lohnschreibernächte, nach dem Fieber, das ihn durchraste, wenn er seine Romanfiguren schuf, sie leiden, sündigen, in Blut und in Schlamm waten ließ' (p. 122) [longing for the tortures and delights of his nights as a paid hack; for the fever, which coursed through him when he created his characters, made them suffer, sin, and wade through blood and mud]. He returns to the city, to the 'seligen Bitternissen seiner Schriftstellerei' (p. 122) [holy hardships of his dabblings]. Lotti's sale of the watches was in this respect futile in that it did not give the Halwigs a fairy-tale ever after in the countryside. The dénouement would be quite cynical if the emphasis with regard to Lotti's renunciation were on the Halwigs' salvation. Instead, the sale of the watches is a highly productive act because, as I have argued, Lotti's new life depends on her ceasing to cling to a mummified past.

Ebner might have constructed a storyline in which Lotti's movement away from the negative potential inherent in her antiquarian relationship to history led to events in which she embraced her 'odd-woman' status and lived triumphantly freed from her past in the 'new' parts of Vienna. Such a plot resolution might easily have been embraced as protofeminist. However, Lotti's marriage to an equal, the birth of a child, and her position as a respected artisan in a community within the city, are outcomes which should not be judged negatively as a movement away from individual fulfilment. It is worth remembering that reform-minded critics of the limits and de-humanizing aspects of the city and city life both now and in the nineteenth century have regularly imagined alternatives which involve spaces and economic structures capable of sustaining community as well as individuality.[31] Such constructs should not be dismissed out of hand as 'conservative', 'archaic', or 'romantic'.[32] Nor should certain plot resolutions such as marriage and family automatically be labelled (and denigrated) as sentimental. At least one early reviewer of *Lotti* praises Ebner precisely as one who writes without sentimentality. Szczepański writes that Lotti is 'eine von den großen, starken und stillen Frauenseelen, die Frau von Ebner-Eschenbach so überzeugend in jeder ihrer Regungen und Handlungen und ohne alle Sentimentalität zu schildern versteht' [one of those great, strong, and quiet female souls, whom Frau von Ebner-Eschenbach is able to portray so convincingly in each of their emotions and strivings and without any sentimentality].[33]

Scholars such as Boetcher Joeres attempt to remove the 'layers of stereotypical presuppositions and labels' in order to 'see what other, less label-bound interpretations are possible' (p. 9). Stripping away labels can free writers such as Ebner from the limitations inherent in such problematical terms as 'conservative', 'progressive', and 'protofeminist'. Ebner then emerges as a complex writer deeply engaged with contemporaneous discourses. As I have shown, *Lotti* deals with powerful economic and social forces affecting life in the nineteenth-century city. Ebner plots a course for her heroine Lotti, 'konservativ wie sie einmal ist' (p. 6) [conservative as she is], that allows Lotti to avoid the dangers of a life-denying conservation of her father's watch collection, representing an antiquarian relationship to history, while conserving her dedication to community, compassion, and family within the changing urban social and economic landscape. It is short-sighted to read Lotti's values only as part of the discourse of female domesticity. Instead, her values need to be examined as part of her era's concerns regarding the social parameters within which an individual can live in modern times as articulated by, for example, Tönnies, Sitte, Nietzsche, and Ebner. A stereotypical, superficial use of the term 'conservative' is insufficient to deal with the intricacies of Ebner's text and Ebner as a writer.

   Given this framework, Ebner and other 'conservative' women of the eighteenth and nineteenth centuries, and the images of women in their work, need further research. Both the celebration of subversive, 'radical' women writers and the abstract analysis of gendered social relations tend to be 'partial' efforts, in both senses of the word. If we agree with Kessler-Harris that from 'a scholarly perspective, few people would argue that we know enough about, or sufficiently understand, the minds of women over time to believe that our data are complete, or complete enough' (p. B7), then we must recognize that, since all women writers helped create, disseminate, preserve, and/or disrupt the social, cultural, and political discourses of their eras, our scholarly efforts must encompass all women writers. New, more nuanced interpretations will follow.

## Notes to Chapter 7

1. Alice Kessler-Harris, 'Do We Still Need a Women's History?', *The Chronicle Review*, supplement to *The Chronicle of Higher Education* (7 Dec. 2007) pp. B6–B7. The shift towards the purportedly more analytical framework of gender studies has received much scholarly comment. For example, Dietz asserts that the analytical framework supplied by gender studies can be so abstract as to erase the specificity of women's history and can obscure the need for political action. Dietz adds another dimension to the discussion by noting that investigating the multiplicity of constructed masculinities circulating in a given era can result in men being at the centre of analysis once more. See Mary G. Dietz, 'Current Controversies in Feminist Theory', *Annual Review of Political Science*, 6 (2003), 399–431. See also Toby L. Ditz, 'The New Men's History and the Peculiar Absence of Gendered Power: Some Remedies from Early American Gender History', *Gender & History*, 16.1 (2004), 1–35, and the chapters by Anne Fleig and Anke Gillier in this volume.
2. Ruth-Ellen Boetcher Joeres, *Respectability and Deviance: Nineteenth-Century German Women Writers and the Ambiguity of Representation* (Chicago: University of Chicago Press, 1998), p. xxvii.
3. Historians have paid attention to 'conservative' figures and eras as part of their attempt to understand the rise of fascism. The titles of books such as Louis L. Snyder's *From Bismarck to Hitler: The Background of Modern German Nationalism* (Williamsport, PA: The Bayard Press, 1935) and William Montgomery McGovern's *From Luther to Hitler: The History of Fascist-Nazi Political Philosophy* (Boston: Houghton Mifflin, 1941) set the tone for this line of scholarly inquiry.
4. Todd Kontje, 'Reawakening German Realism', in *A Companion to German Realism: 1848–1900*, ed. by Todd Kontje (Rochester, NY: Camden House, 2002), pp. 1–28 (p. 1).
5. Charlotte Woodford, 'Realism and Sentimentalism in Marie von Ebner-Eschenbach's *Unsühnbar*', *Modern Language Review*, 101.1 (2006), 151–66 and 'Suffering and Domesticity: The Subversion of Sentimentalism in Three Stories by Marie von Ebner-Eschenbach', *German Life and Letters*, 59.1 (2006), 47–61.
6. Karlheinz Rossbacher, *Literatur und Liberalismus: Zur Kultur der Ringstrassenzeit in Wien* (Vienna: J&V, 1992).
7. *Letzte Chancen: Vier Einakter von Marie von Ebner-Eschenbach*, ed. by Susanne Kord (London: Modern Humanities Research Association, 2005), p. 7.
8. Linda Kraus Worley, 'The Making (and Unmaking) of an Austrian Icon: The Reception of Marie von Ebner-Eschenbach as a Geopolitical Case Study', *Modern Austrian Literature*, 41.2 (2008), 19–39.

9. These readings tend, like much early feminist scholarship, to emphasize 'progressive' or 'feminist' tendencies. Rossbacher points out inaccuracies in some of this scholarship as it takes Ebner to task for not having done more for women's emancipation (p. 370).

10. Ferrel V. Rose, *The Guises of Modesty: Marie von Ebner-Eschenbach's Female Artists* (Columbia, SC: Camden House, 1994); Ulrike Tanzer, *Frauenbilder im Werk Marie von Ebner-Eschenbachs* (Stuttgart: Heinz, 1997); Monika Mánczyk-Krygiel, *An der Hörigkeit sind die Hörigen schuld* (Stuttgart: Heinz, 2002); Katherine Goodman, *Dis/closures: Women's Autobiography in Germany between 1790 and 1914* (New York: Lang, 1986); Norbert Gabriel, ' "... daß die Frauen in Deutschland durchaus Kinder bleiben müssen ...": Die Tagebücher der Marie von Ebner-Eschenbach', in *Des Mitleids tiefe Liebesfähigkeit: Zum Werk der Marie von Ebner-Eschenbach*, ed. by Joseph P. Strelka (Berne: Lang, 1997), pp. 77–95; Susanne Kord, 'Introduction', in *Letzte Chancen: Vier Einakter von Marie von Ebner-Eschenbach* (see n. 7), pp. 1–20 and 'Introduction', in *Macht des Weibes: Zwei historische Tragödien von Marie von Ebner-Eschenbach*, ed. by Susanne Kord (London: Modern Humanities Research Association, 2005), pp. 1–18; Doris M. Klostermaier, *Marie von Ebner-Eschenbach: The Victory of a Tenacious Will* (Riverside, CA: Ariadne, 1997); Edith Toegel, *Marie von Ebner-Eschenbach: Leben und Werk* (New York: Lang, 1997); Peter C. Pfeiffer, 'Im Kanon und um den Kanon herum: Marie von Ebner-Eschenbach', in *Kanon und Kanonisierung als Probleme der Literaturgeschichtsschreibung*, ed. by Peter Wiesinger and Hans Derkits (Berne: Lang, 2003), pp. 113–18; Linda Kraus Worley, ' "Plotting the Czech Lands": Marie von Ebner-Eschenbachs Konstruktionen des Tschechischen', in *Herausforderung Osteuropa: Die Offenlegung stereotyper Bilder*, ed. by Theda Kahl, Elisabeth Vyslonzil, and Alois Woldan (Munich: Oldlenbourg, 2004), pp. 135–48; Claudia Seeling, *Zur Interdependenz von Gender- und Nationaldiskurs bei Marie von Ebner-Eschenbach* (St Ingbert: Röhrig Universitätsverlag, 2008) and Marie Luise Wandruszka, *Marie von Ebner-Eschenbach: Erzählerin aus politischer Leidenschaft* (Vienna: Passagen, 2008).

11. Reinhard Thum, 'Oppressed by Generosity: Dismantling the Gilded Marital Cage in Marie von Ebner-Eschenbach's "Erste Trennung" ', in *Neues zu Altem*, ed. by Sabine Cramer (Munich: Fink, 1996), pp. 57–66; Linda Kraus Worley, 'Telling Stories/Telling Histories: Marie von Ebner-Eschenbach's "Er laßt die Hand küssen" ', in *Neues zu Altem*, ed. by Sabine Cramer (Munich: Fink, 1996), pp. 43–56; Linda Dietrick, 'Gender and Technology in Marie von Ebner-Eschenbachs "Ein Original" ', *Women in German Yearbook*, 17 (2001), 141–64 and Peter C. Pfeiffer, *Marie von Ebner-Eschenbach: Tragödie, Erzählung, Heimatfilm* (Tübingen: Narr Francke Verlag, 2008).

12. Helga H. Harriman, 'Introduction', in *Seven Stories by Marie von Ebner-Eschenbach*, trans. by Helga H. Harriman (Columbia, SC: Camden House, 1986), p. xix.

13. Ebner writes in her diary on April 20, 1884: 'Ida [Fleischl, a close friend of Ebner's] schreibt viel liebes von Heyse, dem die *Muschi* [*Comtesse Muschi: Eine Novelette aus Österreich*] sehr gefallen hat und der mir räth einen Roman aus der wiener [sic] Gesellschaft zu schreiben' [Ida writes many dear things about Heyse, who liked *Muschi* [*Countess Muschi: A Novelette from Austria*] very much and who advises me to write a novel of Viennese society] (Marie von Ebner-Eschenbach, *Tagebücher III: 1879–1889*, ed. by Karl K. Polheim (Tübingen: Niemeyer, 1993), p. 401).

14. I use the term 'urban-based literature' and not 'narrated city' because Ebner's novel does not meet the strict criteria set by Klotz who limits his analyses in *Die erzählte Stadt* (The Narrated City) to those novels which encompass 'die Stadt selber, der sie sich mehr oder minder ausschließlich verschreiben. Wenn sie die Stadt zum Vorwurf nehmen, handeln sie nicht nur davon: ihr Aufbau, ihre Sicht, ihr Stil sind — von Mal zu mal anders — davon geprägt' [the city itself, on which they more or less totally concentrate. Whenever they use the city as a subject, they don't just use it in the plot: their structure, their subject position, their style are — each time differently — formed by the city] (Volker Klotz, *Die erzählte Stadt* (Munich: Hanser, 1969), p. 10).

15. Rose concentrates on Lotti as a female artist who is called to cure (Rose, pp. 86–118); Henn briefly notes that Lotti is a working woman in her introduction to *Lotti, die Uhrmacherin* (Stuttgart: Reclam, 1999), p. xx.

16. Carl E. Schorske, *Fin-de Siècle Vienna: Politics and Culture* (New York: Random House, 1961), p. 31.

17. This biographical fact coupled with Ebner's own collector's passion for watches may well have previously obscured the artistic relevance of place and artefacts in the novel.

18. Marie von Ebner-Eschenbach, 'Lotti, die Uhrmacherin', *Sämtliche Werke*, 6 vols (Berlin: Paetel, 1920), III, 1–123 (p. 10). Further references are to this edition; all translations are my own.

19. Charlotte Brontë, *Jane Eyre* (1847); Adalbert Stifter, *Brigitta* (1844); Louise von François, *Die letzte Reckenburgerin* (1871).

20. Sharon Marcus, *Apartment Stories: City and Home in Nineteenth-Century Paris and London* (Berkeley, CA: University of California Press, 1999).

21. Klotz, for example, reads Raabe's *Die Chronik der Sperlingsgasse* (1857) in terms of a created domestic community versus the alienation of the city in the chapter 'Stadtflucht nach Innen' (pp. 167–93).

22. *Lotti*, p. 6. The novel's opening frame compares Lotti's relationships to her neighbours with relationships among neighbouring countries. Rose integrates this scene into her argument that Ebner employs a rhetoric of diminution in her fiction (pp. 91–98). For further arguments regarding Ebner's rhetoric of diminution, see Elisabeth Endres, 'Marie von Ebner-Eschenbach', in *Frauen: Porträts aus zwei Jahrhunderten*, ed. by Hans Jürgen Schultz (Stuttgart: Kreuz, 1981) and Claudio Magris, *Der habsburgische Mythos in der österreichischen Literatur* (Salzburg: Otto Müller, 1966).

23. *Tagebücher II: 1871–1878*, pp. 256–57.

24. *Tagebücher III*, p. 445. Ebner remained interested in Nietzsche for the rest of her life. As evidenced by numerous diary entries, her opinions varied from the quite negative to the positive. Although she responded to *Jenseits von Gut und Böse* (Beyond Good and Evil) as a 'philosophische Modekrankheit' [philosophical fad illness] in a 1898 diary entry, she struck a more positive note in 1909 when quoting from a review which underscored the new 'Sehnsuchtsbild [sic] vollkommener Güte' [picture of longing of complete goodness] in *Also sprach Zarathustra* (Thus spoke Zarathustra). *Tagebücher V*, p. 86; *Tagebücher VI*, p. 209.

25. Friedrich Nietzsche, *Vom Nutzen und Nachteil der Historie für das Leben* (Stuttgart: Reclam, 1982), pp. 27–28. All references are to this edition.

26. All translations are taken from Friedrich Nietzsche, *Untimely Meditations*, ed. by Daniel Breazeale and trans. by R. J. Hollingdale (Cambridge: Cambridge University Press, 1997), pp. 72–73.

27. James R. Farr, 'The Disappearance of the Traditional Artisan', in *A Companion to Nineteenth-Century Europe, 1789–1914*, ed. by Stefan Berger (Malden, MA: Blackwell, 2006), pp. 98–108 (p. 107).

28. Both Rose and Manczyk-Krygiel underscore these gender disparities. However, Manczyk-Krygiel's assertion that Lotti's tears when Gottfried leaves for London express 'ihren Ärger und Schmerz über die ungleichen Bildungschancen für Männer und Frauen' [her anger and pain concerning the unequal educational opportunities for men and women] is not grounded in the text. Manczyk-Krygiel, *An der Hörigkeit sind die Hörigen schuld*, p. 186.

29. Diary entry of 9 April 1880. *Tagebücher III*, p. 25.

30. For a detailed discussion of this term and character type, see Linda K. Worley, 'The "Odd" Woman as Heroine in the Fiction of Louise von François', *Women in German Yearbook*, 4 (1987), 155–65.

31. See, for example, Andrew Lees, *Cities, Sin, and Social Reform in Imperial Germany* (Ann Arbor, MI: The University of Michigan Press, 2002).

32. One example of such criticism is Schorske's reference to Camillo Sitte's 'archaism' (p. 61) with respect to his urban plans. The limits of such labels are particularly evident in light of the twenty-first century's emphasis on the environment, green spaces, and community.

33. Paul von Szczepański, 'Neues vom Büchermarkt', *Velhagen & Klasings Neue Monatshefte*, 4.4 (1889), 586–91 (p. 586).

# CHAPTER 8

# Nursing and Caretaking Stories for Girls
## Feminist Analysis of a Conservative Genre

*Jennifer Askey*

When, in 1977, Elaine Showalter encouraged feminist literary scholars to turn their attention to literature written by women and begin to trace the development of a feminine literary history — to engage in 'gynocriticism' — feminist scholars of German literature did not take long to heed her call.[1] The last twenty-five years have brought forth a plethora of research on German women writers that illustrates forcefully the role women played in literary movements during the eighteenth and nineteenth centuries.[2] Scholarly articles and monographs on Sophie von La Roche, Bettina von Arnim, Dorothea Schlegel, and others have exposed women's contributions to the development of the novel, the cult of sentimentality, and the ideals of Romanticism.[3] Literary scholars have also examined women writers whose work reflects many of the values and preoccupations of the first women's movement in the nineteenth century.[4] This scholarly work has made a significant contribution to our understanding of the social and intellectual life of women in the eighteenth and nineteenth centuries, and the reclamation of these authors and their reintroduction into the German literary canon has made it richer and more complex.

The intersection of feminist literary studies and literary work influenced by cultural studies opens up new possibilities for reading and interpreting popular literature written by women in the nineteenth century. Whereas many 'reclaimed' authors, such as Gabriele Reuter, Marie von Ebner-Eschenbach, and Fanny Lewald, enjoyed a measure of critical acclaim in their own time, many women writing for a living in the nineteenth century published so-called *Trivialliteratur* (trivial literature): pleasant, one-off reads intended to entertain and to provide conservative moral and social commentary. Overlooking this kind of literature deprives both feminist scholarship in *Germanistik* as well as German cultural studies in general of valuable literary material that in its day sought to address the lives and concerns of a largely female, middle-class, novel-reading public.

It is with this in mind that I turn my attention to the subgenre of women's writing in the nineteenth century known as *Mädchenliteratur* (girls' literature). Malte Dahrendorf describes girls' literature as follows:

> Es stellt eine Literatur dar, die von vornherein auf 'weibliche' Bedürfnisse hin gemacht ist; da diese Bedürfnisse, mehr oder weniger im Unterbewußtsein

wirkend, milieu- und traditionsbedingt sind, paßt sich auch das Mädchenbuch in seinem Weltbild überholten Sozialstrukturen an.[5]

[It represents a literature that is, from its conception, intended to address feminine concerns. Since these concerns, functioning more or less at the subconscious level, are determined by social milieu and tradition, the book for girls accommodates its view of the world to outdated social structures.][6]

Girls' literature did not consist solely of works of fiction, though the texts examined here are all novels. A young reader could find adventure novels, romantic stories, historical fiction, and travel literature all geared to her gender and class, as well as comportment manuals and other guides to proper living. Popular nineteenth-century novels included *Der Trotzkopf* (1865) (translated as *Taming a Tomboy*, 1898) by Emmy Rhoden (1832–1885) and *Backfischchens Leiden und Freuden* (1863) (translated as *Gretchen's Joys and Sorrow*, 1877) by Clementine Helm (1825–96), historical novels and biographies by authors such as Brigitte Augusti (1839–1930) and Elisabeth Halden (1841–1916), and short stories by Ottilie Wildermuth (1817–77) that appeared in children's and family periodicals.[7] These books reflected the conservative social and gender ideals of the middle-class for which they were written. So-called *Backfischbücher*, or books for teenage girls, such as those by Rhoden and Helm, earned their moniker by virtue of their target audience: *Backfische* were literally 'little fish' that were perhaps tempting to catch but too little to keep. Though stylistically formulaic, these novels for girls provide a window onto the concerns and preoccupations of their readers (or their readers' parents) and the conservative, backwards-looking gender ideals they upheld. In their purchase and reading of girls' literature, girls, their friends, and family could align their pleasure reading with the expectations of their social sphere, as well as demonstrate their commitment to conservative or traditional gender and social norms.

Gisela Wilkending explains that girls' literature distinguished itself from literature written for boys, which focused on adventure and conquest, by providing the fantasy of a 'beschränkte Abenteuer' [limited adventure] for the young reading woman.[8] Dagmar Grenz's study of girls' literature in Germany in the eighteenth and nineteenth centuries outlines the limited parameters of girls' literature: the horizons of the world portrayed are narrow; only the family or educational environment of the protagonist is visible to the reader and to the protagonist herself; the protagonist is a girl either of noble birth or from the upper-middle classes and her story is limited to her *Wartezeit*, those difficult years of waiting between the end of schooling and her introduction into society as a young lady.[9] The novels end with this phase of personal and social development, and with promising prospects for the young protagonist's marriage.

In reproducing the context held up as the ideal environment for the production of marriageable young ladies, this literature also reproduced a network of domestic, class-, and nation-focused duty and desire around female protagonists that provided the raw material for a limited adventure for young ladies. Girls' literature was not intended to give girls and young women emancipatory ideas. It was geared to teach young women how to bring their desires — for independence, for love, for emotional connection, for a fulfilling life — into line with the needs of others around them, whether their family or their national community. And this literature was popular in the truest sense of the word. Rhoden's *Trotzkopf* and Helm's *Backfischchens Leiden* sold thousands of copies and remained in print for decades, becoming literary brands that remain in print to this day.[10] Augusti's historical fiction was printed and reissued for more than thirty years after its initial publication in the 1880s, and Wildermuth's stories for girls and children appeared in Cotta's Stuttgart *Morgenblatt* and in monograph form. In addition to the reprint information available on these titles, contemporaneous or near-contemporaneous studies of children's literature can also help scholars today to gauge the reception of girls' literature. Hermann Köster in *Geschichte der deutschen Jugendliteratur* (1906) writes of Wildermuth: 'Sie gehört zu den wenigen Jugendschriftstellerinnen, die aus der Menge herausragen' [She is one of the few female authors of youth literature who stand above the crowd], but also that her work possesses no 'besondere dichterische Qualitäten' [particular literary qualities]. While he found her heart-warming domestic stories superior to girls' literature that concerned itself solely with balls, ball gowns, and girlfriends, he saw little lasting literary merit in her work.[11] Regarding Augusti's historical novels, Köster pronounces: 'Man darf sie, obgleich sie für die reifere weibliche Jugend bestimmt sind, nicht zur Backfischliteratur rechnen, dazu stehen sie doch zu hoch' (p. 318) [One cannot count these as *Backfischliteratur*, although they are written for older girls. For that they are too good]. He dismisses the works of Clementine Helm, whose popularity rested on the *Backfisch* genre, in the following way: 'Es ist keine Frage, daß die Lektüre solcher Bücher, verbunden mit einer falschen Erziehung, in den Köpfen und Herzen unserer Mädchen die größten Verheerungen anrichten kann' (p. 304) [There is no question that reading such books, together with an improper education, can cause the greatest devastation in the heads and hearts of our girls]. Köster's evaluation rests on his understanding of the works' independent aesthetic merit as well as on their depiction of what seems like a fairy-tale world of feminine beauty, fashion, and romance. While he may not hold these women writers in particularly high esteem, his evaluation of and pronouncement on their oeuvre indicates that their readership was large enough to merit critical attention from a historian and scholar of children's literature. The fact that he evaluates their work twenty or more years after its initial publication indicates as well the popularity and longevity of these women's work.

So why was girls' literature by Augusti, Helm, Wildermuth, and others so popular with girls at the end of the nineteenth century? Girls' literature is not protofeminist literature and the present study does not seek to claim otherwise. It is, however, ripe for feminist analysis. What desires and dreams did girls find reproduced in these narratives that they felt applied to their own lives? In the tradition of cultural studies, a consideration of this popular literature for girls can provide a necessary corrective to the focus among feminist scholars of literature and history on canonical German women authors and on the pioneers of the feminist movement.

I will focus on one frequent narrative element in girls' literature which benefits from a feminist analysis of narrative strategy, reader response, and reader identification. Illness and corresponding nursing activities (*Pflege*) play a central role in many stories written for girls, and a close examination of a few nursing storylines can illuminate the intersection of conservative social narratives and the accommodation of teenage wish-fulfilment fantasies. The authors of girls' literature deal in reality and fantasy: they provide empathetic and realistic protagonists through whom the narrative is focalized for the reader and simultaneously nurture the fantasy of combining female autonomy with family and social approval. Narratives in which girls take on womanly obligations in the act of nursing and thus achieve harmony in the family and simultaneously develop romantic relationships which hold out the promise of release from the bonds of childhood model a female reality for their readers in which the exchange of the limitations of female childhood (subjugation to mother, father, educators) for the limitations of female adulthood (subjugation to a husband) can be vicariously experienced as emancipatory. Both feminist literary criticism and children's literature studies — which owe a great deal to feminist approaches to literature — recognize the ability of narrative to teach young readers how to read and interpret their own lives and the possibilities contained therein. Children's literature can and does restrict its vision of the possible to that which is traditional, comfortable, and which upholds the status quo for the society in which that literature is produced and read.

Ottilie Wildermuth's story *Klärchens Genesung* (Little Klara's Convalescence, 1859) represents the most common form of nursing and illness narrative.[12] Klärchen, the young protagonist, falls while playing rambunctiously in the yard. The resulting knee injury keeps her bedridden for almost two years, during which time Klärchen learns patience and piety. She learns to be happy for her friends when they are happy, and to appreciate the fact that she can live her invalid existence in relative warmth and luxury, while other sick children suffer cold and deprivation. Eventually, she believes she understands God's message to her, conveyed through her injury and convalescence:

> 'Nun aber, liebe Mutter, möchte ich für den Himmel leben, nicht nur für die Erde, und wenn ich so in Schmerzen dalag, da hat mir kein Märchen und keine Geschichte so schön und tröstlich geklungen wie die wahren Geschichten vom lieben Heiland; wie er Kranke geheilt und Kinder gesegnet hat und so viel, viel größere Schmerzen gelitten als ich.' (p. 61)

> ['Now, dear Mother, I wish to live for heaven and not for the earth. And as I lay there in pain, no fairy-tale or story was as sweet and comforting to me as the true stories of our dear Saviour — how he healed the sick and blessed children and suffered much, much more pain than I.']

Klärchen recovers, but her physical and emotional suffering has brought her to crucial acceptance of her future as an adult woman — one who exists to serve, who is allowed no personal passions, no self-interest, one who must live for others with little hope of earthly reward.

In this common type of illness narrative the girl's illness can stand in for the awkward stage of adolescence — that period when a young woman may feel her body has betrayed her in some way, or has become unrecognizable. Nursing stories such as Klärchen's focus less on the care given her by others and more on the work she does on herself while ill — on her inward journey towards an acceptance of her role as a young woman in her family and community. Wildermuth's narrative addresses the needs of the community in which both the protagonist and young reader lived. By producing a compliant and domestic female, *Klärchens Genesung* reaffirms the nineteenth-century class and gender discourse that effectively bars women from participation in the public sphere, while rewarding the physical role of mother and caretaker and encouraging girls and women to work on their temperament and piety. Sickbed narratives such as *Klärchens Genesung* use the female body as a symbol both of the inherent weakness of women and of the stubborn or independent traits they must fight to overcome. Here, the female body and its potentially mysterious ailments function as the sign for the troubled situation of the young woman in the family and in society and, under control and 'healthy', as the solution to the same.

For the readers of this type of fiction, the focalization of their reading through that protagonist would give them the opportunity to feel themselves selected for work of great importance.[13] Attainment of the feminine ideal was the greatest goal towards which they could strive, and the emotional work on themselves required during periods of illness or nursing could serve as their calling card in the world of adult femininity. Additionally, as Miriam Bailin discusses in *The Sickroom in Victorian Fiction: The Art of Being Ill* (1994), readers who are engaged in following episodes of sickness and nursing experience vicarious strong feelings and desires: the delicious feelings of gratitude experienced by the patient being tended, if that patient is the focalizing point of the narrative; savouring being the centre of attention, either as nurse or patient; and the freedom from certain moral strictures — those inhibiting physical contact, those determining the gendered division of labour.[14] This complex of readerly desires can go a long way to explaining the popularity of fiction that offered no real adventure, few thrills, and the dubious distinction of coming recommended by parents, teachers, or clergy.

Brigitte Augusti's series of historical novels, *An deutschem Herd* (At the German Hearth, 1885–88), provides examples of another type of nursing narrative that shows readers female characters who grow into adulthood through the act of tending the sick and wounded. The theme of nursing appears in all five volumes of the series, and provides contemporary readers with multiple opportunities to examine the private and public faces of illness and nursing, and the significance of the young woman's role as caregiver.

Limited as women's horizons are in Augusti's texts, the opportunity to care for someone, to take responsibility for their comfort and well-being and to exercise some autonomy in matters of their care is greeted by almost all of Augusti's protagonists with undiluted enthusiasm. When, in *Das Pfarrhaus zu Tannenrode* (The Parsonage at Tannenrode, 1887), young Lenore meets her childhood friend Count Maltheim, he is missing part of a leg and, in general, has aged a great deal through the stress of the Thirty Years War. He wonders whether she still feels warmly towards him, as she had done many years before, given his current weakened state. ' "Es müßte ein sehr niedrig gesinntes Weib sein, das an ehrenvollen Wunden einen Anstoß nähme," versetzte Lenore unwillig, "eine edle Frau würde darin nur Ehrenzeichen sehen und stolz darauf sein" ' ['It would be a woman of a very nasty disposition who took offence at honourable wounds,' Lenore reluctantly countered, 'a noble woman would only see in them medals of honour and be proud of them'].[15] In the same novel, Hanna Violarius marries a veteran of the same war, Konrad, whom she tends during an illness. As their nurse–patient relationship develops, it becomes evident that Hanna's activities in the sickroom contribute to her growing feelings of self-worth and autonomy. Gabriele, the young protagonist in the last volume of Augusti's series, *Die Erben von Scharfeneck* (The Heirs of Scharfeneck, 1888), spends her free time one winter during the French Revolution tending to a French count who fled France during the Terror. While some members of her household worry that the Frenchman will exercise undue influence on Gabriele, her mother praises her daughter's commitment to her 'Christenpflicht und echtes Frauenwerk, die Kranken zu pflegen, die Betrübten zu trösten' [sense of Christian duty and true woman's work, to care for the sick and to comfort the aggrieved].[16]

Nursing becomes an essential component of the identity of these three characters as women and as members of their middle-class households. Performing their Christian duty, as Gabriele's mother calls it, solidifies their status in the family and their community as proper young ladies. Additionally, caring for the sick advertises the caretaker's availability and suitability for marriage. Both the protagonists and the intended readers of girls' literature are, ideally, unmarried but marriageable middle-class young women, who had little to do in the months or years between being officially introduced to society and their marriage. If, during this time, the opportunity arose for a young woman to be useful and distinguish herself by providing care to a wounded man, it should come as no surprise that she typically welcomed it.

Augusti's texts romanticize the practice of caregiving. This romanticization is twofold: on the one hand, the work involved in caretaking is portrayed as a joy, or at least as merely a small inconvenience for the young woman; and, on the other, nursing and caretaking often lead to actual romance. Lenore, for example,

> hatte es nicht immer leicht mit ihrem Gatten, den ein dreißigjähriges Kriegsleben aller häuslichen Ordnung und Sitte entfremdet hatte, dem manche dunkle Erinnerung auf der Seele lastete, und dem die alten Wunden auch körperlich manche Stunde voll Schmerz und Pein bereiteten. Aber Lenore behielt immer guten Mut, ihre Liebe und ihr Vertrauen waren durch nichts zu erschüttern, immer war sie bereit, ihrem Gatten zu trösten und zu pflegen, zu zerstreuen und zu erheitern, und so wurde sie ihm mit jedem Tage teurer und unentbehrlicher. (p. 222)

> [did not always have it easy with her spouse, whom thirty years of life at war had robbed of all domestic order and manners, whose soul suffered under many a dark memory, and whose old wounds also caused him many an hour of physical pain and suffering. But Lenore always maintained good courage; her love and her trust could be brought down by nothing. She was always prepared to comfort and tend to her spouse, to divert and amuse him, and thus she became dearer and more essential to him with each passing day.]

Through their caregiving, these young female characters are able to assure for themselves a position of superlative importance in the family arena. Their husbands, the texts suggest, cannot do without their emotional and physical support. This gives these young women a sense of self-worth that should not be underestimated. The seductiveness, as it were, of the sickroom for readers marking time in a *Wartezeit* of their own involves the lure of a realm of independence and social significance usually unavailable to women outside the home. Nursing and caretaking, it would appear, dissolve some of the normal strictures of late nineteenth-century German middle-class society.

This is also the contention made by Bailin in her study of nursing in *The Sickroom in Victorian Fiction*. She argues that sickroom scenes in the works of Charles Dickens, George Eliot, Charlotte Brontë, and others suggest that a woman tending an ill man affords both caregiver and patient the opportunity to cast aside some of the social rules regarding their gender role and express more freely their wishes and desires — both physical and emotional (p. 22). Both the physical intimacy of the patient/nurse relationship and the secluded setting of tending activities — usually in a bedroom — create a singular atmosphere within the typically repressive nineteenth-century household.

Both desire and duty are reproduced and reaffirmed in Augusti's nursing narratives. Whether by the promise of autonomy or by the manner of their weakened charges, the young women in them are seduced into tending to the emotional and physical injuries of the men in their care. Hanna invests all her time and energy in Konrad's welfare. Scrupulously following the doctor's orders and demonstrating to other members of the household that she is, indeed, old enough and responsible enough to take on this burden, Hanna asserts herself and, at the same time, becomes indispensable to Konrad. This relationship of need develops in private and initially thwarts the expectations of their families — as with Lenore and Maltheim, the groom is much older than his desired bride and one member of the couple has much more money than the other. But the foundation built in the sickroom eventually translates into a relationship that affirms their social and familial roles and provides a guarantee of future happiness within patriarchal society. As each of the characters in the sickroom narrative finds his or her needs met through the other, their private relationship is publicly reintegrated into their social circle through marriage, according to Bailin (p. 23). The sickroom nurse in this scenario heals both physical and social wounds.

What Hanna and Konrad are unwilling to discuss, amidst the joy of their private, intense relationship, is its physical nature. Here they exhibit the restraint on the subject of sexuality and intimacy typical of such novels in the nineteenth century, but there is no escaping the sexual nature of Hanna and Konrad's nurse–patient relationship. When Konrad dismisses a suitor for Hanna, he remarks to another family member standing nearby:

> 'Später mögt Ihr ihn trösten, und ich zweifle nicht, daß es Euch trefflich gelingen wird, denn er ist noch jung, und die ganze Welt steht ihm offen. Ich aber könnte ohne meine Hanna nicht mehr leben, sie versteht das Pflegen gar zu gut.'
> Wieder verbarg Hanna ihr glückselig errötendes Antlitz an Bertas Schulter.
> (p. 165)

> ['You can comfort him later and I do not doubt that you will succeed splendidly therein; for he is still young and the whole world is open to him. I, however,

could no longer live without my Hanna. She understands how to nurse me far
too well.'
    Again, Hanna buried her happily reddening face in Berta's shoulder.]

In this passage, the sexual nature of Hanna and Konrad's nursing relationship
peeks through the economic and social rationale offered for their decision to wed.
Her body — the blood rushing to her cheeks — reveals the sexuality she cannot
express.

    The nurse–patient relationship as displayed in Augusti's novels imposes a strict
division of labour and emotional behaviour on the pair involved. The wounded man
will subject his female caregiver to bouts of moodiness and difficulty, requiring his
caregiver's emotional support, and also will experience physical difficulties that
necessitate her constant physical attention. The young woman as nurse incorporates
the needs and desires of the patriarchal systems of family, nation, and war into her
own emotional household and makes them her own. Nursing involves the acting
out of familiar, patriarchal social and familial habits, coded as feminine. These
actions, in turn, give rise to and gratify a particular constellation of desires, also
defined as specifically female in patriarchal culture. The desire to care for others,
the desire for authority in the domestic arena, and the desire for familial harmony
even at the expense of individual autonomy all appear and are satisfied in these
narratives.

    Clementine Helm, who wrote *Backfischchens Leiden und Freuden* (1863), a bestseller
and the book that gave a name to a whole subgenre of girls' literature (*Backfischliteratur*),
also composed *Lillis Jugend* (Lilli's Youth, 1871), the fictional, first-person account
of a young girl's coming of age. *Lillis Jugend* shares some features with *Backfischchens
Leiden*, in that it emphasizes important lessons in comportment and social behaviour
that girls in their early teens need to learn. However, Lilli's narration of the trials
and tribulations of her youth and the lessons she learned devotes more time and
space to the sickroom than to the schoolroom, music room, or parlour.

    When young Lilli and her mother come to live with Uncle Walter, his daughter
Adele, and his mother-in-law, referred to simply as Großmama (grandma), Lilli is
an over-enthusiastic, bossy, self-centred little girl. Adele, her cousin, on the other
hand, is a sickly, delicate, quiet child. Lilli describes her in not very flattering
terms: 'Durch diese ihre stete Kränklichkeit und Schwäche hatte sie etwas
Grilliges, Verdrießliches in ihrem Wesen erhalten, und statt des frischen, kindlichen
Jugendmuthes lagerte eine ängstliche, drückende Schwere auf dem armen Kinde,
welche es still und wenig anziehend machte' (p. 17) [Due to her constant sickliness
and weakness, she had something capricious and sullen about her and instead of
lively, childish spirit there loomed an anxious, oppressive weight on the poor child,
which made her quiet and not very attractive]. *Lillis Jugend* follows the path towards
self-improvement and maturity that each of these girls — cousins, of the same age,
living in the same house — does or does not take. Helm leaves little doubt that the
sickroom is an ideal place to absorb the lessons a young woman must learn. Lilli
informs the reader in the opening lines of the book that her childhood experiences
have made her who she is as an adult. The fact that she is a happy woman and
feels confident in sharing her childhood journey with young readers prepares the

intended reader to read Lilli's story as a success story. Lilli's sickroom duties, which might otherwise appear somewhat forced and unpleasant, are presented within a narrative of personal happiness.

Lilli's initial childish selfishness and boyish behaviour are the first hurdles she must overcome. This task is accomplished by sharing responsibility for poor Adele's happiness. First, she takes on the role of Adele's protector: 'Besonders meiner Schwester gegenüber machte es mir, wie schon erwähnt, großes Vergnügen, die Rolle eines kleinen Ritters gegen seine Dame zu spielen' (p. 29) [Particularly with regard to my sister it pleased me greatly, as I mentioned previously, to play the role of the little knight towards his lady].[17] This knights and ladies comparison is maintained throughout the course of Lilli and Adele's relationship and bears witness to Lilli's resistance to her feminine role. Lilli enjoys being the dominant partner in this sisterhood and, although she finds adapting her own behaviour to Adele's quiet and capricious ways a challenge, the rewards — family approval and Adele's love and devotion — are clearly worth the effort.

Tending to Adele's needs only accomplishes a portion of Lilli's maturation process. Rising to the much larger challenge of nursing the formidable and disapproving grandmother in her final illness completes Lilli's transformation from selfish child and tomboy to nurturing woman. Lilli wins her grandmother's approval by looking after her expertly and patiently:

> Jetzt lächelte sie mir immer häufiger zu, hatte oft ein freundlich Wort oder einen dankbaren Blick, und bald wollte sie von niemand anderem Arznei oder Speise und Getränk annehmen. [...] Wie unsäglich mich solche Anerkennung beglückte vermag ich nicht auszusprechen. (p. 136)

> [Now she smiled at me more and more frequently and often had a friendly word or a thankful glance, and soon she would take medicine, food, and drink from no one but me. [...] How unspeakably happy this recognition made me, I cannot put into words.]

Her grandmother's recognition of Lilli's maturation and growing selflessness leads her to entrust Lilli with Adele's further care. In the spirit of self-sacrifice reinforced by the positive attention bestowed on her nursing activities, Lilli swears to her grandmother that she will take care of Adele after grandmother dies, 'sollte es auch das Glück meines eigenen Lebens kosten' (p. 140) [even if it should cost me my own life's happiness]. This promise of ultimate self-sacrifice will be tested later in Lilli's life and because she adheres to her promise to the older woman, she receives the ultimate reward of a happy marriage to the man of her dreams.

Before that happy event can take place, however, Lilli must watch Adele nurse Waldemar, the man they both love, back to health after a train accident. As with many nursing narratives, Adele falls in love with Waldemar while she tends to his wounds. Significantly, her love is directed at a non-responsive, almost comatose man. 'Aber der kranke, schwache, hülflose Waldemar, der siech und hülfsbedürftig vor ihr lag in aller Hinfälligkeit eines schwer Kranken und Verwundeten, der erregte ihr weder Scheu noch Beklommenheit, und seinem matten Auge konnte sie ohne Angst und Erröthen begegnen' (p. 257) [But the sick, weak, and helpless Waldemar, who lay before her infirm and needy with the decrepitude helplessness of the severely ill and wounded — he called forth neither shyness nor anxiety in her and she could meet his dull eyes without fear or blushing]. Lilli explains in her narration that it is precisely Waldemar's incapacitation that allows the shy and awkward Adele to show her affection through caretaking. It also allows him to feel gratitude, in the guise of love, for his nurse and marry her.

But the physical and emotional hardiness required of the nurse ultimately prove too much for Adele. Emotionally she never leaves her cocoon and remains unable to engage fully in adult married life with Waldemar. They never set up house together: Adele cannot separate from her paternal family. Physically, nursing Waldemar back to health exacts a toll on Adele that leads to her early death. Lilli, Waldemar, and Adele's father all concur that Adele failed to reach maturity. Lilli refers to her as 'unschuldig' [innocent] and 'ein Engel' [an angel] (p. 285) and Waldemar reflects that, in his memories of his married life with her, she appears to him as merely a child (p. 294). Following a period of mourning and awkwardness, Waldemar and Lilli permit themselves to express their love for one another and they marry. Unlike the childlike and sickly Adele, Lilli has always been robust. Her childhood energy has been subdued by her time spent in the sickroom tending to Adele and her grandmother and she now appears a composed young lady, mature enough to enjoy a union of the hearts (and bodies) with Waldemar.

As is often the case with regard to the girls' novel of this period, these stories of nursing are typically 'restrictive texts', which allow little scope for active reader judgements, as opposed to some other types of children's texts which, according to critic John Stephens, 'enable critical and thoughtful responses'.[18] In them, the interpretative possibilities open to the reader are limited. By restricting themselves to the exploration of existing social realities, nursing narratives in girls' literature provide a generally closed interpretation of nursing as a duty or phase to pass through on the way to marriage, an activity that demonstrates outwardly a girl's inner feminine virtues.

Lilli, both the protagonist and narrator of *Lillis Jugend*, ends the novel with the words, 'Es war unser Hochzeitstag!' (p. 300) [It was our wedding day!]. Regarding her reconciliation with her grandmother in the sickroom, she says, 'und innig dankte ich Gott, [...] daß die einzige Klippe aus meinem jungen Leben hinweggenommen wurde' (p. 137) [and I earnestly thanked God that the sole hurdle had been removed from my young life]. Thus integrated into the maturation narrative typical of *Backfischbücher*, Lilli's nursing activities can only be interpreted by the reader as part of her learning to become a mature adult woman, and therefore marriageable. Similarly, although Gabriele, in *Die Erben von Scharfeneck* by Brigitte Augusti, is obviously smitten with the injured Count Maltheim, her tending at his bedside is interpreted by her mother as 'Christian duty'. The fact that Gabriele's infatuation quickly fades as she continues to tend to the Count reinforces for the reader the connection between nursing activity and social and familial approval. Although the task becomes less seductive as Gabriele learns more about the Count's character, she continues to nurse him, thus displaying her own sense of responsibility.

Girls' literature did not explicitly or implicitly thematize the professionalization of caretaking, which may have opened an interpretative window onto nursing as a route to increased individual and financial autonomy for women in this era. Instead, nursing is confined to the middle-class home in girls' literature. Girls and young women who possessed the time and leisure to care for others in the home belonged primarily to families affluent or desirous enough to keep the women in the family from engaging in paid employment. Thus, their private nursing activity takes place in the context of their lives as domestic and familial creatures: they are daughters, nieces, sisters, cousins. By reading girlhood narratives that feature protagonists who mirror their own familial and economic realities, middle-class girls could learn to associate nursing and tending with domestic responsibility rather than economic and social independence.

The limiting of interpretative possibilities in conservative social narratives for women continued within certain, gender-focused genres in the twentieth century. In her groundbreaking study of women readers, *Reading the Romance: Women, Patriarchy, and Popular Literature* (1984), Janice Radway demonstrated how a specific population of women readers used romance novels as a kind of support system. As Radway describes them, romance novels are an 'exploration of the meaning of patriarchy for women' and, as such, can suggest ways of navigating one's path through it successfully.[19] By reading tales of strong, independent women who find happiness, love, and personal fulfilment within the bounds of traditional patriarchal family structures, Radway's readers were able to find strategies for their own emotional success in their patriarchal culture. It is in Radway's sense that I believe nursing and caretaking activities in nineteenth-century girls' literature deserve scrutiny, as activities that potentially provide young girls with the possibility of limited agency and limited adventure and the potential to be recognized as an adult and valuable. As a realm of freedom fashioned from the materials of restriction, nursing mediates what are essentially conflicting desires: to go beyond one's designated and restrictive social role and the largely internalized injunction to renounce desire; to give voice to aggressive impulses towards independence and sexuality and to stifle those impulses in the name of the society that elicited them.

Although the narrative voice in girls' literature generally promotes a closed interpretation of the text and leaves little room for opposing fantasies,[20] stories of nursing and caretaking do leave room for, and even produce, fantasies of a sexual nature. Particularly well suited to teenage readers' concerns and preoccupations during the years in which they are marking time until marriage, these narratives produce and affirm female desire, but in a safe and non-rebellious manner, by symbolically displacing sexual desire onto desire for family, community approbation, or for a weakened and non-threatening male figure. The 'limited adventure' in girls' literature, to return to Wilkending's terminology, is that of overcoming childish traits and taking on the obligations of womanhood. While these novels narrate stories in which the desire for social integration into the adult family and community is rewarded, they also draw upon and reproduce a girl's desire for love and the potential rewards of adult sexuality. Some important characteristics of adult womanhood are expressed through the description of nursing the sick in books for girls: physical and emotional fortitude, selfless devotion, unflagging attentiveness. The physicality of these characteristics suggests a strong correlation between the rigours of the sickroom and the rigours of the bedroom and its attendant consequences in childbirth. Lenore and Hanna, who nurse their soldiers back to health, make the transition with their husbands from the sickroom to the bedroom. Integration into the adult world of sexuality comes into view as a potential adventure in these books for girls.

Gabriele Reuter's *Aus guter Familie* (From a Good Family), the bestselling novel of 1895, provides an example of the possible tension between the closed interpretation of female possibilities in nineteenth-century literature for girls and the evolving social and educational landscape for women at the end of the century. While I do not want to equate Reuter's novel with the lighter fare that comprised the body of literature written for girls and young women around this time, Reuter is very much concerned with what girls and young women read, what they do in their spare time, and what paths to individual agency present themselves to them. Given that, her novel's ruminations on nursing are useful in this context. Mimi is cousin to the protagonist of the novel, Agathe. Agathe is adrift in a world that has no place for her and her ambition, intelligence, and talent. Mimi escapes Agathe's plight by pursuing a career as a nurse in a Protestant religious order. This action is interpreted as a flight from her proper feminine duty by members of Agathe's family. Agathe's father, in particular, finds Mimi's desire entirely selfish, a distraction from her fundamental duty to serve her family.[21] Agathe finds, however, that caring for her own ageing parents in the home does not satisfy her: 'Unermeßliche Räume in ihrem Herzen wurden dadurch nicht ausgefüllt' (p. 219) [Caring for them didn't fill the immeasurable empty places in her heart].[22] This discord between Mimi's desire to leave her family and enter into nursing activity by choice and Agathe's family's desire that she serve her family by tending to them in the home demonstrates the tension inherent in the discourse around nursing. The dominant patriarchal culture sought to confine nursing to the domestic arena, where the desire it incited could be contained, managed, or integrated into existing patriarchal family structures. Mimi's plan to pursue nursing as a religious profession removes her from the domestic cycle of desire and duty, making her nursing activity a betrayal of her feminine obligations to her home.

Caretaking and nursing narratives such as those in Augusti, Helm, or Wildermuth's texts provide their readers with strategies for dealing with the difficulties and injustices of their own lived existence. By romanticizing nursing and illness, Augusti's narrative takes an unpleasant situation common in the readers' own era — the care and tending of wounded veterans of the wars of the 1860s and 1870s and the constant reminder of the ravages of war — and turns it into an opportunity for personal development by creating empathetic characters who use nursing as a way to assert their adulthood and capability. Even if her nineteenth-century readers were not in a position to care for someone in the way Hanna and Lenore are, their education and religious instruction emphasized the importance and propriety of women and girls contributing to charity and donating time and goods to private and religious welfare organizations. Similarly, Lilli's self-improvement through selfless devotion to others earns her the man of her dreams by the end of *Lillis Jugend*. Nursing and tending to the sick represent the apogee of charity and, in the domestic context, serve as sufficient indication of a girl's good breeding and gentle spirit — key marriageable attributes.

The seductive promise of power hinted at in Augusti's narratives, however, in the end serves to enforce the limited role of the married adult woman. Although their nursing work is more externally focused than the work of the girls who themselves are sick, such as Klärchen or Adele, and is thus more apt to be recognized as a valuable contribution to the family, community, or nation, these girls — Lili, Hanna, Lenore — are ultimately at work on themselves. Although they have each grasped the potential of nursing to allow them to expand their narrow sphere of activity and to gain some sort of authority and autonomy, the romantic relationships developed through nursing merely serve to reintegrate them into the restrictive, Victorian moral space that it appeared nursing might allow them to escape.

Whether these protagonists are working on themselves as they struggle with illness or practising self-sacrifice by working for others, each of them is learning how to reproduce allowable and socially productive desires in the service of their families and community. Regardless of the type of nursing (or even simple charity) in which a young girl is engaged, she is first and foremost acting as a representative of her class and gender. Thus, the autonomy described in some nursing scenarios in girls' literature reveals itself as superficial and untenable. The desires produced and reproduced in nursing and its narration are the conservative desires of the patriarchal status quo. The limited adventures described in girls' literature reveal for current feminist scholarship the strategies of the traditional gender order for retaining and solidifying the participation of young women in that order, even in the face of external social and political changes in women's public lives. Through a critical examination of this conservative literature, its history, and its priorities, feminist scholarship in German literature can begin to paint a more nuanced picture of women's lives, their fantasies, and their creative expression in the nineteenth century. By continuing to expand our focus beyond the protofeminist, we can see and appreciate the productive force of desire within the patriarchal system in the creative expression of authors and the instrumentalization of that desire in readers by means of identification and focalization. That this production of desire was in the service of the status quo, and not of emancipation, makes it no less valuable a tool for understanding female experience in the nineteenth century.

## Notes to Chapter 8

1. Elaine Showalter, *A Literature of their Own: British Women Novelists from Brontë to Lessing* (Princeton, NJ: Princeton University Press, 1977).
2. Ruth-Ellen Boetcher Joeres, *Die Anfänge der deutschen Frauenbewegung: Louise Otto-Peters* (Frankfurt am Main: Fischer Taschenbuch, 1982).
3. See for example Claire Baldwin, *The Emergence of the Modern German Novel: Christoph Martin Wieland, Sophie von La Roche, and Maria Anna Sagar* (Rochester, NY: Camden House, 2002); Margaretmary Daley, *Women of Letters: A Study of Self and Genre in the Personal Writing of Caroline Schlegel-Schelling, Rahel Levin Varnhagen, and Bettina Von Arnim* (Columbia, SC: Camden House, 1998); Laura Martin, *Harmony in Discord: German Women Writers in the Eighteenth and Nineteenth Centuries* (Oxford: Lang, 2001).
4. See for example Kay Goodman, *Beyond the Eternal Feminine: Critical Essays on Women and German*

*Literature* (Stuttgart: Akademischer Verlag Hans-Dieter Heinz, 1982); Ludmila Kaloyanova-Slavova, *Übergangsgeschöpfe: Gabriele Reuter, Hedwig Dohm, Helene Böhlau und Franziska von Reventlow* (New York: Lang, 1998); Ruth-Ellen Boetcher Joeres and Marianne Burkard, *Out of Line/ausgefallen: The Paradox of Marginality in the Writings of Nineteenth-Century German Women* (Amsterdam: Rodopi, 1989); Carol Diethe, *Towards Emancipation: German Women Writers of the Nineteenth Century* (New York: Berghahn Books, 1998); Karin Tebben, *Beruf: Schriftstellerin: Schreibende Frauen im 18. und 19. Jahrhundert* (Göttingen: Vandenhoeck & Ruprecht, 1998); Margaret Ward, *Fanny Lewald: Between Rebellion and Renunciation* (New York: Lang, 2006).

5. Malte Dahrendorf, *Das Mädchenbuch und seine Leserin: Jugendlektüre als Instrument der Sozialisation.* 3rd edn (Weinheim and Basle: Beltz, 1978), p. 20.

6. All translations are my own unless otherwise stated.

7. Emmy Rhoden, *Der Trotzkopf: Eine Pensionsgeschichte für junge Mädchen* (Stuttgart: G. Weise, 1885); Clementine Helm, *Backfischchen's Leiden und Freude: Eine Erzählung für junge Mädchen* (Leipzig: Wigand, 1863). For Wildermuth's publication history see Rosemarie Wildermuth, *Ottilie Wildermuth: 1817–1877* [Für die Ausstellung von Februar–Mai 1986 im Schiller-Nationalmuseum Marbach], Marbacher Magazin 37 (1986); Brigitte Augusti [Auguste Plehn], *An deutschem Herd: Kulturgeschichtliche Erzählungen aus alter und neuer Zeit mit besonderer Berücksichtigung des Lebens der deutschen Frauen*, 5 vols (Leipzig: Ferdinand Hirt & Sohn, 1885–88), I: *Edelfalk und Waldvöglein* (1885); II: *Im Banne der Freien Reichsstadt* (1886); III: *Das Pfarrhaus zu Tannenrode* (1887); IV: *Die letzten Maltheims* (1888); V: *Die Erben von Scharfeneck* (1888).

8. Gisela Wilkending, *Kinder- und Jugendbuch* (Bamberg: C. C. Buchner, 1987), p. 164.

9. See Dagmar Grenz, *Mädchenliteratur: Von den moralisch-belehrenden Schriften im 18. Jahrhundert bis zur Herausbildung der Backfischliteratur im 19. Jahrhundert* (Stuttgart: Metzler, 1981).

10. Emmy von Rhoden, *Der Trotzkopf* (Würzburg: Arena, 2002); Clementine Helm, *Backfischchens Leiden und Freuden* (Munich: Weismann, 1981; BiblioBazaar, 2009).

11. Hermann L. Köster, *Geschichte der deutschen Jugendliteratur* [Reprint of 1927 edition] (Munich: Verlag Dokumentation, 1972), p. 305. Further references to this work are given in parentheses in the text.

12. Ottilie Wildermuth, 'Klärchens Genesung: Eine wahre Geschichte', in *Ottilie Wildermuth's Erzählungen* (Konstanz: Christlicher Buch- und Kunstverlag Carl Hirsch, 1908), pp. 53–65.

13. Although many studies of women's literature and children's literature rely on the assumption of reader identification with the protagonist, the term 'focalization' allows for a more nuanced understanding of the reader/text interaction.

14. Miriam Bailin, *The Sickroom in Victorian Fiction: The Art of being Ill* (Cambridge and New York: Cambridge University Press, 1994), p. 7.

15. Augusti, *Das Pfarrhaus zu Tannenrode*, 10th edn (Leipzig: Ferdinand Hirt & Sohn, 1910), p. 218. Further references to this work are given in parentheses in the text.

16. Augusti, *Die Erben von Scharfeneck*, 13th edn (Leipzig: Ferdinand Hirt & Sohn, 1913), p. 41.

17. Although Adele is her cousin, she and Lilli refer to one another as 'sisters' in their new family constellation.

18. John Stephens, 'Analysing Texts: Linguistics and Stylistics', in *Understanding Children's Literature*, 2nd edn, ed. by Peter Hunt (London: Routledge, 2005), pp. 73–85 (p. 84).

19. Janice Radway, *Reading the Romance: Women, Patriarchy, and Popular Literature* (Chapel Hill: University of North Carolina Press, 1984), p. 75.

20. Wilkending, *Kinder- und Jugendbuch*, p. 164.

21. Gabriele Reuter, *Aus guter Familie: Leidensgeschichte eines Mädchens* (Berlin: S. Fischer, 1897), p. 108.

22. This translation is from C. Lynne Tatlock's translation of the novel, *From a Good Family* (Columbia, SC: Camden House, 1999), p. 125.

CHAPTER 9

# Writing Back, More Truth than Fiction

## Henriette Frölich's
## *Virginia oder die Kolonie von Kentucky* (1820)

*Stephanie Hilger*

The feminist effort of recovering literature by women writers has shown that, while there had always been women writing, in the early nineteenth century women entered the literary marketplace in greater numbers, a trend that had begun in the eighteenth century and would be continued in the twentieth century.[1] The reasons for this development are manifold and vary among countries and literary traditions in the European context. They include greater literacy, the increasing prominence of the genre of fiction, the gradual change from a patronage system to writing as a remunerated activity, and women's claims to a voice in the public sphere during an era that was undergoing momentous political and social change. The significant number of writing and publishing women at that time meant that women writers could not be considered a homogeneous group and that their literary production was diverse and varied. While some women wrote for a comparatively small circle of friends, others wrote for publication and some of these achieved a certain degree of financial success and sometimes even fame.[2] Those who published their writings did so anonymously, pseudonymously, under their husband's name, or their own. Some published politically progressive literature, while others were more conservative in their ideas. Interestingly enough, it is precisely the quantity and diversity of women's literary production that has contributed to their critical neglect in the traditional canon over the course of the centuries.

Contemporary male authors experienced women's entry into the literary sphere as a threatening reality undermining their monopoly on intellectual prestige and financial reward. In the German context, this can be seen especially acutely in Goethe and Schiller's discussions of women writers as 'dilettantes' and their acerbic characterizations of specific women authors.[3] Their comments acknowledge the increasing presence of women as writers while undermining their contribution to literary discourse by either belittling their literary production or attacking their character. Goethe and Schiller's dismissal of female contemporaries was instrumental in cementing their status as *the* authors of the late eighteenth and early nineteenth centuries. The nineteenth-century critic Heinrich Laube coined the period designation 'Weimarer Klassik' [Weimar Classicism], thereby further strengthening this perception in the subsequent writing of German literary history.[4] The concept of Weimar Classicism established a cult of genius, which centred on Goethe and Schiller and their work at the court of Weimar. There resulted a de facto exclusion of all those authors — men and women — who were not working on 'classical' themes in Weimar, which profoundly shaped the subsequent writing of German literary history. The term 'classical' not only referred to the themes of this literature but also expressed a value judgement about those who worked, to use Katherine Goodman and Edith Waldstein's phrase, 'in the shadow of Olympus'.[5]

One of the effects of women's supposed shadow existence was the perception that they were blocked from the rays of creative inspiration and were, therefore, limited to imitating the works produced by those sitting on the summit of the mountain of genius. Women's contribution to literary and intellectual discourse was seen as imitative rather than creative. This perception betrays a gendered interpretation of the profoundly intertextual nature of eighteenth- and nineteenth-century literature. During this period, authors responded to each other, often across national and language borders, in a so-called 'Republic of Letters', a transnational intellectual community. The interactions of participants in this realm were not limited to general intellectual discussions but also extended to explicit and open responses to specific texts and authors.

Writers passionately responded to and, in the absence of copyright restrictions, liberally borrowed from, each other, especially when it came to authoring a novel, a form still perceived as new and therefore malleable. Writing a response to or a continuation of a famous text was another widely adopted strategy for drawing attention to a text and publicizing it. Both male and female authors engaged in this type of response, yet their intertextual engagement has been evaluated differently depending on their gender. Male writers who explicitly engaged other authors' works were perceived as participating in an exchange in the public sphere. By contrast, women were seen as imitators, not partaking in public discussions but, instead, practising their writing in a private setting. Their writing was not read as an intellectual contribution to the public realm but as private handiwork akin to the act of stitching from a pre-printed pattern, trying to imitate the model as perfectly as possible.[6]

One productive way of recovering the ways in which women authors' responses to other texts contribute to discussions in the public sphere is to wed feminist approaches with the concept of 'writing back' from postcolonial theory. This concept, most explicitly theorized in Bill Ashcroft, Gareth Griffiths, and Helen Tiffin's *The Empire Writes Back* (1989), uncovers power dynamics in the process of writing and publication at times of social and political upheaval.[7] Parallels can be drawn between authors in the postcolonial period and women writers in the late eighteenth and the early nineteenth centuries, that is, the time from the French Revolution to the end of Napoleon's rule. Postcolonial literature emerged at a time when the justification for colonial rule was being questioned. Authors living under colonial rule found themselves in the paradoxical position of being both fluent in and at the same imprisoned by the colonizer's discourse. One way to an independent voice was first to acknowledge and then to question the colonizer's literary tradition by rewriting and responding to its important works. One of the best-known examples is the Nigerian writer Chinua Achebe's *Things Fall Apart* (1958), which challenges the premise of Joseph Conrad's *Heart of Darkness* (1899), one of the most important, controversial, and influential narratives of empire. While not all postcolonial authors 'wrote back' in this explicit way, many of them, educated in the colonial system, used the master's tools in order to uncover the flawed foundations of the master's house. Using a well-known text as an anchoring point caused an ambivalent reception; it ensured visibility yet also exposed authors to harsh criticism from the literary establishment. In a manner that perhaps foreshadows the postcolonial writers who questioned the colonizer's discourse of enlightened benevolence, women authors of the late eighteenth and early nineteenth centuries scrutinized the paradoxical deployment of the Revolutionary concepts of liberty and equality in contemporary discourse by 'writing back' to it. They questioned the application of the concept of fraternity as solidarity between men to the exclusion of women in the literary sphere. By 'writing back', late eighteenth- and early nineteenth-century women authors responded to some of the literary and political premises of well-known and canonical texts, usually those written by the male 'greats' of the time, such as Goethe and Schiller. The concept of 'writing back' allows for the recovery of the political dimension of women authors' writing by freeing their contributions from traditional literary histories, which tend to place them in the shadow of Olympus.

One example of this strategy of 'writing back' to the conventions and prescriptions of Weimar Classicism is Henriette Frölich's (1768–1833) *Virginia oder die Kolonie von Kentucky: Mehr Wahrheit als Dichtung* (More Truth than Fiction), published in 1820 under the pseudonym Jerta in Berlin. This text explicitly invokes Goethe's writings, on two different yet related levels. The novel can be described as a *Bildungsroman* (novel of education) in epistolary format. *Virginia* thereby implicitly responds to both *Wilhelm Meisters Lehrjahre* (Wilhelm Meister's Apprenticeship, 1795/96) and *Die Leiden des jungen Werther* (The Sorrows of Young Werther, 1774), the two late eighteenth-century texts that had become literary reference points in the early nineteenth-century German fictional tradition. The female heroine, Virginia, writes a series of letters to her cousin Adèle from the moment she leaves her homeland, France, in 1814, to the establishment of a colony in Kentucky in 1817. Since the letters are bundled for the practical purpose of transmitting them across the ocean, they resemble diary entries and, in many respects, even a fictional autobiography outlining the *Bildung* of its female subject. The subtitle of the novel — *Mehr Wahrheit als Dichtung* (More Truth than Fiction) — echoes the subtitle of Goethe's autobiography, *Aus meinem Leben: Dichtung und Wahrheit* (From My Life: Fiction and Truth), and thereby engages conventions from the autobiographical genre and its representation of *Bildung*.[8] Frölich not only reverses the word order of Goethe's *Dichtung und Wahrheit*, the first volumes of which had already appeared by the time *Virginia* was published, she also inserts a comparative construction, claiming that there is more truth than fiction in *her* text, a novel. She thereby comments cynically on Goethe's autobiography and draws attention to the tenuous line between truth and fiction in both genres. Frölich's title page claims that the novel is 'herausgegeben von Jerta' [edited by Jerta].[9] This type of reference was a conventional move by eighteenth- and nineteenth-century authors, geared both at conferring an element of truth to a fictional text in order to generate interest among the reading public and at providing a layer of protection for the author. As in this case, this strategy was often complemented by pseudonymous or anonymous publication. Frölich 'writes back' to various literary discourses and thereby presents a fictional autobiography, anchored in actual historical events, that centres on the *Bildung* of a female heroine. With this text, Frölich challenges the assumption of the male subject as the centre of two prominent early nineteenth-century genres, autobiography and the *Bildungsroman*.

Frölich responds to Goethe's portrayal of *Bildung* as an exclusively male process — represented by the male protagonist and autobiographical subject in *Wilhelm Meister* and *Dichtung und Wahrheit* — with her choice of a female protagonist. In contrast to Goethe's novel, where the female figures are secondary characters who illustrate Wilhelm's development and mainly figure as his love interests, in Frölich's text, the eponymous heroine Virginia is the focus of the story. In addition, Frölich closely intertwines Virginia's private story with late eighteenth- and early nineteenth-century public history. Frölich's novel is anchored in a specific historical moment; the life of the fictional protagonist is a reflection of true historical events. The first part of the novel is set in France; the second takes place in North America. The protagonist is born in the chaos on the day the Bastille falls, on 14 July, 1789:

> So kam der Julius heran, dieser so oft beschriebene und in der Weltgeschichte ewig merkwürdige Monat [...] Tief in sich gekehrt, ging sie auch am 14. Julius mittags auf ihrem gewöhnlichen Spaziergange auf und nieder [...] Das Getümmel nimmt zu. Von allen Seiten das Geschrei: 'Nieder mit der Bastille, nieder!' Kanonen werden aufgepflanzt, die Türme vom Zeughaus und vom Garten werden eingestoßen, Löcher in die Mauern gebrochen. Meine Mutter fängt an zu begreifen, was vorgeht [...] alles verkündigt eine beschleunigte Entbindung. (28)

> [The month of July came along, this month which has been so often described and will remain forever strange in world history [...] Deeply lost in thought, she [Virginia's mother] walked to and fro on her usual walk at noon on 14 July [... ] The tumult is increasing. From everywhere there are cries: 'Down with the Bastille, down with it!' Canons are set up, the towers of the arsenal and the garden are rammed, holes are broken into the walls. My mother begins to understand what is happening [...] everything is announcing an accelerated delivery.][10]

The protagonist's birth is embedded in public history and becomes an integral part of it. After the delivery, her father — overcome by Republican enthusiasm — names his daughter after the Roman heroine: 'Virginia, Virginia! du teures Pfand der neuen Freiheit. Roms Virginia sprengte durch ihren Tod Roms Bande; du verbürgst mir durch den Augenblick deiner Geburt die Freiheit deines Vaterlandes' (p. 29) [Virginia, Virginia! You are a precious token of this new freedom. Rome's Virginia broke the shackles of Rome with her death; the moment of your birth guarantees the freedom of your fatherland]. Frölich uses the convention of a fictional family narrative to present the historical events of the French Revolution. Her subtitle, *Mehr Wahrheit als Dichtung*, can be understood in this sense; Frölich claims that there is more truth than fiction in her description of the conditions surrounding the protagonist's birth than there is in Goethe's autobiography. In *Dichtung und Wahrheit*, the birth of the autobiographical subject Goethe is presented in the following terms:

> Am 28. August 1749, Mittags mit dem Glockenschlage zwölf, kam ich in *Frankfurt am Main* auf die Welt. Die Konstellation war glücklich; die Sonne stand im Zeichen der Jungfrau, und kulminirte für den Tag; Jupiter und Venus blickten sie freundlich an, Merkur nicht widerwärtig; Saturn und Mars verhielten sich gleichgültig: nur der Mond, der so eben voll ward, übte die Kraft seines Gegenscheins um so mehr, als zugleich seine Planetenstunde eingetreten war. Er widersetzte sich daher meiner Geburt, die nicht eher erfolgen konnte, als bis diese Stunde vorübergegangen.[11]

> [On 28 August, 1749, at midday, as the clock struck twelve, I came into the world, in Frankfurt-on-the-Main. My horoscope was propitious: the sun stood in the sign of the Virgin, and had culminated for the day; Jupiter and Venus looked on him with a friendly eye, and Mercury not adversely; while Saturn and Mars kept themselves indifferent; the moon alone, just full, exerted the power of her reflection all the more, as she had then reached her planetary hour. She opposed herself, therefore, to my birth, which could not be accomplished until this hour had passed.][12]

Goethe describes his own birth as a cosmic event. The macrocosmic planetary order directly influences the birth of Johann Wolfgang in the microcosm of Frankfurt; the stars and the planetary constellations need to align perfectly for the birth of the genius of Weimar Classicism. This hyperbolic description reflects the early nineteenth-century cult of male genius. Frölich's description of her heroine's birth also transcends the private realm of the family, yet Virginia's birth is not tied to planetary constellations but to more believable historical chaos and social upheaval, which interrupt the mother's leisurely walk and thereby hasten the delivery. Frölich's text is fictional, yet a comparison of the descriptions of Virginia's and Goethe's birth underlines the claim of Frölich's subtitle that there is more truth and plausibility in her story than in Goethe's superlative autobiography.

Virginia's birth parallels the birth of a new social system. Her father's exclamation 'Virginia, Virginia!' echoes the calls for liberty, equality, and fraternity heard not only in the streets of Paris, but throughout Europe. This narrative constellation allows Frölich to participate in debates on politics, from which women were often excluded, especially when it came to writing, rather than merely talking about, social and political change. The genre of the novel presented women in the early nineteenth century with the opportunity to contribute to public discussions in a forum that, in contrast to pamphlets and treatises, did not claim to be explicitly political. With her novel, Frölich engages in debates on women's rights and women's education, which, although an integral part of Revolutionary ideals, were often sidelined by the Revolution's fraternal underpinnings. Frölich politicizes the fictional genre by 'writing back' to the assumption that the concepts of *Bildung* (education) and *Mündigkeit* (the individual's capacity for critical thinking and action)

WRITING BACK, MORE TRUTH THAN FICTION    133

are cornerstones in the narratives of male, but not female, fictional protagonists and autobiographical subjects. Frölich reflects on the meaning of these concepts for women by writing a novel about a female protagonist who lives at a time when those exact ideas are open to negotiation and debate. Frölich's ensuing conclusions regarding the status of women as equal political subjects are as ambivalent as the position of women authors on the early nineteenth-century literary scene.

Political change and social experiments stand at the centre of Frölich's novel and are intimately linked to the protagonist's *Bildung*. In the first part of the novel, Virginia's father, a French aristocrat fighting for Revolutionary ideals, provides her with an example of a self-sufficient, egalitarian society that explicitly contradicts *ancien régime* hierarchies. The father, a representative of progressive ideas about gender and class, establishes a 'Paradis' (p. 19) on an estate in the Provence that he inherited from his mother. The previous tenant had neglected the estate; its farmers were in effect indentured servants. Virginia's father divides the land among the farmers and demands a modest rent, determined by the farmers themselves. As a result of his patriarchal benevolence 'Wohlstand kehrte in seine reinliche Hütte zurück, Gesundheit und Kraft sprach sich in seiner regsamen Gestalt aus' (pp. 18–19) [prosperity returned to his [the farmer's] clean hut and his lively countenance expressed health and strength]. This idyllic life in a utopian setting comes to an abrupt halt after the death of Virginia's entire family. Her mother dies after she learns of her son's death in battle; then, her father perishes fighting for Napoleon. Frölich's novel is an example of what Lynn Hunt calls a family romance of the French Revolution, a narrative in which public political events are reflected through the prism of a family narrative, in this case one that focuses on the daughter.[13] Virginia's life is inextricably intertwined with Revolutionary events. Left without protection, Virginia is placed under the guardianship of an uncle who forces her to renounce her father's estate. He attempts to compel Virginia, whom he characterizes as a 'trotzige Republikanerin' (p. 109) [obstinate republican], to live according to her class privileges. As a result of her uncle's wish that she marry his son, Virginia flees and boards a ship to America, because 'das Gefühl der Freiheit überwog jede andre Empfindung' (p. 113) [the desire for freedom surpassed any other feeling]. The personal is political in *Virginia oder die Kolonie von Kentucky*; the female protagonist's private life is closely tied to turn-of-the-century public events. Having grown up on her father's egalitarian estate, Virginia cannot return to the reactionary life that her uncle envisions for her.

The first part of the novel thematizes the father's vision of social justice and an alternative form of government on his French estate. The second part discusses the same Revolutionary ideals in the context of his daughter's participation in European emigration to North America. Virginia and Mucius, her French suitor, with whom she is reunited in the New World, become part of a diverse group of European immigrants, many of whom have fled Europe, which is described as the 'gärende[r] Weltteil' (p. 164) [fermenting continent]. Soon, these immigrants plan on establishing a colony on the banks of the Ohio River, inspired by Rousseauist ideals. Virginia becomes the immigrants' 'Heldin' (p. 168) [heroine]; she voices their desire for freedom and contentment : 'ich sehne mich in die Urwälder zurück, in die Freiheit des Goldenen Zeitalters' (p. 168) [I am longing for the primeval forests, for the freedom of the Golden Age]. One of the colonizers, a German called Walter, inherited land from his mother, which she won in a lottery. Ellison, the ship's captain, and Mucius buy the adjoining land and, together with Walter and the others, they establish a new European colony, which they expect to be self-sufficient and independent:

> Dann aber werden wir aller Außenhülfe entsagen, und die junge Kolonie wird für ihre Bedürfnisse selbst sorgen. Hierzu werden alle nötigen Vorkehrungen getroffen. Alles ist voll Leben und Tätigkeit, wir alle sind nur von einem großen Gedanken begeistert. Mucius entwirft den Plan zu einem kleinen Staate, in welchem Freiheit und Gleichheit verwirklicht werden sollen; jeder Abschnitt des Entwurfs wird der Generalversammlung, in welcher auch wir Weiber eine halbe Stimme haben, vorgelegt und, nach Stimmenmehrheit, angenommen oder abgeändert, und ich denke, es wird eine Verfassung zustande kommen, woran mehrere Menschenalter nichts zu flicken finden werden. (p. 169)

> [Then we will no longer require any external help and the young colony will take care of its own needs. All necessary arrangements are being made for this purpose. Everything is full of life and activity, and we are all motivated by one grand idea. Mucius is developing a plan for a small state, in which liberty and equality will be realized; every paragraph of the draft is presented to the general assembly, in which we women also have half a vote and it is, following the majority of the votes, either accepted or modified and I think a constitution will come into being which several future generations will have no cause to mend.]

Self-sufficiency is the driving principle of the new state and the motivating factor for its new inhabitants. This material foundation is complemented by a constitution which is based on two of the mottos of the French Revolution, liberty and equality. While the third concept, fraternity, is not explicitly mentioned here, its presence is palpable in the exact workings of the general assembly. In it, Virginia specifies, women 'also' have half a vote. This element of the colony's constitution has triggered the most debate among modern critics of the novel. Ute Brandes argues that 'Frölich optimistically assigns equal constitutional rights which predate those of German women by one century'.[14] Similarly, Mechthilde Vahsen concludes that, as a result of this law, women in the colony are assigned a public identity as political subjects and can exercise their democratic rights, although only to a limited degree.[15] Cindy Brewer approaches the novel from the perspective of a twenty-first-century reader and observes that 'Frölich disappoints our modern sentiments with the limitations of [the colony's] societal structure'.[16] Todd Kontje takes Brewer's observation one step further and characterises Frölich's political programme as 'half-hearted feminism'.[17] The debate surrounding Frölich's feminism is emblematic of contemporary discussions of all women writers of the period and reflects modern-day expectations regarding female authorship in the early nineteenth century. This debate not only highlights the ambivalence of the term 'feminist', it also poses the question whether women writers are necessarily feminist just because they are female. Contextualizing the protagonist's comment in a time when women were not allowed to vote *at all* is a first step towards understanding Frölich's contribution to political and social debate. From this perspective, giving women half a vote was quite a revolutionary and a 'feminist' demand, especially considering the fact that, in most Western European countries, universal suffrage was not extended to women for another century. Moreover, Virginia's statements need not be those of the author; there is no necessary seamless overlap between author and heroine just because both are women. Even if we read Virginia as the author's spokesperson in the novel, the text itself exceeds this reading. In fact, the ending of the above-cited passage highlights the paradox of women's half-vote, whether Frölich intended it or not. Virginia's comment that the new constitution will be one in which generations will not find anything to mend draws attention to itself. This statement implicitly questions the ideals of liberty and equality by highlighting the fraternal underpinnings of a supposedly democratic society that falls short of its own ideals because, in it, women only have half a vote. The remaining ambivalence with regard to women's voting rights points at the highly contested nature of such issues in the early nineteenth century and the incomplete realization of the Enlightenment ideals of individual autonomy and self-determination.

The novel's ambivalence with respect to gender equality is also evident in its description of women's education. Virginia grows up on her father's utopian estate and receives an education that is untypical for women at the time:

> Ich lernte fast von selbst lesen [...]. Meine Mutter schaffte mir Puppen an und anderes Spielgerät, ich wußte eben nichts damit anzufangen [...]. Mein Vater erhielt, durch einen Zufall, ein altes Werk, welches meine kindische Aufmerksamkeit auf sich zog. Es war eine Weltgeschichte [...]. Ich wendete mich an meiner Vater, und dieser erklärte mir die Bilder einfach, aber wahr [...]. Ich übte mich unermüdet, und in kurzem las ich fertig in meiner lieben Geschichte [...]. Ich kann im eigentlichsten Sinne sagen, ich bin unter den Heroen der Vorwelt herangewachsen. Sie waren meine Vorbilder [...] (pp. 34–35)

> [I learnt to read nearly on my own [...]. My mother gave me dolls and other toys; I did not know what to do with them [...]. My father obtained, by chance, an old book that attracted my childish curiosity. It was a history of the world [...]. I turned to my father, and he explained the images to me in simple, but faithful terms [...]. I practised tirelessly and in a short time I read the whole of this dear history of mine [...] I can truly say that I grew up amidst the heroes of ancient times. They were my models [...]]

Virginia's father encourages his daughter's desire for learning whereas her mother loses patience with Virginia. She even develops animosity towards her daughter, who gradually becomes her husband's main confidante and discussion partner: 'Sie liebte diese Unterhaltungen nicht sehr, sahe auch meine fortschreitende Ausbildung nicht allzu gern' (p. 38) [She did not like these conversations very much; neither did she look favourably upon my progressing education]. Virginia's 'Ausbildung' [education], the type of education typically reserved for men, stands in contrast to her mother's traditional role as a 'gute Mutter, eine gute Hausfrau, eine Wohltäterin der Dürftigen' (p. 38) [good mother, a good housewife, a benefactress to the needy]. In the early years of their marriage, the father had hoped his wife would become his intellectual partner: 'Er hatte oft versucht, sie dafür auszubilden, aber mit wenig Erfolg' (p. 38) [He had often tried to educate her for this purpose, but with little success]. Again, the word 'ausbilden' [to educate] assumes a central position in a novel that argues for the importance of *Bildung*, in the sense of an intellectual education that reflects Enlightenment ideals, for men and women. The mother was educated in the convent, 'nach der Sitte der Zeit' (p. 38) [according to the custom of the time]; hers is a traditional education of the past. By contrast, Virginia is portrayed as a female figure of the present who does not feel fulfilled by her mother's daily activities:

> Aber wenn ich wieder zurücktrat in den alltäglichen Gang des häuslichen Lebens, da fühlte ich meine Tätigkeit plötzlich gelähmt. Die kleinen, immer wiederkommenden Sorgen des Haushalts vermochten nicht, meine Seele zu füllen, und mein Geist kehrte heißhungrig in die Ideenwelt zurück. (pp. 41–42)

> [But when I returned to the daily course of home life, I felt that my power to act was suddenly paralysed. The small, ever-recurring household worries could not fill my soul and my mind returned ravenously to the world of ideas.]

Virginia experiences the contrast between the masculine realm of ideas and the feminine world of household duties. She realizes that traditional gender roles do not accord women a spot in public history:

> Ich weinte nur zuweilen im stillen darüber, daß ich ein Mädchen war, eins der unbedeutenden Wesen, von welchen die Geschichte so wenig sagt, während die Taten der Männer jedes Blatt füllen. Nur als Opfer werden sie genannt. Iphigenia, Virginia — nur als Opfer für große Zwecke. (p. 37)

> [I sometimes cried in secret about the fact that I was a girl, one of those insignificant creatures about whom history says so little, while the deeds of men fill every page. They are only mentioned as victims. Iphigenia, Virginia — only as victims of great causes.]

Virginia's opposition to the idea of passive femininity, represented not least by Goethe's *Iphigenie auf Tauris*, is the motivating factor in her decision to emigrate. Her desire for an active social role is founded on the education she received from her father, the benevolent patriarchal figure on the European continent. Virginia's 'Bildung', her education, is closely linked to the 'Bildung', the establishment, of a new colony on the American continent.

   In the colony, education seems not to be segregated according to gender lines at first sight. However, equal education in such subjects as reading, writing, mathematics, natural sciences, and world history only extends to the twelfth birthday:

> [S]pielend [sollen] die Kräfte der Kinder, sowohl leiblich als geistig, ausgebildet und beide Geschlechter, bis zum zwölften Jahre, ganz gleich beschäftigt und unterrichtet werden [...]. Mit dem zwölften Jahre werden die Mädchen zur Haushaltung und zu künstlichen Arbeiten mit der Nadel und auf dem Webstuhl angeführt, die Knaben lernen die höheren Wissenschaften und die toten Sprachen [...]. (pp. 195–96)

> [The physical and mental strength of the children shall be developed playfully and the two sexes shall be occupied and taught in exactly the same way until their twelfth year [...]. When they reach twelve years the girls will be taught housekeeping and artificial work with the needle and the loom; the boys will study the higher sciences and ancient languages [...].]

In Kentucky, the children's 'Ausbildung' is equal only until they reach puberty. Then, gender-specific instruction commences: the girls learn the practical use of the needle, while the boys acquire knowledge of a more theoretical kind. Here again the novel only goes half-way. The novel's presentation of the issue of education is marked by the same ambivalence as its discussion of voting. In comparison to early nineteenth-century historical realities, the educational system in the fictional colony is advanced and, one could even say, progressive and protofeminist. Yet total equality is absent. Frölich's portrayal of voting and the educational system in this novel raises a number of questions: Does Frölich agree with the limitations imposed on equality or does she, instead, criticize them by exposing an underlying assumption that only men can be fully-fledged citizens? Is the author strategically arguing for gradual progress in order not to alienate her contemporaries? Is Kentucky to be read as an actual colonial project or rather, as Gerhard Steiner argues, a 'Sinnbild, in dem sie alle ihre politischen Hoffnungen und Forderungen zum Ausdruck bringt' [allegory, in which she expresses all her political hopes and demands]?[18] Frölich creates a 'colonial fantasy', to use Susanne Zantop's analytical concept, yet the fantasy remains ambivalent with respect to issues of gender equality.[19] It is precisely this ambivalence that makes *Virginia oder die Kolonie von Kentucky* uncomfortable and disconcerting reading in the twenty-first century.

By highlighting rather than neatly resolving the debates surrounding women's rights, Frölich's 1820 novel mirrors the political realities of the early nineteenth century. Living and writing in Berlin at that time, Frölich experienced both the optimism of the German Wars of Liberation and the ensuing restoration of feudal-aristocratic privileges; she also witnessed the curtailment of individual rights and of gender equality.[20] As Joan Landes points out, women's position in the public sphere was becoming increasingly tenuous in the post-Revolutionary period.[21] Landes analyses French public discourse, but her observations can also be applied to the political atmosphere in German-speaking lands. Women were silenced in a predominantly male, bourgeois public sphere, in which only men could become complete citizens. Contemporary discourse projected women into a realm of domestic virtue that was imagined as separate from the public sphere. The novel's ambivalent presentation of the position of women in an imagined new world reflects the mixing of Revolutionary idealism with the discourse on women's domesticity. Frölich thematizes the increasing silencing of women's voices during this time with the genre of the novel, which allowed her to participate in the political debate on gender without explicitly appearing to do so. Henriette Frölich's novel is, therefore, one example of how women authors politicized the genre of fiction in the early nineteenth century in order to 'write back' and respond not only to specific authors but also to debates that were of direct relevance to them.

Virginia's ambivalent position in the colony parallels that of the author in the literary sphere of her time. On the one hand, the genre of fiction was a medium with which Frölich could enter the public sphere of political and social debate, yet, on the other, she was aware of the power of those literary figures residing on the early nineteenth-century Mount Olympus. Her awareness of these figures is expressed in her decision to send her play, *Rosenmädchen* (Rose Girl), to Goethe in the hope of it gaining his approval. She addresses him as 'Euer Exzellenz' [your excellency] and describes his judgement as the 'höchste Tribunal' [highest tribunal]. She asks 'im Namen der Kunst um ein einziges beifälliges oder abmahnendes Wort' [for a single encouraging or admonishing word in the name of art], aware that Goethe's reviews, which were often disseminated in important literary journals, could make or break a writer's career. Frölich claims to be calm in the expectation of his judgement and promises to defer to it, adopting the type of feminine passivity that her protagonist laments: 'Nun aber kann ich ruhig sein. Ich werde Wahrheit finden!' [Now I can be calm. I will find the truth!].[22] There is no record of Goethe's reaction to Frölich's letter. Are we supposed to conclude, as suggested by Gerhard Steiner, that it must have been positive since she continued writing? Or should we rather assume that Goethe never responded? In either case, Frölich's relation to literary authority was an ambivalent one. Her strategy of 'writing back' reflects this ambivalence. By means of this strategy Frölich engages the dominant literary discourse of the early nineteenth century, challenging the assumption of the male subject as the centre of two prominent early nineteenth-century genres, autobiography and the *Bildungsroman*, by claiming that her novel contains 'mehr Wahrheit als Dichtung'. At the same time, Frölich's 'writing back' acknowledges existing power dynamics in the literary sphere, simultaneously reinforcing and questioning the authority of those who lay claim to 'Dichtung' and 'Wahrheit'. Like her heroine, Frölich strategically navigates gender prescriptions of her time. It is precisely this aspect that makes Frölich's novel fascinating if unsettling reading in the early twenty-first century. *Virginia oder die Kolonie von Kentucky* questions those clear-cut categories of 'progressive' and 'conservative' that are often deployed in the recovery of women authors from previous centuries and forces us to reconsider their meaning.

## Notes to Chapter 9

1. Estimates of the actual number of women writing and publishing during this period vary, yet scholars agree that there was a significant increase. For the German context, see, for example, Barbara Becker-Cantarino, *Der lange Weg zur Mündigkeit: Frau und Literatur (1500–1800)* (Stuttgart: Metzler, 1987); Gisela Brinker-Gabler, *Deutsche Dichterinnen vom 16. Jahrhundert bis zur Gegenwart: Gedichte und Lebensläufe* (Frankfurt am Main: Fischer Taschenbuch Verlag, 1978); *Deutsche Literatur von Frauen*, ed. by Gisela Brinker-Gabler, 2 vols (Munich: Beck, 1988); Helen Fronius, *Women and Literature in the Goethe Era, 1770–1820: Determined Dilettantes* (Oxford: Clarendon Press, 2007); Susanne Kord, *Ein Blick hinter die Kulissen: Deutschsprachige Dramatikerinnen im 18. und 19. Jahrhundert* (Stuttgart: Metzler, 1992); and Susanne Kord, *Sich einen Namen machen: Anonymität und weibliche Autorschaft, 1700–1900* (Stuttgart: Metzler, 1996).

2. For examples of late eighteenth- and early nineteenth-century women authors, see Stephanie Hilger, *Women Write Back: Strategies of Response and the Dynamics of European Literary Culture, 1790–1805* (Amsterdam and New York: Rodopi, 2009).

3. See Helen Fronius, *Women and Literature*, for a detailed discussion of Goethe and Schiller's exchange on 'dilettantes'. Also see Stephanie Hilger, 'Epistolarity, Publicity, and Painful Sensibility: Julie de Krüdener's *Valérie*', *French Review*, 79.4 (2006), 737–48, and Stephanie Hilger, 'The Murderess on Stage: Christine Westphalen's *Charlotte Corday* (1804)', in *Women and Death 3: Women's Representations of Death in German Culture since 1500*, ed. by Anna Richards and Clare Bielby (Rochester, NY: Camden House, 2010).

4. Heinrich Laube, *Geschichte der deutschen Literatur* (Stuttgart: Hallberger'sche Verlagshandlung, 1839).

5. *In the Shadow of Olympus: German Women Writers around 1800*, ed. by Katherine R. Goodman and Edith Waldstein (Albany: State University of New York Press, 1992).

6. For case studies of women authors' intertextual response and their contemporaries' reaction to it, see Hilger, *Women Write Back*.

7. Bill Ashcroft, Gareth Griffiths, and Helen Tiffin, *The Empire Writes Back: Theory and Practice in Post-colonial Literatures* (London: Routledge, 1989).

8. For a discussion of the position of Goethe's autobiography in the history of the genre see Ortrun Niethammer, *Autobiographien von Frauen im 18. Jahrhundert* (Tübingen: Francke, 2000).

9. Henriette Frölich, *Virginia oder Die Kolonie von Kentucky: Mehr Wahrheit als Dichtung* (Berlin: Aufbau-Verlag, 1963), p. 7. All further references will be to this edition and will be made parenthetically in the text.

10. All translations of foreign-language material are mine, unless otherwise noted.

11. Johann Wolfgang Goethe, *Aus meinem Leben: Dichtung und Wahrheit*, in *Johann Wolfgang Goethe — Sämtliche Werke*, XIV (Frankfurt am Main: Deutscher Klassiker Verlag, 1986), p. 15.

12. Johann Wolfgang Goethe, *Autobiography: The Truth and Fiction Relating to My Life*, in *The Complete Works of Johann Wolfgang von Goethe in Ten Volumes*, I, trans. by John Oxenford (New York: P. F. Collier and Son, 1900), p. 9.

13. Lynn Hunt, *The Family Romance of the French Revolution* (Berkeley: University of California Press, 1992).

14. Ute Brandes, 'Escape to America: Social Reality and Utopian Schemes in German Women's Novels around 1800,' in *In the Shadow of Olympus*, pp. 157–71 (p. 168).

15. Mechthilde Vahsen, *Die Politisierung des weiblichen Subjekts: Deutsche Romanautorinnen und die Französische Revolution 1790–1820* (Berlin: Erich Schmidt Verlag, 2000), p. 183.

16. Cindy Brewer, 'The Emigrant Heroine: Gender and Colonial Fantasy in Henriette Frölich's *Virginia oder Die Kolonie von Kentucky*', *Seminar*, 42.3 (2006), 194–210 (p. 204).

17. Todd Kontje, *Women, the Novel, and the German Nation 1771–1871: Domestic Fiction in the Fatherland* (Cambridge: Cambridge University Press, 1998), p. 113.

18. Gerhard Steiner, 'Nachwort', in Henriette Frölich, *Virginia oder Die Kolonie von Kentucky: Mehr Wahrheit als Dichtung* (Berlin: Aufbau-Verlag, 1963), pp. 205–33 (p. 232).

19. Susanne Zantop, *Colonial Fantasies: Conquest, Family, and Nation in Precolonial Germany, 1770–1870* (Durham, NC and London: Duke University Press, 1997).

20. In the late eighteenth century, the Frölich residence became a salon for Berlin Enlightenment thinkers. In 1792, Henriette's husband, the lawyer Carl Wilhelm Frölich, published *Über den Menschen und seine Verhältnisse* (About Man and his Conditions), a political treatise on collective property, inspired by the utopian socialism of French thinkers such as François-Noël Babeuf. For more information on Henriette Frölich's life in early nineteenth-century Berlin, see Gerhard Steiner's afterword to *Virginia*.

21. Joan Landes, *Women and the Public Sphere in the Age of the French Revolution* (Ithaca: Cornell University Press, 1988).

22. Frölich's letter to Goethe is reproduced in Steiner, 'Nachwort', p. 213.

# CHAPTER 10

# Contestations of Normativity

## Rereading Nineteenth-Century Authors with Current Moral Philosophy

*Annette Bühler-Dietrich*

Judith Butler's recent publications *Undoing Gender* (2004) and *Giving an Account of Oneself* (2005) deal with gender and with moral philosophy; they stress the interconnectedness of human beings. In *Undoing Gender*, a collection of essays already published elsewhere, she tackles the issue of gender and sex norms with regard to conceptions of sexuality and gender which exceed the sex–gender binary. Such forms of living in between tend to be either ignored or punished. Butler suggests it is an ethical imperative to acknowledge these forms of living, in order to make for a liveable life for all human beings. In addition, she conceives of sexuality as that site which makes us aware that we are fundamentally and physically related to the other. Butler continues a line of thought which she had developed in *The Psychic Life of Power* (1997). There she explores how Foucault's notion of subjectivation (*assujetissement*), a coming-into-being of the subject that occurs when he/she is implicated in normative power structures, needs to be supplemented with the subject's desire for these structures. The subject is brought forth by these structures of subjection. Desire, however, works both with and subversively against these strictures. In *Undoing Gender*, Butler examines the way in which these norms preclude certain forms of life. Finally, in *Giving an Account of Oneself*, she questions the norm of giving a coherent account of one's life. Drawing on psychoanalysis, she argues for a foundational non-narratability of subjectivity. Since the subject is unable to put her life into a coherent narrative, psychoanalytic transference witnesses these gaps in subjectivity without needing or wanting to close them. A different attitude to the other follows, which includes an awareness of the necessary inconsistencies in the other's account.

Butler questions the possibility of a self-identical individual and posits a different ethics towards the other arising from the chance afforded by this lack of self-identity. Insofar as she displaces the issue from normativity to desire and then to the primary origins of the subject, she further interrogates how the subject comes into being through the other from the very start. In *Undoing Gender*, Butler positions her reasoning clearly within the project of social transformation. Social transformation can be achieved if the imbrication with the other leads to a different responsibility for the other.[1]

Butler's rethinking of gender norms and ethics takes up an issue which was already prominent in feminist writings around 1900. Male writers of this period struggled to define 'woman' and women authors took issue with the definitions which were inscribed upon them.[2] Within women's writing, two different strands can be distinguished and were discerned at the time: there were radical feminist writers such as Hedwig Dohm (1833–1919) and Rosa Mayreder (1858–1938) on the one hand, and conservative women authors, so-called 'anti-feminists', such as Ellen Key (1849–1926), Lou-Andreas Salomé (1861–1937), and Laura Marholm (1854–1928)[3] on the other. Since the latter argued from biology, radical feminist writers criticized them severely. In their criticism, they disregarded the radical potential which can be found in the reasoning of the conservative authors against whom they were polemicizing. The writings of both groups of authors aim at delineating a space for articulation and living which they consider to be feminine. In the following discussion, I will show how Rosa Mayreder and Laura Marholm, representatives from either side of the spectrum, work at a definition of femininity which contests male norms of femininity at the time. In spite of the different historical circumstances, Butler's moral philosophy and her work on gender can help us grasp the specific project of female articulation which Mayreder and Marholm share.

Around 1900, both Rosa Mayreder and Laura Marholm published important works on femininity. Mayreder published the essays *Zur Kritik der Weiblichkeit* (On the Critique of Femininity) in 1905, Marholm published a series of books, among them *Das Buch der Frauen* (Modern Women, 1895) and *Zur Psychologie der Frau I und II* (Studies in the Psychology of Woman, 1903).[4] Both women were prolific writers. Marholm earned her living with translations from Scandinavian languages as well as with reviews of Scandinavian writings, which, during the period of Naturalism, were of great interest to the German audience. Mayreder, in contrast to Marholm, led an affluent life, during which she founded the 'Allgemeiner Österreichischer Frauenverein' (General Austrian Women's Society), co-edited the journal *Dokumente der Frauen* (Women's Documents), and became a representative of the International Women's League for Peace and Liberty after 1919. In addition to her important treatises *Zur Kritik der Weiblichkeit* and *Geschlecht und Kultur* (Sex and Culture, 1923), she published prose fiction and the libretto to Hugo Wolf's opera *Der Corregidor* (1896). Whereas Marholm, who was born in Riga, settled in Denmark on her own when quite young and became close friends with leading Scandinavian intellectuals such as Georg Brandes (1842–1927), Arne Garborg (1851–1924), and, ultimately, her husband Ola Hansson (1860–1925), Mayreder remained in Vienna, a European centre for the exposition of various theories of femininity at the time. Two very different attitudes to femininity resulted. While Mayreder kept on publishing until the end of her life, Marholm had stopped publishing by 1905, after suffering severe bouts of paranoia, and spending half a year in the Munich lunatic asylum.

Whereas Mayreder's work has sparked some interest in recent years, which has led to new editions of some of her works, Marholm's works have not been republished. While her *Buch der Frauen* can be found in libraries and second-hand bookshops, her fiction is hard to track down.[5] Comparatively little critical literature has been published on Marholm. Useful, however, is Susan Brantly's monograph *The Life and Writings of Laura Marholm* (1991), which includes several formerly unpublished Swedish documents in English translation.[6] Individual quotations by Marholm are occasionally discussed in secondary works dealing with the period, such as Nike Wagner's *Geist und Geschlecht* (1981), but they tend to perpetuate the stereotypes about Marholm which were already prevalent during her lifetime.[7] By contrast, Mayreder's contribution to Austrian feminism is remarked upon in a number of publications.[8]

Marholm attracted severe criticism from radical feminists of her period, because she considered women to be determined by their biology. According to her, procreation is the chief aim and work of woman: 'Die beste Arbeit, die das Weib leisten kann und in der sich seine Produktivität ganz und gar ungeschmälert und dauerhaft zeigt, das ist das Kind' [The best work woman can do is the child. In it, her productivity is displayed entirely undiminished and shown to be enduring].[9] Therefore, she regards women's endeavours to enter the formerly male professions as a service to male capitalism, not as an achievement for women.[10] For Marholm, women should find fulfilment in their sexuality, as well as in motherhood. In *Buch der Frauen*, it is a lack of sexual fulfilment which she claims to be at the centre of women's artistic deficit. She argues as follows:

> Aber das alleinstehende Weib kann mit der Konvenienz nicht brechen, denn diese ist seine einzige Stütze. Und die Konvenienz ist nicht bloß außer ihm, sie ist auch in ihm. Sie ist zugleich seine intimste weibliche Scham, sie ist die Richtschnur seines Empfindens, von der es nicht [sic] befreit, außer der Liebe. Darum ist, je höher das Weib begabt ist, in desto höherem Grade die Liebe ihr großes Los.

> [But the single woman cannot break with convention, since it is her only source of support. And convention is not only external to her, it is also within her. It is at the same time her most intimate female shamefulness, it is the guiding principle of her emotions, and nothing will free her from it but love. Therefore, the more gifted woman is, the more love is her great destiny.][11]

It is, however, not marriage, but sexual pleasure woman needs to find, as Marholm argues with regard to the mathematician and writer Sonja Kowalewska (1850–91).[12] Only in love, according to Marholm, can woman come into her own and find a voice of her own:

> Und kommt für das durchschnittlich gutveranlagte Weib schon alles darauf an, welcher Mann für sie der Gebende wird, wieviel mehr für das Weib-Genie, in dem das Weib und das Genie zugleich geweckt wird, frei wird, Weib und Genie wird unter der Umarmung des Mannes.

> [And if, for the averagely gifted woman, everything depends on which man becomes her provider, how much more this is the case for the genius-woman, in whom womanhood and genius are awakened and freed at the same time, who becomes woman and genius through the embrace of a man.][13]

Only through sexuality can female genius be awakened. Yet in Marholm's idea of sexuality, it cannot be any embrace, but only one fed by unmitigated desire.[14]

Marholm's distinct enemy is bourgeois marriage. Since it is 'klug berechnet' [cleverly calculated],[15] it is without the love for which woman, according to Marholm, is made.[16] This love needs to be unconditional. Its effect might be good or bad:

> je höher des Weibes Leib und Geist und Seele entwickelt ist, desto weniger kann es des Mannes entraten, der ihr großes Glück ist oder ihr großes Unglück, aber in allen Fällen der einzige Sinn ihres Lebens. Denn des Weibes Inhalt ist der Mann.

> [the more developed a woman's body, mind and soul, the less she can do without man. He is her happiness or her great misfortune, but in any case the only meaning of her life. For woman's content is man.][17]

It is sentences like the latter which evoked vehement protest among radical feminists of the period and make one wonder still. Yet Marholm's attitude to man, procreation, and sexuality deserves closer scrutiny. She observes a fundamental deficit in women's life and art and she sees a relation between sexuality on the one hand and artistic creation on the other. Outside exigencies — the lack of social structures for single women, the necessity to secure a living through marriage — are responsible for the current state of affairs. Thus her thinking, even if it centres on biology, allows for a social regulation of gender as well.[18] Additionally, nowhere does she grant man as social being a position which makes him superior to women. Instead, it is the social being man whom woman avoids: 'Das Weib rottet sich in Massen zusammen, um sich zu schützen vor dem Manne als Beutejäger, vor dem Speculirwüthigen, dem Alles, was in seinen Gesichtskreis fällt, nur als gute Prise in Betracht kommt' [Woman gathers in masses in order to protect herself from man the hunter and speculator, who considers everything in his radius only as a good steal].[19]

It is rather the idea of man Marholm favours, an 'Ich, das über das Weib herrscht, nicht als ein Einzelwesen mit einzelnen Ansprüchen, sondern als Glied einer Lebenskette' [ego, who rules over woman, not as an individual being with individual demands, but as part of the chain of life].[20] Marholm accords a position to man which exceeds any concept of individual man. Instead, it is man as progenitor, as representative of the genus she envisions, man as lover, not as husband. Although for her sexuality and procreation are writ large at the centre of women's lives, it is not marriage which guarantees the sort of fulfilment she highlights again and again. When she stresses the innate relationship between woman and man, she makes a radical, albeit conservative argument: she does away with individualism and instead refers the subject to his or her dependency on the other. While bourgeois society shapes this dependency in terms of economics, Marholm attacks such a conflation of economics and sexuality. Marriage to her is neither tied to premarital abstinence nor is it forcibly a lifelong commitment. Instead, it is a physical, bodily dependency on the other.

Marholm's focus on eroticism is striking in light of the rather anti-sensual attitude we will see in Mayreder. It also needs to be separated from Marholm's insistence on motherhood. Even though she claims that motherhood is woman's ultimate destiny, sexuality exists in its own right for her.[21] Her theory of femininity makes her develop an ethics which focuses on the relation to the other as source of fulfilment.

Even though Marholm grounds her thinking in procreation, the consequences she draws suggest a need for social transformation.[22] Instead of supporting abstinence and monogamy with the Norwegian writer Björnstjerne Björnson (1832–1910), who had run a campaign for premarital sexual abstinence, Marholm favours Garborg's proposal for facilitated divorce legislation.[23] Her claim that woman finds fulfilment in man and in procreation is associated neither with financial support nor with any desire for permanence. It is a specific social situation she attacks: while women wither away in hapless marriages on which they depend for their living, men seek pleasure outside marriage.[24]

In contrast to her critique of Björnson, Marholm's musings in *Zur Psychologie der Frau* are rather general. Accordingly, it is a female typology she develops, one which is not related to a specific national situation. In this typology, she distinguishes between 'la détraquée' [the hysterical one], 'la cérébrale' [the cerebral one], and 'la grande amoureuse' [the great lover].[25] While they are biological types, they are nevertheless determined by the social situation; thus the cerebral type might be an 'amoureuse manquée' [a failed lover]. Marholm considers 'la cérébrale' to be the woman who starts to write, who engages in the women's rights movement, and who continues to seek a kind of fulfilment she cannot find in her work. The women Marholm discusses in *Buch der Frauen* are such 'cérébrales'. But they exist because of the current social situation:

> Unsere gegenwärtigen Culturverhältnisse sind so, daß das Weib sich immer nur frei *von etwas*, aber nicht frei *zu etwas* zu fühlen vermag; — und welcher, selbst von unseren vorgeschrittensten und verfeinertsten Männern, würde dem Weibe die Enthüllung seines ganzen Wesens ohne eine unangenehme Betroffenheit einräumen? Das Weib, das sich so zeigt, wird ihm *fremd*; denn er hat in seinen Nerven das Gedächtniß aller der Vorschriften, die in Literatur und Kunst und Leben über das wahre, echte und zulässige Weibsein gemacht worden sind.

> [Our current cultural situation is such that women are always only free *from something*, but they do not feel free *to do something* — and who, even among our most progressive and sophisticated men, would allow women to reveal their entire being without feeling unpleasantly affected? The woman who is thus revealed to him becomes a *stranger*, because he has in his nerves the memory of all the definitions of true, genuine, and reliable womanhood which literature, art, and life have suggested.][26]

Since culturally constructed and sedimented images determine how men perceive women, woman's sexuality in particular is strictly regulated:

> Das moderne Weib kann nicht lieben. Oder was darunter verstanden wird: es kann sich nicht vergessen, nicht das Bewußtsein seiner selbst verlieren, sich nicht hingeben in einer Extase, sich auch nicht unterwerfen. Ja, das Weib liebt nicht mehr, sondern das Weib denkt und das Weib urtheilt.

> [Modern woman cannot love. Or at least as love is understood: she cannot forget herself, cannot lose her consciousness of herself, cannot abandon herself in ecstasy, cannot subordinate herself. Yes, woman does not love anymore, woman thinks and judges.][27]

Instead of losing herself in self-abandon, woman closes herself off. Marholm opposes love and thought, because women's thoughts nowadays are monitored by discursive gender prescriptions. To these Marholm opposes another concept of femininity which is tied to an ecstatic idea of sexuality, one which is not predominantly procreative. Whereas Marholm's *Buch der Frauen* focuses more on sexuality and artistic creation, she turns towards procreation in *Zur Psychologie der Frau*. Marholm's high esteem for motherhood is equally for such a loss of self in favour of the other:

> Es wird zu allen Zeiten Frauen geben, die früh und aus eigenem Entschlusse verzichten werden auf eigenes Leben, um in Anderer Leben zu leben, aus dem Wesen des Weibes heraus, das Extase ist, und aus jenem noch tieferen Gefühle im Wesen des Weibes: unser Keiner lebt sich selber; Gefäße sind wir und Trägerinnen für Anderer Inhalt, wir tragen nun eigene oder fremde Frucht.

> [At all times there will be women who early on decide for themselves to renounce a life of their own in order to live in the life of others, due to the essence of woman, which is ecstasy, and due to that even deeper feeling in women's being: none of us lives for herself, we are vessels for and bearers of another's content, whether we carry our own or another's fruit.][28]

Marholm's attack on 'Ichsucht' (egotism) might seem strange when one considers women's concurrent struggle for emancipation.[29] Yet her critique of current gender norms makes it clear that it is not a return to the previous situation she favours.[30] Instead, she delineates an alternative society of nurturing. Marholm dreams of a secular 'Schwesterschaft des Lebens' (sorority of life),[31] where women take professional care of their kin. While charitable work was widespread among well-to-do women in Germany at that time,[32] Marholm disparages 'die tändelnde Pose müssiggängerischer Wohlthätigkeit' [the dallying pose of idle benevolence] and asks for a true commitment which creates a social heterotopos.[33]

Phrases like 'Gefäße sind wir und Trägerinnen für Anderer Inhalt' called forth vehement criticism from nineteenth-century feminists.[34] But Marholm's idea that woman's needs go beyond being a self-identical subject is useful for identifying a more radical potential in her. While woman faces social impediments on all sides, she experiences an excess which comes to bear in sexuality and in motherhood. Marholm's awareness of an excess within the subject which prevents closure brings her closer to Butler's recent publications, even though Butler does not share Marholm's preoccupation with motherhood. Butler focuses on the failure of self-identity and on the 'ethical enmeshment' with the other in order to bring forth a different ethical and political attitude towards the other.

> Let's face it. We're undone by each other. And if we're not, we're missing something. [...] And so when we speak about *my* sexuality or *my* gender, as we do (and as we must) we mean something complicated by it. Neither of these is precisely a possession, but both are to be understood as *modes of being dispossessed*, ways of being for another, or, indeed, by virtue of another.[35]

And she continues:

> The particular sociality that belongs to bodily life, to sexual life, and to becoming gendered (which is always, to a certain extent, becoming gendered *for others*) establishes a field of ethical enmeshment with others and a sense of disorientation for the first-person, that is, the perspective of the ego.[36]

It is this perspective of the ego which Marholm rejects. Instead, she emphasizes the ecstatic subject, who enjoys fulfilment by way of 'being dispossessed' by the other. In contrast to Butler, however, Marholm reserves this ecstasy for woman.

Brantly writes that Marholm's critics rejected her treatment of sexuality: 'Marholm's advocacy of the feminine sex drive was shocking at a time when the scientific community held that women barely had one at all'.[37] Helene Lange reproaches her for having drawn woman as 'das hysterische Geschlechtswesen' [the hysterical sex][38] — a severe judgement at the height of the diagnosis of hysteria in women.[39] Woman was seen as an overtly sexual being by female writers neither within nor outside the women's movement, with the exception of Lou Andreas-Salomé. The protest Marholm's fiction writing met with must be understood in this context.[40] In addition, Marholm's writings were welcomed by those very male writers, such as Paul Möbius (1853–1907) or Max Runge (1849–1909), who had restricted woman to biology all along.[41]

In her essay 'Reaktion in der Frauenbewegung' (Reactions within the Women's Movement, 1899), Hedwig Dohm writes in response to Lou Andreas-Salomé:

> Wie käme ich dazu, meine ganz individuelle Veranlagung zum Maßstab der ganzen Frauenwelt zu machen? Damit verfiele ich ja in den Fehler der Frauen, die mit sich alle anderen Frauen identifizieren. Nein, die Frauen in ihrer Gesamtheit lassen sich nicht unter einen Hut bringen.

> [How could I possibly arrive at the idea of turning my individual disposition into the measure of all womanhood? If I did so, I would be making the same mistake as those women who identify all other women with themselves. No, women in their entirety cannot all be grouped together.][42]

Dohm's statement is distinctively modern, if we consider the efforts of the late 1980s and early 1990s to pluralize the feminist subject. Her criticism applies not only to Lou Andreas-Salomé but also to Marholm and to Mayreder. Both create typologies of woman and attach clear judgements to these types.

As discussed above, for Marholm it is the relation between sexuality, intelligence, and social circumstances which brings forth different types of women. By contrast, Mayreder distinguishes between 'primitive Weiblichkeit' [primitive womanhood] and 'differenzierte Weiblichkeit' [differentiated womanhood]. Primitive womanhood depends on man sexually and desires subordination; Mayreder sees these women as fulfilling the 'primitive teleologische Geschlechtsnatur' [primitive teleological sexual nature] which aims at procreation.[43] The women Marholm depicts are for Mayreder representatives of primitive womanhood.[44] By contrast, it is personality which determines differentiated womanhood:

> Das Weib aber, das aus eigener Machtvollkommenheit über sich als Geschlechtswesen verfügen will und dieses Recht der Persönlichkeit kraft innerer Notwendigkeit zum obersten Gesetz seines Lebens macht [...] wird als Typus der differenzierten Weiblichkeit gelten können [...]. Denn das entscheidende Merkmal ist die Entwicklung des Persönlichkeitsbewußtseins, das die primitive teleologische Geschlechtsnatur aufhebt — am umfassendsten dann, wenn es auch die erotische Eigenart des Individuums durchdringt.

> [The woman, however, who out of a sense of her own independence wants

to be in control of herself as sexed being and who, of inner necessity, makes this right to a personality the highest law of her life [...] can be considered the type of differentiated womanhood [...]. For the most important feature is the development of a consciousness of personality which negates primitive, teleological sexual nature — most extensively when it also penetrates the erotic character of the individual.][45]

Mayreder is clearly in favour of differentiated womanhood. All through her writing, she insists on personality as the prime value in life which permits woman to rise above the ascription 'Gattungswesen' [species]. When, in *Geschlecht und Kultur*, she later ponders 'Das Wesen der Liebe' [the essence of love] she tries to separate eroticism and love. Again, she subordinates sexuality to love:

> in den ersten Stadien jener Geschlechtsliebe, bei welcher die seelischen Momente der Anziehung überwiegen, ist das sexuelle Moment so untergeordnet, daß es nicht als etwas Ursprüngliches, als primäre Ursache, sondern eher als etwas Hinzukommendes, Sekundäres erscheint.

> [in the early stages of that sexual love in which the attractions of personality dominate, the sexual element is subordinate, so that it does not appear as something fundamental, as primary cause, but rather as something additional, as something secondary.][46]

Mayreder's investigation of gender and sexuality is far more learned than Marholm's. Like Butler, who takes Hegel's phenomenology as a model of self-transformation by the encounter with the other,[47] Mayreder goes back to Hegel:

> Hegel hat daher als das erste Moment in der Liebe bezeichnet, 'daß ich keine selbständige Person für mich sein will, und daß, wenn ich dies wäre, ich mich mangelhaft und unvollständig fühle.' [...] Um den Preis, daß die egoistische Isolierung aufgehoben wird, nimmt der Liebende die Gefahr, in fremdes Leid verstrickt zu werden, willig auf sich.

> [For that reason, Hegel has described the first moment in love as the feeling 'that I do not wish to be an independent person for myself, and that I would feel incomplete and deficient if I were one'. [...] In order to lose this egotistical isolation, the lover gladly runs the risk of becoming involved in someone else's suffering.][48]

While Mayreder reserves this state for love, Butler sees egotistical isolation as itself impossible:

> If I am struggling *for* autonomy, do I not need to be struggling for something else as well, a conception of myself as invariably in community, impressed upon by others, impressing them as well, and in ways that are not always clearly delineable, in forms that are not fully predictable?[49]

For Butler, the subject is structured by the set of norms which govern subjectivation but also by physical exposure to the other. The issue of autonomy is reformulated, as the quotation above shows. Butler's writings thus destabilize the idea of autonomy in two ways: on the one hand she continues Foucault's idea that the subject comes into being by being subjected to norms.[50] On the other she shifts the focus in such a way that bodiliness becomes the basis for a different relation to the self: one of 'undoing': 'If the way I am undone by the other conflicts with social norms, I might no longer be recognizable as a subject'.[51] Butler has queer and transgender subjects in mind,[52] and Mayreder refers to one such instance of non-recognition: by calling emancipated women 'Mannweiber' [man-women], men tried to disparage them.[53]

Fantasies allow alternative identities to be envisioned: 'Fantasy is what allows us to imagine ourselves and others otherwise; it establishes the possible in excess of the real; it points elsewhere, and when it is embodied, it brings the elsewhere home'.[54] Fantasies which are enacted physically can change social reality; as fantasies they articulate desire.[55] By contrast, Mayreder leads her own struggle in accordance with the women's movement of her time. It is the opposition between body and mind and the distinction between different types of intelligence which govern her thinking: 'Das Element der Bewegung aber, das Element der Erneuerung und Entwicklung, wird durch Einzelne repräsentiert, durch Individualitäten. Die Individualität ist die Quelle, aus welcher alle neuen Erkenntnisse, alle neuen Bedürfnisse, alle neuen Daseinsmöglichkeiten entspringen' [The element of movement, however, the element of renewal and development, is represented by individuals, by individualities. Individuality is the source from which all new insights, all new needs, all new possibilities of existence spring].[56]

As part of this progress, physical needs are relinquished: 'Für hochgestimmte Seelen ist nichts unerträglicher als die Vorstellung von der Gebundenheit durch das Geschlecht' [To elevated souls, nothing is more unbearable than the idea of being bound by one's sex].[57] But those souls are the strong ones and their way of living is not that of the multitude.[58] Her close study of Nietzsche comes to the fore here. Yet she allows for a possible alteration of femininity, if social circumstances and the prevailing norms change.[59] Both Mayreder and Marholm thus attack the 'corset' of norms and customs, but their way of moving beyond them is very different.

Mayreder's persistent denial of sexuality goes hand in hand with her glorification of individualism. Both attitudes eventually testify to the validity of the gender norms of her time for Mayreder herself. As we can see from her diary, in life she struggled with the kind of love which renounces sexuality, although she celebrated it in her writings. Mayreder wrote *Zur Kritik der Weiblichkeit* in part during her love affair with Paul Kubin. As a married woman, she refused to consummate the affair. Kubin's ensuing visits to a brothel, quite typical for Viennese men at that time,[60] make the split between physical and psychic needs — which Mayreder herself fought to the detriment of sensuality — apparent: 'aber die Vorstellung, daß der Leib, auf welchen ich mit übermenschlicher Anstrengung verzichtet habe, an eine bezahlte Unwürdige vergeudet werden soll, bringt mich außer mich' [but the idea that the body which I have renounced with superhuman effort should be wasted on some unworthy, paid woman, makes me very angry].[61] When Mayreder dismisses Marholm's acceptance of pre-marital male sex and prostitution, her public and private animosity are both in evidence.[62] In her opinion, being paid for sex reduces woman to a 'willenloses Werkzeug der männlichen Übermacht' [a helpless tool of male dominance][63] and is thus opposed to the idea of a free personality Mayreder wants to foster.

Since Mayreder's prime values are personality and individuality, qualities she sees in opposition to the sex drive of the genus, her idea of the relation between sexuality and art differs considerably from that of Marholm. For Mayreder, sexuality is necessary for art through sublimation: 'Jeder Künstler, so führte sie aus, lebe von der Sublimierung seiner Sexualität, er brauche starke Impulse, Eindrücke, die über das Durchschnittliche hinausgehen, das sei notwendig für jede Art der Kreativität' [every artist, she explains, lives by sublimating his sexuality; he needs strong impulses, impressions above and beyond the average; this is necessary for any kind of creativity], writes Schmölzer, summing up an unpublished diary entry by Mayreder.[64] By contrast, Marholm sees sexual pleasure as essential to female creativity.[65]

In spite of their different evaluation of phenomena, Mayreder and Marholm witness a similar conflict in female artists of their time. Both, for example, write about Marie Bashkirtseff (1860–84), a young Russian artist whose diaries were published posthumously in 1887. For Marholm, Bashkirtseff's artistic deficits are due to her virginity: '[S]ie blieb gefangen ihr Lebenlang in dem, was größer war als alle ihre Möglichkeiten — in der *großen Unwissenheit* des jungen Mädchens' [All her life, she remained a prisoner of that which was greater than all her possibilities — of the great ignorance of the young girl].[66] By contrast, Mayreder sees Bashkirtseff, as she does Sonja Kowalewska, as an example of female 'dyscrasia', a mixture of the desire for intellectual independence and sexual subordination.[67] Mayreder uses this medical terminology idiosyncratically but persistently in her writings, giving them an aura of scientificity. For Mayreder Bashkirtseff is important because of 'die außerordentliche Ausbildung des reflexiven Denkens' [the extraordinary refinement of her capacity for reflection].[68] Mayreder clearly constructs Bashkirtseff as a mirror image of herself. Her own diaries display the same self-reflexivity she sees in Bashkirtseff and even her own sexuality displays traits of the dyscrasia she sees in the young Russian artist.[69] For Marholm Bashkirtseff embodies the prototypical 'Psychologie des jungen Mädchens' [psychology of the young girl].[70] Mayreder's impulse is to liberate Bashkirtseff's diaries from Marholm's misreading. Yet once again she so openly opposes personality to sexuality that rather than giving a more adequate description of Bashkirtseff she imposes her specific point of view on her.

In spite of the differences between them, both authors share certain assumptions: both consider the impact of social circumstances on the way 'woman' is constructed. They envisage various social changes which could bring about a different kind of womanhood. Both, however, also start from the assumption that woman's character is dependent on biology. While Marholm calls for social circumstances which make sexual fulfilment possible, Mayreder erects personality as the bulwark against the upsurge of any 'teleological' needs caused by the genus 'woman'. Insofar as both thinkers see gender as constructed but sex as natural, they interrupt a sex–gender continuity which can be found in male writers like Möbius, but continue to depend on thinking a female biological essence.[71]

Although in other ways Marholm and Mayreder contest the norms and conventions of their time, their thinking functions in accordance with the heterosexual matrix. When Mayreder conceives of androgyny, it is strictly metaphorical. As a combination of female and male traits, it transcends the character restrictions of either sex. Yet she abhors the blurring of sex inscriptions and sees it as a form of degeneracy. Whereas Butler tries to prepare the way for a livable minority life in between sex and gender ascriptions, Mayreder writes: 'Jede Abweichung von der physiologischen Norm macht das Individuum zu einem unvollkommenen Wesen; die körperliche Zwitterhaftigkeit ist widerwärtig, weil sie eine Unzulänglichkeit, eine unterbrochene und mißglückte Bildung darstellt' [Every deviation from the physiological norm turns the individual into an incomplete being; physical androgyny is disgusting, because it represents a deficit, an interrupted and failed form].[72] Although the late nineteenth century proved to be increasingly obsessed with homosexual and transgender practices, they were relegated to the realm of pathology.[73]

For Marholm, androgyny isn't really a topic. In spite, or because, of her focus on heterosexuality she does not address the homosexual practices depicted early on in Reuter's *Aus guter Familie* when she discusses the book.[74] She does, however, diagnose an altered relation between women which becomes manifest in a different style of writing:

> Und sie empfinden für einander mit ihren entwickelten vibrierenden Nerven wie noch nie Weib für Weib empfunden, ein Empfinden bis in den Herzpunkt des Wesens der anderen, ein Mitschwingen, wie sonst nur das Weib für den Mann vibrierte und mitschwang.

> [And they feel for each other with these highly developed, vibrating nerves in a way woman has never felt for woman; a feeling that penetrates to the heart of the other, a vibration, a resonance, of a kind woman so far has only experienced for man.][75]

Consequently, another kind of feminine expression ensues which goes beyond the imitation of male models. 'Weibpersönlichkeit' [female personality] and a new sensibility for other women thus go hand in hand.[76] This 'vibration' for another woman is considered a positive development by Marholm; its logical continuation is in fact her idea of a matriarchal heterotopos as refuge for unwed women.

While Mayreder, the less conservative woman writer, in the end remains within bourgeois norms, Marholm's idea of female sexuality leads her to develop a vision of feminine creativity and sociality which gestures towards a utopian way of living. Her concept of female creativity is reminiscent of Woolf's statement in *A Room of One's Own* (1929):

> The book has somehow to be adapted to the body, and at a venture one would say that women's books should be shorter, more concentrated, than those of men, and framed so that they do not need long hours of steady and uninterrupted work.[77]

Her idea of sociality relies on a strongly biologistic view of woman. Yet her vision of sexuality goes beyond the realms of bourgeois decency, as the reactions of her surroundings show. It is the 'antifeminist' Marholm who explodes bourgeois gender norms which deny woman overt sexuality. Marholm is aware of the undoing of the subject by sexuality which Butler discusses. By turning it into a diagnostic tool for literary criticism, she argues against a predominance of the mind and personality in art, in direct opposition to Mayreder.

At the outset of *Undoing Gender*, Butler writes:

> If my doing is dependent on what is done to me or, rather, the ways in which I am done by norms, then the possibility of my persistence as an 'I' depends upon my being able to do something with what is done with me.[78]

Within the male gender discourse of the late nineteenth century, Marholm and Mayreder can clearly be seen as doing something with what is done with them. Both struggle to redefine femininity according to their own point of view. As such, they are part of a group of women writers about whom Mayreder writes:

> Dieses subjektive Verfahren verleiht ihren Aussagen besonderes Gewicht. [...] Einen praktischen Wert, etwa als Richtschnur und Erziehungskanon, haben diese Aussagen schon deshalb nicht, weil die Vertreterinnen der spezifischen Weiblichkeit unter sich nicht einig sind, was man eigentlich darunter zu verstehen hat.

> [This subjective way of proceeding gives weight to their statements. [...] These statements do not have any practical value, for example as guiding principle or educational canon, not least because the representatives of the specific types of femininity cannot agree amongst themselves about how precisely these are defined.][79]

Even though Mayreder takes the position of outside observer in this quotation, in fact she is implied by it. Although she claims that women's theories of femininity have no practical value, they have an impact on discourses on femininity. In this respect they potentially open up new possibilities for women. As Butler writes:

> That it [feminism] asks how we organize life, how we accord it value, how we safeguard it against violence, how we compel the world, and its institutions, to inhabit new values, means that its philosophical pursuits are in some sense at one with the aim of social transformation.[80]

I contend that even the so-called 'antifeminist' Marholm asks such questions just as vehemently as Mayreder. Even though both women's roots in biologistic thinking are out of date, each in her own way deserves close scrutiny today. Their battle with sex and gender norms is one which is still fought today, as Butler makes us aware again and again.

## Notes to Chapter 10

1. Butler continues this line of thought in her most recent publication, *Frames of War: When is Life Grievable?* (London: Verso, 2010).
2. Notorious for their definitions of womanhood are Paul Möbius (1853–1907) and Otto Weininger (1880–1903). Both Möbius's *Ueber den physiologischen Schwachsinn des Weibes* (On Woman's Physiological Mental Deficiency, 1900) and Weininger's *Geschlecht und Charakter* (Sex and Character, 1903) were widely read at the time.
3. Erroneously, *Lexikon deutschsprachiger Schriftstellerinnen 1800–1945*, ed. by Gisela Brinker-Gabler, Karola Ludwig, and Angela Wöffen (Munich: dtv, 1986), claims that Marholm died in 1905.
4. Both books appeared in English translation: Laura Marholm, *Modern Women*, trans. by Hermione Ramsden (London: J. Lane; Boston: Roberts Brothers, 1896); Laura Marholm, *Studies in the Psychology of Woman*, trans. by Georgia A. Etchison (Chicago: H. S. Stone, 1899). The latter publication is a translation of the first edition of *Zur Psychologie der Frau*. All translations in this article, however, are my own.

5. Now a copy of her novel *Frau Lily als Jungfrau, Gattin und Mutter* (1897), is available at *Open Library:* <http://openlibrary.org/b/OL23435426M/Frau_Lilly_als_Jungfrau_Gattin_und_Mutter>, viewed 29.04.2010.

6. Susan Brantly, *The Life and Writings of Laura Marholm* (Basel: Helbing & Lichtenhahn, 1991).

7. See Nike Wagner, *Geist und Geschlecht: Karl Kraus und die Erotik der Wiener Moderne* (1981; Frankfurt am Main: Suhrkamp, 1987), pp. 86–89, on Mayreder and Marholm. In 1992, two articles appeared on Marholm's relation to German naturalists: Peter Sprengel, ' "Entgleisungen" in Hauptmanns Nachlaß: Zur Thematisierung weiblicher Sexualität bei Ola Hansson und Laura Marholm', *Orbis Litterarum*, 47 (1992), 31–51, and Bengt Algot Sorensen, 'Laura Marholm, Fr. Nietzsche und G. Hauptmanns *Einsame Menschen*', *Orbis Litterarum*, 47 (1992), 52–62. Recently Sarah Colvin discussed Marholm's play *Karla Bühring* (1895) in her *Women and German Drama: Playwrights and their Texts, 1860–1945* (Rochester, NY: Camden House, 2003), pp. 75–102.

8. See Hilde Schmölzer's biography *Rosa Mayreder: Ein Leben zwischen Utopie und Wirklichkeit* (Vienna: Promedia, 2002); Katrin Schmersahl's discussion in *Medizin und Geschlecht: Zur Konstruktion der Kategorie Geschlecht im medizinischen Diskurs des 19. Jahrhunderts* (Opladen: Leske + Budrich, 1998); the introduction to the recent edition of her diaries by Harriet Anderson, 'Einleitung', in Rosa Mayreder, *Tagebücher 1873–1937*, ed. by Harriet Anderson (Frankfurt am Main: Insel, 1988), pp.10–40; and the afterword to the republished essays by Eva Geber, 'Rosa Mayreder: Visionäre Theoretikerin des Feminismus', in Rosa Mayreder, *Zur Kritik der Weiblichkeit: Essays*, ed. by Eva Geber (1905; Vienna: Mandelbaum, 1998), pp. 261–74; also Eva Geber, 'Der Verlust der Hoffnung', in Rosa Mayreder, *Geschlecht und Kultur: Essays*, ed. by Eva Geber (1923; Vienna: Mandelbaum, 1998), pp. 321–30.

9. Laura Marholm, *Zur Psychologie der Frau*, 1, 2nd enlarged edn (Berlin: Carl Duncker, 1903), p. 311. There is a second volume of *Zur Psychologie der Frau* (Berlin: Carl Duncker, 1903). It discusses among other things novels by Paul Bourget and Barbey d'Aurevilly. I will only quote from volume 1 here. All translations are my own.

10. See Marholm, *Psychologie der Frau*, I, pp. 284–99.

11. Laura Marholm, *Das Buch der Frauen: Zeitpsychologische Porträts*, 4th edn (Paris, Leipzig, and Munich: Albert Langen, 1896), p. 54.

12. Ibid., pp. 172–73.

13. Ibid., p. 172.

14. 'Keiner begehrte ihrer mit dem Urtrieb des Mannes zum Weibe' (Ibid., p. 170).

15. Ibid., p. 48.

16. Marholm sees Gabriele Reuter's heroine Agathe in *Aus guter Familie* (1896) as an example of a wrong, bourgeois attitude to love. See Marholm, *Psychologie der Frau*, 1, 167–76.

17. Marholm, *Buch der Frauen*, p. 48.

18. See for example her article 'Zur Frauenfrage: Die beiden Seiten der Medaille', *Freie Bühne*, 12 (1890), 585–89.

19. Marholm, *Psychologie der Frau*, I, p. 282.

20. Ibid., p. 283.

21. Kowalewska, for example, was wife and mother and still she lacked the experience of being a lover ('Geliebte'); see Marholm, *Buch der Frauen*, p. 173.

22. Brantly situates this attention to sexuality and social transformation in the discursive atmosphere of the Friedrichshagener Dichterkreis [Friedrichshagen circle of writers]: 'In the tiny suburb, three special interests permeated the air, which no doubt had their effect on the Hanssons: Socialism, the interrelatedness of science and literature, and the relationship between the sexes' (Brantly, *Marholm*, p. 89). Marholm and her husband lived in Friedrichshagen from 1891 to 1893.

23. Laura Marholm, 'Björnson als Sittlichkeitsapostel', *Die Gegenwart*, 33 (1888), 100–03.

24. It is women's situation she criticizes when she reviews Reuter's *Aus guter Familie*: 'Das Verdienstliche in diesem Buche liegt nun darin, dieses innere Leben anschaulich zu machen. Es ist gewiß nicht complicirt; es ist ganz einfach, es besteht eben im Warten' [The merit of this book is that it makes visible this inner life. It is certainly not complicated, it is very simple, it consists of waiting], (Marholm, *Psychologie der Frau*, I, p. 171).

25. See Marholm, *Psychologie der Frau*, I, pp. 36–65, for an extended description of these types.

26. Ibid., p. 55.
27. Ibid., p. 53.
28. Ibid., p. 326.
29. Ibid., p. 325.
30. Whenever she looks for models, it is to the Middle Ages, to a pre-Reformation society.
31. Marholm, *Psychologie der Frau*, I, p. 328.
32. See Ute Frevert, 'Kulturfrauen und Geschäftsmänner: Soziale Identitäten im deutschen Bürgertum des 19. Jahrhunderts', in *'Mann und Weib und Weib und Mann': Geschlechter-Differenzen in der Moderne* (Munich: Beck, 1995).
33. Marholm, *Psychologie der Frau*, I, p. 327.
34. Mayreder attacks similar statements by Marholm in *Zur Kritik der Weiblichkeit: Essays* (1905; Vienna: Mandelbaum, 1998), pp. 142–44.
35. Butler, *Undoing Gender* (New York: Routledge, 2004), p. 19.
36. Ibid., p. 25.
37. Brantly, *Marholm*, p. 108.
38. Lange, quoted in Brantly, *Marholm*, p. 109.
39. Sprengel describes Gerhart Hauptmann's reaction to Laura Marholm, whom he treated in a parody, the point of attack of which was Marholm's discussion of sexuality. See Peter Sprengel, '"Entgleisungen" in Hauptmanns Nachlaß', pp. 31–51.
40. See Brantly, *Marholm*, pp. 107–14.
41. On Runge see ibid., p. 110. Möbius reads Marholm selectively and overlooks Marholm's perception of the influence of social circumstances on the construction of gender. See Möbius, *Ueber den physiologischen Schwachsinn des Weibes*, 3rd edn (Halle: Carl Marhold, 1901), p. 17.
42. Dohm, 'Reaktion in der Frauenbewegung', *Die Zukunft*, 29 (1899), 279–91, repr. in Hedwig Dohm, *Ausgewählte Texte: Ein Lesebuch zum Jubiläum ihres 175. Geburtstages mit Essays und Feuilletons, Novellen und Dialogen, Aphorismen und Briefen*, ed. by Nikola Müller and Isabel Rohner (Berlin: trafo, 2006), pp. 136–51 (p. 140).
43. Mayreder, *Zur Kritik*, pp. 162–63.
44. Ibid., pp. 153–54.
45. Ibid., p. 163.
46. Mayreder, *Geschlecht und Kultur*, p. 263.
47. Butler elaborates on Hegel repeatedly in the works under consideration here, especially *Giving an Account of Oneself* (New York: Fordham University Press, 2005), pp. 26–30.
48. Mayreder, *Geschlecht und Kultur*, p. 252.
49. Butler, *Undoing Gender*, pp. 21–22.
50. A concise description of Foucault's impact on Butler can be found in Vicki Kirby, *Judith Butler: Live Theory* (London: Continuum, 2006), pp. 108–28.
51. See Butler, *Giving an Account*, p. 30.
52. Butler, *Undoing Gender*, p. 29.
53. Mayreder, *Zur Kritik*, p. 160.
54. Butler, *Undoing Gender*, p. 29.
55. Ibid., p. 29.
56. Mayreder, *Zur Kritik*, p. 81.
57. Ibid., p. 257.
58. 'Es ist ein Vorrecht der Starken, das Leben nach eigenen Impulsen zu gestalten, allein es kann keine Maxime für die Schwachen, also für die Mehrzahl bilden' [It is the prerogative of the strong to shape life according to their own impulses; they cannot, however, make maxims for the weak, for the majority] (Mayreder, *Zur Kritik*, p. 89).
59. Ibid., p. 91.
60. They were in fact recommended by his doctor; see Mayreder, *Tagebücher 1873–1937*, p. 72.
61. Ibid., pp. 72–73. With Kubin's visits to the brothel, prostitution, one of the key topics in Mayreder's public speeches, became a personal threat as well as a social evil. On Mayreder's battle against prostitution see Schmölzer, 'Prostitutionsdebatte', in *Rosa Mayreder*, pp. 119–23.
62. Mayreder, *Zur Kritik*, p. 162.
63. Mayreder, *Geschlecht und Kultur*, p. 107.

64. Schmölzer, *Mayreder*, pp. 160–61.
65. See Marholm, *Buch der Frauen*, pp. 172–73.
66. Marholm, *Buch der Frauen*, p. 23.
67. See Mayreder, *Zur Kritik*, p. 158, and Mayreder, 'Eine andere Marie Baschkirtseff', *Das Magazin für Litteratur*, 67 (1898), 778–83 (p. 779).
68. Mayreder, 'Baschkirtseff', p. 781.
69. On her diaries, see Anderson, 'Einleitung', p. 28.
70. Marholm, *Buch der Frauen*, p. 24.
71. On Mayreder's biologistic thinking see Schmölzer, *Mayreder*, pp. 232–33.
72. Mayreder, *Zur Kritik*, pp. 242–43.
73. One of the notorious texts in this respect is Richard von Krafft-Ebing's *Psychopathia Sexualis* (1886).
74. Agathe and Eugenie share a strong affective and physical relationship, in which displaced heterosexuality might cooperate with homosexuality. See Gabriele Reuter, *Aus guter Familie: Leidensgeschichte eines Mädchens*, ed. by Katja Mellmann, 1: *Text* (1895; Marburg: Verlag LiteraturWissenschaft.de, 2006), p. 41. On Reuter see Marholm, *Psychologie der Frau*, I, pp. 167–76.
75. Marholm, *Buch der Frauen*, p. 130.
76. Ibid., p. 126.
77. Virginia Woolf, *A Room of One's Own*, with a foreword by Mary Gordon (1929; Orlando, FL: Harcourt Brace Jovanovich, 1989), p. 78.
78. Butler, *Undoing Gender*, p. 3.
79. Mayreder, *Zur Kritik*, p. 139.
80. Butler, *Undoing Gender*, p. 205.

CHAPTER 11

# 'Race', Gender, Nation

## Colonial(ist) Constructions of Alterity and Identity in Frieda von Bülow's Autobiographical Writings from German East Africa

*Katharina von Hammerstein*

Whilst travelling by boat to German East Africa in June 1893, Frieda von Bülow (1857–1909) wrote to her best friend Lou Andreas-Salomé: 'mit jedem Tag überkommt mich [...] wieder jenes herrliche Freiheits- und Lebensgefühl, nach dem ich mich in unseren eigenen, von 1000 Schranken durchzogenen feindlichen Verhältnissen so lange vergebens gesehnt habe' [every day this wonderful feeling of liberty and life comes over me again [...], which I had longed for in vain for so long in our own hostile circumstances, characterized by a thousand barriers].[1] The limitations of women's lives in Wilhelminian Germany are juxtaposed with the independence and positive sense of self of an (admittedly white) woman in the recently founded German colony of East Africa; she expresses an elation which she had already felt during her first stay six years previously when she was working there as an independent woman.[2] Her letter to Andreas-Salomé identifies Bülow as a critic of the restrictive gender system in late nineteenth-century Germany. On the face of it one might therefore expect her life and works to be ideal subjects for feminist study. Furthermore, both of her stays in German East Africa prove that Bülow's own actions went far beyond the narrowly confined sphere for female activity in her time: in 1887/88 she worked as an organizer of medical stations in Zanzibar and on the East African coast in the service of the German-National Women's League,[3] co-founded by Bülow herself in 1886, and in 1893/94 she was the first female owner of a plantation in Tanga.[4] Then, of course, there are her numerous novels, novellas, reviews, and journal and newspaper articles on themes associated with colonial life and, later, on the woman question in Germany. The latter found a readership in the women's movement and its periphery. Many of these pieces were published in Germany, in the journal edited by Helene Lange under the universalist title *Die Frau: Monatsschrift für das gesamte Frauenleben unserer Zeit* (The Woman: Monthly Magazine for the Whole of Female Life in Our Times).

So Frieda von Bülow left behind a considerable feminist legacy. And yet her endeavours, both in word and in deed, to broaden the scope of life for women around 1900 have not earned her a place in the annals of feminist historical writing or literary history. She was interested not just in feminist issues, but also in issues of the day that have come under harsh scrutiny in the twentieth and twenty-first centuries, namely questions surrounding the ideological, political, and economic concepts of nationalism and colonialism. Perhaps these interests, and perhaps also her love for the colonialist Carl Peters[5] (then the most popular colonialist in Germany, but now infamous), served to disqualify her as the subject of early feminist research. In its initial phases, feminist literary research was focused on unearthing role models. It began by concentrating on works by female authors neglected in the traditional literary canon, but which represented models of progressive female emancipation. Consequently, Bülow's texts, which undoubtedly deal with women's issues, but which often combine a kind of German-nationalistic feminism with the then widespread racist-colonial discourse, were initially ignored by feminist literary scholarship.

Recently postcolonial critics from Israel, the United States, and South Africa have paid moderate attention to Bülow's work, concentrating mainly on a few of her colonial novels.[6] Her non-fictional, autobiographical writings from her time in German East Africa were for a long time almost entirely ignored, if we exclude the comments made by her first biographer, Sophie Hoechstetter (1910)[7] and a brief mention of her *Reisescizzen und Tagebuchblätter aus Deutsch-Ostafrika* (Travel Sketches and Diary Entries from German East Africa, 1889) in Lora Wildenthal's well-researched literary volume *German Women for Empire* (2001).[8] But interest in Frieda von Bülow's life and work seems to have grown again in the past few years, including in Germany, particularly since papers belonging to the Münchhausen-Bülow family have been made accessible in the Berlin State Library.[9] One of the reasons for this popularity may be the fact that the connections between feminist and postcolonial research methods have proved so fruitful; intercultural encounters from the past are being re-evaluated anew in the twenty-first century, no doubt inspired by the increasing intercultural exchange in our own world society. Monika Czernin's well-researched biography of Bülow and my own new editions of Bülow's *Reisescizzen* as well as two of her journal articles about daily life in German East Africa now provide a more easily accessible foundation for further research.[10] The colonial past, and its connections with the debate on women's rights around 1900, have become the focus for research much later in Germany than in Great Britain or France. In the light of this fact it would seem inappropriate now to focus the efforts of feminist research only on those female literary forebears who happen to meet our current criteria for 'political correctness', whilst disregarding those women writers who are further removed from today's mores and ideology.

This essay will not examine the details of Frieda von Bülow's life, which have remained fairly unknown for a long time despite her extensive oeuvre now: her biography can easily be found.[11] Bülow became Germany's first female colonial novelist on the strength of her personal experience of East Africa, where she spent nearly two years between 1887 and 1894. In this capacity she became an active co-producer of the German colonial image of Africa, a collage of spaces and dreams of sovereignty, exoticism, and adventure. It is easy to see in Bülow's literary

'Africanism' an illustration of Edward Said's thesis about a European scientific and literary orientalism which supported colonial structures of power by constructing an ideologically tainted concept of 'knowledge' and a definition of reality based on binary opposites — on the one hand, the familiar, the European, the West, 'Us', and on the other, the Unfamiliar, the Orient, the East, the Other.[12]

For the purposes of my study of the contrast between a German-nationalistic self-identity, i.e. a German-patriotic 'Us', and a native alterity — a 'Them' — in East Africa at the beginning of German colonial rule, as this contrast is represented in her texts, Bülow's under-researched autobiographical writings are more profitable than her novels. Her *Reisescizzen und Tagebuchblätter aus Deutsch-Ostafrika*, her travel writings, published in journals and newspapers between 1887 and 1898, and her letters are all to be seen in the context of a German national and colonial policy of expansion, following the famous Berlin Congo Conference of 1884–85, in the course of which European colonial powers divided Africa up amongst themselves. Germany claimed, and received, authority over Togo, Cameroon, German East Africa, and German Southwest Africa. Bülow's writings from German East Africa, which encompasses the area today occupied by the states of Tanzania, Rwanda, and Burundi, are the first written expressions of a white, German woman direct from the German African colonies.[13] Other white female voices follow after the turn of the century, and then they emanate primarily from the settlers' colony of German Southwest Africa (today's Namibia), focusing, among other things, on the debate about German womanhood as the carrier of German culture and saviour of German racial purity in the colonies.[14] At the end of the nineteenth century, Bülow is the first to add a white, female perspective to German-African colonial literature, whilst at the same time contributing to those far-reaching and intertwined national, social, political, and historical projects: nationalism, colonialism, and feminism.

What interests me most in her narratives is how the cultural *difference* between a German female self and the East African other, which is constructed on the content level of the texts, is related to the imaginary *community* (in Benedict Anderson's sense),[15] which is constructed on a communicative level between the female writer and her German readership through the process of reading.[16] How are the central categories of nation, 'race' (or rather ethnicity), and gender linked, i.e. how are nationalistic-racist thinking on difference, and the striving for autonomy of the white, German woman and female writer connected?

For today's readers, Bülow's autobiographical writings from East Africa offer insights into the hierarchically constructed colon(ial)ists' discourse based on 'racial' or ethnic concepts of difference, as she chats in a judgemental manner about flora and fauna, the country and its people. At the same time — albeit from the per-spective of a white, German woman writer — the texts open up perspectives on intercultural encounters between German colonials and the colonized Arabic, Indian, African, and other local men and women in 'contact zones'. This is a term coined by Mary Louise Pratt to mean 'social spaces where disparate cultures meet, clash, and grapple with each other, often in highly asymmetrical relations of domination and subordination — like colonialism, slavery, or their aftermaths'.[17] Instead of viewing colonials and the colonized as opposites, Pratt emphasizes the shared nature of colonial space even under the tense preconditions of an inequality of power. In her discussions about the dialogical nature of intercultural colonial encounters, Pratt refers, of course, to cultures and not to 'races'.

I consciously place the term 'race', which in Bülow's day was used by the European and American colonial powers as a pseudoscientific justification for a supposedly natural, hierarchical classification of humanity into white rulers and non-white subjects, in inverted commas. The term has today become scientifically and politically questionable and has to be regarded as a social construct. Nonetheless, even in the nineteenth century it was almost never used in a primarily biological sense, founded exclusively on origin.[18] According to Birthe Kundrus it was instead a 'multi-dimensional' concept which encompassed physical characteristics as well as dimensions like nationality, social status, and above all cultural and habitual ascriptions.[19] In Bülow's autobiographical texts from German East Africa the term 'race' hardly features at all, despite numerous descriptions of the physical characteristics of representatives of East African ethnicities.[20] But a self-defined cultural identity of white Germanness is still clearly contrasted with a stereotypical and collective definition of East African ethnicities by the German observer.

Let us turn our attention to the way in which a sense of community, and of national identity, is constructed on a communicative level between Bülow and her German, primarily female readership, before moving on to an analysis of the ascriptions of otherness. The female narrator, writing from Africa, presents herself as well established in the white colonial community, which consists mostly of male representatives of European missions, trade, diplomacy, and military. She uses phrases such as 'wir deutschen Frauen' [we German women][21] and 'wir Deutschen' [we Germans],[22] offers innumerable gushing outbursts about 'noch nie dagewesene Erfolge' [unparalleled successes],[23] and talks of the 'bevorzugteste gesellschaftliche Stellung' [most favoured social position] of the Germans and in particular of the German East African Company, led by Carl Peters, in the Sultan state of Zanzibar and on the East African coast.[24] Such formulations create both gender solidarity and solidarity based on national pride between the female narrator from distant Africa and her male and female readers in the German homeland. Comparisons with German cultural phenomena such as cathedrals, castles, the Rhine, and the Siebengebirge,[25] as well as comments about the consumption of 'Münchner Hofbräu' [beer brewed in Munich],[26] 'Metwurst' [a cold minced meat],[27] and Christmas Stollen[28] are woven into the text to underline the connection between the colonials and the fatherland; they create archetypical German points of reference which help the German readership gain an impression of the lives of the white, German compatriots in East Africa. The distant colony appears less alien by being discursively integrated into the German Reich.

In terms of the content of Bülow's writings, a racializing 'imperial gaze'[29] characterizes the representation of the colonized natives by the narrator. The inhabitants of East Africa are on the one hand subsumed into 'das [eine] Volk der Araber, Indier, Perser, Aegypter, Goanesen und Suaheli' [[one] tribe of Arabs, Indians, Persians, Egyptians, Goaneses, and Suaheli][30] and are on the other hand neatly divided into ethnic groups, whose characteristics are invariably derived from their ethnicity, regardless of individual personal characteristics, thereby being essentialized and inscribed as fixed and unchangeable. There is talk of 'Neger-Armseligkeit, indischen von Unsauberkeit strotzenden Kramläden und arabischen Schutthaufen' [negro-poverty, Indian corner shops brimming with filthiness, and Arabic rubbish heaps].[31] By means of these ascriptions of poverty, dirt, and decay, an image of native backwardness is juxtaposed with an image of the progress of flourishing European (in this case British) culture.[32]

Africans are depicted in Bülow's texts as cheerful, vain, loveably workshy servants, waiters, and missionary pupils, out of tune with the German work ethos, and inclined to dance. Just how dependent on the labour of these people German colonials actually were becomes clear, however, when the (always undifferentiated) mass of workers, rowers, or water carriers who were in the employ of the author are described. They are also mentioned as being the slaves of Arabic masters, and shown to be friendly and helpful inhabitants of idyllic, scenic villages. In contrast to the image of German energy and adult responsibility, Africans are frequently infantilized in the disparaging descriptions of the author, who promptly gives her African and Arabic servants German names like 'Liese' or 'Carl Schmidt', disregarding their actual identity, and implicitly excluding them from the community of political equals.[33] Frequent comparisons with animals, especially faithful and clever dogs,[34] suggest not only the demeaning of black people versus white people, but also a supposedly natural tendency of black people towards willing subordination to a master or mistress.

Indians, presented as a rich and therefore materialist and independent class of merchants and traders, find the least favour in Bülow's feudal-aristocratic judgement. They are characterized as mercenary, avaricious, and weak 'Erzschwindler' [conmen *par excellence*],[35] antisemitically regarded as being on a par with the German Jews: 'Was der Jude beim deutschen Landvolk ist, das ist der Indier unter den Schwarzen' [The Indian is to the black what the Jew is to the German rural population]; they are accused of using 'unreelle Geschäftskniffe' [shady business tactics]. Bülow also warns that they are 'gefährliche Konkurrenten für die europäischen Kaufleute' [dangerous rivals for the European traders].[36] In this manner an emotionally charged picture emerges of a suspicious, dishonest opponent, which taps into, and reinforces, the anti-Semitism which was rife back home in Germany. Parallels with anti-Semitic descriptions are also expressed in the generalized depiction of the way 'an Indian' looks. His 'Gesichtsausdruck [ist] habgierig und lauernd. Es fehlt ihm das Sanfte des Guanesen, die heitere Gutherzigkeit und Leichtigkeit des Schwarzen, der Anstand und die edle Würde des Arabers. Von all diesen ostafrikanischen *Typen* ist der Inder der mindest sympathische' [[his] facial expression is avaricious and lurking. He lacks the gentleness of the Goanese, the cheerful good nature and ease of the black man, the decency and noble dignity of the Arab. Of all of these East African *types* the Indian is the least likeable].[37] This characterization, based on physical attributes as well as personality traits, which uses the grammatical singular to describe representatives of individual ethnic groups, thereby essentializing them further, reflects the discursive proximity of Bülow's text to contemporary racial taxonomy.

By contrast, if equally generalizing, in Bülow's texts Arabs are furnished 'meist mit edlen Gesichtszügen' [usually with noble facial features][38] and as the local elite and political partners for German colonial ambitions, they receive a certain degree of respect. In her journal article 'Unser Wali' (Our Wali, 1895/96), Bülow cites the thoughts of an educated Arab on the subject of the mutual supremacy of Germans and Arabs over the black Africans. The racist views normally held by the author herself are here expressed by a native, and therefore receive an apparent corroboration from someone with local knowledge:

> Wir gebildeten Menschen sind ja im Grunde überall die gleichen. Ihr Europäer glaubt an Gott, und wir glauben an Gott. Wir Araber kennen alle eure Propheten. Wir kennen Abraham und Moses und David und Salomo und verehren sie. Ihr und wir, das ist im Grunde das nämliche. 'Sawa, sawa'. — Die Schwarzen dagegen haben keinen Begriff von Gott. Sie kümmert nur das eine: Essen und Trinken. Sie sind darum etwas von uns ganz Verschiedenes, — näher den Tieren.

> [We educated people are all the same at heart. You Europeans believe in God, we believe in God. We Arabs know all of your prophets. We know Abraham and Moses and David and Salomon and revere them. You and us, we are the same at heart. 'Sawa, sawa'. — The blacks, on the other hand, have no concept of God. They only know one thing: eating and drinking. They are therefore something quite different from us, — closer to animals.][39]

Although a native 'we' and a German 'you' — now from reversed perspectives — are juxtaposed, this text nonetheless propagates an elitist class-consciousness which goes beyond national boundaries, becomes intertwined with a hierarchical racial consciousness, and excludes black people from any kind of relationship of equality on the basis of their supposedly more primitive, animal-like state of development.

Bülow's narrator is clearly class-conscious and mentions repeatedly that she is addressed as 'Baronin' (baroness), thereby identifying herself as a member of the German aristocracy and as a welcome guest in castles of Arab noblemen, who are as respectful as they are hospitable. Above all she emphasizes that she was twice the recipient of the munificence of the Sultan Barghash bin Said of Zanzibar, who allowed her to travel on his private 'Dhau' (a sailing boat). But even in these descriptions of intercultural contact with people considered her 'equal' at least in terms of class, her writing is infiltrated by disparaging jokes about the primitive living conditions in Arab castles, or the plush interior and the omnipresent cockroaches in the sultan's cabin (which was vacated especially for her).[40] Displaying a clear sense of superiority based on her ethnicity or 'race', nationality, and culture, Bülow establishes herself as the equal of the ruling Arab elite and indeed the sultan — while arrogantly looking down upon the backward and unsanitary way of life of those same local rulers and reducing them to mere vassals of German colonial interests.

Even where Bülow's texts reveal a mixture of physical-racial and ethno-cultural systems of differentiation, the latter on the basis of cultural specificities such as language, behaviour, customs, and dress,[41] the emphasis on the commonality of the German cultural experience nonetheless results in a conscious separation from that which is culturally other in German East Africa. This differentiation goes hand in hand with a hierarchy, whereby access to power as well as exclusion from power derive from an enhancement of the value of self alongside the devaluing of the 'other'.

In Bülow's texts there is no evidence, with very rare exceptions, of a sense of female solidarity with non-European women beyond the 'racial' divides. On the contrary, in obvious rivalry with local women she constructs models of contrasting femininity, where the native women's erotic charisma is set in contrast to her own education, independence, chummy resilience, and valiant willingness to act for the national and colonial enterprise.[42] However, this model of femininity appears almost 'masculine' in the context of gender discourse around 1900 and also distances her from the contemporary ideal of domestic femininity and from the 'dem bürgerlichen Projekt Nation innewohnenden Geschlechterdualismus' [gender dualism inherent in the bourgeois project of nation-building] in late nineteenth-century Germany.[43]

Overall, Bülow's narratives are characterized by a condescending and patronizing tone towards both the male and female non-European natives. Emphasizing the alterity of the colonized, a welcome contrast which bolsters a German national sense of self, Bülow in her writing creates an image of cultural and 'racial' superiority as well as patriotic community which bridges the spatial distance between Africa and Europe.

Yet Bülow's racist projections of the East African other, based on difference and separation, also display elements of *inter*cultural exchange in the context of the represented 'contact zones', and contain indications that these simplistic racist patterns are latently undermined. For example, Bülow counteracts the stereotype of the supposedly ungrateful blacks by observing 'daß die vermeintlich erteilten Wohlthaten [der Weißen von den Schwarzen, KvH] nicht als solche empfunden worden sind' [that the benefits which the black people apparently received from the white people were in fact not perceived as such].[44] Furthermore, readers learn a great deal about the East African class system and East African 'race' relations, gender relations, and religious beliefs, which often manifest themselves in 'dasturi' (Swahili for custom and convention). Naturally, these observations are presented through the subjective lens of Bülow's text. She writes for example that the carrying of water is regarded amongst the blacks as 'Weiberbeschäftigung' [women's work],[45] explains what Ramadan is,[46] declares herself to be impressed by the judicial fairness of an Arabic wali (governor) in favour of a black man,[47] and mentions again and again her own attempts to speak Swahili, which allow her slightly better to communicate with the local population and understand their mentality.[48]

Bülow's texts are important not only for what they say, but also for what they don't say at all, or only in passing: military exercises, the arrival of battleships from various European nations, and bellicose confrontations with natives. Only occasionally do Bülow's narratives hint at hesitant local resistance[49] — for example in her representation of a fearful, but self-confident Arabic wali faced with a declaration that the administration on the East African coast would be handed over from Zanzibar to Germany (*Reisescizzen*, 'Eine unblutige Eroberungsfahrt' (An Unbloody Voyage of Exploration)); in the ironic description of a strike by the female water-carriers (*Reisescizzen*); in the belittling report about a revolt by slaves belonging to the overseer of Bülow's chalk quarry ('Allerhand Alltägliches' (All Kinds of Everyday Stories)); or in the casual mention of a festive reception for 'siegreich vom Kilima Ndscharo heimkehrende Krieger' [victorious warriors returning from the Kilimanjaro].[50] Not once is the legality of the colonialization of East Africa questioned, despite the historically proven fact that the process of colonialization (in particular through Carl Peters) was forceful. Bülow's texts purport to be reliable eyewitness accounts, yet they either deliberately misrepresent, or perhaps totally misread, the colonial situation. Despite, or maybe precisely because of, Bülow's acute powers of observation the Germans are portrayed as good, peaceful, mostly welcome (or at least respected on the basis of their military and cultural superiority), inclined towards harmonious relations with the natives, innocent of any brutal measures and therefore also not exposed to any retaliatory threats from the natives. The fact that the texts suggest nothing disquieting with regard either to native or German conduct facilitates the readers' identification with their colonial compatriots who were actively involved in the expansion of their common fatherland all the way to Africa.

This adamant insistence on the construction of a conflict-free, harmonious encounter between Germans and natives in the East African 'contact zones' and, at the same time, on a hierarchical concept of difference can be seen, on the content level, as a leitmotif in Bülow's narratives from German East Africa. From today's perspective this may appear to be a contradictory representation, but it fulfils several functions on the level of communication between the author and her readership, functions connected with the far-reaching processes of colonialism, nationalism, and feminism. As printed media, Bülow's texts participate in the construction of a white, German national identity by representing hierarchical and yet apparently unproblematic colonial conditions. Around 1890, this national identity is defined by an ethnic, German community of origin, that is, by a process of homogenization within and a separation from that which is 'other', in this case from the ethnic, 'racial', and cultural alterity of the population of German East Africa. 'Ausgrenzung fungiert als Bestandteil der [nationalen, KvH] Selbstkonstitution' [exclusion functions as a component of the constitution of the [national] self].[51] The almost pathological need to represent these potentially conflicting tendencies as harmonious in Bülow's texts is testimony to the fact that the expansionist success and the hegemony of the Europeans (including the Germans) in Africa depended on an absence of conflict — or at least on the limited nature of any resistance — in the colonial space. Emphasis on the physical and therefore unchangeable difference between the European and native ethnicities and 'races' also provides a justification for the apparently 'natural' rejection of any claim to equality.

But this biological argument is also the principal argument used in the nineteenth century to justify gender differences and therefore the exclusion of women from equality. Consequently, members of the female sex, *inferior* in the German motherland, feel an even greater need (as Bülow and other women who followed in her footsteps in the colonies clearly did)[52] to insist in the colonies that they belonged to the *superior*, white 'race' and German nation.[53] It is only this allegiance and their participation in colonialism on the side of the white rulers which gives these women access to positions of authority and independence (as rulers over the colonized), something which they were still being denied in Europe.

Bülow's literary efforts, which are juxtaposing German *identity* with East African *alterity*, thus do not just promote a German national body of thought, but also the conquering of spaces in which an independent white German woman might be active. The colony, so went the feminist argument of the day, opened up spheres of self-determined activity and thus space for self-realization for white women which were far removed from the 'thousand barriers' preventing them flourishing back home in Germany. It was here that this 'herrliche Freiheits- und Lebensgefühl' [wonderful sense of freedom and life] about which Bülow raved when writing to her friend Lou Andreas-Salomé in 1893, as cited in the opening paragraph of this chapter, could thrive.[54]

It is in the freedom-loving white woman's sense of belonging to the supposedly 'superior' German 'race' or ethnicity that we find that dangerous liaison between colonial racism, German jingoism, and bourgeois feminism at the turn of the century, a mixture that historical research and the women's movement have long ignored. The emancipation of German women in the colonies, so often enthusiastically welcomed and propagated by writers who enthused about opportunities for personal self-development, about professional as well as domestic authority, and about making a contribution to the patriotic project, was based on a racist concept of self and other and a world-view which legitimized European, including German, claims to power. It could only be achieved at the expense of colonized men and women; in Africa, at the expense of 'the blacks'.

It is because of this connection between colonial racism and white women's emancipation that Bülow's writing contains very few examples of solidarity with native women. As a believer in German nationalistic feminism she adhered to the concept of a clear racial (racist) polarization and hierarchy between Germans and natives. Publishing her views on East African conditions very widely in newspaper and journal articles, travelogues, and novels, Bülow helped spread and confirm the belief held by her German readership back home that a supposedly natural hierarchy existed between people of different colour and ethnic background.

So what can my study of Bülow's autobiographical writings from German East Africa and her literary and therefore communicative participation in the projects of colonial expansion, nation-building, and female emancipation in the late nineteenth century contribute to a review of feminist literary criticism today? Scholars of literature, culture, and history could, and indeed should, continue critically to evaluate unknown as well as canonized women writers, and apply new theoretical and methodological approaches, regardless of our sympathy or otherwise for the moral, political, or aesthetic positions expressed in the texts. This means not selecting just the likeable or popular female forbears in accordance with today's ideologies. Texts by conservative or from today's perspective 'politically incorrect' women writers (among whom there are protofeminists) can tell us much about history and literature, not least about that *liaison dangereuse* between the women's movement, nationalism, and colonialism around 1900. Monika Czernin comments on this conjunction specifically in the life and works of Bülow, and on our response to her from today's perspective:

> Alle drei Bewegungen waren Frieda wichtig, alle drei bedeuteten für sie einen Glück verheißenden Aufbruch, Mitgestaltung an einer Verbesserung des Lebens, Kampf für das Gute, ja das Beste. Dass wir heute davon nur noch den Feminismus als positive Entwicklung beschreiben und ihn von den anderen Strömungen abtrennen wollen, ist unsere gefärbte Brille, mit deren Hilfe wir das 19. Jahrhundert nach unseren Vorstellungen retuschieren.

> [All three movements proved important to Frieda, all three meant for her a new departure which promised happiness, an involvement in efforts to improve life, a battle for what was good, indeed for that which was best. The fact that today we regard feminism as the only positive development amongst these and that we want to separate it from the other trends is the product of our coloured spectacles, through which we try to reconstruct the nineteenth century in line with our own preferences.][55]

Analysing these historical, discursive, and practical overlaps makes us aware of our own ideological concepts and of their historically conditioned nature. It also reminds us to read historical interdependencies in *their* historical context. Many gender-critical women around 1900 did not see beyond that which was closest to their interests: the success of German national hegemony suggested itself more readily as the foundation for their own sense of freedom than any kind of female solidarity across 'racial' and ethnic boundaries. It would be many decades before ideas about intercultural exchange and movements subscribing to a concept of 'diversity' and to respect for members of different ethnicities arose. Even today, such ideas and beliefs are not shared by all.

Future research will have to investigate more closely the sense in which the white, German feminist movement was complicit with white, German dominance, and will also have to highlight the ambiguities, caesuras, and traces of subversion which can be found, despite their nationalistic-feminist self-interest, in the writings of colonial(ist) women authors. The interweaving of feminism with hegemonial ideologies — in Bülow's case the connection of feminism and a racist, colonialist concept of difference — may in fact be the most important aspect of these texts for our purposes today. They prompt readers and scholars to reflect on their position at a time of neocolonialism and globalization. They raise questions such as these: Do I as a white German-American female academic with a permanent post have to consider the possibility that my allegiance to the West may be greater than my allegiance to the gender which I share with women from poorer parts of the world? To what extent am I — despite being committed to a sense of intercultural female solidarity — complicit with the wealth and power of the so-called First World? What economic and political foundations are providing *my* 'Freiheits- und Lebensgefühl' [sense of freedom and life]? Where are the differences — or maybe in the light of neocolonial developments, parallels — between the privileges enjoyed by a white, Western woman today and those enjoyed by Frieda von Bülow a century ago? Such questions, to cite Theodor Fontane, are 'ein weites Feld' [a broad area].[56]

## Notes to Chapter 11

1. Cited from Monika Czernin, *'Jenes herrliche Gefühl der Freiheit': Frieda von Bülow und die Sehnsucht nach Afrika* (Bremen: Ullstein, 2008), p. 262. Some of the correspondence between Frieda von Bülow and Lou Andreas-Salomé can be found in the Universitätsbibliothek Göttingen and also in collected papers no. 371 Münchhausen/Bülow, in the Staatsbibliothek zu Berlin, Preußischer Kulturbesitz, Box 6. The correspondence has not yet been published.

2. In Bülow's text *Reisescizzen und Tagebuchblätter aus Deutsch-Ostafrika* (1889), a diary entry from 29 August 1887 from Dar-es-Salaam reads: 'Ich kann aber in Wahrheit versichern, daß ich mich, so weit meine Erinnerung reicht, noch nie so frisch und geistig wohl befunden habe, wie hier in diesen ganz primitiven Verhältnissen' [I can say in all truthfulness that I cannot recall ever having been as energetic and mentally well as I am here in these very primitive conditions] (Frieda von Bülow, *Reisescizzen und Tagebuchblätter aus Deutsch-Ostafrika* (Berlin: Walther & Apolant, 1889), pp. 119–20). Citations from Bülow's text in this chapter are from the original 1889 edition, as page references for the new edition by Katharina von Hammerstein (Berlin: Trafo, forthcoming) are not yet available.

3. On Bülow's first visit to Africa, see Lora Wildenthal, *German Women for Empire, 1884–1945* (Durham, NC: Duke University Press), pp. 13–53; Czernin, *Bülow* and Katharina von Hammerstein, '"Ein segenspendendes Werk zur Ehre der deutschen Nation": Vorschlag einer Lesart von Frieda von Bülows kolonial-nationalistischen Aufzeichnungen aus Deutsch-Ostafrika', in Frieda von Bülow, *Reisescizzen und Tagebuchblätter aus Deutsch-Ostafrika*, ed. by Katharina von Hammerstein (Berlin: Trafo, forthcoming).

4. Frieda von Bülow and her youngest sister Sophie inherited their brother Albrecht's plantation and chalk quarry. He had been Reichskommissar for the German East African Kilimanjaro territory and died in battle in 1892 near Moschi. Her energetic commitment to a project of this kind as a single, German woman was itself unusual, but not necessarily doomed to fail. However, colonial policies pursued by Berlin which favoured large-scale state efforts, rather than small-scale enterprises, eventually forced Bülow to hand over her business in Tanga. See Wildenthal, *Empire*, p. 65, and Czernin, *Bülow*, p. 332. Several of Bülow's autobiographical journal and newspaper articles and novels engage with her experiences in 1893–94 in Tanga.

5. For more details on the colonialist Carl Peters, see von Hammerstein, '"Ein segenspendendes Werk"' and the index of the new edition of Bülow, *Reisescizzen*; see also Wildenthal, *Empire*; Arne Perras, *Carl Peters and German Imperialism, 1856–1918: A Political Biography* (Oxford and New York: Clarendon Press, 2004) and Carl Peters, *Die Gründung von Deutsch-Ostafrika: Kolonialpolitische Erinnerungen und Betrachtungen* (Berlin: C. A. Schwetschke und Sohn, 1906).

6. See Joachim Warmbold, 'Germania in Africa: Frieda Freiin von Bülow, "Schöpferin des deutschen Kolonialromans"', *Jahrbuch des Instituts für deutsche Geschichte* [Tel-Aviv University], 15 (1986), 309–36, and *'Ein Stückchen neudeutsche Erd ...': Deutsche Kolonial-Literatur. Aspekte ihrer Geschichte, Eigenart und Wirkung, dargestellt am Beispiel Afrikas* (Frankfurt am Main: Haag + Herchen, 1982), translated as *Germania in Africa: Germany's Colonial Literature* (New York, Berne, Frankfurt am Main, Paris: Lang, 1989); Marcia Klotz, 'White Women and the Dark Continent: Gender and Sexuality in German Colonial Discourse from the Sentimental Novel to the Fascist Film' (PhD Dissertation, Stanford University 1994) and 'Memoirs from a German Colony: What do German Women Want?', in *Eroticism and Containment: Notes from the Flood Plain*, ed. by Carol Siegel and Ann Kibbey (New York: New York University Press, 1994), pp. 154–87; Friederike Eigler, 'Engendering German Nationalism and Race in Frieda von Bülow's Colonial Writings', in *The Imperialist Imagination: German Colonialism and its Legacy*, ed. by Sara Friedrichsmeyer, Sara Lennox, and Susanne Zantop (Ann Arbor: University of Michigan Press, 1998), pp. 68–85; Russel Berman, *Enlightenment of Empire: Colonial Discourse in German Literature* (Lincoln, NB and London: University of Nebraska Press, 1998), pp. 172–202; Lora Wildenthal, *Empire* and '"When Men Are Weak": The Imperial Feminism of Frieda von Bülow', *Gender & History*, 10.1 (1998), 53–77; Ingrid Laurien, '"A Land of Promise?" Autobiography and Fiction in Frieda von Bülow's East-African Novels', in *Africa and Europe: En/Countering Myths: Essays on Literature and Cultural Politics*, ed. by Carlotta von Maltzan (Frankfurt am Main: Peter Lang, 2003), pp. 203–14.

7. Sophie Hoechstetter, *Frieda Freiin v. Bülow: Ein Lebensbild* (Dresden: Carl Reissner, 1910).

8. 'It [Bülow's *Reisescizzen*] is a lighthearted account of adventurous encounters with exotic peoples, romantic ruins, festivities, and experiences with medical care of Europeans and locals' (Wildenthal, *Empire*, p. 28).

9. At the time of writing, collected papers 371 Münchhausen-Bülow, situated in the Staatsbibliothek zu Berlin, Preußischer Kulturbesitz, which contain 10 boxes and 7 handwritten volumes, were only partially catalogued.

10. Frieda von Bülow, 'Eine unblutige Eroberungsfahrt an der ostafrikanischen Küste' and 'Allerhand Alltägliches aus Deutsch-Ostafrika', ed. by Katharina von Hammerstein, in *Kolonialer Alltag in Ostafrika in Dokumenten*, ed. by Ulrich van der Heyden (Berlin: Trafo, 2009), pp. 159–74 and 175–93 as well as von Hammerstein, 'Briefe von Frieda von Bülow: Einführung', ibid., pp. 149–57.

11. See the biographies by Czernin (2008) and Hoechstetter (1910) as well as *Zwei Blüten an einem Zweig: Beiträge zu Leben und Wirken der Schriftstellerinnen Frieda und Margarethe von Bülow*, ed. by Maria Helene von Hatzfeld (Ingersleben: Heimatmuseum, *c.* 2000); Katharina von Hammerstein, 'Frieda von Bülow', in *Fembio: Frauenbiographieforschung*, ed. by Luise Pusch (Hanover: Institut für Frauenbiographieforschung, 2007), <http://www.fembio.org/biographie. php/frau/biographie/frieda-von-buelow/>; von Hammerstein, ' "Ein segenspendendes Werk" '; Katja Kaiser, 'Neudietendorf: Frieda von Bülow, die koloniale Frauenfrage und koloniale Frauenorganisationen', in *Kolonialismus hierzulande: Eine Spurensuche in Deutschland*, ed. by Ulrich van der Heyden and Joachim Zeller (Erfurt: Sutton Verlag, 2007), pp. 171–76; Marianne Bechhaus-Gerst, 'Die Kolonialschriftstellerin Frieda von Bülow', in *Frauen in den deutschen Kolonien*, ed. by Marianne Bechhaus-Gerst and Mechtild Leutner (Berlin: Ch. Links Verlag, 2009), pp. 66–69, 238–39.

12. See Edward Said, *Orientalism* (New York: Pantheon Books, 1978).

13. The memoirs of the Sultan of Zanzibar's sister (who had married a German) had been published shortly before this: Emily Said-Ruete (née Princess Salme of Oman and Zanzibar), *Leben im Sultanspalast: Memoiren aus dem 19. Jahrhundert*, a reprint of *Memoiren einer arabischen Prinzessin*, 2 vols (Berlin: Luckhardt, 1886), ed. and with an afterword by Annegret Nippa (Hamburg: Die Hanse/Europäische Verlagsanstalt, 2007; original: Frankfurt am Main: Athenäum, 1989). See also Julius Waldschmidt and Ulrich van der Heyden, *Kaiser, Kanzler und Prinzessin: Ein Frauenschicksal zwischen Orient und Okzident*, 2nd edn (Berlin: Trafo, 2006).

14. See Katharina Walgenbach, *'Die weiße Frau als Trägerin deutscher Kultur': Koloniale Diskurse über Geschlecht, 'Rasse' und Klasse im Kaiserreich* (Frankfurt am Main and New York: Campus, 2005) and Anette Dietrich, *Weiße Weiblichkeiten: Konstruktionen von 'Rasse' und Geschlecht in deutschen Kolonien* (Bielefeld: Transcript Verlag, 2007).

15. Benedict Anderson, *Imagined Communities: Reflections on the Origin and Spread of Nationalism*, rev. edn (London and New York: Verso, 1991).

16. On reading autobiographical texts as communicative acts, see Gabriele Jancke, *Autobiographie als soziale Praxis: Beziehungskonzepte in Selbstzeugnissen des 15. und 16. Jahrhunderts im deutschsprachigen Raum* (Cologne, Weimar, and Vienna: Böhlau, 2002).

17. Mary Louise Pratt, *Imperial Eyes: Travel Writing and Transculturalism* (New York: Routledge, 1992).

18. See Dieter Gosewinkel, 'Rückwirkungen des kolonialen Rasserechts? Deutsche Staatsangehörigkeit zwischen Rassestaat und Rechtsstaat', in *Das Kaiserreich transnational: Deutschland in der Welt 1871–1914*, ed. by Sebastian Conrad and Jürgen Osterhammel (Göttingen: Vandenhoeck & Ruprecht, 2004), pp. 236–56.

19. See Birthe Kundrus, *Moderne Imperialisten: Das Kaiserreich im Spiegel seiner Kolonien* (Cologne: Böhlau, 2003), pp. 222, 276–77.

20. For example, in Bülow's *Reisezcizzen* there is only one ironic mention of the 'edle Rasse' [noble race] of a stubborn Mascat donkey (20 September 1887) and the attitude of a female English missionary is quoted thus: 'Wir wollen die Neger keineswegs zu Engländern machen, sondern zu Christen. Im übrigen sollen sie die Eigentümlichkeiten ihrer Race behalten. Wir studieren darum sorgfältig ihre Gebräuche und ihre Sprache. Allen Unterricht erteilen wir in Kisuaheli' [We don't want to turn the negroes into English people, but into Christians. Apart from that,

they ought to retain the peculiarities of their race. This is why we are studying their customs and their language closely. We do all the teaching in Swahili] (19 June 1887). The English term 'race' is here used in the context of cultural and communicative parameters such as language and customs.

21. Bülow, *Reisescizzen*, 7/8 July 1887, 1889 edn, p. 51.
22. Ibid., 30 June and 16 November 1887, 1889 edn, pp. 49 and 163.
23. Ibid., 21 July 1887, 1889 edn, pp. 68–69.
24. Ibid., 30 June 1887, 1889 edn, p. 49.
25. The Siebengebirge is a German range of hills to the east of the Rhine, south-east of Bonn, literally 'seven mountains'.
26. Ibid., 14 July 1887, 1889 edn, p. 62.
27. Ibid., 19 August 1887, 1889 edn, p. 97.
28. Ibid., 25 December 1887, 1889 edn, p. 180.
29. Ann Kaplan, *Looking for the Other: Feminism, Film, and the Imperial Gaze* (New York und London: Routledge, 1997).
30. Bülow, *Reisescizzen*, 20 June 1887, 1889 edn, p. 34.
31. Ibid., 19 June 1887, 1889 edn, p. 29.
32. Bülow is referring to the British mission in Zanzibar city. Despite competing for hegemony in East Africa, there are fundamental overlaps between the German and British colonial discourses:

Die obsessive Beschäftigung mit dem eigenen weißen Nationalprestige, der komplexe Versuch, eine nationale Identität auch und gerade über überseeischen Besitz herauszubilden, 'die weiße Frau' als Kulturretterin oder die Radikalisierung rassistischer Haltungen um 1900 lassen sich z.B. genauso in der britischen Kolonialdiskussion feststellen.

[An obsessive interest in their own white national prestige, the complex endeavour to construct a national identity despite, and indeed because of, overseas property, the image of 'the white woman' as a saviour of culture, or the radicalization of racist attitudes around 1900 are evident in the British colonial discourse as well.]

(cited from Birthe Kundrus, 'Die imperialistischen Frauenverbände des Kaiserreichs: Koloniale Phantasie- und Realgeschichte im Verein', *Basler Afrika Bibliographien* (Namibia Resource Center–Southern Africa Library, BAB Working Paper), 3 (2005), p. 22)
33. Bülow, *Reisescizzen*, 30 August and 12 September 1887, 1889 edn, pp. 120 and 132.
34. Ibid., 19 August 1887, 22 September, and 15 January 1888, 1889 edn, pp. 93, 105, 141, and 193. See also Frieda von Bülow, 'In der Station', *Daheim*, 24.9 (1888), p. 138.
35. Bülow, *Reisescizzen*, 24 June and 19 August 1887, 1889 edn, pp. 44–45 and 88.
36. Frieda von Bülow, 'Unpolitische Briefe, Tanga, 31. Juli 1893', *Tägliche Rundschau, Unterhaltungs-Beilage*, 217 (15 September 1893), pp. 866–67.
37. Frieda von Bülow, 'Am Werkeltag in Deutsch-Ostafrika', *Die Frau: Monatsschrift für das gesamte Frauenleben unserer Zeit*, 3.12 (September 1896), p. 743, my emphasis.
38. Bülow, *Reisescizzen*, 20 June 1887, 1889 edn, p. 34.
39. Frieda von Bülow, 'Unser Wali: Skizze aus dem deutsch-ostafrikanischen Leben', *Die Frau: Monatsschrift für das gesamte Frauenleben unserer Zeit*, 3 (1895–96), p. 485.
40. Bülow, *Reisescizzen*, 25 July 1887, 1889 edn, p. 70.
41. On the definition of ethnicity, see Reinhart Kößler and Tilman Schiel, 'Nationalstaaten und Grundlagen ethnischer Identität', in *Nationalstaat und Ethnizität*, ed. by Reinhart Kößler and Tilman Schiel (Frankfurt am Main: IKO Verlag für interkulturelle Kommunikation, 1994), pp. 1–22.
42. See Hammerstein, 'Bülow' (2007).
43. Ute Planert, 'Vater Staat und Mutter Germania: Zur Politisierung des weiblichen Geschlechts im 19. und 20. Jahrhundert', in *Nation, Politik und Geschlecht: Frauenbewegungen und Nationalismus in der Moderne*, ed. by Ute Planert (Frankfurt am Main and New York: Campus, 2000), pp. 15–65 (p. 48).

44. Bülow, *Reisescizzen*, 23 June 1887, 1889 edn, p. 38.

45. Ibid., 12 January 1888, 1889 edn, p. 191.

46. Ibid., 20 June 1887, 1889 edn, p. 33.

47. Ibid., 16–17 September 1887, 1889 edn, pp. 135–37.

48. On intercultural exchanges in Bülow's *Reisescizzen*, see Hammerstein, ' "Ein segenspendendes Werk" '.

49. On allusions to military conflicts and local resistance in Bülow's *Reisescizzen*, see Hammerstein ' "Ein segenspendendes Werk" '.

50. Frieda von Bülow, 'Ostafrikanische Briefe: Dar-es-Salaam, 11. September 1893', *Tägliche Rundschau, Unterhaltungs-Beilage*, 254 (28 October 1893), pp. 1013–14 (p. 1014).

51. Planert, 'Vater Staat', p. 17.

52. Worth mentioning are the women who wrote about their experiences in German South-West Africa, e.g. Clara Brockmann, Ada Cramer, Margarethe von Eckenbrecher, Helene von Falkenhausen, Orlana Holm, and Elsa Sonnenberg.

53. See Frances Gouda, 'Das "unterlegene" Geschlecht der "überlegenen" Rasse: Kolonialgeschichte und Geschlechterverhältnisse', in *Geschlechterverhältnisse im historischen Wandel*, ed. by Hanna Schissler (Frankfurt am Main and New York: Campus, 1993), pp. 185–203.

54. Cited from Czernin, *Bülow*, p. 262.

55. Ibid., p. 81.

56. This saying, which stems from Theodor Fontane's *Effi Briest* (1894–95), is repeatedly used by the character of Herr von Briest when he is pressed for an opinion on (too) complicated matters of life.

# BIBLIOGRAPHY

AGORNI, MIRELLA, 'The Voice of the "Translatress": From Aphra Behn to Elizabeth Carter', *Yearbook of English Studies*, 28 (1998), 181–95

ALIMADAD-MENSCH, FARANAK, *Gabriele Reuter: Porträt einer Schriftstellerin* (Berne: Lang, 1984)

ALLISTON, APRIL, *Virtue's Faults: Correspondences in Eighteenth-Century British and French Women's Fiction* (Stanford, CA: Stanford University Press, 1996)

ANDERSON, BENEDICT, *Imagined Communities: Reflections on the Origin and Spread of Nationalism*, rev. edn (London and New York: Verso, 1991)

ANON., 'Beantwortung der Frage: Dürfen Weiber gelehrte Kenntnisse haben? oder: Sind Weiblichkeit und wissenschaftliche Geistesbildung zu vereinigen? Ein Versuch', *Journal von deutschen Frauen für deutsche Frauen*, 1 (1805), 21–35

ARDIS, ANN L., *Modernism and Cultural Conflict, 1880–1922* (Cambridge: Cambridge University Press, 2002)

ARMSTRONG, NANCY, *Desire and Domestic Fiction* (New York: Oxford University Press, 1987)

ARYGYLE, GISELA, 'The Horror and Pleasure of Un-English Fiction: Ida von Hahn-Hahn and Fanny Lewald in England', *Comparative Literature Studies*, 44.1–2 (2007), 144–65

ASHCROFT, BILL, GARETH GRIFFITHS, and HELEN TIFFIN, *The Empire Writes Back: Theory and Practice in Post-colonial Literatures* (London: Routledge, 1989)

BAILIN, MIRIAM, *The Sickroom in Victorian Fiction: The Art of being Ill* (Cambridge and New York: Cambridge University Press, 1994)

BALDWIN, CLAIRE, *The Emergence of the Modern German Novel: Christoph Martin Wieland, Sophie Von La Roche, and Maria Anna Sagar* (Rochester, NY: Camden House, 2002)

BASSNETT, SUSAN, *Comparative Literature: A Critical Introduction* (Oxford: Blackwell, 1993)

—— *Translation Studies*, 3rd edn (London: Routledge, 2002)

BÄUMER, KONSTANZE, 'Reisen als Moment der Erinnerung: Fanny Lewald (1811–1889) *Lehr- und Wanderjahre*', *Amsterdämer Beiträge zur Neueren Germanistik*, 28 (1989), 137–57

BAUMGARTNER, KARIN, 'In Search of Literary Mothers across the Rhine: The Influence of Mme de Genlis and Mme de Staël on the Writing of Helmina von Chézy', *Women's Writing* (special issue on 'Women Readers in Europe: Readers, Writers, Salonnières, 1750–1900'), 18.1 (2011)

BEAULIEU, JEAN-PHILIPPE, ed., *D'une écriture à l'autre: Les femmes et la traduction sous l'ancien régime* (Ottawa: Presses de l'Université d'Ottawa, 2004)

BECHHAUS-GERST, MARIANNE, 'Die Kolonialschriftstellerin Frieda von Bülow', in *Frauen in den deutschen Kolonien*, ed. by Marianne Bechhaus-Gerst and Mechtild Leutner (Berlin: Ch Links Verlag, 2009), pp. 66–69, 238–39

BECKER-CANTARINO, BARBARA, '"Gender Censorship": On Literary Production in German Romanticism', *Women in German Yearbook*, 11 (1995), 81–97

BECKER-CANTARINO, BARBARA, *Der lange Weg zur Mündigkeit: Frau und Literatur (1500–1800)* (Stuttgart: Metzler, 1987)

—— 'Goethe as a Critic of Literary Women', in *Goethe as a Critic of Literature*, ed. by Karl J. Fink and Max L. Baeumer (Lanham, NY and London: University Press of America, 1984), pp. 160–81

——*Meine Liebe zu Büchern: Sophie von La Roche als professionelle Schriftstellerin* (Heidelberg: Winter, 2008)

BECKER-CANTARINO, BARBARA, *Schriftstellerinnen der Romantik: Epoche — Werk — Wirkung* (Munich: Beck, 2000)

——'"Outsiders": Women in German Literary Culture of Absolutism', *Jahrbuch für internationale Germanistik*, 2 (1984), 147–58

BELGUM, KIRSTEN, 'Domesticating the Reader: Women and *Die Gartenlaube*', *Women in German Yearbook*, 9 (1994), 91–111

BELGUM, KIRSTEN, 'E. Marlitt: Narratives of Virtuous Desire', in *A Companion to German Realism*, ed. by Todd Kontje (Rochester, NY: Camden House, 2002), pp. 259–82

BENNHOLDT-THOMSEN, ANKE, and ALFREDO GUZZONI, *Gelehrsamkeit und Leidenschaft: Das Leben der Ernestine Christine Reiske, 1735–1798* (Munich: Beck, 1992)

[BERLEPSCH, EMILIE VON], *Caledonia: Von der Verfasserin der Sommerstunden. Eine malerische Schilderung der Hochgebirge in Schottland*, 4 vols (Hamburg: Hoffmann, 1802–04)

BERLEPSCH, EMILIE VON, 'Fortsetzung: Ueber einige zum Glück der Ehe nothwendige Eigenschaften und Grundsätze', *Neuer Teutscher Merkur*, June (1791), pp. 113–34

——*Sommerstunden* (Zurich: Orell, Gessner, Füssli und Compagnie, 1794)

——'Ueber einige zum Glück der Ehe nothwendige Eigenschaften und Grundsätze', *Neuer Teutscher Merkur*, May (1791), pp. 63–102

BERMAN, RUSSEL, *Enlightenment of Empire: Colonial Discourse in German Literature* (Lincoln, NB and London: University of Nebraska Press, 1998)

BERTSCHIK, JULIA, *Mode und Moderne: Kleidung als Spiegel des Zeitgeistes in der deutschsprachigen Literatur (1770–1945)* (Cologne: Böhlau, 2005)

BESSERER HOLMGREN, JANET, *The Women Writers in Schiller's 'Horen': Patrons, Petticoats, and the Promotion of Weimar Classicism* (Newark, DE: University of Delaware Press, 2007)

BITTERMANN-WILLE, CHRISTA and HELGA HOFMANN-WEINBERGER, 'Erstklassige Schriftstellerinnen zweiter Güte? Literarische Bestseller österreichischer Autorinnen vom 19. Jahrhundert bis zum Zweiten Weltkrieg', in *Biblos: Beiträge zu Buch, Bibliothek und Schrift*, ed. by Austrian National Library (Vienna: Phoibos Verlag, 2005), pp. 19–39

BLACKWELL, JEANNINE, 'Sophie von La Roche and the Black Slave Poet Feuerbach: A Study in Sentimentality, Enlightenment, and Outsiderdom', in *The Enlightenment and its Legacy*, ed. by Sara Friedrichsmeyer and Barbara Becker-Cantarino (Bonn: Bouvier, 1991), pp. 105–15

BLAND, CAROLINE and ELISA MÜLLER-ADAMS, eds, *Schwellenüberschreitungen: Politik in der Literatur von deutschsprachigen Frauen 1780–1918* (Bielefeld: Aisthesis, 2007)

BLAU DuPLESSIS, RACHEL, 'Marble Paper: Toward a Feminist "History of Poetry"', in *Modern Language Quarterly*, 65.1 (2004), 93–129

BOCK, GISELA, *Frauen in der europäischen Geschichte: Vom Mittelalter bis zur Gegenwart* (Munich: Beck, 2000)

BOETCHER JOERES, RUTH-ELLEN, *Die Anfänge der deutschen Frauenbewegung: Louise Otto-Peters* (Frankfurt am Main: Fischer Taschenbuch, 1982)

——*Respectability and Deviance: Nineteenth-Century German Women Writers and the Ambiguity of Representation* (Chicago: University of Chicago Press, 1998)

——'Scattered Thoughts on Current Feminist Literary Critical Work in Nineteenth-Century German Studies', *Women in German Yearbook*, 17 (2001), 225–44

——'"That girl is an entirely different character!" Yes, but is she a feminist? Observations on Sophie von La Roche's *Geschichte des Fräuleins von Sternheim*', in *German Women in the Eighteenth and Nineteenth Centuries: A Social and Literary History*, ed. by Ruth-Ellen Boetcher Joeres and Mary Jo Maynes (Bloomington: Indiana University Press, 1986), pp. 137–56

——and MARIANNE BURKARD, *Out of Line/ausgefallen: The Paradox of Marginality in the Writings of Nineteenth-Century German Women* (Amsterdam: Rodopi, 1989)

BOETCHER JOERES, RUTH-ELLEN and MARY JO MAYNES, eds, *German Women in the Eighteenth and Nineteenth Centuries* (Bloomington: Indiana University Press, 1986)

[BOHL, JOHANNA SUSANNA], 'Winde und Männer: Antwort eines Frauenzimmers auf Dr. Sheridans Wolken und Weiber', *Der Teutsche Merkur*, July (1782), pp. 3–8

BÖHME, HARTMUT and PETER MATUSSEK, LOTHAR MÜLLER, *Orientierung Kulturwissenschaft: Was sie kann, was sie will* (Hamburg: Rowohlt 2002)

BOVENSCHEN, SILVIA, *Die Imaginierte Weiblichkeit: Exemplarische Untersuchungen zu kulturgeschichtlichen und literarischen Präsentationsformen des Weiblichen* (Frankfurt am Main: Suhrkamp, 1979)

BRAITHWAITE, ANN, 'The Personal, the Political, Third-Wave and Postfeminisms', *Feminist Theory*, 3.3 (2002), 335–44

BRANDES, ERNST, *Betrachtungen über das weibliche Geschlecht und dessen Ausbildung in dem geselligen Leben*, 3 vols (Hanover: Buchhandlung der Gebrüder Hahn, 1802)

[BRANDES, ERNST], *Ueber die Weiber* (Leipzig: Weidmanns Erben und Reich, 1787)

BRANDES, ERNST, 'Schriftstellerey der Weiber', in *Betrachtungen über das weibliche Geschlecht und dessen Ausbildung in dem geselligen Leben* (Hanover: Buchhandlung der Gebrüder Hahn, 1802), pp. 1–87

BRANDES, HELGA, 'Das Frauenzimmer-Journal: Zur Herausbildung einer journalistischen Gattung im 18. Jahrhundert', in *Deutsche Literatur von Frauen, 1: Vom Mittelalter bis zum Ende des 18. Jahrhunderts*, ed. by Gisela Brinker-Gabler (Munich: Beck, 1988), pp. 452–68

BRANDES, UTE, 'Escape to America: Social Reality and Utopian Schemes in German Women's Novels around 1800', in *In the Shadow of Olympus: German Women Writers Around 1800*, ed. by Katherine R. Goodman and Edith Waldstein (Albany: State University of New York Press, 1992), pp. 157–71

—— *Schriftstellerinnen der Romantik: Epoche — Werke — Wirkung* (Munich: Beck, 2000)

BRANTLY, SUSAN, *The Life and Writings of Laura Marholm* (Basle: Helbing & Lichtenhahn, 1991)

BRAUN, CHRISTINA VON and INGE STEPHAN, 'Gender@Wissen. Einführung', in *Gender@ Wissen: Ein Handbuch der Gender-Theorien*, ed. by Christina von Braun and Inge Stephan (Cologne, Weimar, and Vienna: Böhlau 2005), pp. 7–45

BREGER, CLAUDIA, and DOROTHEA DORNHOF, and DAGMAR VON HOFF, , 'Gender Studies/ Gender Trouble: Tendenzen und Perspektiven der deutschsprachigen Forschung', *Zeitschrift für Germanistik*, N.F. 1 (1999), 72–113

BREWER, CINDY, 'The Emigrant Heroine: Gender and Colonial Fantasy in Henriette Frölich's *Virginia oder Die Kolonie von Kentucky*', *Seminar*, 42.3 (2006), 194–210

BRINKER-GABLER, GISELA, *Deutsche Dichterinnen vom 16. Jahrhundert bis zur Gegenwart: Gedichte und Lebensläufe* (Frankfurt am Main: Fischer Taschenbuch Verlag, 1978)

BRINKER-GABLER, GISELA, ed., *Deutsche Literatur von Frauen*, 2 vols (Munich: Beck, 1988)

BRINKER-GABLER, GISELA, KAROLA LUDWIG, and ANGELA WÖFFEN, eds, *Lexikon deutsch-sprachiger Schriftstellerinnen 1800–1945* (Munich: dtv, 1986)

BRINKER-GABLER, GISELA, 'Einleitung. Frauen Schreiben. Überlegungen zu einer ausgewählten Exploration literarischer Praxis', in *Deutsche Literatur von Frauen*. Vol. 1 Vom Mittelalter bis zum Ende des 18. Jahrhunderts, ed. by Gisela Brinker-Gabler (Munich: Beck, 1988), pp. 11–36

BROOKS, PETER, 'Aesthetics and Ideology: What Happened to Poetics?', in *Aesthetics and Ideology*, ed. by George Levine (New Brunswick, NJ: Rutgers University Press, 1994)

BROWN, HILARY, '"Als käm Sie von der Thems und von der Seyne her": Luise Gottsched als Übersetzerin', in *Übersetzungskultur im 18. Jahrhundert: Übersetzerinnen in Deutschland, Frankreich und der Schweiz*, ed. by Brunhilde Wehinger and Hilary Brown (Hanover: Wehrhahn, 2008), pp. 37–52

—— *Benedikte Naubert (1756–1819) and her Relations to English Culture*, Modern Humanities Research Association Texts and Dissertations, 63; Bithell Series of Dissertations, 27 (Leeds: Maney, 2005)

——'Luise Gottsched and the Reception of French Enlightenment Literature in Germany', in *Translators, Interpreters, Mediators: Women Writers 1700–1900*, ed. by Gillian Dow (Oxford: Lang, 2007), pp. 21–36

——'Luise Gottsched the Satirist', *Modern Language Review*, 103 (2008), 1036–50

——'The Reception of the Bluestockings by Eighteenth-Century German Women Writers', *Women in German Yearbook*, 18 (2002), 620–31

——'Women and Classical Translation in the Eighteenth Century', *German Life and Letters*, 59 (2006), 344–60

BROWN, HILARY, and GILLIAN DOW, EDS, *Readers, Writers, Salonnières: Female Networks in Europe, 1700–1900* (Oxford: Lang, forthcoming)

BROWN, SARAH ANNES, 'Women Translators', in *The Oxford History of Literary Translation in English*, ed. by Peter France and Stuart Gillespie, 5 vols (Oxford: Oxford University Press, 2005–), III, *1660–1790*, ed. by Stuart Gillespie and David Hopkins (2005), pp. 111–20

BÜLOW, FRIEDA VON, 'Allerhand Alltägliches aus Deutsch-Ostafrika' [*Die Frau: Monatsschrift für das gesamte Frauenleben unserer Zeit*, 2.1 (1894), 25–30 and 2.2 (1994), 93–97], new ed. by Katharina von Hammerstein, in *Kolonialer Alltag in Ostafrika in Dokumenten*, ed. by Ulrich van der Heyden (Berlin: Trafo, 2009), pp. 175–93

——'Am Werkeltag in Deutsch-Ostafrika', *Die Frau: Monatsschrift für das gesamte Frauenleben unserer Zeit*, 3.12 (1896), pp. 740–45

——'Eine unblutige Eroberungsfahrt an der ostafrikanischen Küste' [*Daheim: Ein deutsches Familienblatt mit Illustrationen*, 24.2 (1888), 22–24 and 24.3 (1888), 38–40], new ed. by Katharina von Hammerstein, in *Kolonialer Alltag in Ostafrika in Dokumenten*, ed. by Ulrich van der Heyden (Berlin: Trafo, 2009), pp. 159–74

——'In der Station', *Daheim*, 24.9 (1888), 135–39

——'Ostafrikanische Briefe: Dar-es-Salaam, 11. September 1893', *Tägliche Rundschau, Unterhaltungs-Beilage*, 254 (28 October 1893), pp. 1013–14

——*Reisescizzen und Tagebuchblätter aus Deutsch-Ostafrika* (Berlin: Walther & Apolant 1889), new edn by Katharina von Hammerstein (Berlin: Trafo, forthcoming)

——*Reisescizzen und Tagebuchblätter aus Deutsch-Ostafrika*, ed. by Katharina von Hammerstein (Berlin: Trafo, forthcoming)

——'Unpolitische Briefe, Tanga, 31.7.1893', *Tägliche Rundschau, Unterhaltungs-Beilage*, 217 (15 September 1893), pp. 866–67

——'Unser Wali: Skizze aus dem deutsch-ostafrikanischen Leben', *Die Frau: Monatsschrift für das gesamte Frauenleben unserer Zeit*, 3 (1895/96), 483–85

BUTLER, JUDITH, *Bodies that Matter: On the Discursive Limits of 'Sex'* (New York: Routledge, 1993)

——*Frames of War: When is Life Grievable?* (London: Verso, 2010)

——*Gender Trouble: Feminism and the Subversion of Identity* (New York: Routledge, 1990)

——*Giving an Account of Oneself* (New York: Fordham University Press, 2005)

——'Performative Acts and Gender Constitution: An Essay in Phenomenology and Feminist Theory', *Theatre Journal*, 40.4 (1988), 519–31

——*The Psychic Life of Power: Theories in Subjection* (Stanford: Stanford UP, 1997)

——*Undoing Gender* (New York: Routledge, 2004)

BUTLER, JUDITH and JOHN GUILLORY, KENDALL THOMAS, *What's Left of Theory: New Work on the Politics of Literary Theory* (London and New York: Routledge, 2000)

CAINE, BARBARA, and GLENDA SLUGA, *Gendering European History* (London: Leicester University Press, 2000)

CASALE, RITA, 'Die Vierzigjährigen entdecken den Feminismus: Anmerkungen zur Epistemologisierung politischer Theorien', *Feministische Studien*, 26.2 (2008), 197–207

CHOW, REY, 'Poststructuralism: Theory as Critical Self-consciousness', in *The Cambridge Companion to Feminist Literary Theory*, ed. by Ellen Rooney (Cambridge: Cambridge University Press, 2006), pp. 195–210

CLARK, SUZANNE, *Sentimental Modernism: Women Writers and the Revolution of the Word* (Bloomington: Indiana University Press, 1991)

COCALIS, SUSAN L., 'Acts of Omission: The Classical Dramas of Caroline von Wolzogen and Charlotte von Stein', in *Thalia's Daughters: German Women Dramatists from the Eighteenth Century to the Present*, ed. by Susan L. Cocalis and Ferrel Rose (Tübingen: Francke, 1996), pp. 77–98

COCHRAN, TERRY, 'The Knowing of Literature', *New Literary History*, 38 (2007), 127–43

COHEN, MARGARET, *The Sentimental Education of the Novel* (Princeton, NJ: Yale University Press, 1999)

COLVIN, SARAH, *Women and German Drama: Playwrights and their Texts, 1860–1945* (Rochester: Camden House, 2003)

CULLENS, CHRIS[TINE E.], 'Female Difficulties, Comparativist Challenge: Novels by English and German Women, 1752–1814', in *Borderwork: Feminist Engagements with Comparative Literature*, ed. by Margaret R. Higonnet (Ithaca: Cornell University Press, 1994), pp. 100–19

—— '"Female Difficulties": Novels by English and German Women, 1755–1814' (unpublished doctoral dissertation, Stanford University, 1989)

CULLER, JONATHAN, 'Feminism in Time: A Response', *Modern Language Quarterly*, 65.1 (2004), 117–94

CZERNIN, MONICA, *'Jenes herrliche Gefühl der Freiheit': Frieda von Bülow und die Sehnsucht nach Afrika* (Bremen: Ullstein, 2008)

DAGMAR, JANK, *Anmerkungen zum Teilnachlaß von Sophie Pataky (1860–?) im Archiv der deutschen Frauenbewegung in Kassel* [1999]. Retrieved February, 18, 2009, from <http://forge.fh-potsdam.de/~ABD/jank/sophie_pataky.pdf>

DAHRENDORF, MALTE, *Das Mädchenbuch und seine Leserin: Jugendlektüre als Instrument der Sozialisation* (Weinheim and Basle: Beltz, 1978)

DALEY, MARGARETMARY, *Women of Letters: A Study of Self and Genre in the Personal Writing of Caroline Schlegel-Schelling, Rahel Levin Varnhagen, and Bettina Von Arnim* (Columbia, SC: Camden House, 1998)

DAMRAU, PETER, 'Eliza Haywoods *Geschichte des Fräuleins Elisabeth Thoughtless* (1756): Frühe Selbsterkenntnis und Ehekritik in der englischen Übersetzungsliteratur', *German Quarterly*, 82.4 (2009), 425–46

DAWSON, RUTH P., *The Contested Quill: Literature by Women in Germany 1770–1800* (Newark, DE: University of Delaware Press, 2002)

—— '"Der Weihrauch, den uns die Männer streuen": Wieland and the Women Writers in the *Teutscher Merkur*', in *Christoph Martin Wieland: Nordamerikanische Forschungsbeiträge zur 250. Wiederkehr seines Geburtstages 1983*, ed. by Hanjörg Schnelle (Tübingen: Niemeyer, 1984), pp. 225–49

DIETRICH, ANETTE, *Weiße Weiblichkeiten: Konstruktionen von 'Rasse' und Geschlecht in deutschen Kolonien* (Bielefeld: Transcript Verlag, 2007)

DIETRICK, LINDA, 'Gender and Technology in Marie von Ebner-Eschenbachs "Ein Original"', *Women in German Yearbook*, 17 (2001), 141–64

DIETZ, MARY G., 'Current Controversies in Feminist Theory', *Annual Review of Political Science*, 6 (2003), 399–431

DIJK, SUZAN VAN and KERSTIN WIEDEMANN, 'La nécessité d'une approche internationale de la réception sandienne: Des réactions allemandes réutilisées par la critique néerlandaise', *Œuvres & Critiques* (special issue on 'George Sand: La réception hors de France au XIXe siècle'), 28.1 (2003), 188–211

DIJK, SUZAN VAN and OTHERS, eds, *'I have heard about you': Foreign Women's Writing Crossing the Dutch Border* (Hilversum: Uitgeverij Verloren, 2004)

DITZ, TOBY L., 'The New Men's History and the Peculiar Absence of Gendered Power:

Some Remedies from Early American Gender History', *Gender & History*, 16.1 (2004), 1–35

DOHM, HEDWIG, 'Reaktion in der Frauenbewegung', *Die Zukunft*, 29 (1899), 279–91, repr. in Hedwig Dohm, *Ausgewählte Texte: Ein Lesebuch zum Jubiläum ihres 175. Geburtstages mit Essays und Feuilletons, Novellen und Dialogen, Aphorismen und Briefen*, ed. by Nikola Müller and Isabel Rohner (Berlin: trafo, 2006), pp. 136–51

DOW, GILLIAN, *Translators, Interpreters, Mediators: Women Writers 1700–1900* (Oxford: Lang, 2007)

EAGLETON, MARY, *Figuring the Woman Author in Contemporary Fiction* (New York: Palgrave Macmillan, 2005)

EAGLETON, TERRY, *After Theory* (New York: Basic Books, 2003)

EBNER-ESCHENBACH, MARIE VON, *Tagebücher*, ed. by Karl K. Polheim, 6 vols (Tübingen: Niemeyer, 1989–97)

EBNER-ESCHENBACH, MARIE VON, 'Lotti, die Uhrmacherin', *Sämtliche Werke* (Berlin: Paetel, 1920), III, 1–123

EIGLER, FRIEDERIKE, 'Engendering German Nationalism and Race in Frieda von Bülow's Colonial Writings', in *The Imperialist Imagination: German Colonialism and its Legacy*, ed. by Sara Friedrichsmeyer, Sara Lennox, and Susanne Zantop (Ann Arbor: University of Michigan Press, 1998), pp. 68–85

ELLIOTT, EMORY, 'Introduction: Cultural Diversity and the Problem of Aesthetics', in *Aesthetics in a Multicultural Age*, ed. by Emory Elliott, Louis Freitas Caton, and Jeffrey Rhyne (Oxford: Oxford University Press, 2002), pp. 3–27

ELLIOTT, JAKE, 'The Currency of Feminist Theory', *Periodical of the Modern Language Association*, 121.5 (2006), 1697–1703

ENDRES, ELISABETH, 'Marie von Ebner-Eschenbach', in *Frauen: Porträts aus zwei Jahrhunderten*, ed. by Hans Jürgen Schultz (Stuttgart: Kreuz, 1981)

[ERATH, FRÄULEIN VON], TRANS., *Leben und Thaten verschiedener berühmter Feldherren: Nebst dem Leben des M. Porcius Cato, und Titus Pomponius Atticus* (Frankfurt and Leipzig: Kochendörffer, 1766)

EVANS, RICHARD J., *The Feminist Movement in Germany 1894–1933* (London, Beverly Hills: Sage, 1976)

FARR, JAMES R., 'The Disappearance of the Traditional Artisan', in *A Companion to Nineteenth-Century Europe, 1789–1914*, ed. by Stefan Berger (Malden, MA: Blackwell, 2006), pp. 98–108

FEBEL, GISELA, 'Frauenbiographik als kollektive Biographik', in *Frauenbiographik: Lebensbeschreibungen und Porträts*, ed. by Christian von Zimmermann and Nina von Zimmermann (Tübingen: Gunter Narr, 2005), pp. 127–44

FETTERLEY, JUDITH, *The Resisting Reader: A Feminist Approach to American Fiction* (Bloomington: Indiana University Press, 1978)

FISCHER, BERNARD, *Der Verleger Johann Friedrich Cotta: Chronologische Verlagsbibliographie 1787–1832. Aus den Quellen bearbeitet* (Munich: K. G. Saur, 2003)

FISCHER, CHRISTIAN AUGUST, 'Über den Umgang der Weiber mit Männern' (Leipzig: Gräfl, 1800)

FLEIG, ANNE, *Handlungs-Spiel-Räume: Dramen von Autorinnen im Theater des ausgehenden 18. Jahrhunderts*, Epistemata: Reihe Literaturwissenschaft (Würzburg: Königshausen & Neumann, 1999)

—— 'Zwischen Ausschluss und Aneignung: Neue Positionen in der Geschlechterforschung zur Aufklärung', *Das achtzehnte Jahrhundert*, 26.1 (2002), 79–89

FLEIG, ANNE and HELGA MEISE, 'Das Geschlecht der Innovation: Bedeutung und Reichweite der Verknüpfung von Gattungs- und Geschlechterdiskurs bei Gellert, Sulzer und Wieland', *Das achtzehnte Jahrhundert*, 29.2 (2005), 159–78

FREVERT, UTE, *Frauen-Geschichte zwischen bürgerlicher Verbesserung und neuer Weiblichkeit* (Frankfurt am Main: Suhrkamp, 2001)

——*Mann und Weib und Weib und Mann: Geschlechter-Differenzen in der Moderne* (Munich: Beck, 1995)

FRIEDRICHS, ELISABETH, *Die deutschsprachigen Schriftstellerinnen des 18. und 19. Jahrhunderts: Ein Lexikon* (Stuttgart: Metzler, 1981)

FRÖLICH, HENRIETTE, *Virginia oder Die Kolonie von Kentucky: Mehr Wahrheit als Dichtung* (Berlin: Aufbau-Verlag, 1963)

FRONIUS, HELEN, '"Nur eine Frau wie ich konnte so ein Werk schreiben": Reassessing German Women Writers and the Literary Market 1770–1820', in E. Müller-Adams, and E. Bland, eds, *Frauen und der literarische Markt 1780–1918* (Bielefeld: Aithesis, 2007), pp. 29–52

——'Der reiche Mann und die arme Frau: German Woman Writers and the Eighteenth-Century Literary Market', *German Life and Letters*, 56 (2003), 1–19

——*Women and Literature in the Goethe Era, 1770–1820: Determined Dilettantes* (Oxford: Clarendon Press, 2007)

GABRIEL, NORBERT, '"... daß die Frauen in Deutschland durchaus Kinder bleiben müssen ...": Die Tagebücher der Marie von Ebner-Eschenbach', in *Des Mitleids tiefe Liebesfähigkeit: zum Werk der Marie von Ebner-Eschenbach*, ed. by Joseph P. Strelka (Berne: Lang, 1997), pp. 77–95

GALLAS, HELGA and ANITA RUNGE, *Romane und Erzählungen deutscher Schriftstellerinnen um 1800: Eine Bibliographie mit Standortnachweisen* (Stuttgart: Metzler, 1993)

GALLAS, HELGA and MAGDALENE HEUSER, *Untersuchungen zum Roman von Frauen um 1800* (Tübingen: Niemeyer, 1990)

GENEVRAY, FRANÇOISE, 'Vassili Botkine, George Sand et l'alliance intellectuelle franco-allemande', *Œuvres & Critiques* (special issue on 'George Sand: La réception hors de France au XIXe siècle'), 28.1 (2003), 49–75

GERIG, MAYA, *Jenseits von Tugend und Empfindsamkeit: Gesellschaftspolitik im Frauenroman um 1800* (Cologne, Weimar, and Vienna: Böhlau, 2008)

GIESLER, BIRTE, *Literatursprünge: Das erzählerische Werk von Friederike Helene Unger* (Göttingen: Wallstein, 2003)

[GILDEN, HENRIETTE ERNESTINE CHRISTIANE VON], 'An den Verfasser des Gedichts: das Walzen. (Im 2ten Stücke des Teutschen Merkurs 1793, wie auch an Herrn Menschen-schreck im Bürgerschen Musen-Allmanach dieses Jahres. S. 159)', *Der Neue Teutsche Merkur*, May (1793), pp. 95–97

GILLEIR, ANKE and ALICIA C. MONTOYA, 'Introduction: Toward a New Conception of Women's Literary History', in *Women Writing Back/Writing Women Back: Transnational Perspectives from the Late Middle Ages to the Dawn of the Modern Era*, ed. by Anke Gilleir, Alicia C. Montotya, and Suzan van Dijk (Leiden and Boston: Brill, 2010), pp. 1–20

GNÜG, HILTRUD and RENATE MÖHRMANN, 'Vorwort', in *Frauen — Literatur — Geschichte: Schreibende Frauen vom Mittelalter bis zur Gegenwart*, ed. by Hiltrud Gnüg and Renate Möhrmann (Stuttgart: Metzler, 1999), pp. ix–xii

GOETHE, JOHANN WOLFGANG, *Aus meinem Leben: Dichtung und Wahrheit*, in *Johann Wolfgang Goethe — Sämtliche Werke*, XIV (Frankfurt am Main: Deutscher Klassiker Verlag, 1986)

——*Autobiography: The Truth and Fiction Relating to My Life*, in *The Complete Works of Johann Wolfgang von Goethe in Ten Volumes*, I, trans. by John Oxenford (New York: P. F. Collier and Son, 1900)

——*Werke: Hamburger Ausgabe*. ed. by Erich Trunz, VII: *Wilhelm Meisters Lehrjahre* (Munich: Deutscher Taschenbuch Verlag, 1988)

GOLDSMITH, ELIZABETH C. and DENA GOODMAN, eds, *Going Public: Women and Publishing in Early Modern France* (Ithaca: Cornell University Press, 1995)

GOODMAN, KATHERINE, *Dis/closures: Women's Autobiography in Germany between 1790 and 1914* (New York: Lang, 1986)

GOODMAN, KATHERINE R. and EDITH WALDSTEIN, eds, *In the Shadow of Olympus: German Women Writers around 1800* (Albany: State University of New York Press, 1992)

GOODMAN, KAY, *Beyond the Eternal Feminine: Critical Essays on Women and German Literature* (Stuttgart: Akademischer Verlag Hans-Dieter Heinz, 1982)

GOSEWINKEL, DIETER, 'Rückwirkungen des kolonialen Rasserechts? Deutsche Staatsangehörigkeit zwischen Rassestaat und Rechtsstaat', in *Das Kaiserreiche transnational: Deutschland in der Welt 1871–1914*, ed. by Sebastian Conrad and Jürgen Osterhammel (Göttingen: Vandenhoeck & Ruprecht, 2004), pp. 236–56

GOTTSCHED, LUISE, *Briefe*, ed. by Dorothea von Runckel, 3 vols (Dresden: Harpeter, 1771–72)

——*Der Frau Luise Adelgunde Victoria Gottschedin, geb. Kulmus, sämmtliche kleinere Gedichte*, ed. by Johann Christoph Gottsched (Leipzig: Breitkopf, 1763)

——trans., *Neue Sammlung auserlesener Stücke, aus Popens, Eachards, Newtons und andrer Schriften* (Leipzig: Breitkopf, 1749)

——trans., *Zwo Schriften, welche von der Frau Marquis von Chatelet, gebohrner Baronessinn von Breteuil, und dem Herrn von Mairan, beständigem Sekretär bey der französischen Akademie der Wissenschaften, Das Maaß der lebendigen Kräften betreffend, gewechselt worden* (Leipzig: Breitkopf, 1741)

GOUDA, FRANCES, 'Das "unterlegene" Geschlecht der "überlegenen" Rasse. Kolonial-geschichte und Geschlechterverhältnisse', in *Geschlechterverhältnisse im historischen Wandel*, ed. by Hanna Schissler (Frankfurt am Main and New York: Campus, 1993), pp. 185–203

GRENZ, DAGMAR, *Mädchenliteratur: Von den moralisch-belehrenden Schriften im 18. Jahrhundert bis zur Herausbildung der Backfischliteratur im 19. Jahrhundert* (Stuttgart: Metzler, 1981)

GROSS, HEINRICH, *Deutschlands Dichterinnen und Schriftstellerinnen: Eine literarhistorische Skizze*, 2nd edn (Vienna: Carl Gerolds Sohn, 1882)

GUBAR, SUSAN, 'Feminism Inside Out', *Periodical of the Modern Language Society*, 121.5 (2006), 1711–16

——'What Ails Feminist Criticism?', *Critical Inquiry*, 24.4 (1998), 879–902

HABERMAS, REBEKKA, *Frauen und Männer des Bürgertums (1750–1850): Eine Familiengeschichte* (Göttingen: Vandenhoeck & Ruprecht, 2000)

HACKER, LUCIA, *Schreibende Frauen um 1900: Rollen, Bilder, Gesten* (Berlin: LIT, 2007)

HAMMERSTEIN, KATHARINA VON, 'Briefe von Frieda von Bülow: Einführung', in *Kolonialer Alltag in Deutsch-Ostafrika in Dokumenten*, ed. by Ulrich van der Heyden (Berlin: Trafo, 2009), pp. 149–57

——'Frieda von Bülow', in *Fembio: Frauenbiographieforschung*, ed. by Luise Pusch (Hanover: Institut für Frauenbiographieforschung, 2007), <http://www.fembio.org/biographie. php/frau/biographie/frieda-von-buelow/>

——'"Ein segenspendendes Werk zur Ehre der deutschen Nation." Vorschlag einer Lesart von Frieda von Bülows kolonial-nationalistischen Aufzeichnungen aus Deutsch-Ostafrika', in Frieda von Buelow, *Reisescizzen und Tagebuchblätter aus Deutsch-Ostafrika*, ed. by Katharina von Hammerstein (Berlin: Trafo, forthcoming)

HARK, SABINE, *Dissidente Partizipation: Eine Diskursgeschichte des Feminismus* (Frankfurt am Main: Suhrkamp 2005)

HARPHAM, GEOFFREY GALT, 'Aesthetics and the Fundamentals of Modernity', *Aesthetics and Ideology*, ed. by George Levine (New Brunswick, NJ: Rutgers University Press, 1994), pp. 124–52

HARRIMAN, HELGA H., 'Introduction', in *Seven Stories by Marie von Ebner-Eschenbach*, trans. by Helga H. Harriman (Columbia, SC: Camden House, 1986), pp. xi–xxxv

——'Women Writers and Artists in Fin-de-Siècle Vienna', *Modern Austrian Literature: Journal of the International Arthur Schnitzler Research Association*, 23 (1993), 1–19

HATZFELDT, MARIA HELENE VON, ed., *Zwei Blüten an einem Zweig: Beiträge zu Leben und Wirken der Schriftstellerinnen Frieda und Margarethe von Bülow* (Ingersleben: Heimatmuseum, c. 2000)

HAYES, JULIE CANDLER, *Translation, Subjectivity, and Culture in France and England, 1600–1800* (Stanford, CA: Stanford University Press, 2009)

HELM, CLEMENTINE, *Backfischchen's Leiden und Freuden: Eine Erzählung für junge Mädchen* (Leipzig: Wigand, 1863)

HELM, CLEMENTINE, *Lillis Jugend: Eine Erzählung für junge Mädchen* (Leipzig [u.a.]: Anton, 1871)

HENN, MARIANNE, 'Nachwort', in Marie von Ebner-Eschenbach, *Lotti, die Uhrmacherin*, ed. by Marianne Henn (Stuttgart: Reclam, 1999), pp. 149–66

HIGONNET, MARGARET R., 'Comparative Literature on the Feminist Edge', in *Comparative Literature in the Age of Multiculturalism*, ed. by Charles Bernheimer (Baltimore: The Johns Hopkins University Press, 1995), pp. 115–64

HILGER, STEPHANIE, 'Epistolarity, Publicity, and Painful Sensibility: Julie de Krüdener's *Valérie*', *French Review*, 79.4 (2006), 737–48

—— 'The Murderess on Stage: Christine Westphalen's *Charlotte Corday* (1804)', in *Women and Death 3: Women's Representations of Death in German Culture since 1500*, ed. by Anna Richards and Clare Bielby (Rochester, NY: Camden House, 2010)

—— *Women Write Back: Strategies of Response and the Dynamics of European Literary Culture, 1790–1805* (Amsterdam and New York: Rodopi, 2009)

[HIPPEL, THEODOR GOTTLIEB VON], *Ueber die bürgerliche Verbesserung der Weiber* (Frankfurt und Leipzig [no publisher], 1794)

HOECHSTETTER, SOPHIE, *Frieda Freiin v. Bülow: Ein Lebensbild* (Dresden: Carl Reissner, 1910)

HOELLER, HILDEGARD, *Edith Wharton's Dialogue with Realism and Sentimental Fiction* (Gainesville: University Press of Florida, 2000)

HOF, RENATE, *Die Grammatik der Geschlechter: Gender als Analysekategorie der Literaturwissenschaft* (Frankfurt am Main and New York: Campus 1995)

HOFF, DAGMAR VON, *Dramen des Weiblichen: Deutschsprachige Dramatikerinnen um 1800* (Opladen: Westdeutscher Verlag 1989)

HONEGGER, CLAUDIA and CAROLINE ARNI, 'Vorwort', in *Gender: Die Tücken einer Kategorie*, ed. by Claudia Honneger (Zürich: Chronos 2001), pp. 7–13

HOWE, PATRICIA, '"Das Beste sind Reisebeschreibungen": Reisende Frauen um die Mitte des neunzehnten Jahrhunderts und ihre Texte', in *Reisen im Diskurs: Modelle der literarischen Fremderfahrung von den Pilgerberichten bis zur Postmoderne*, ed. by Anne Fuchs and Theo Harden (Heidelberg: Carl Winter, 1995), 301–20

HUNT, LYNN, *The Family Romance of the French Revolution* (Berkeley: University of California Press, 1992)

HUNT, PETER, ed., *Understanding Children's Literature: Key Essays from the International Companion Encyclopedia of Children's Literature* (London: Routledge, 1999)

JACOB, MARIANNE, *Die Anfänge bibliographischer Darstellung der deutschen Literatur des 19. Jahrhunderts: Untersuchungen zur Vorgeschichte des Deutschen Schriftsteller-Lexikons 1830–1880* (Berlin: PhD dissertation, Faculty of Philosophy, Humboldt University, 2003)

JANCKE, GABRIELE, *Autobiographie als soziale Praxis: Beziehungskonzepte in Selbstzeugnissen des 15. und 16. Jahrhunderts im deutschsprachigen Raum* (Cologne, Weimar, and Vienna: Böhlau, 2002)

JANNIDIS, FOTIS and GERHARD LAUER, MATIAS MARTINEZ, SIMONE WINKO, EDS, *Rückkehr des Autors: Erneuerung eines umstrittenen Begriffs* (Tübingen: Niemeyer 1999)

JIRKU, BRIGITTE E., *'Wollen sie mit Nichts ... ihre Zeit versplittern?': Ich-Erzählerin und Erzählstruktur in von Frauen verfassten Romanen des 18. Jahrhunderts* (Frankfurt am Main: Lang, 1994)

JUNG, URSULA, 'The Reception of Germaine de Staël and George Sand among Female Novelists in Nineteenth-Century Spain', in *Readers, Writers, Salonnières: Female Networks in Europe, 1700–1900*, ed. by Hilary Brown and Gillian Dow (Oxford: Lang, forthcoming)

KAISER, KATJA, 'Neudietendorf: Frieda von Bülow, die koloniale Frauenfrage und koloniale Frauenorganisationen', in *Kolonialismus hierzulande: Eine Spurensuche in Deutschland*, ed. by Ulrich van der Heyden and Joachim Zeller (Erfurt: Sutton Verlag, 2007), pp. 171–76

KALOYANOVA-SLAVOVA, LUDMILA, *Übergangsgeschöpfe: Gabriele Reuter, Hedwig Dohm, Helene Böhlau und Franziska von Reventlow* (New York: Peter Lang, 1998)

KAPLAN, ANN, *Looking for the Other: Feminism, Film, and the Imperial Gaze* (New York and London: Routledge, 1997)

KECK, ANNETTE and MANUELA GÜNTER, 'Weibliche Autorschaft und Literaturgeschichte: Ein Forschungsbericht', *Internationales Archiv für die Sozialgeschichte der Literatur*, 26.2 (2001), 201–33

KEITH-SMITH, BRIAN, *An Encyclopedia of German Women Writers 1900–1933: Biographies and Bibliographies with Exemplary Readings*, I–X (Lewiston, NY: Mellen Verlag, 1997–98)

KEITH-SMITH, BRIAN, *German Women Writers 1900–1933: Twelve Essays*, Bristol German Publications, 3 (Lewiston, NY: Mellen Verlag, 1993)

KESSLER-HARRIS, ALICE, 'Do We Still Need a Women's History?', *The Chronicle Review*, supplement to *The Chronicle of Higher Education*, (7 Dec. 2007), B6–B7

KINNEBROCK, SUSANNE, 'Revisiting Journalism as a Profession in the Nineteenth Century: Empirical Findings on Women Journalists in Central Europe', *Communications: The European Journal of Communication Research*, 34 (2009), 107–24

—— 'Schreiben für die (politische) Öffentlichkeit — Frauen im Journalismus um 1900', in *Frauen in der literarischen Öffentlichkeit 1780–1918*, ed. by Caroline Bland and Elisa Müller-Adams (Bielefeld: Aisthesis, 2007), pp. 143–67

KIRBY, VICKI, *Judith Butler: Live Theory* (London: Continuum, 2006)

KLINGER, CORNELIA, GUDRUN-AXELI KNAPP, and BIRGIT SAUER, EDS, *Achsen der Ungleichheit: Zum Verhältnis von Klasse, Geschlecht und Ethnizität* (Frankfurt am Main: Campus 2007)

KLOSTERMAIER, DORIS M., *Marie von Ebner-Eschenbach: The Victory of a Tenacious Will* (Riverside, CA: Ariadne, 1997)

KLOTZ, MARCIA, 'Memoirs from a German Colony: What do German Women Want?', in *Eroticism and Containment: Notes from the Flood Plain*, ed. by Carol Siegel and Ann Kibbey (New York: New York University Press, 1994), pp. 154–87

—— 'White Women and the Dark Continent: Gender and Sexuality in German Colonial Discourse from the Sentimental Novel to the Fascist Film' (PhD Dissertation, Stanford University 1994)

KLOTZ, VOLKER, *Die erzählte Stadt* (Munich: Hanser, 1969)

KNAPP, GUDRUN-AXELI, ' "Intersectionality" — ein neues Paradigma feministischer Theorie? Zur transatlantischen Reise von "Race, Class, Gender" ', *Feministische Studien*, 23.1 (2005), 68–81

KOLOCH, SABINE, 'Madeleine de Scudéry in Deutschland: Zur Genese eines literarischen Selbstbewußtseins bürgerlicher Autorinnen', in *Gender Studies in den romanischen Literaturen: Revisionen, Subversionen*, ed. by Renate Kroll and Margarete Zimmermann, 2 vols (Frankfurt am Main: dipa, 1999), I, 213–55

KONTJE, TODD, 'History as Melodrama in Felix Dahn's *Ein Kampf um Rom*', in *The Late Nineteenth-Century German Bestseller*, ed. by Charlotte Woodford and Benedict Schofield (Rochester, NY: Camden House, forthcoming)

—— 'Introduction: Reawakening German Realism', in *A Companion to German Realism: 1848–1900*, ed. by Todd Kontje (Rochester, NY: Camden House, 2002), pp. 1–28

KONTJE, TODD, *Women, the Novel, and the German Nation 1771–1871: Domestic Fiction in the Fatherland* (Cambridge: Cambridge University Press, 1998)

[KÖPKEN, FRIEDRICH VON], 'Das Walzen', *Der Neue Teutsche Merkur*, February (1793), pp. 216–18

KORD, SUSANNE, *Ein Blick hinter die Kulissen. Deutschsprachige Dramatikerinnen im 18. und 19. Jahrhundert* (Stuttgart: Metzler, 1992)

——'The Innocent Translator: Translation as Pseudonymous Behavior in Eighteenth-Century German Women's Writing', *Jerome Quarterly*, 9.3 (1994), 11–13

——'Introduction', in *Letzte Chancen: Vier Einakter von Marie von Ebner-Eschenbach*, ed. by Susanne Kord (London: Modern Humanities Research Association, 2005), pp. 1–20

——'Introduction', in *Macht des Weibes: Zwei historische Tragödien von Marie von Ebner-Eschenbach*, ed. by Susanne Kord (London: Modern Humanities Research Association, 2005), pp. 1–18

——*Sich einen Namen machen: Anonymität und weibliche Autorschaft, 1700–1900* (Stuttgart: Metzler, 1996)

——*Women Peasant Poets in Eighteenth-Century England, Scotland and Germany: Milkmaids on Parnassus* (Rochester, NY: Camden House, 2003)

KÖSSLER, REINHART and TILMAN SCHIEL, 'Nationalstaaten und Grundlagen ethnischer Identität', in *Nationalstaat und Ethnizität*, ed. by Reinhart Kößler and Tilman Schiel (Frankfurt am Main: IKO Verlag für interkulturelle Kommunikation, 1994), pp. 1–22

KÖSTER, HERMANN, *Geschichte der deutschen Jugendliteratur in Monographien* (Munich: Verlag Dokumentation, 1972)

KRAFFT-EBING, RICHARD VON, *Psychopathia sexualis* (14th edn, 1912; Munich: Matthes & Seitz, 1997)

[KREUTZFELD, JOHANN GOTTLIEB], 'Wolken und Weiber oder *A New Simile for the Ladies*, nach Dr. Sheridan', *Der Teutsche Merkur*, May (1782), pp. 97–100

KRUG, MICHAELA, *Auf der Suche nach dem eigenen Raum: Topographien des Weiblichen im Roman von Autorinnen um 1800* (Würzburg: Königshausen und Neumann 2004)

KUHLES, DORIS and ULRIKE STANDKE, *Journal des Luxus und der Moden 1786–1827: Analytische Bibliographie mit sämtlichen 517 schwarz-weißen und 976 farbigen Abbildungen der Original-zeitschrift* (Munich: K. G. Saur, 2003)

KUNDRUS, BIRTHE, 'Die imperialistischen Frauenverbände des Kaiserreichs: Koloniale Phantasie- und Realgeschichte im Verein', *Basler Afrika Bibliographien* (Namibia Resource Center-Southern Africa Library. BAB Working Paper), 3 (2005), 1–23

——*Moderne Imperialisten: Das Kaiserreich im Spiegel seiner Kolonien* (Cologne: Böhlau, 2003)

KUZNIAR, ALICE A., ed., *Outing Goethe and his Age* (Stanford, CA: Stanford University Press 1996)

LA ROCHE, SOPHIE VON, *Geschichte des Fräuleins von Sternheim* [1771], ed. by Barbara Becker-Cantarino (Stuttgart: Reclam, 1983)

——*History of Lady Sophia Sternheim*, trans. by Crista Baguss Britt (New York: State University of New York Press, 1991)

——*The History of Lady Sophie Sternheim*, trans. by Joseph Collyer, ed. by James Lynn (London: Pickering & Chatto, 1991)

LACHMANSKI, HUGO, *Die deutschen Frauenzeitschriften des achtzehnten Jahrhunderts* (Berlin: Paul, 1900)

LANDES, JOAN, *Women and the Public Sphere in the Age of the French Revolution* (Ithaca: Cornell University Press, 1988)

LAUBE, HEINRICH, *Geschichte der deutschen Literatur* (Stuttgart: Hallberger'sche Verlagshandlung, 1839)

LAURIEN, INGRID, ' "A Land of Promise?" Autobiography and Fiction in Frieda von Bülow's East-African Novels', in *Africa and Europe: En/Countering Myths: Essays on Literature and Cultural Politics*, ed. by Carlotta von Maltzan (Frankfurt am Main: Lang, 2003), pp. 203–14

LEES, ANDREW, *Cities, Sin, and Social Reform in Imperial Germany* (Ann Arbor, MI: The University of Michigan Press, 2002)

LEVINE, GEORGE, 'Introduction: Reclaiming the Aesthetic', in *Aesthetics and Ideology*, ed. by George Levine (New Brunswick, NJ: Rutgers University Press, 1994), pp. 1–30

LEVINSON, MARJORIE, 'What is New Formalism?', *Periodical of the Modern Language Association*, 122.2 (2007), 558–70

LEYDECKER, KARL, 'Divorce and the Rise of the Women's Novel in Germany', in *After Intimacy: The Culture of Divorce in the West since 1789*, ed. by Karl Leydecker and Nicholas White (Oxford: Lang, 2007), pp. 11–29

——and NICHOLAS WHITE, eds, *After Intimacy: The Culture of Divorce in the West since 1789* (Oxford: Lang, 2007)

LIEBRAND, CLAUDIA, *Kreative Refakturen: Annette von Droste-Hülshoffs Texte* (Freiburg: Rombach, 2008)

LOREY, CHRISTOPH and JOHN PLEWS, ed., *Queering the Canon: Defying Sights in German Literature and Culture* (Columbia, SC: Camden House, 1998)

LOSTER-SCHNEIDER, GUDRUN and GABY PAILER, EDS, *Lexikon deutschsprachiger Epik und Dramatik von Autorinnen 1730–1900* (Tübingen and Basle: Francke, 2006)

LUKAS, WOLFGANG, ' "Entsagung": Konstanz und Wandel eines Motivs in der Erzählliteratur von der späten Goethezeit zum frühen Realismus', in *Zwischen Goethezeit und Realismus — Wandel und Spezifik in der Phase des Biedermeier*, ed. by Michael Titzmann (Tübingen: Niemeyer, 2002), pp. 113–49

MAGRIS, CLAUDIO, *Der habsburgische Mythos in der österreichischen Literatur* (Salzburg: Otto Müller, 1966)

MÁNCZYK-KRYGIEL, MONIKA, *An der Hörigkeit sind die Hörigen schuld* (Stuttgart: Heinz, 2002)

MANDAL, ANTHONY, and BRIAN SOUTHAM, eds, *The Reception of Jane Austen in Europe*, The Athlone Critical Traditions Series: The Reception of British and Irish Authors in Europe, 14 (London: Continuum, 2007)

MARCUS, SHARON, 'Feminist Criticism: A Tale of Two Bodies', *Periodical of the Modern Language Association*, 121.5 (2006), 1722–28

MARCUS, SHARON, *Apartment Stories: City and Home in Nineteenth-Century Paris and London* (Berkeley, CA: University of California Press, 1999)

MARHOLM, LAURA, 'Björnson als Sittlichkeitsapostel', *Die Gegenwart*, 33 (1888), 100–03

——*Das Buch der Frauen: Zeitpsychologische Porträts*, 4th edn (Paris, Leipzig, and Munich: Albert Langen, 1896)

MARHOLM, LAURA, *Frau Lily als Jungfrau, Gattin und Mutter* (Berlin: Duncker, 1897), <http://openlibrary.org/b/OL23435426M/Frau_Lilly_als_Jungfrau_Gattin_und_Mutter> [accessed 29 April 2010]

——*Modern Women*, trans. by Hermione Ramsden (London: J. Lane; Boston: Roberts Brothers, 1896)

——*Studies in the Psychology of Woman*, trans. by Georgia A. Etchison (Chicago: H. S. Stone, 1899)

——'Zur Frauenfrage: Die beiden Seiten der Medaille', *Freie Bühne*, 12 (1890), 585–89

——*Zur Psychologie der Frau*, I, 2nd enlarged edn (Berlin: Carl Duncker, 1903)

——*Zur Psychologie der Frau*, II (Berlin: Carl Duncker, 1903)

MARLITT, EUGENIE, *Goldelse* (first publ. Leipzig: Ernst Keil, 1867; Berlin: Sammlung Zenodot Bibliothek der Frauen, 2007)

MARTIN, LAURA, *Harmony in Discord: German Women Writers in the Eighteenth and Nineteenth Centuries* (Oxford and New York: Peter Lang, 2001)

MARTINO, ALBERTO, *Die deutsche Leihbibliothek: Geschichte einer literarischen Institution (1756–1914)* (Wiesbaden: Harrassowitz, 1990)

MAST, THOMAS, 'Gender, Class, Jewishness, and the Problem of Self in Fanny Lewald's

*Jenny*: Jenny's "schielender Blick"', *Focus on Literatur: A Journal for German-Language Literature*, 2.1 (1995), 31–50

[MAUVILLON, JAKOB], *Mann und Weib nach ihren gegenseitigen Verhältnissen geschildert: Ein Gegenstück zu der Schrift: Ueber die Weiber* (Leipzig: Dykische Buchhandlung, 1791)

MAY, ANJA, *Wilhelm Meisters Schwestern: Bildungsromane von Frauen im ausgehenden 18. Jahrhundert* (Königstein im Taunus: Helmer, 2006).

MAYREDER, ROSA, 'Eine andere Marie Baschkirtseff', *Das Magazin für Litteratur*, 67 (1898), 778–83

—— *Geschlecht und Kultur: Essays*, afterword by Eva Geber (1923; Vienna: Mandelbaum, 1998)

—— *Tagebücher 1873–1937*, ed. and intro. by Harriet Anderson (Frankfurt am Main: Insel, 1988)

—— *Zur Kritik der Weiblichkeit: Essays*, ed. with an afterword by Eva Geber (1905; Vienna: Mandelbaum, 1998)

McGOVERN, WILLIAM MONTGOMERY, *From Luther to Hitler: The History of Fascist-Nazi Political Philosophy* (Boston: Houghton Mifflin, 1941)

MEISE, HELGA, *Die Unschuld und die Schrift: Deutsche Frauenromane im 18. Jahrhundert* (Berlin: Guttandin & Hoppe, 1983; 2nd edn Frankfurt am Main: Helmer 1992)

MEISE, HELGA, ' "Hirnkinder": Gattungsvorgabe und hybride Schreibweise in Sophie von La Roches "Pomona für Teutschlands Töchter" ', in *'Bald zierliche Blumen — bald Nahrung des Verstands'. Lektüren zu Sophie von La Roche*, ed. by Monika Lippke, Matthias Luserke-Jaqui, and Nikola Rossbach (Hannover: Wehrhahn, 2008), pp. 123–41

MILLER, NANCY K., 'The Text's Heroine: A Feminist Critic and her Fictions', in *Conflicts in Feminism*, ed. by Marianne Hirsch and Evelyn Fox Keller (New York: Routledge, 1990), pp. 112–20

MILLETT, KATE, *Sexual Politics* (New York: Doubleday, 1970)

MÖBIUS, PAUL J., *Ueber den physiologischen Schwachsinn des Weibes*, 3rd edn (Halle: Carl Marhold, 1901)

MOI, TORIL, 'The Challenge of the Particular Case: Bourdieu's Sociology of Cultural and Literary Criticism', in Toril Moi, *What is a Woman? And Other Essays* (Oxford: Oxford University Press, 2001), pp. 300–12

—— ' "I am not a woman writer": About Women, Literature and Feminist Theory Today', *Feminist Theory*, 9.3 (2008), 259–71

NENON, MONIKA, 'Nationalcharakter und Kultur: Die Reiseberichte von Sophie von La Roche', *Carleton Germanic Papers*, 24 (1996), 57–72

NIEBERLE, SIGRID, 'Rückkehr einer Scheinleiche? Ein erneuter Versuch über die Autorin', in *Rückkehr des Autors: Zur Erneuerung eines umstrittenen Begriffs*, ed. by Fotis Jannidis, Gerhard Lauer, Matias Martinez, and Simone Winko (Tübingen: Niemeyer 1999), pp. 255–72

NIETHAMMER, ORTRUN, *Autobiographien von Frauen im 18. Jahrhundert* (Tübingen: Francke, 2000)

NIETZSCHE, FRIEDRICH WILHELM, *Jenseits von Gut und Böse* (1886)

—— *Menschliches, Allzumenschliches*, I: *Ein Buch für freie Geister* (1878)

—— *Untimely Meditations*, ed. by Daniel Breazeale and trans. by R. J. Hollingdale (Cambridge: Cambridge University Press, 1997), pp. 72–73

—— *Vom Nutzen und Nachteil der Historie für das Leben* (Stuttgart: Reclam, 1982)

NIGG, MARIANNE, *Biographien der österreichischen Dichterinnen und Schriftstellerinnen: Ein Beitrag zur deutschen Literatur in Österreich* (Korneuburg: Julius Kühlkopfs, 1893)

NÜNNING, ANSGAR, 'Welten-Weltbilder-Weisen der Welterzeugung: Das Wissen der Literatur und die Aufgabe der Literaturwissenschaft', *Germanisch-Romanische Monatsschrift*, 59.1 (2009), 65–90

NÜNNING, ANSGAR and VERA NÜNNING, *Erzählanalyse und Gender Studies* (Stuttgart: Metzler, 2004)

OFFEN, KAREN, *European Feminisms, 1700–1950: A Political History* (Stanford, CA: Stanford University Press, 2000)

OPITZ, CLAUDIA, 'Gender — eine unverzichtbare Kategorie der historischen Analyse: Zur Rezeption von Joan W. Scotts Studien in Deutschland, Österreich und der Schweiz', in *Gender: Die Tücken einer Kategorie*, ed. by Claudia Honegger and Caroline Arni (Zürich: Chronos, 2001), pp. 95–115

——'Nach der Gender-Forschung ist vor der Gender-Forschung: Plädoyer für die historische Perspektive in der Geschlechterforschung', in *Was kommt nach der Genderforschung? Zur Zukunft der feministischen Theoriebildung*, ed. by Rita Casale and Barbara Rendtorff (Bielefeld: Transcript, 2008), pp. 13–28

ORNAM, VANESSA VAN, *Fanny Lewald and Nineteenth-Century Constructions of Femininity* (New York: Lang, 2002)

OSINSKI, JUTTA, *Einführung in die feministische Literaturwissenschaft* (Berlin: Erich Schmidt Verlag, 1998)

PAILER, GABY and GUDRUN LOSTER-SCHNEIDER, *Lexikon deutschsprachiger Epik und Dramatik von Autorinnen (1730–1900)* (Tübingen: Francke, 2006)

PATAKY, SOPHIE, *Lexikon deutscher Frauen der Feder: Eine Zusammenstellung der seit dem Jahre 1840 erschienenen Werke weiblicher Autoren, nebst Biographien der lebenden und einem Verzeichnis der Pseudonyme*, I–II (Berlin: Pataky [Eigenverlag], 1898)

PERRAS, ARNE, *Carl Peters and German Imperialism, 1856–1918: A Political Biography* (Oxford and New York: Clarendon Press, 2004)

PETERS, CARL, *Die Gründung von Deutsch-Ostafrika: Kolonialpolitische Erinnerungen und Betrachtungen* (Berlin: C. A. Schwetschke und Sohn, 1906)

PFEIFFER, PETER C., 'Im Kanon und um den Kanon herum: Marie von Ebner-Eschenbach', in *Kanon und Kanonisierung als Probleme der Literaturgeschichtsschreibung*, ed. by Peter Wiesinger and Hans Derkits (Berne: Lang, 2003), pp. 113–18

——*Marie von Ebner-Eschenbach: Tragödie, Erzählung, Heimatfilm* (Tübingen: Narr Francke Verlag, 2008)

PIERETTI, MARIE-PASCALE, 'Women Writers and Translation in Eighteenth-Century France', *French Review*, 75.3 (2002), 474–88

PLAIN, GILL and SUSAN SELLERS, 'Introduction to Part III', in *A History of Feminist Literary Criticism*, ed. by Ellen Rooney

PLANERT, UTE, 'Vater Staat und Mutter Germania: Zur Politisierung des weiblichen Geschlechts im 19. und 20. Jahrhundert', in *Nation, Politik und Geschlecht: Frauenbewegungen und Nationalismus in der Moderne*, ed. by Ute Plantert (Frankfurt am Ma\in and New York: Campus, 2000), pp. 15–65

PLEHN, AUGUSTE (pseud. of BRIGITTE AUGUSTI), *An Deutschem Herd: Kulturgeschichtliche Erzählungen aus alter und neuer Zeit mit besonderer Berücksichtigung des Lebens der deutschen Frauen: Für das reifere Mädchenalter*, 5 vols (Leipzig: F. Hirt, 1891)

POCKELS, CARL FRIEDRICH, *Contraste zu dem Gemälde der Weiber: Nebst einer Apologie derselben gegen die Befehdung im goldenen Kalbe: Ein Anhang zu der Charakteristik des weiblichen Geschlechts* (Hanover: Ritschersche Buchhandlung, 1804)

——'Beantwortung der Frage: Dürfen Weiber gelehrte Kenntnisse haben? oder: Sind Weiblichkeit und wissenschaftliche Geistesbildung zu vereinigen? Ein Versuch', *Journal von deutschen Frauen für deutsche Frauen*, 1 (1805), 21–35

POPP, ADELHEID, *Jugend einer Arbeiterin* (Berlin and Bonn: Dietz, 1983)

PRATT, MARY LOUISE, *Imperial Eyes: Travel Writing and Transculturalism* (New York: Routledge, 1992)

RADWAY, JANICE, *Reading the Romance: Women, Patriarchy, and Popular Literature* (Chapel Hill: University of North Carolina Press, 1984)

RECKE, ELISA VON DER, 'An Herrn J. M. Preißler, Professor bei der kgl. dänischen Akademie der Künste, nebst Vorwort der Herausgeber und Nachschrift der Autorin', *Berlinische Monatsschrift*, 5 (1786), 385–98

REISKE, ERNESTINE CHRISTINE, trans., *Hellas* (Mitau: Hinz, 1778)

——trans., *Zur Moral* (Leipzig: Buchhandlung der Gelehrten, 1782)

REUTER, GABRIELE, *Aus guter Familie: Leidensgeschichte eines Mädchens* (1895; Berlin: Fischer, 1986)

——*Aus guter Familie: Leidensgeschichte eines Mädchens*, ed. by Katja Mellmann, I: *Text* (1895; Marburg: Verlag LiteraturWissenschaft.de, 2006)

——*From a Good Family* (Columbia, SC: Camden House, 1999)

——*Liselotte von Reckling* (Berlin: Fischer, 1904)

——*Vom Kinde zum Menschen* (Berlin: Fischer, 1921)

RHODEN, EMMY, *Der Trotzkopf: Eine Pensionsgeschichte für junge Mädchen* (Stuttgart: G. Weise, 1885)

RICHARDS, ANNA, ' "Double-voiced Discourse" and Psychological Insight in the Work of Therese Huber', *Modern Language Review*, 99.2 (2004), 416–29

——'The Eighteenth Century', review chapter in *The Year's Work in Modern Language Studies 69 (2006 and 2007)* (London: Maney, 2008) and in *The Year's Work in Modern Language Studies 70 (2008)* (London: Maney, 2009)

——'Sense and Sentimentality? Margarete Böhme's *Tagebuch einer Verlorenen* (1905) in Context', in *Commodities of Desire: The Prostitute in Modern German Literature*, ed. by Christiane Schönfeld (Rochester, NY: Camden House, 2000), pp. 98–109

——*The Wasting Heroine in German Fiction by Women 1770–1914* (Oxford, Oxford University Press, 2004)

——*Women and Death 3: Women's Representations of Death in German Culture since 1500*, ed. by Anna Richards and Clare Bielby (Rochester, NY: Camden House, 2010)

RICHEL, VERONICA C., *Luise Gottsched: A Reconsideration* (Berne: Lang, 1973)

RICHTER, SIMON, *Missing the Breast: Gender, Phantasy, and the Body in the German Enlightenment* (Seattle: University of Washington Press, 2006)

ROBBINS, RUTH, *Literary Feminisms* (London: Macmillan, 2000)

ROONEY, ELLEN, 'Introduction', in *The Cambridge Companion to Feminist Literary Theory*, ed. by Ellen Rooney (Cambridge: Cambridge University Press, 2006), pp. 1–26

ROSE, FERREL V., *The Guises of Modesty: Marie von Ebner-Eschenbach's Female Artists* (Columbia, SC: Camden House, 1994)

ROSSBACH, NIKOLA, ed., *'bald zierliche Blumen — bald Nahrung des Verstands': Lektüren zu Sophie von La Roche* (Hanover: Wehrhahn 2008), pp. 123–41

ROSSBACHER, KARLHEINZ, *Literatur und Liberalismus: Zur Kultur der Ringstrassenzeit in Wien* (Vienna: J&V, 1992)

ROSSLYN, WENDY, *Feats of Agreeable Usefulness: Translations by Russian Women 1763–1825* (Fichtenwalde: Göpfert, 2000)

RUNGE, ANITA, *Literarische Praxis von Frauen um 1800: Briefroman, Autobiographie, Märchen* (Hildesheim, Zurich, and New York: Olms, 1997)

RUSSELL J. REISING, 'Can Cultured Reading Read Culture? Toward a Theory of Literary Incompetence', *Tulsa Studies in Women's Literature*, 10.1 (1991), 67–77

SAGARRA, EDA, 'Gegen den Zeit- und Revolutionsgeist: Ida Gräfin Hahn-Hahn und die christliche Tendenzliteratur im Deutschland des 19. Jahrhunderts', in *Deutsche Literatur von Frauen*, II, ed. by Gisela Brinker-Gabler (Munich: Beck, 1988), pp. 105–19

SAGARRA, EDA, *A Social History of Germany, 1648–1914* (London: Methuen, 1977)

SAID, EDWARD, *Orientalism* (New York: Pantheon Books, 1978)

SAID-RUETE, EMILY (née Princess Salme of Oman and Zanzibar), *Leben im Sultanspalast: Memoiren aus dem 19. Jahrhundert*, a reprint of *Memoiren einer arabischen Prinzessin*, 2 vols (Berlin: Luckhardt, 1886), ed. and with an afterword by Annegret Nippa (Hamburg:

Die Hanse/Europäische Verlagsanstalt, 2007; original: Frankfurt am Main: Athenäum, 1989).

SCHABERT, INA, 'No Room of One's Own: Women's Studies in English Departments in Germany', *Periodical of the Modern Language Association*, 119.1 (2004), 69–79

SCHEIDELER, BRITTA, *Zwischen Beruf und Berufung: Zur Sozialgeschichte der deutschen Schriftsteller von 1880 bis 1933* (Frankfurt am Main: Buchhändler-Vereinigung, 1997)

SCHIETH, LYDIA, *Die Entwicklung des deutschen Frauenromans im ausgehenden 18. Jahrhundert: Ein Beitrag zur Gattungsgeschichte* (Frankfurt am Main: Lang, 1987)

SCHLAFFER, HANNELORE, 'Weibliche Geschichtsschreibung: Ein Dilemma', *Merkur: Deutsche Zeitschrift für Europäisches Denken*, 40.3 (1986), 256–60

SCHLEINER, LOUISE, 'Voicing the Subject: Early Modern Women's Strategies within Discourse Domains', in *Writing the History of Women's Writing: Toward an International Approach*, ed. by Suzan van Dijk and others (Amsterdam: Royal Netherlands Academy of Arts and Sciences, 2001), pp. 163–69

SCHMERSAHL, KATRIN, *Medizin und Geschlecht: Zur Konstruktion der Kategorie Geschlecht im medizinischen Diskurs des 19. Jahrhunderts* (Opladen: Leske + Budrich, 1998)

SCHMID-BORTENSCHLAGER, SIGRID, *Österreichische Schriftstellerinnen 1800–2000: Eine Literaturgeschichte* (Darmstadt: Wissenschaftliche Buchgesellschaft, 2009)

SCHMID-BORTENSCHLAGER, SIGRID and HANNA SCHNEDL-BUBENICEJ, *Österreichische Schriftstellerinnen 1880–1938: Eine Bio-Bibliographie* (Stuttgart: Heinz, 1982)

SCHMIDGEN, WOLFRAM, 'Reembodying the Aesthetic', *Modern Language Quarterly*, 66.1 (2005), 55–84

SCHMÖLZER, HILDE, *Rosa Mayreder: Ein Leben zwischen Utopie und Wirklichkeit* (Vienna: Promedia, 2002)

SCHORSKE, CARL E., *Fin-de Siècle Vienna: Politics and Culture* (New York: Random House, 1961)

SCHÖSSLER, FRANZISKA, *Einführung in die Gender Studies* (Berlin: Akademie Verlag 2008)

SCHUBERT, FRANK, *Die Stellung der Frau im Spiegel der Berlinischen Monatsschrift*, Abhandlungen zur Philosophie, Psychologie und Pädagogik, 150 (Bonn: Bouvier, 1980)

SCHULZE, JUTTA and PETRA BUDKE, *Schriftstellerinnen in Berlin 1871–1945: Ein Lexikon zu Leben und Werk* (Berlin: Orlanda-Frauenverlag, 1995)

SCHUTTE WATT, HELGA, 'Woman's Progress: Sophie La Roche's Travelogues 1787–1788', *The Germanic Review*, 69.2 (1994), 50–60

SCOTT, JOAN W., 'Die Zukunft von gender: Fantasien zur Jahrtausendwende', in *Gender. Die Tücken einer Kategorie*, ed. by Claudia Honegger and Caroline Arni (Zurich: Chronos, 2001), pp. 39–63

SCOTT, JOAN W., 'Gender: A Useful Category of Historical Analysis', *American Historical Review* 5, 91 (1986), 1053–76 [German translation: 'Gender: Eine nützliche Kategorie der historischen Analyse', in *Selbstbewußt Frauen in den USA*, ed. by Nancy Kaiser (Leipzig: Reclam, 1994), pp. 27–74]

SEELING, CLAUDIA, *Zur Interdependenz von Gender- und Nationaldiskurs bei Marie von Ebner-Eschenbach* (St Ingbert: Röhrig Universitätsverlag, 2008)

SHOWALTER, ELAINE, 'Feminist Criticism in the Wilderness', in *The New Feminist Criticism: Essays on Women, Literature and Theory*, ed. by Elaine Showalter (London: Virago, 1986), pp. 243–70

——*A Literature of their Own: British Women Novelists from Brontë to Lessing* (Princeton NJ: Princeton University Press, 1977)

——*A Literature of their Own: From Charlotte Brontë to Doris Lessing*, 2nd edn (London: Virago, 1999)

SIEGEL, MONIKA, ' "Ich hatte einen Hang zur Schwärmerey ...": Das Leben der Schriftstellerin und Übersetzerin Meta Forkel-Liebeskind im Spiegel ihrer Zeit' (unpublished doctoral thesis, University of Darmstadt, 2001)

SIMON, SHERRY, *Gender in Translation: Cultural Identity and the Politics of Transmission* (London: Routledge, 1996)

SITTER, CARMEN, *'Die eine Hälfte vergißt man(n) leicht!': Zur Situation von Journalistinnen in Deutschland* (Pfaffenweiler: Centaurus, 1998)

SMITH, THERESA ANN, *The Emerging Female Citizen: Gender and Enlightenment in Spain* (Berkeley: University of California Press, 2006)

—— 'Writing out of the Margins: Women, Translation, and the Spanish Enlightenment', *Journal of Women's History*, 15.1 (2003), 116–43

SNYDER, LOUIS L., *From Bismarck to Hitler: The Background of Modern German Nationalism* (Williamsport, PA: The Bayard Press, 1935)

SORENSEN, BENGT ALGOT, 'Laura Marholm, Fr. Nietzsche und G. Hauptmanns *Einsame Menschen*', *Orbis Litterarum*, 47 (1992), 52–62

SPENCER, JANE, *The Rise of the Woman Novelist: From Aphra Behn to Jane Austen* (Oxford: Blackwell, 1986)

SPIEKERMANN, MARIE-LUISE, 'Dorothea Margareta Liebeskind (1765–1853): Übersetzerin zwischen wissenschaftlicher Literatur und Unterhaltungsromanen englischer Autorinnen', in *Übersetzungskultur im 18. Jahrhundert: Übersetzerinnen in Deutschland, Frankreich und der Schweiz*, ed. by Brunhilde Wehinger and Hilary Brown (Hanover: Wehrhahn, 2008), pp. 141–64

SPIVAK, GAYATRY CHAKRAVORTY, *Death of a Discipline* (New York: Columbia University Press, 2003)

SPRENGEL, PETER, '"Entgleisungen" in Hauptmanns Nachlaß: Zur Thematisierung weiblicher Sexualität bei Ola Hansson und Laura Marholm', *Orbis Litterarum*, 47 (1992), 31–51

STARK, SUSANNE, 'Women and Translation in the Nineteenth Century', *New Comparison*, 15 (1993), 33–44

STARNES, THOMAS C., *Der Teutsche Merkur: Ein Repertorium* (Sigmaringen: Jan Thorbecke, 1994)

STAVES, SUSAN, *A Literary History of Women's Writing in Britain, 1660–1789* (Cambridge: Cambridge University Press, 2006)

STEINER, GERHARD, 'Nachwort', in Henriette Frölich, *Virginia oder Die Kolonie von Kentucky: Mehr Wahrheit als Dichtung* (Berlin: Aufbau-Verlag, 1963), pp. 205–33

STEMPER, DAGNY, *Das Leben der schleswig-holsteinischen Schriftstellerin Ernestine Voß (1756–1834): Eine Analyse zu Biographie und Werk auf der Grundlage ihres autographischen Nachlasses* (Frankfurt am Main: Lang, 2006)

STEPHAN, INGE, '"Gender": Eine nützliche Kategorie für die Literaturwissenschaft', *Zeitschrift für Germanistik*, N.F. 1 (1999), 23–35

STEPHAN, INGE and CHRISTINA VON BRAUN, EDS, *Gender-Studien: Eine Einführung* (Stuttgart: Metzler 2000)

STEPHAN, INGE and CHRISTINA VON BRAUN, EDS, *Gender@Wissen: Ein Handbuch der Gender-Theorien* (Cologne, Weimar, and Vienna: Böhlau, 2005) Stocksieker Di Maio, Irene, 'Jewish Emancipation and Integration: Fanny Lewald's Narrative Strategies', in *Autoren damals und heute: Literaturgeschichtliche Beispiele veränderter Wirkungshorizonte*, ed. by Gerhard P. Knapp (Amsterdam: Rodopi, 1991)

STOCKSIEKER DI MAIO, IRENE, 'Jewish Emancipation and Integration: Fanny Lewald's Narrative Strategies', in *Autoren damals und heute: Literaturgeschichtliche Beispiele veränderter Wirkungshorizonte*, ed. by Gerhard P. Knapp (Amsterdam: Rodopi, 1991)

TANZER, ULRIKE, *Frauenbilder im Werk Marie von Ebner-Eschenbachs* (Stuttgart: Heinz, 1997)

TEBBEN, KARIN, *Beruf: Schriftstellerin. Schreibende Frauen im 18. und 19. Jahrhundert* (Göttingen: Vandenhoeck & Ruprecht, 1998)

—— *Deutschsprachige Schriftstellerinnen des Fin de siècle* (Darmstadt: Wissenschaftliche Buchgesellschaft, 1999)

TGAHRT, REINHARD, and OTHERS, eds, *Weltliteratur: Die Lust am Übersetzen im Jahrhundert Goethes*, Marbacher Kataloge, 37 (Munich: Kösel, 1982)

THUM, REINHARD, 'Oppressed by Generosity: Dismantling the Gilded Marital Cage in Marie von Ebner-Eschenbach's "Erste Trennung"', in *Neues zu Altem*, ed. by Sabine Cramer (Munich: Fink, 1996), pp. 57–66

TODD, JANET, *The Sign of Angellica: Women, Writing and Fiction, 1660–1800* (New York: Columbia University Press, 1989)

TOEGEL, EDITH, *Marie von Ebner-Eschenbach: Leben und Werk* (New York: Lang, 1997)

TOMPKINS, JANE, *Sensational Designs: The Cultural Work of American Fiction 1790–1860* (New York: Oxford University Press, 1985)

TULLY, CAROL, 'Women on the Verge of a Cultural Breakthrough: German Hispanism, Translation and Gender in the Nineteenth Century', keynote speech at WIGS and WISPS Annual Conference on 'Friendship', held at Swansea University, 13 November 2010

UJMA, CHRISTINA, 'England und die Engländer in Fanny Lewalds Romanen und Reiseberichten', in *The Novel in Anglo-German Context: Cultural Cross-Currents and Affinities*, ed. by Susanne Stark (Amsterdam: Rodopi, 2000), pp. 145–56

VAHSEN, MECHTHILDE, *Die Politisierung des weiblichen Subjekts: Deutsche Romanautorinnen und die Französische Revolution 1790–1820* (Berlin: Erich Schmidt Verlag, 2000)

VENUTI, LAWRENCE, *The Scandals of Translation: Towards an Ethics of Difference* (London: Routledge, 1998)

—— *The Translator's Invisibility: A History of Translation*, 2nd edn (London: Routledge, 2008)

WAGNER, NIKE, *Geist und Geschlecht: Karl Kraus und die Erotik der Wiener Moderne* (Frankfurt am Main: Suhrkamp, 1987)

WALDSCHMIDT, JULIUS and ULRICH VAN DER HEYDEN, *Kaiser, Kanzler und Prinzessin: Ein Frauenschicksal zwischen Orient und Okzident*, 2nd edn (Berlin: Trafo, 2006)

WALGENBACH, KATHARINA, *'Die weiße Frau als Trägerin deutscher Kultur': Koloniale Diskurse über Geschlecht, 'Rasse' und Klasse im Kaiserreich* (Frankfurt am Main and New York: Campus, 2005)

WANDRUSZKA, MARIE LUISE, *Marie von Ebner-Eschenbach: Erzählerin aus politischer Leidenschaft* (Vienna: Passagen, 2008)

WARD, MARGARET E., 'The Personal is Political — The Political becomes Personal: Fanny Lewald's Early Travel Literature', in *Politics in German Literature*, ed. by Beth Bjorklund and Mark E. Cory (Columbia: Camden House, 1998), pp. 60–82

—— *Fanny Lewald: Between Rebellion and Renunciation* (New York: Lang, 2006)

WARMBOLD, JOACHIM, 'Germania in Africa: Frieda Freiin von Bülow, "Schöpferin des deutschen Kolonialromans"', *Jahrbuch des Instituts für deutsche Geschichte* [Tel-Aviv University], 15 (1986), 309–36

WARMBOLD, JOACHIM, *'Ein Stückchen neudeutsche Erd' ...': Deutsche Kolonial-Literatur. Aspekte ihrer Geschichte, Eigenart und Wirkung, dargestellt am Beispiel Afrikas* (Frankfurt am Main: Haag + Herchen, 1982), trans. as *Germania in Africa: Germany's Colonial Literature* (New York, Berne, Frankfurt am Main, and Paris, 1988)

WEBSTER GOODWIN, SARAH, 'Cross Fire and Collaboration among Comparative Literature, Feminism, and the New Historicism', in *Borderwork: Feminist Engagements with Contemporary Literature*, ed. by Margaret Higonnet (Ithaca: Cornell University Press, 1994), pp. 247–66

WECKEL, ULRIKE, *Zwischen Häuslichkeit und Öffentlichkeit: Die ersten deutschen Frauenzeitschriften im späten 18. Jahrhundert und ihr Publikum* (Tübingen: Niemeyer, 1998)

WEEDON, CHRIS, *Gender, Feminism, and Fiction in Germany, 1840–1914* (New York and Berne: Lang, 2006)

—— 'Of Madness and Masochism: Sexuality in Women's Writing at the Turn of the

Century', in *Taboos in German Literature*, ed. by David Jackson (Oxford: Berghahn, 1996), pp. 79–95

WEHINGER, BRUNHILDE, and HILARY BROWN, eds, *Übersetzungskultur im 18. Jahrhundert: Übersetzerinnen in Deutschland, Frankreich und der Schweiz* (Hanover: Wehrhahn, 2008)

WEHLER, HANS-ULRICH, *Deutsche Gesellschaftsgeschichte*, III: *Von der 'Deutschen Doppelrevolution' bis zum Beginn des Ersten Weltkriegs 1849–1914* (Munich: Beck, 1995)

WEIGEL, SIGRID, 'Der schielende Blick: Thesen zur Geschichte weiblicher Schreibpraxis', in *Die verborgene Frau: Sechs Beiträge zu einer feministischen Literaturwissenschaft*, ed. by Sigrid Weigel and Inge Stephan (Berlin: Argument, 1983), pp. 83–137.

WEININGER, OTTO, *Geschlecht und Charakter: Eine prinzipielle Untersuchung* (1903; Munich: Matthes & Seitz, 1980)

WIEGMAN, ROBYN, 'Difference and Disciplinarity', in *Aesthetics in a Multicultural Age*, ed. by Emory Elliott, Louis Freitas Caton, and Jeffrey Rhyne (Oxford: University Press, 2002), pp. 135–56

——'On Being in Time with Feminism', *Modern Language Quarterly*, 65.1 (2004), 161–76

WIELAND, CHRISTOPH MARTIN, 'Deutschland's Dichterinnen', *Neuer Teutscher Merkur* (April 1803), pp. 258–74

WILDENTHAL, LORA, *German Women for Empire, 1884–1945* (Durham, NC: Duke University Press, 2001)

——'"When Men Are Weak": The Imperial Feminism of Frieda von Bülow', *Gender & History*, 10.1 (1998), 53–77

WILDERMUTH, OTTILIE, *Ottilie Wildermuth's Erzählungen* (Konstanz: Christlicher Buch- und Kunstverlag Carl Hirsch, 1908)

WILDERMUTH, ROSEMARIE, *Ottilie Wildermuth: 1817–1877* [Für die Ausstellung von Februar– Mai 1986 im Schiller-Nationalmuseum Marbach] (Marbach: Schiller-Nationalmuseum, 1986)

WILKENDING, GISELA, *Kinder- und Jugendbuch* (Bamberg: C. C. Buchner, 1988)

WOODFORD, CHARLOTTE, 'Realism and Sentimentalism in Marie von Ebner-Eschenbach's *Unsühnbar*', *Modern Language Review*, 101.1 (2006), 151–66

——'Suffering and Domesticity: The Subversion of Sentimentalism in Three Stories by Marie von Ebner-Eschenbach', *German Life and Letters*, 59.1 (2006), 47–61

WOOLF, VIRGINIA, *A Room of One's Own*, foreword by Mary Gordon (1929; Orlando, FL: Harcourt Brace Jovanovich, 1989)

WORLEY, LINDA KRAUS, 'The Making (and Unmaking) of an Austrian Icon: The Reception of Marie von Ebner-Eschenbach as a Geopolitical Case Study', *Modern Austrian Literature*, 41.2 (2008), 19–39

——'The "Odd" Woman as Heroine in the Fiction of Louise von François', *Women in German Yearbook*, 4 (1987), 155–65

——'"Plotting the Czech Lands": Marie von Ebner-Eschenbachs Konstruktionen des Tschechischen', in *Herausforderung Osteuropa: Die Offenlegung stereotyper Bilder*, ed. by Theda Kahl, Elisabeth Vyslonzil, and Alois Woldan (Munich: Oldenbourg, 2004), pp. 135–48

——'Telling Stories/Telling Histories: Marie von Ebner-Eschenbach's "Er laßt die Hand küssen"', in *Neues zu Altem*, ed. by Sabine Cramer (Munich: Fink, 1996), pp. 43–56

ZANTOP, SUSANNE, *Colonial Fantasies: Conquest, Family, and Nation in Precolonial Germany, 1770–1870* (Durham, NC and London: Duke University Press, 1997)

ZIMMERMANN, MARGARETE, 'Literaturgeschichte/Literaturgeschichtsschreibung', in *Metzler Lexikon Gender Studies Geschlechterforschung: Ansätze — Personen — Grundbegriffe*, ed. by Renate Kroll (Stuttgart and Weimar: Metzler, 2002), pp. 237–38

# INDEX

*For Product Safety Concerns and Information please contact our EU representative GPSR@taylorandfrancis.com Taylor & Francis Verlag GmbH, Kaufingerstraße 24, 80331 München, Germany*

T - #0096 - 090625 - C0 - 247/170/10 [12] - CB - 9781906540869 - Matt Lamination